POWERSCAPE

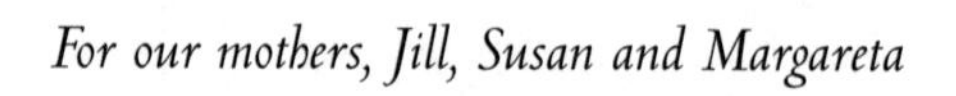

For our mothers, Jill, Susan and Margareta

POWERSCAPE

Contemporary Australian politics

Ariadne Vromen, Katharine Gelber and *Anika Gauja*

Illustrations by Fiona Katauskas

First published in 2009

Allen & Unwin
83 Alexander Street
Crows Nest NSW 2065
Australia
Phone: (61 2) 8425 0100
Fax: (61 2) 9906 2218
Email: info@allenandunwin.com
Web: www.allenandunwin.com

National Library of Australia
Cataloguing-in-Publication entry:

Vromen, Ariadne.
Powerscape: contemporary Australian politics/Ariadne Vromen; Katharine Gelber; Anika Gauja.

2nd ed.

ISBN: 9781741756258 (pbk.)

Includes index.
Bibliography.

Australia – Politics and government – 20th century.
Australia – Politics and government – 21st century.

Other Authors/Contributors:
Gelber, Katharine.
Gauja, Anika.

320.0994

Illustrations by Fiona Katauskas
Typeset in 11.5/15 pt Centaur MT by Midland Typesetters, Australia
Printed in Australia by Ligare Pty Ltd, Sydney

10 9 8 7 6 5 4 3 2 1

CONTENTS

PART II POLITICAL ACTORS

PART III POLICY PROCESSES

Visit the Powerscape website at <www.allenandunwin.com/powerscape>

TABLES

FIGURES

ACKNOWLEDGEMENTS

We set ourselves two ambitious tasks in writing this book. In choosing to write about Australian politics we had to recognise that Australians learn little about their political system through school. Therefore the first challenge for us was to present introductory institutional information in a lively and interesting way. Our second challenge was to capture the dynamism and complexity of Australian political processes and relate them to everyday political experiences. Most books on Australian politics tend to do one or the other. In *Powerscape* we provide our attempt to find an approach that meets both these challenges.

Since the first edition we have received useful feedback on what we tried to do with *Powerscape*, from both students and lecturers. The Australian political landscape has continued to change, including the recent change in federal government, and this is reflected in the new examples we have focused on. In the second edition we have added two new chapters on political institutions and policy-making.

Allen & Unwin has been a very supportive publisher, and we'd like to thank them for their invaluable assistance and expertise. The special contribution made by cartoonist Fiona Katauskas has made the book more accessible and original. The second edition has also benefited from the talent of our third author, early career researcher Anika Gauja. As a result this has been a women-only project—a somewhat unique event in Australian political science literature.

We would like to thank individuals who either provided us with constructive comments on the development of the first edition, or gave us useful suggestions for development and expansion into the second edition. Thank you to: Rebecca Albury, Nick Economou, Kim Huynh, Carol Johnson, Matt McDonald, Diarmuid Maguire, Susan Park, Shelly Savage, Rodney Smith and John Warhurst.

Ariadne thanks her family for their ongoing support, especially Diarmuid and his boys. She also thanks the movie group girls and Zelda for providing welcome distraction. Katharine would like to thank the Gilbert + Tobin Centre of Public Law,

UNSW, at which she was a Visiting Fellow in 2008 while parts of this book were written. Since the first edition she and Lou have welcomed into the world their son Simon, who makes it all worth it. Anika would like to thank her family for all their support, as well as 'team extreme', the 'agents' and the 'Sydney gang'.

INTRODUCTION

The study of politics is a bit like trying to catch the wind. It is very powerful, you can see its effects all around you, but it is hard to grab hold of and difficult to measure. Politics is all around us, whether or not we consider ourselves 'political'. Perhaps without realising it, we are all members of a number of political communities, including the country to which we belong and the State in which we live. We do not always get a choice about our membership of some political communities. For example, many people acquire their citizenship simply by being born in a particular country. They did not ask for it, but having it grants them privileges, such as the freedom to travel, or the provision of social welfare, and also imposes responsibilities on them, such as paying taxes. Those who do not have automatic entitlement to citizenship are obliged to apply for it through complicated legal and administrative procedures, with no guarantee their request will be granted. The political community, in this instance, is a nation, in the sense of a physical, geographically defined entity. However, this is not the only way to define a political community; other ways include shared identities, common histories or mutual experiences.

Between and within political communities there are continuous interactions. A feature of these interactions is that there are always winners and losers, privileged and underprivileged, haves and have-nots. The study of politics is the study of the interactions of this unequal power between individuals and groups within a political community—how they happen, why they happen, and why some people or groups do better out of the system than others. It is a discipline that tries to make the intangible tangible, the seemingly chaotic systematic, and the apparently random ordered. It seeks to describe, analyse and explain the complex phenomena that affect collective decision-making in a society, the values the people hold and the choices they make. It also tries to discern the assumptions and perspectives that inform people's decisions, values and choices.

In this book we argue that political interactions and decision-making events take place in a continuous process of contestation. There is ongoing dispute over values and choices within any political system that reflects people's engagement with the system at many levels—the formal institutions of parliament and government, by pressure groups, through social networks and as individuals.

In Australia (as in all political communities) some people's values and choices win out over others'. Sometimes the political party you vote for wins government, sometimes it loses. Sometimes the school you attend gets more funding, sometimes it gets less. Sometimes new roads are built that make cars travel to and from work faster, sometimes a new train line is built instead. The study of politics is the study of how and why these decisions occur, and how and why people argue in favour of one choice over another. Ultimately, it is a study of power, or more specifically of relationships of power.

The study of politics is the study of interactions of unequal power between individuals and (formal and informal) institutions, groups and organisations within a community.

This book examines a range of political actors engaging within various arenas (both formal and informal) within Australian politics. We will discuss the use of power by and within democratic institutions, policy-making processes, mechanisms of representation and participatory forums. We have included chapters on a wide range of participants within our political system, to provide information on the breadth of political activity and engagement within Australian politics. Throughout the book we use the term 'political actors' to describe the individuals, groups and organisations involved in contemporary Australian political processes. This term demonstrates that active involvement in Australian politics is not limited to politicians and government, but also includes public servants, the media, businesses in the private sector, and community organisations. A related feature of this book is that we consider political engagement not just in formal terms such as voting at elections or lobbying politicians, but also in terms of affecting public attitudes and behaviour, creating new forms of participation and active citizenship, and challenging the political status quo.

Outline of this book

This book has been organised in three parts that enable us to investigate contemporary Australian politics from a power perspective—the Powerscape. Each of the parts is based on a theme: 'Power and Democracy', 'Political Actors' and 'Policy Processes'. There are fourteen chapters, and each chapter begins with a snapshot intended to be an example of a power struggle that illuminates the information and analysis presented in the text that follows. The snapshot raises questions that will be answered in the chapter and often also introduces you to important actors within the area or theme being discussed. Studying the chapter will enable you to assess, analyse and understand the material presented in the snapshot, and see it as a microcosm of the broader issues and themes under discussion. Chapters also contain boxes with definitions of key terms, and highlighted examples to help illustrate the points being made.

In the first chapter, 'Power and politics', of Part I, we discuss the concept and utilisation of power within Australian politics. In Chapter 2, 'Liberal democracy in Australia', we move on to outline the democratic framework within which Australian politics operates—our liberal–democratic system of government—and focus on the central points and assumptions of liberal–democratic systems generally. This allows us to argue how liberal and democratic values interact in ways that are a salient and positive feature of Australian politics. Chapter 3, 'Frameworks for governing', explains the core institutional elements of our governmental system, and shows how they provide arenas for interaction and participation. We argue that, while the text of the constitutional document and the core institutions are important, developing an in-depth understanding of the system of government as a whole involves examining its implications as well as changing interpretations and expectations of government. Chapter 4, 'Parliaments', outlines the design of the federal and State Australian parliaments. It looks at the way in which parliaments give an institutional expression to some of the ideas underpinning liberal democracy, and the challenges they face in doing so. It also highlights the work of individual parliamentarians and how they view their representative and legislative duties. In Chapter 5, 'Electoral systems', we posit that these systems adapt and change as new players, new political events and new expectations for representative politics challenge the traditional two-party system. We put forward interpretations of the electoral system that focus on the ways we vote and the ways in which we understand election outcomes. Taken together, Part I provides the core conceptual, theoretical and institutional material essential to grasping the mechanics of Australian politics.

Part II provides an overview of the range and power of political actors involved in contemporary politics in Australia. In Chapter 6, 'Political parties', we trace the role of both established major parties and new minor parties within the electoral landscape, and outline how they compete within the electoral system. We suggest that political parties are changing. The chapter highlights new issues in the analysis of party systems and current understandings of the ideological positions taken by parties. In Chapter 7, 'News and media', we provide ways of understanding how the media shape and produce information. The media communicates the political landscape to the public in complex ways, and understanding those processes is important in understanding how some political issues become represented as important and others do not, and how the media influence this decision-making. We also focus here on new media, including the Internet. In Chapter 8 we examine 'Individual engagement', to provide an analytical framework for studying the political behaviour and influence of individuals within Australian politics. This provides a context to develop understandings of how people interact with the system in ways that can be considered 'political' even though they themselves might not consciously or formally be regarded as political activities. Chapters 9 and 10, 'Pressure groups' and 'Social movements' respectively, look more specifically at the strategic behaviour of business and community-oriented pressure groups and social movements in engaging with the political system and seeking to achieve political and social change. These chapters tell the story of a dynamic political system and of high levels of public engagement. They are something of an antidote to the prevailing view that political participation in the twenty-first century in many liberal–democratic systems of government is subdued, or even absent. Instead, these chapters tell a story of critical, strategic, complex and targeted interactions by political actors that shape political processes.

Part III provides an overview of the context within which policy decisions are made and implemented in Australia. This begins in Chapter 11 where we consider Australian 'federalism', and demonstrate that a complete assessment of our federalism requires recognising and examining more than the formal institutions; it also requires analysing the processes at work in the dynamics of our system. We argue that examining opportunities for political engagement within the federal system recognises the complex processes involved in contemporary federal dynamics. Chapter 12, 'Policy analysis', shows that while policy-making is often portrayed as the decisions made by a government as to whether it should do A or B, in reality it is a continually contested, inherently 'messy' activity involving a diverse range of political actors and interests that need to be reconciled. We develop a framework for analysing real-life policy issues that recognises and accommodates the complexity of policy-making. In Chapter 13, 'Policy delivery', we argue that although the contemporary framework for policy delivery encourages the participation of a wider range of actors, such as business and community organisations, than ever before in Australian politics, the forms of action they may take are constrained by the political and economic framework within which their engagement takes place. The final chapter of the book, 'Australia in the world', examines foreign policy from the perspective of the role Australia is playing in the world. We argue that since the late 1990s Australian foreign policy has demonstrated an extraordinary synergy with that of the United States. We argue that at the same time Australia's external policies and practices are more and more affected by domestic, internal political debates, and that understanding our place and role in the world requires an understanding of Australia's domestic politics—the two are intimately linked.

Understanding power in contemporary Australian politics

This book examines relationships of power in detail by looking at formal and informal political arenas, the increasing engagement of a variety of players in the political process, and internal and external factors influencing policy-making. We do not see power as a top-down, elitist procedure whereby those who have power impose their decisions and their decision-making processes on those in relatively less influential positions. We do not see power in primarily institutional terms—as mediated through formal institutions of government. Nor do we see power in pluralist terms—assuming everyone has equal opportunity to participate in and engage with the system.

We see power from a participatory perspective. We view participation as important, no matter at which level it occurs, because when people participate in and engage with political processes, they are attempting to shape their own future. This perspective is informed by the multifaceted definition of power we have already provided. We also see power as a relationship, as a thing that is 'exercised rather than possessed' (Foucault 1995, p. 26). But having said this, we recognise the reality that people do not automatically have equal power to participate in and engage with our contemporary political system. Inequalities exist, and the institutions and frameworks for governing can perpetuate inequalities.

The story that unfolds in this book is a story of contestation over these inequalities, over who will win and who will lose, and of the right to participate in and dispute decisions of government. Ultimately, this story is a positive one. Despite the (at times considerable) criticism raised within our book of specific aspects of contemporary Australian political practice, we focus on the dynamism and engagement at work within that system. Our hope is that this dynamism and engagement will continue to pressure the system at the points needed to achieve better outcomes—domestically and internationally—for those currently lacking in power and those currently exercising it. The contemporary Powerscape of Australian politics undergoes continuous change. The elements of that change explored in this book give reason for optimism that change will continue to be pursued by, and therefore be beneficial for, a great many of the people who currently contest dominant modes of power.

PART I
POWER AND DEMOCRACY

CHAPTER 1
POWER AND POLITICS

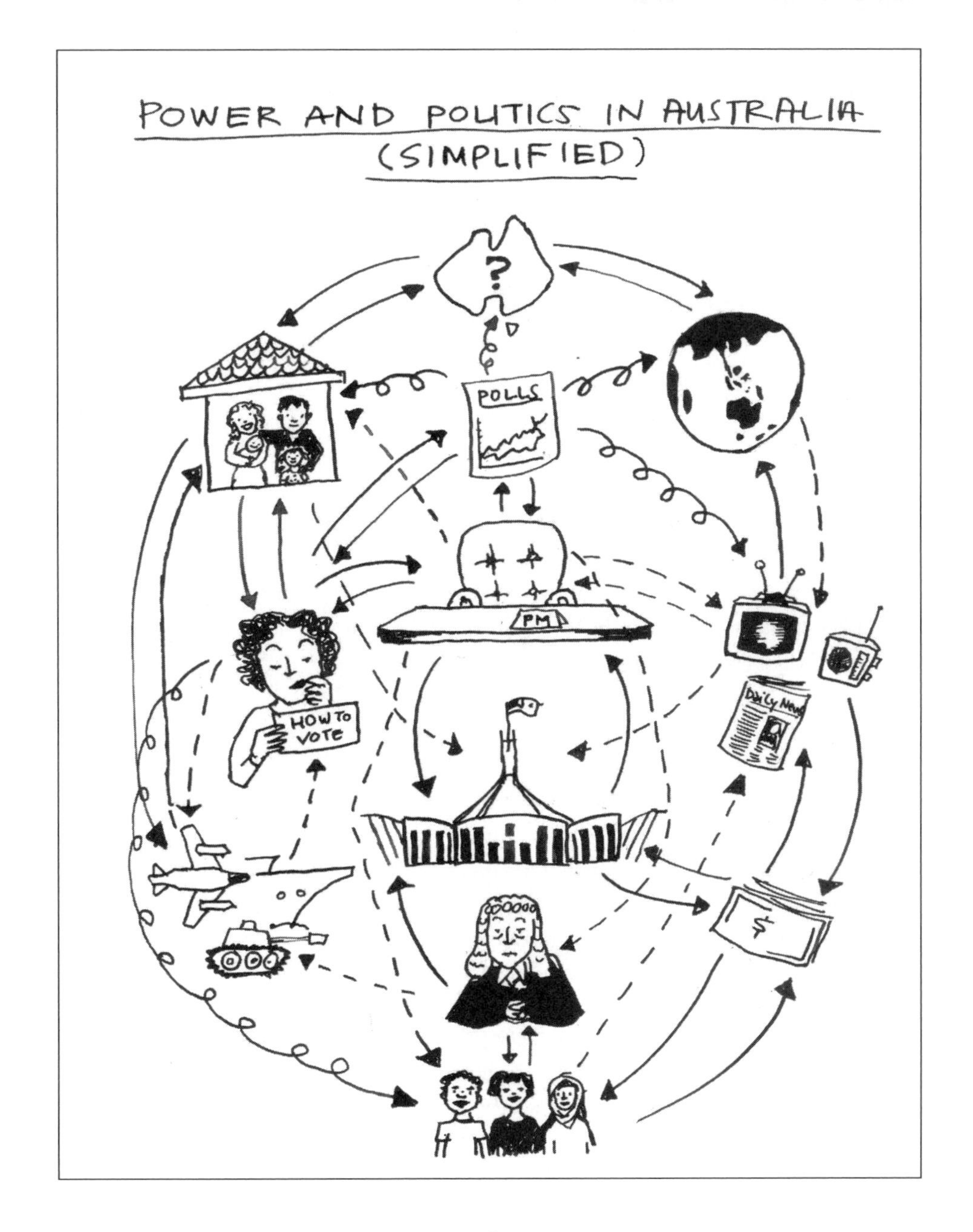

This chapter presents the study of politics as the study of power, and more specifically relationships of power between people, groups and institutions. It recognises that the study of politics is the study of situations of relative inequalities of power, and that power is an essentially contested concept. We present a three-dimensional view of power that informs the analysis in the rest of the book.

Topics covered in this chapter include:

- the study of politics is essentially the study of relationships of power
- power is ubiquitous, but intangible and hard to measure
- a three-dimensional view of power enables more complex interactions to be analysed and understood
- power can be present in capacity or exercise; thus it can be overt or covert, conscious or unconscious, and individual or collective.

SNAPSHOT The Australian Prime Minister: leading the power game?

The Prime Minister is regarded as the most powerful political leader in Australia. As the leader of the elected government and the highest representative of the people, he or she (in December 2007 Australia had its first female Prime Minister when newly elected Deputy Prime Minister Julia Gillard took on the role of Acting Prime Minister for three days) is called upon to play a variety of leadership roles.

Within days of being sworn into office on 3 December 2007, Prime Minister Kevin Rudd declared:

> the government has a plan to move Australia forward by boosting long-term productivity growth for the future. The Government has a plan to tackle Australia's future challenges and I want to begin implementing that plan as soon as possible ... I do not under-estimate the degree of difficulty involved in this ambitious agenda. But the time has come now to roll our sleeves up and get to work. (Rudd 2007a)

Then on the opening day of the new parliament on 12 February 2008, the traditional owners of Australia were honoured and for the first time ever a welcome to country was performed by first Australians (Rudd 2008a).

On the next day, the first sitting day of the new parliament, the Prime Minister apologised to indigenous people for the Stolen Generation and made commitments to reduce disadvantage faced by indigenous communities within the next five to ten years (Rudd 2008b). The apology was an historic occasion.

In these statements and actions, the Prime Minister has acknowledged that he is a political leader who exercises discretion in decision-making and exerts individual political power. The job of Prime Minister involves leading public debate, changing laws and regulations, representing Australia, giving speeches and media interviews, and addressing the community. In doing these things the Prime Minister recognises that he or she is expected to develop policy that gives expression to the people's values and aspirations. Since Kevin Rudd is now leading the first national Labor government for more than a decade, he feels he has a mandate for change. He will also be continuously lobbied and pressured by other members of government, parliamentarians, the media and the general public.

How far is the Prime Minister able to exercise independent leadership, and how much is he affected by other players, issues and ideas within the Australian political system? How does the Prime Minister respond to competing demands and still retain the role of a political leader?

To understand the Prime Minister's role, we can examine three arenas within which contestation over power takes place. These are:

- the formal, institutional arena of decision-making within parliament
- the broader political context within which decisions are made about what issues need to be brought to parliament and in what form, and
- the full range of competing ideas and values championed by the Prime Minister and others within Australian politics when trying to have their voice heard.

The first arena influencing the Prime Minister is the formal institutional arena within which he operates and makes decisions. The Prime Minister makes formal decisions within the parliamentary system as the leader of the political party that forms government. In this formal sense the Prime Minister's power to make decisions is clear. He leads the putting of proposals to parliament for a vote. It is easy to see when the Prime

Minister has achieved his intention and when he has not, by looking at whether his party's proposals are passed by the parliament. But this does not tell us the whole story about how the Prime Minister operates within the Australian political system.

In order to understand some of the broader pressures the Prime Minister faces, it is necessary to examine a second arena. This is the broader formal context within which decisions are made. It includes the activities of other members of the Prime Minister's party in providing advice from their areas of expertise and trying to bring up proposals of their own for the party to adopt and then take to the parliament for approval. The process of considering which ideas to take to the parliament, and in what form, is lengthy and complicated. The media also play an important role in raising awareness of some political issues and pressuring the government to respond. Media coverage of political and community issues can force the government to respond to specific concerns, for example about crime levels or the state of schools. Consultations between the government and members of the community can inform the positions the government adopts. For example, Kevin Rudd consulted indigenous people on the wording of the apology before it was made. In order to understand how much power the Prime Minister really has, it is necessary to examine all of these pressures on his leadership. But even these two arenas do not tell us everything about how the Prime Minister operates because they do not provide us with the full context within which decision-making takes place and power is possessed and exercised.

As well as responding to parliamentary, party, media and community pressures, the Prime Minister is also expected to provide leadership in the sense of having a vision for Australia's future. How does he or she do this? A Prime Minister's vision for Australia's future is based in his or her overall ideals, values and preferences. In the contemporary political environment in Australia, arguments about decisions and policy at a parliamentary level tend to reflect larger differences in ideas. An ideology by which Kevin Rudd claims to be informed is social justice—the idea that his role requires that power be 'balanced by social responsibility and a duty to the less fortunate' (*Canberra Times* 2007, p. 16). Time will tell whether this ideology survives other influences on the Prime Minister. Other influential ideological perspectives that will affect political decision-making include neo-liberalism—a belief in the importance of free market competition and a promotion of choice through market systems—and globalisation—the extent to which Australia is becoming integrated with global economic and social concerns. There are of course other ideologies and debates that influence the Prime Minister's decision-making and views on the world. These influences tend to operate in invisible and covert ways. This means that underlying beliefs can affect decision-making without us even being aware of them.

Understanding how the Prime Minister exercises leadership therefore requires an examination of all three arenas within which pressure is possessed and exerted both overtly and covertly. What do these arenas represent? How can they be explained? What is the role of power in understanding politics?

The study of politics

The study of politics is at least several thousand years old (Dahl 1964, p. 2). During this time society has become more complex, with the emergence of representative parliamentary forms of government, a large bureaucracy and the development of new norms for relations between states internationally. As these momentous changes have occurred and demands on government have increased, a constant theme in every political society has been the presence of, and attempt to harness, power.

There are many ways of studying power, but power is ultimately less an entity than a (potential or actual) relationship. Power is about relationships between people, singly and collectively, who more often than not possess differing levels of power. More specifically, politics is the study of relationships between people and institutions possessing different levels of power, and attempts to alter these levels in terms of access, process and outcomes. Power is therefore a ubiquitous theme in political science literature.

But calculations of power are difficult to make. This renders the study of politics particularly open to interpretation. It is for this reason that some people argue that the study of politics is not a 'science' at all; 'real' science, also called hard science, is characterised by testable theorems and the conducting of experiments that produce hard data from which analysts may deduce the answer to a question. Social sciences, in which the study of politics is located, are far less exact. It is difficult, if not impossible, to conduct experiments on human beings from which all other factors except those under study may be eliminated. For example if a political scientist were to ask what the causes of poverty in a particular community might be, and were to find a relationship between impoverishment and lack of access to publicly funded education, the researcher may wish to deduce that some kind of causal link exists between the provision of publicly funded education and an ability to earn enough money to live comfortably. However, the same study may also find that impoverished families had more children than rich families. Would this imply that having more children induced poverty? Conversely, would it imply that impoverished families tend to have more children? These implications need to be assessed using other methods and tests, which means that finding answers is usually not straightforward. In the end answers in the social sciences tend to be informed by the values the researcher holds as well as the nature and method of the study undertaken.

For these reasons, Dahl regards the study of politics as both science and art (1964, p. 2). It is a science in the sense that an idea or an answer may be developed and assessed via the scientific research methods of observation, interview, survey, questionnaire or statistical analysis. For example if you wanted to discover whether a policy directed at people with disabilities had increased their rate of finding full-time work, you could count the number of people with disabilities in full-time jobs before and some time after the policy was implemented, and interview some of those people to discover what factors had helped them secure their employment. But the study of politics is also an art in the sense that it is based on skills that can be learned and practised. In this context, this book seeks to provide students of Australian politics with the skills necessary to study the Australian political system, its dynamics and framework, its central components, and the engagement of individuals, groups, organisations and institutions with it.

In political science, some concepts are known as 'essentially contested' (Lukes 2005, p. 14). This means something quite specific. A contested concept is one whose definition is under dispute. This means that different researchers will apply different frameworks, assumptions and even values to that concept, to understanding and applying it. This is true of the idea of power. However, power is more than just a contested concept: it is an *essentially* contested one. This means that resolution of the debate over the meaning of power is impossible, in the sense that no one true meaning of the term exists (Heywood 2004, p. 5). Instead, different meanings of the term can be upheld as valid within different contexts and arguments. In trying to provide a definition of power here, then, we are not trying to establish the one true meaning of power. What we are doing is outlining a particular conception of power that we find persuasive. We will also clarify why we find it persuasive.

What is power?

Lukes' analysis of power, first published thirty years ago but still influential today, differentiates three ways of understanding power as one-dimensional, two-dimensional and three-dimensional (2005). Each of these ways of understanding power sheds light on particular elements in interactions within political communities. Moreover, each is relational; that is to say power is defined not as an entity or a thing, but as an observable feature of, or capacity within, disagreements and interactions between people. The cause of those disagreements is not at issue here. Disagreements may emerge over differences in ideological perspective, values or cultural attitudes, for example. What is at issue here is the observation of power at work in communication and interaction between people, whether it be in the form of an actual exercise of power or in the mere presence of a capacity to exercise such power.

Lukes first describes a view of power that he regards as 'one-dimensional'. This is a view in which power is understood through observing decision-making processes, or observing behaviour in the making of concrete decisions. The focus of the study of politics and power is therefore formal political institutions such as parliaments. In this view, decision-making occurs because of instances of direct and observable conflict or because there are issues that are controversial and therefore invoke conflict (2005, pp. 16–19). For example, observing the outcome and process of decisions about education funding would enable us to decide whether power had been successfully exercised by an advocate for greater government funding for private schools or an advocate for reduced government funding for private schools. We would examine who was able to win majority support for their point of view within the policy circles where such decisions are made. Table 1.1 describes the one-dimensional view of power.

Although this seems at first a logical and clear way of deciding who is able to possess or exert power in a given situation, Lukes criticises this one-dimensional view for making assumptions about decision-making that might not be true. He particularly criticises the assumption that open conflict is an essential condition

TABLE 1.1 One-dimensional power

Concept of power	Power as decision-making
Where is power exercised?	The formal political arena, institutions of politics such as the parliament
How do we measure power?	By counting votes and the outcomes of decisions

Source: adapted from Hay 2002, p. 180.

for the exercise of power. Lukes points out that it is possible to observe power at work in arenas even where there is no direct or observable conflict. For example, power is at work when a student completes their homework and assignments for their teacher. They are obeying the school rules, but it is unlikely that there was overt conflict when the teacher exercised power over the students.

In other situations the exercise of power may be invisible because the range of options presented in decision-making may not reflect all possibilities, but only those that are dominant or considered 'safe'. Alternative decisions or options may not be expressed openly (Lukes 2005, p. 22). In these instances, the opportunity for observing open conflict is reduced or absent. Yet it would be wrong to assume that just because no overt instance of conflict can be observed, there is no power differential at work. Indeed, power can be successfully deployed in instances where conflict is subdued or even absent.

These concerns have given rise to Lukes' second conceptualisation of power, which he calls 'two-dimensional'. This view adds depth to the conceptualisation of power discussed so far by recognising that, within any political community, there are ways of raising barriers to the participation of some people in expressing their views. This means that some means of expressing choices and preferences are more powerful than others. Those put forward by the most powerful group tend to become discussed as viable, and their participation is privileged (Lukes 2005, pp. 20–1). To the extent that this scenario is true, it means that in decision-making processes, everyone's views and desires are not equally represented. Some people have less opportunity to interact with decision-making processes than others, which lessens their chances of ensuring that their values or preferences win in the decision-making process even before it has begun. Those people are excluded from political decision-making.

In this understanding of how power may be exercised, types of power can be described in several ways. Lukes begins to do this, but others have added to his typology. The following list, therefore, has been adapted from both Lukes (2005, pp. 21–2) and Smith (1997a, pp. 19–21), and ranks types of power from the more covert to the more overt.

- Influence occurs where a person is encouraged to comply with another's wishes without any threat or force being used. An example is when a teacher asks students to do their school work.
- Inducement is when a person is encouraged to do something by being offered a reward in return. This could be a pay rise or public accolades.
- Persuasion is more overt than inducement, and involves the open communication by one person of their wishes to another, in a manner that persuades them to do what is asked of them. In their ideal form, parliamentary debates are a form of persuasion in which parliamentarians attempt to persuade their counterparts that their policy proposal is better than others' on the basis of the viability of the arguments presented.
- Manipulation occurs where a person complies even if they are not aware that they are being required to do so. The real meaning of the person using their power over others is hidden. An example of manipulation is a politician deliberately lying to their constituents to get elected to parliament, if they later reveal that their real policy agenda was different from that presented to the public before the election.
- Authority is used when a person is encouraged to comply with another's wishes because they believe them to be legitimate and reasonable. Another way to describe it is that a person possesses authority when other people obey them without requiring any further means of persuasion. For example, when a minister requests a public servant to undertake a task that is reasonable and within their job description, the public servant will undertake that task without resistance because the minister has the authority to request them to do it.
- Coercion occurs where a person complies with the wishes of another in response to a threat. This could include the police refusing to allow protesters entry to a cordoned area on security grounds. The protesters know that if they breach the cordon, they will be arrested and charged with trespass. Some may choose not to comply and engage instead in civil disobedience, but in doing so they make a conscious decision to resist the coercive power of the police.

- Force occurs where a person complies because they have no choice not to. This type of power can include physical compulsion such as using a weapon to force compliance. It includes governments engaging in armed warfare.

Except for the last two types, there may be no observable conflict in many of these situations because power is exercised covertly. Nevertheless, it would be wrong to assume that power is not present in a capacity or that it is not being exercised in all of these examples. Indeed, subtle and pervasive forms of power can be very powerful. In this sense, the two-dimensional view of power is more convincing than the one-dimensional view, and it adds depth to our understanding of power. Table 1.2 describes the two-dimensional view of power.

However, there are criticisms even of this view of power. The main criticism of the two-dimensional view is that it still relies, albeit tacitly, on an assumption that power is generated in situations of conflict and that the exercise of power involves a person ensuring, or being able to ensure, another's compliance with their own wishes.

Lukes' solution to this dilemma is to advocate a three-dimensional view of power. In this view, it is recognised that compliance can be secured not just by a person influencing others to agree with their wishes but also by the potential range of wishes available to all individuals being limited and structured by the social and cultural forces, ideas and values within which political activity takes place. This occurs through socialisation, whereby individuals are shaped by a set of belief systems and social practices that they accept because they are transmitted to them by parents, school or the media.

But individual socialisation is not the only way ideas influence choices and the formation of preferences. Ideas, values and ideologies influence us in ways we are

TABLE 1.2 Two-dimensional power

Concept of power	Power as decision-making and agenda-setting
Where is power exercised?	Formal political arena and informal processes that privilege some political players and exclude others
How is power measured?	By examining the informal processes which contribute to agenda-setting and exclusion

Source: adapted from Hay 2002, p. 180.

often not conscious of and lead us to hold certain views. Sometimes dominant ideas in a society can suppress dissent and produce an appearance of consensus. Lukes reminds us that 'the most effective and insidious use of power is to prevent ... conflict from arising in the first place' (2005, p. 27). Where consensus exists, it may not be a genuine consensus but rather a manifestation of power. In the three-dimensional view of power, before decision-making even takes place, dominant ideas, values and beliefs affect the range of choices regarded as viable. Table 1.3 describes the three-dimensional view of power.

Although the three-dimensional view emphasises invisible manifestations of power, is it also conceivable that rulers could intentionally shape the preferences of their subjects through the use of ideological power? Lukes says it is, but at the same time he reiterates the point that power can operate even where there is no deliberate manipulation involved: 'Power can be at work, inducing compliance by influencing desires and beliefs, without being "intelligent and intentional"' (2005, p. 136).

Lukes has also responded to criticism that his third dimension of power seems to cast people as passive 'dopes' who are oblivious to their circumstances and cannot know their real interests. If they are taken in by the views around them without knowing it, doesn't that make them passive and easily manipulated? Is this an insufficient view of people's capacity for independent thought and decision-making? Lukes answers this by saying that power's third dimension can be only partially effective; it can be resisted as well as complied with, and compliance can be willing or unwilling. The complex range of responses to the third

TABLE 1.3 Three-dimensional power

Concept of power	Power as decision-making, agenda-setting and preference shaping. Power is expressed in values, ideas and ideologies
Where is power exercised?	In society generally, in all interactions between political actors within a community
How is power measured?	Three-dimensional power is largely invisible. It shapes preferences and values through ideas and values, and is expressed in discourse

Source: adapted from Hay 2002, p. 180.

dimension of power include the possibility that 'one can *consent* to power and *resent* the mode of its exercise' (2005, p. 150).

Having discussed all three dimensions of power, we can understand the three-dimensional view of power by presenting it visually and by looking at a concrete example of power in practice. This helps us to understand that the three-dimensional view does not ignore the insights of the first two ways of understanding power. On the contrary, it integrates them while also looking at broader factors influencing the way power is exercised in society. The third dimension is cumulative and includes the insights of the first two. Figure 1.1 captures the essence of this multi-dimensional view of power.

FIGURE 1.1 Politics and power in three dimensions

Three-dimensional view
Two-dimensional view
adds notion that some views are privileged and others marginalised or excluded, so power can be covert
One-dimensional view
focuses on decision-making which represents direct, observable conflict
includes understanding that social and cultural factors and values limit the potential range of choices, values and preferences in subtle and cumulative ways

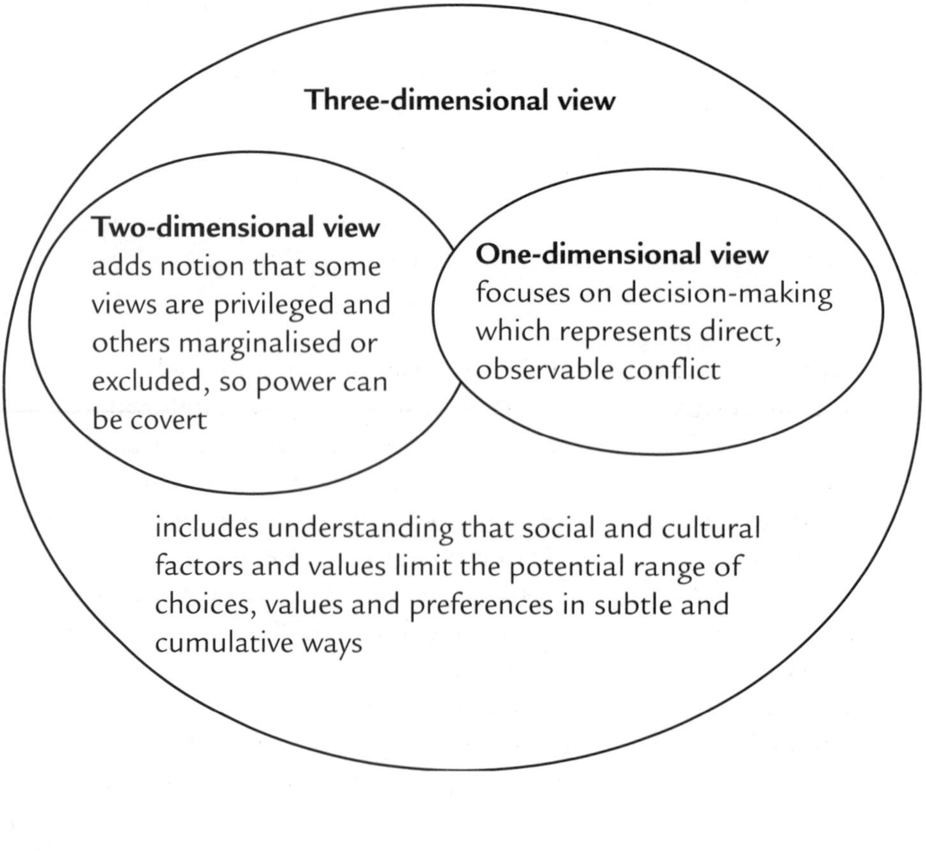

Three-dimensional power in operation: education

In the 2007 federal election campaign, Kevin Rudd promised that his government, if elected, would introduce an 'education revolution'. Central to this was funding to ensure that all year 9 to 12 students around the nation have computers and broadband access, which would cost $1 billion over four years. At the Labor Party federal election campaign launch in Brisbane on 14 November, Rudd stated:

> Nation building requires vision. And the cornerstone of my vision for Australia's future is an education revolution. I spoke about Australia's need for an education revolution in my very first speech to Parliament nearly 10 years ago. I have been speaking about it all year. Because I believe passionately in the power of education. I believe education is the engine room of equity. The engine room of opportunity. And the engine room of the economy . . . We need nothing less than an education revolution now. A revolution in the quantum of our national investment across the entire education spectrum. And a revolution in the quality of those investments—to improve radically the performance of the education system . . .
>
> Today I announce that if elected, Federal Labor will undertake a ground-breaking reform by providing every Australian secondary school student in years nine to 12 with access to their own computer at school. This is an education revolution. (Rudd 2007b)

After the election, the Rudd Labor government moved to implement this policy. It initiated a national audit of existing computer infrastructure to identify the schools most in need, and discussed the policy at a Council of Australian Governments meeting in December. At that meeting it was agreed that schools with the scarcest resources would be the first to be allocated funds (Ferrari 2007). In addition, a cyber safety policy is to be implemented, and the professional development of existing and trainee teachers will need to be adjusted to provide teachers with the skills to use computers as a teaching tool (Gillard 2007).

The scheme has been criticised on a number of grounds. Education expert Kevin Donnelly has argued that there is little research demonstrating the educational benefits of having computers in schools (Donnelly 2007a).

> He also criticised what he sees as the Labor party's 'utilitarian' approach to education in which education is seen as useful because it contributes to economic productivity, rather than because of its inherent ability to cultivate individuals' creativity and intellectual life by enhancing knowledge (Donnelly 2007b).

What were the competing demands on the Prime Minister that led to his decision to implement the 'education revolution' policy, and what does the introduction of this scheme tell us about power in contemporary Australian politics?

In the one-dimensional view of power, the introduction of this scheme tells an observer that the Prime Minister successfully campaigned for and then introduced a new policy that implemented changes to secondary education throughout the country. He did so immediately after winning an election in which he campaigned on the issue. This represents a clear exercise of authoritative, observable, decision-making power.

If the introduction of the scheme were to be viewed through a two-dimensional view of power, the picture becomes a little more complicated. In a two-dimensional view we may develop a different understanding of how power was exercised by examining broader influences on the introduction of this scheme, and which appear to have been more influential or dominant. For example, in its campaign platform the Labor Party expressed the belief that 'To stay competitive in a digital economy Australia must accept the fact that computer technology is no longer just a key subject to learn, it is now the key to learning in almost every subject' (ALP 2007a). In making this claim it drew on research conducted by the federal Department of Communication, Information Technology and the Arts (DCITA 2004) showing how critical the use of information technology is in many industries and jobs, and cited research by the Organisation for Economic Cooperation and Development (OECD 2006 cited in ALP 2007b, p. 5) on computer use in schools in forty-one countries, which indicated that a third of Australia's secondary students are taught information technology in an environment where a shortage of resources hinders their learning. The OECD report also claimed that investment in information technology can lead to a greater competitive advantage in global markets, and that in countries where computer use is usual, young people who do not have access to computers are at risk of significant disadvantage in education and in life, and tend to be 'low performing' (2006, pp. 8, 17, 61).

Nevertheless, the same report indicated that on many indicators Australian students' use of and access to computer technology ranked very highly, with Australian students typically having had access to computers and the internet for longer than students in many other countries and Australia ranked third highest (after Denmark and Liechtenstein) for the percentage of students reporting that they had access to a computer. The number of users per computer is comparatively low, although rural locations fared worse than urban centres (OECD 2006, pp. 18–19, 20, 26, 29).

These research findings could be taken as an indication that greater government support is needed to enable students to have access to computer technology in their everyday schooling. On the other hand, since Australia is already performing quite well in comparison with other OECD countries, arguments could be made that the policy insufficiently recognises existing infrastructure and performance given the very large amount of money that has been committed. A two-dimensional view of power allows us to look at the introduction of this policy with a more critical view of the factors affecting its introduction and likely success.

A three-dimensional view of power would look even more broadly at the scheme as an example of the implementation of social values and ideals. In the debate around the scheme we can see differences between the Prime Minister's belief that providing computer access for all will ensure equity and equal opportunity to secondary students, and that it will enhance economic performance. On the other hand a belief has been expressed that investment in education ought not to rely on calculations of its usefulness to the economy, but that instead education should be seen as an intrinsic good that enhances each individual's own potential. These larger debates concern fundamental values and underlying philosophical views over how best to allocate government resources: collectively or individually, for the social good or for individual benefit.

Understanding the development of this policy within a three-dimensional view demonstrates that the introduction of the education revolution by the Rudd Labor government represented complex interactions over power. Understanding this policy in the three-dimensional view allows us to analyse and begin to understand why competing claims exist that appear to contradict each other, and that there is little 'truth' in political debates. Rather, debates expressing differing views about how political interactions take place and who exercises power within them need to be analysed.

Understanding power in this way does not mean that we prescribe how power ought to be exercised. Rather, in adopting a three-dimensional view we are recognising the competing dimensions of power and ways of seeing what is taking place in political dynamics. We are not prescribing a way of viewing Australian political practice, rather we are providing the tools to make readers capable of analysing Australian political practice well.

Key aspects of power

To summarise, there are some key aspects of understanding power in the way that Lukes advocates. These include that power:

- can be exercised covertly or overtly
- can be exercised individually and collectively
- can exist as a capacity, even where conflict is not observable
- can be exercised in ways that are not directly observable and quantifiable, and
- is an expression of underlying social and cultural processes and ideas.

This preferential understanding of power acknowledges all the forces at work in a complex society. This definition of power is multifaceted, and relying upon it to examine a political community such as Australia provides a framework within which a range of actors may be examined as legitimate constituent parts of the study of politics. This definition provides an analytical framework that not only permits us but also requires us to look beyond the formal institutions of politics that are normally the focus of Australian politics studies, and include extra-parliamentary organisations, newly emerging social groups, and individuals who interact with the system.

Ultimately, the choice of how one understands power depends to a large extent on how one understands these related factors about society, including how individuals and groups interact with the political system, how conflict is mediated within and between institutions, and the ways in, and extent to, which non-institutional political forces are able to gain purchase in the political landscape.

Lukes describes power as a concept 'which is ineradicably value-dependent' (2005, p. 30). Because a person's view of power is so closely related to their overall framework for understanding politics, it is important to clarify it at the beginning of this book. Assessing power in three dimensions enables us to recognise the multiple forces at work at formal and informal levels of interaction within political communities, which affect individuals' and groups' ability to interact with political and policy processes, their likelihood of success and the formation of their values, desires and preferences.

Summary

- Power is an essentially contested concept, which is best understood as a multifaceted capacity in relationships between people, processes and institutions.
- Understanding how power is mediated requires examining power in a three-dimensional way, taking into account the unconscious shaping of preferences, desires and values as well as covert and overt types of power exertion and capacity.
- Australian political processes are undergoing continuous engagement with, and deliberation over, power.

Further reading

Foucault, Michel 1995, *Discipline and Punish: The Birth of the Prison,* 2nd edn, Vintage Books, New York.

Lukes, Steven 2005, *Power: A Radical View,* 2nd edn, Palgrave Macmillan, Basingstoke, Hampshire; 1st edn 1974.

Morriss, Peter 2002, *Power: A Philosophical Analysis,* 2nd edn, Manchester University Press, Manchester.

Reynolds, Paul 1991, *Political Sociology: An Australian Perspective,* Longman Chesire, Melbourne.

CHAPTER 2
LIBERAL DEMOCRACY IN AUSTRALIA

This chapter introduces liberal democracies as complex societies that contain elements of both liberal and democratic ideas and values. The conceptualisations and categorisations of these elements and the ways in which they combine are overlapping, making a clear distinction between them impossible. However, a distinctive feature of liberal democracies is that their liberal and democratic elements interact in ways that are a salient and potentially positive feature of Australian politics. In the contemporary era, because liberal democracy has become synonymous with economic liberalism and promotion of the free market, it is important to consider how other liberal and democratic values and ideas may be enhanced, developed and preserved.

Liberal democracies are complex societies in which people often disagree over fundamental concepts and values. Describing a liberal democracy in general, and in Australia in particular, is not straightforward. What we will try to do in this chapter is to outline some of the key elements of liberal democratic political systems, and locate these elements within debates about Australian politics. We will outline and critique some of the key concepts and ideas associated with liberalism and democracy and explore the 'hybrid' system called liberal democracy. We will demonstrate that a feature of liberal democracies is continuous tension and conflict between liberal and democratic values, and between different conceptions of what these mean and how they interact. Moreover, we will argue that this conflict is beneficial insofar as it raises underlying issues that are important in public debate, such as opportunities for political engagement and how individual freedom can be protected. This conflict also makes clear the need to preserve both liberal and democratic aspects of Australian political culture in order for the system as a whole to operate well. In the contemporary era, there is a tendency for principles of economic liberalism to be dominant in Australian liberal democratic practice. We will argue that this is challengeable and that economic liberalism should not automatically be regarded as the paramount consideration in the operation of liberal democracy in Australia. In this context, we will highlight some important new work being undertaken on how to revitalise Australian democracy.

Topics covered in this chapter include:

- that liberal democracies contain values that have their origins in two distinct and overlapping sets of ideas: liberal and democratic

- that liberal and democratic elements often conflict within liberal democratic systems, and this tension produces opportunities for political interaction and engagement
- that liberal democracy has developed in a unique way in Australia
- the outlook for liberal democracy in the contemporary era
- ideas for enhancing the democratic and liberal elements of Australian political practice.

SNAPSHOT Controlling individual liberty to enhance community safety

Since the passage of new anti-terrorism legislation in 2005 it has become possible to subject people to 'control orders'. Under a control order a person's movements can be controlled and their everyday activities can be overtly and closely monitored. They can be prohibited or restricted from specific places, prevented from leaving the country, ordered to be at a specific place at a certain time of day for a specific period, required to wear a tracking device, prevented from communicating with some other people, prevented from using communication devices, prevented from undertaking certain activities including at their work, and required to report to authorities. These are significant restrictions on individual liberty.

The grounds for issuing a control order are where reasonable grounds exist to believe that doing so would substantially assist in preventing a terrorist act, or where the person concerned had provided training to, or received training from, a listed terrorist organisation. The details of preventative detention and control orders are listed in Division 104 of the *Criminal Code* (Cwlth). Applications for control orders are made by the Australian Federal Police (AFP) with the consent of the Attorney-General, and granted by the Federal Court (McDonald 2007, p. 106).

The introduction of control orders was justified by the federal government in the context of new anti-terrorism legislation passed in the wake of the London underground and bus bombings in July 2005. When announcing the proposed legislation, the then Prime Minister John Howard declared that it was 'designed to enable us to better deter, prevent, detect and prosecute acts of terrorism' (Howard 2005).

Yet critics opposed the measures on grounds including that they eroded the presumption of innocence and lowered the threshold for coercive powers to be used by the state, permitted arbitrary interference in people's affairs, and that the existence of a similar regime in the UK before the London bombings had not prevented their occurrence (Chong et al. 2005, pp. 4, 15).

In December 2007 David Hicks became the second Australian to be subjected to a control order after his release from prison (*Age* 2007). Before that, Hicks had been 'Detainee 002', placed in the US detention centre for suspected terrorists in Guantanamo Bay, Cuba, after his arrest in Afghanistan. He was detained on suspicion of having cooperated and trained with Al-Qaeda. It was reported that he had met Osama bin Laden.

In March 2007 Hicks pleaded guilty at a US Military Commission hearing held in Guantanamo Bay to one count of providing material support for terrorism. In exchange for this guilty plea, plus a signed statement that he had suffered no 'illegal' treatment during his incarceration and agreement to a one-year gag during which he could not discuss his case publicly, Hicks received a seven-year sentence with all but nine months suspended. In May he was transferred to Yatala prison in Adelaide (Daskal 2007) to serve his remaining time.

On 29 December 2007 Hicks was released from Yatala and immediately subjected to a control order. His control order included a 12 p.m. to 6 a.m. curfew and a requirement to report to Port Adelaide police station three times a week (AAP & Munro 2007). He was not allowed to leave the country, and he had to provide police with details of his one permitted email address, telephone line and mobile phone number (Roberts & Walker 2007).

The *Age* editorialised that Hicks' release closed a 'shameful chapter in Australian history, one in which the government had neglected its responsibility to protect citizens' rights and uphold fundamental issues of justice including the presumption of innocence (*Age* 2007). The Law Council of Australia ran a long-term campaign advocating fair treatment for David Hicks during his detention, including a speedy and fair trial process (see <www.lawcouncil.asn.au/hicksjustice.html>). Its independent observer of the Hicks Military Commission, Lex Lasry, argued that the new 'criminal justice paradigm' that developed in the US and Australia in response to terrorist attacks implies that 'individual rights can be compromised whenever the executive of a government considers it necessary' (Lasry 2007, p. 4). On the other hand, former Minister for Foreign Affairs Alexander Downer expressed 'no regrets' about the government's handling of the Hicks case and said Hicks' actions in cooperating with terrorists had been 'evil' (*Herald-Sun* 2007).

The Hicks case in its entirety reflects the overlaps, inconsistencies and interdependencies between liberal and democratic values and concerns. On the one hand, his and others' right to individual liberty is paramount. Those liberties—including freedom of movement, freedom of association, the rule of law and the right to a fair trial—ought not to be abrogated without clear and reasonable grounds. On the other hand, his admissions that he trained with Al-Qaeda and associated with known terrorists do pose a potential risk to the public. With control orders, the government is attempting to prevent harm to the community and protect public safety, and is thus responding to community fears about terrorism. However, individuals who are subject to control orders have their fundamental liberties seriously abridged, including freedom of movement and freedom of association. Critics argue that the abridgement of these fundamental liberties can be justified only in exceptional circumstances, that the circumstances required to issue the control order are insufficient and that the range of restrictions on liberties is too wide.

This means that where his (or others') liberties are to be abrogated, the means by which restrictions on liberty are implemented need to be transparent and reviewable, the length of time they are imposed needs to be proportional, and the scope of restrictions needs to be appropriate. Determining the balance between these competing requirements is not easy, but it is a central feature of the tensions between liberal demands and democratic demands in a liberal democracy.

Defining a liberal democracy

'Liberal democracy' is a term used to describe many states around the world that share some characteristics in common. Hague and Harrop (2001) classify modern liberal democracies according to such factors as the existence of a representative government and the extent to which dissent and freedom may be expressed. They produce the classifications shown in Table 2.1, which contain both liberal and democratic ideas.

The term 'state' has different meanings in different contexts. The term can be used to mean a country, a nation or a nation-state and to mean a system of government or political system. It can also be used to describe individual 'States' within the Australian federal system, such as New South Wales and Victoria. For the purposes of this book, the term 'state' is intended to mean a political system. When 'State' appears in this book with a capital 'S' it is intended to mean a State of Australia, such as Tasmania or Queensland.

TABLE 2.1 Types of modern democracies

Type of government	Central characteristics	Examples
Established democracy	Representative and limited government, accepted framework for political competition	Australia, Canada, France, Germany, Italy, Netherlands, New Zealand, Norway, Sweden, United Kingdom
New democracy	Representative institutions are adopted, but pre-democratic traditions persist including limited freedom and rights	Post-communist countries in Eastern Europe, post-military states in Africa and Latin America
Authoritarian rule	Rulers are not accountable to the people or to the law, media are controlled, participation is limited	Military governments, ruling monarchies

Source: adapted from Hague & Harrop 2001, p. 14.

Liberal democracies are relatively new historical entities. The ideas of liberalism became prevalent in the late seventeenth and eighteenth centuries, in opposition to the notion of divine right, the idea that monarchs were imbued by God or by nature with the right to rule (Pateman 1979, p. 6). The idea that people themselves could devise a set of rules by which they would agree to be governed led to the development of a philosophy based on the rights of the individual. Democratic theory emerged in the nineteenth century, and was based on the idea of popular participation in decision-making. Their combination into the idea of a liberal democratic political order, and in particular into representative and democratic forms of government, took hold significantly in the twentieth century (Emy & Hughes 1993, p. 230; Dryzek 2000, p. 9; Heywood 2004, pp. 225–9; Kukathas et al. 1990, p. 17). This is not to suggest that all or even most countries in the world are liberal democracies, but rather that the normative claims of proponents of liberal and democratic principles and forms of government have commanded a significant worldwide audience: to call a country 'illiberal' or 'undemocratic' is a harsh criticism indeed.

A normative argument is prescriptive; it is in favour of a specific norm or standard of behaviour.

Historically, liberal democracies arose at the same time as the emergence and consolidation of industrialisation and market-based economies. This included the development of ever more complex societies within which individual freedom to pursue one's own interests has gone hand in hand with demands for greater public involvement and participation in decision-making. In other words, there is a close, or 'symbiotic', relationship between the economic systems that characterise liberal democracies and their political systems (Emy & Hughes 1993, pp. 84, 232).

Liberal democracies are thus 'hybrid' systems, which combine liberal and democratic elements. Defining these elements is a complicated and multifaceted task. Generally speaking, liberalism is concerned with preserving freedom for individuals to pursue their own interests while democracy is concerned with ensuring that power is popularly exercised, that power ultimately rests with the people. The combining of these two core elements in institutions and participatory forums is what constitutes a society as liberal democratic.

In order to understand the relationship between liberalism and democracy better, it is necessary to outline some of the core elements of liberal and democratic schools of thought. Both liberal and democratic theories have played a critical role in the formation of contemporary ideals, institutions, legal and constitutional conventions, and policy in Australia. We will attempt to delineate some of the core principles and ideas that have informed the development of liberal democracies in general, and show these as a continuum of ideas that inform each other and are closely interrelated. This will provide a framework within which to discuss later the implementation of these ideas in Australia.

Liberalism and democracy

The core of the liberal world-view is the individual. Liberalism focuses on the roles and concerns of individuals, and views them as self-developing and involved in the rational pursuit of maximising their own interests. Society is regarded as an aggregate of individuals, rather than as having an independent identity discrete from the sum of its parts. The appropriate role for the state is to protect the freedom necessary for individuals to pursue the maximisation of their own, rationally conceived interests (Emy & Hughes 1993, pp. 246–7). There are several elements to this conception.

Society is an aggregate of individuals

A core liberal idea is that society is made up of an aggregate of individuals, and is not conceived of as a collective entity. This view was expressed in an extreme form in 1987 by the then British Prime Minister Margaret Thatcher, who declared, 'There's no such thing as society' (Kingdom 1992, p. 1). Critics argue that this emphasis on the individual is a weakness of liberal theory, because it is unable to account for group identities and collective needs.

Individuals are rational self-maximisers

Within liberal thought, it is argued that individuals should be able to develop their own capacities to the greatest extent possible, and that the best way for this to happen is to let individuals make their own rational choices as to what would suit them best. It is assumed that individuals will make rational choices, which means choosing to maximise their personal interests. It is often assumed in contemporary society that this means choosing to pursue wealth and a career, but spending time with family and friends or in leisure or exercise can also be regarded as 'rational' choices in individual development. It is also argued that individuals need to be able to exercise fully their opportunities to self-develop and to develop their own capacities, so that they may participate freely and creatively within society.

Individuals require freedom

In order to self-develop, individuals should be as free as possible from arbitrary interference in their affairs. Thus a corollary to the previous point is that individuals require a sphere of freedom within which to make their own choices as to how to act.

The idea of freedom or liberty is central to liberal discourse, and forms the basis for contemporary arguments in favour of civil liberties and human rights. The idea of a 'sphere of liberty' was famously developed by John Stuart Mill (1806–1873), who argued that people must be free to develop their own capacities, free from interference by government (Rees 1985, p. 48; Gray in Mill 1991). This idea has been embodied in legal principles regarding individual integrity, famously expressed by Blackstone in his *Commentaries on the Laws of England* in 1830, when he stated that the 'right of personal security consists in a person's legal and uninterrupted enjoyment of his [*sic*] life, his limbs, his body, his health, and his reputation' (2001, p. 96). Mill argued that each person should be left free to make their own choices about how to live their life, as long as their pursuit of their own interests does not harm or injure the interests of others. Government interference is justified where necessary to prevent harm; in fact Mill said that the prevention of harm is the 'sole end' that justifies interfering in an individual's freedom (1991, pp. 14, 83).

There are some difficulties with this harm principle, in particular the problem of judging when a person's activities affect only themselves and when they may begin to harm or injure another person (Gray 1983, pp. 48–56). For example, when does a person's behaviour in public constitute harm, and at what point should police be expected to intervene to maintain public order? Also, if a person does harm or injure another person, it is difficult to judge what kind of response should result. Mill differentiates between legal restrictions and/or responding through public opinion (1991, p. 9). For example, criminologists have developed mechanisms of 'shaming' by holding a conference between the offenders and the harmed community, as an alternative response to court proceedings for some harms including youth violence (Sherman, Strang & Woods 2000; Braithwaite 1989). In indigenous communities 'circle sentencing' is being used as an alternative to traditional sentencing approaches for indigenous adults. In circle sentencing the offenders, a magistrate, other community members and family or victims of the offender meet in a circle to discuss the offence and reach agreement on the appropriate penalty. This model is intended to improve community confidence in the sentences decided upon and the criminal justice system (Gamble 2005). There are differences of opinion over whether some harms such as petty theft or bullying are better responded to with punishment or with alternative approaches. The question of an appropriate response to harm is a continuous problem in liberal societies, which try to balance individual rights with the rules and regulations necessary for society to work.

A distinction is sometimes made between 'negative' and 'positive' liberty. Negative liberty is seen as freedom from restraint, whereas positive liberty is seen as freedom to undertake certain human activities. This distinction was first developed by Isaiah Berlin (1969). Today, although the negative conception of liberty is dominant in liberal democracies (Skinner 1984, pp. 194–5), many scholars are developing enlarged concepts of liberty that challenge this distinction. For the purposes of this book, the terms 'liberty' and 'freedom' will be used interchangeably. They will be used in the broadest sense, to mean both freedom from interference or restraint, and freedom to undertake activities.

All individuals must abide by a clear set of rules, which is imposed on everyone equally

Another core liberal idea is the doctrine of the 'rule of law', which means that an objective set of rules is developed in society, which all individuals must obey. All must obey the rules equally, and they may not be arbitrarily applied. All these rules are publicly known and written down.

Some rules are granted the status of 'laws'. These include:

- constitutional law—the text and interpretation of the Australian Constitution
- statutory law (also called legislation or statutes)—the body of law established by parliaments, including criminal law and anti-discrimination law

- common law—the law developed by precedent within court judgments.

For example, courts publish their judgments, and all State governments in Australia provide detailed information on their home pages about the rules in that particular State and about the legal system that adjudicates and enforces the rules. At the Queensland government entry point of <www.qld.gov.au> visitors can click on 'Law and Safety'. At the Victorian government entry point of <www.vic.gov.au> visitors can click on 'Law and Justice'.

The rules are not arbitrary. This means the police or the courts should not be able on a whim to apply them to one person and not to another; they are supposed to apply to all people equally. In practice, this is not always the case. Unofficial and at times unconscious differential application of rules and laws can result from the kinds of cultural and social influences and manifestations of power that we discussed in Chapter 1. Nevertheless, in principle the rules should be applied equally. The rules can also be checked by other institutions. For example, when there is a dispute over the meaning of the rules in the Constitution, the dispute is arbitrated by the High Court of Australia (see Chapter 3).

A limited role for government

Because it is important to preserve freedom for individuals, liberal theory tends to emphasise a limited role for government. Indeed, within liberal theory government is regarded with suspicion: government is a necessary evil, needed to enforce the rules agreed upon by society, to administer society, and to take care of those who are least able to take care of themselves. But government has a natural tendency towards self-aggrandisement and therefore its role should be limited as far as possible. Government should be prevented from interfering in areas where individual enterprise is a more appropriate means of achieving goals. This idea of limited government has been institutionalised in liberal democracies in modern representative forms of government that embody a separation of powers, in order to prevent any single branch of government from becoming too powerful (see Chapter 3).

The idea of limited government finds its strongest expression in economic ideas of the free market. When applied in this way, the type of liberalism being discussed is qualified as 'economic liberalism'. Early nineteenth-century liberal political economists advocated the idea that government intervention to redistribute wealth was wrong, and that individuals should to the greatest degree possible be left to their own endeavours with the free market providing incentive and reward (Arblaster 1994, p. 88). A major contributor to the idea of a free market was Adam Smith (1723–1790), who argued that the market worked best when free from government interference. Instead, the market would guide itself by an 'invisible hand' of demand and supply. This is often called the doctrine of *laissez-faire*. We will return to this idea later when we discuss how it has developed in contemporary Australian politics.

Another implication of the idea of a limited role for government is that individuals should be especially free to conduct their own affairs in private, in areas where the state has no role to intervene. This implies a distinction between private and public affairs. Private activities are those that take place in a domestic arena that is immune from government activity, such as the family, at home or with friends. The public sphere is an arena within which government may more readily regulate individuals' activities, and includes work, communities and the formal arena of politics such as elections and parliament. The difficult distinction between public and private arenas can be seen in the example of the review of privacy laws discussed below, which was considered necessary because of the changing nature and scope of the public/private divide in a technologically enhanced and security-conscious world. This demonstrates the difficulty of drawing a clear dividing line between the two spheres in contemporary politics.

Privacy laws

In January 2006 the federal Attorney-General asked the Australian Law Reform Commission (ALRC) to conduct an inquiry into the *Privacy Act 1988* (Cwlth). The reasons for the inquiry included that since the passage of that legislation understandings of the need for, and the risks posed to, privacy had changed due to advances in information, communication, data storage and surveillance technology and the greater interaction between federal, State and territory laws. The ALRC released a series of issues papers and a discussion paper that invited submissions and comments from members of the public. They have held public meetings and hosted a website inviting public input. The inquiry was completed in March 2008.

Source: <www.alrc.gov.au/inquiries/current/privacy/index.htm>.

The idea of a private/public split is central to liberal thought and has been criticised, in particular by feminist theorists, because women have historically tended to be relegated to the private sphere and thereby placed in an inferior position in politics (van Acker 1999, p. 25). For example, feminists have argued that if a woman is subjected to violence within her home this should be regulated and responded to by the police. Historically, violence against a woman in her own home used to be regarded as a private matter and police would not intervene (Smith, L. 1993, p. 19). Feminist scholarship has raised awareness that if violence within the home is treated as a 'private' issue, this prevents action from being taken against abusers. Since the 1970s significant changes to law and police procedures in regard to domestic violence have resulted from these arguments, and a critique of the private/public split has become a mainstream critique of liberal theory.

A strong civil society

A further implication from the limited role for government is the need for autonomous community organisations within civil society (Kukathas et al. 1990, p. 15). These are organisations independent of government in which individuals can organise themselves around common interests and cooperate to achieve common goals. In this way, the institutions of politics are not limited to the institutions of government, such as the parliament and the High Court, but include other institutions like local clubs, charities and sporting organisations. There are many examples of community organisations in Australian society, including the Salvation Army, the Smith Family, the Cancer Council and Volunteering Australia. Community organisations such as these are important because they build links between individuals and allow them to work cooperatively in areas of mutual interest. This has been called building 'social capital', building networks of trust and reciprocity which help individuals to form bonds and cooperate to achieve goals (Cox 1995, p. 15).

These networks and groups are a focus of this book because we see individuals' participation in community organisations as important to the mediation of power within Australian society. The modes of participation are changing and transforming (see Part II), which is leading to new forms of social capital. This is an important part of our argument because it stands in contrast to the dominant view, which is that the institutions of civil society are in decline. We argue instead that participation in and engagement with politics are taking place in new ways and by a broad range of political actors.

If these are the core concerns of liberal ideas, what can we say about democratic concerns? Democracy, broadly speaking, is a political order designed to ensure that the people are able to govern themselves, to participate in public decision-making. The idea of democracy meaning popular rule was famously encapsulated by Abraham Lincoln in the Gettysburg Address, when he advocated 'government of the people, by the people, and for the people' (cited in Heywood 2004, p. 221). Because the ways in which this might occur can vary hugely, democracy is 'a concept before it is a fact' (Arblaster 1994, p. 3). Some of the core elements of democracy include that it embodies government by all the people, including minorities, which produces decisions in the general interest by assumed or explicit consent. There are several elements to this conception.

Government by the people

In a democratic system, the people are their own decision-makers, but this straightforward normative claim is difficult to implement in complex and populous societies. The tasks of governing are complex and specialised, which precludes direct forms of democracy where all individuals are able to participate directly in decision-making, for example by voting in a plebiscite or referendum on every policy issue and decision. For these reasons liberal democracies have developed complex forms of indirect representative democracy.

In indirect forms of democracy, the people's rule is mediated by representatives who are elected and who are supposed to be prevented from acquiring too much power (via institutional design based on the idea of a separation of powers) and hence becoming remote from the input of those whom they represent (Arblaster 1994, pp. 59–60). This means that democracy requires regular free and fair elections with multiple candidates. It is essential to have multiple candidates so that the voters have choice between representatives and policies, although often in contemporary democracies it has been argued that the policy differences between major political parties are only marginal (see Chapter 6). The Australian Constitution states that members of parliament must be 'directly chosen by the people' (sections 7 and 24), and Australia holds regular free and fair, multiparty elections in every State and Territory as well as federally (see Chapter 5).

In this account of one of the implications of indirect democracy, we can see an interdependence with the liberal idea of restrained governmental power. In this instance the restraint is not for the purpose of protecting individual freedom, but rather for the purpose of ensuring that elected representatives abide by the wishes of those whom they represent. This is an example of the interdependence between liberal and democratic values.

Majorities and minorities should be taken into account

If a core principle of democracy is rule by the people, this implies all people. Yet in large societies consensus is impossible to achieve. Although elected representatives claim to be representing the majority that voted them in, sometimes this majority can be as small as 50 per cent plus one. This is an inherent difficulty with indirect democracy, and it means that the principle of rule by the people can be properly realised only by taking into account minority as well as majority wishes. If minorities are transient, then this state of affairs is relatively easy to accept since each person will find that they may be in a minority on some issues but with the majority on others. In this way, most people's wishes might be catered for most of the time. For example, an individual may find their wishes are in a minority on the question of whether government should ban the use of plastic bags to protect the environment, but that their wishes concur with the majority on the question of whether the government should provide paid parental leave to all workers. On individual issues many people may find that their views concur with the majority often enough for them to feel that their interests are adequately represented. But this cannot be guaranteed.

In addition, the presence of persistent minority views is problematic. If some people are in the minority all of the time, if their views are marginalised and their needs are not met, then they are not in any real sense governing themselves, and this undermines democracy (Arblaster 1994, pp. 66–8). This can occur with marginalised and alienated communities whose needs are not met in a range of policy areas. For example, it has been reported by the Human Rights and Equal Opportunity Commission that the Australian indigenous community suffers in comparison with the non-indigenous community in a range of measures of standard of living. This includes:

- a life expectancy approximately twenty years lower than non-indigenous people

- a death rate more than twice that of the whole Australian population
- an infant mortality rate twice the rate of all Australians
- twice the likelihood of hospitalisation for serious health problems
- less than half the rate of completion of year 12 at school
- three times the unemployment rate
- 62 per cent of the average weekly income of all Australians
- half the home ownership rate
- fifteen times the adult imprisonment rate of non-indigenous adults (HREOC 2005, pp. 29–30).

This means that indigenous people's needs are not being met and implies that the continued marginalisation of indigenous people in all social and economic policy areas poses a democratic problem for Australia. Indigenous people face more obstacles than non-indigenous people in pursuing their individual development.

Democracy produces decision-making in the general interest

Because decision-making in democracy is supposed to be undertaken by all people, whether directly or via their representatives, this implies that the decisions produced by democratic means are in the 'general interest'. Unlike liberal theory, which conceives of society as an aggregate of individuals, democratic theory recognises that an inclusive process of collective thinking and decision-making can lead to the realisation of distinctive, shared values and experiences. In this way, democratic theory is a collective ideal that emphasises the group over the individual. This is an instance in which democratic theory is clearly differentiated from liberal theory, and it has implications for the workings of liberal democracies because individual and group preferences can conflict.

But the ideal of a 'general interest' is also heavily contested, especially in light of the permanent and large-scale minority views in large and complex societies. Often when a claim is made that a policy is in the 'general' or 'national' interest, this can be questioned (see discussion in Chapter 14). If permanent disagreement exists, then it may not be possible to reach consensus on what 'national interest' is in contemporary, multilayered political communities.

Even in a relatively uncontroversial policy area assessing collective interests against individual ones is not straightforward. To give a simple example, an individual's wish to drive their own car at the speed they choose must be weighed against the collective interests of public safety and costs to the health system. This is why governments tend to restrict the speeds at which people may drive, especially in residential and densely populated areas. On the other hand, some individual interests are also recognised because individuals are still allowed to drive at appropriate speeds that are fast enough potentially to cause harm. This is an instance of government regulation in which both the general interest and individual interests are taken into account and attempts are made by regulators to protect both. Since safety is such a high public concern, there are few who openly argue against any speed limit policy in urban areas. However, considerable disagreement exists regarding the details of such a policy—details such as exactly what the speed limit should be, or whether speed limits should be standardised to assist motorists to know what the speed limit is in any given area (e.g. Nixon 2007). Additionally some people still oppose the idea of speed limits, such as occurred in the Northern Territory when highways that previously had no speed limit were limited to 130kph (Toohey 2007).

Representatives should represent the interests of their constituents

We have already said that democratic theory implies that in an indirect democracy, representatives must represent the wishes, or interests, of their constituents. But we have not yet discussed *how* this might occur, a question that is far from straightforward. In representative theory there are several different ways of thinking about how a representative might represent their constituents. Put another way, there are different ways of thinking about the relationship between the representative and the represented (Arblaster 1994, pp. 80–2). The first way of conceptualising this relationship is that the representative is entrusted by those whom they represent to make informed decisions, by relying upon their own experience and understanding of which policy might be the best in the circumstances. The representative relies on their own informed and independent judgement of what is best. This is called the 'trustee' model of representation, and it derives from the ideas of Edmund Burke (Sawer 1998, pp. 28–9). In this model, the judgement of the individual is paramount, and we can again see an example of a close and symbiotic link between the liberal idea of individual freedom—in the prioritising of individual judgement—and the democratic idea of rule by the people—in the idea of representative government.

This contrasts markedly with a second understanding of how representation works, namely the delegate model. In this understanding the representative is delegated by those who elected them to represent their wishes in policy and decision-making. This has also been called the 'mouthpiece' model (Sawer 1998, p. 28). So for example if a representative campaigned and was elected on a platform of lowering tax thresholds, by constituents who believed that lowering tax thresholds was essential, the delegate would be expected to vote in parliament in support of this. This means the representative is 'instructed' in how to vote in parliamentary decision-making by those who elected them (Arblaster 1994, p. 80). In the 2007 federal election this model was promoted by a new political party called Senator Online whose sole platform was that, if elected, their senators would take internet polls on all bills put to parliament and vote according to the majority view expressed in those polls (<www.senatoronline.org.au>).

This understanding of how a representative might operate raises challenges for defining democratic forms of representation. Is it more or less democratic for an elected representative to be instructed on how to vote before they enter parliament? Is it more or less democratic to allow a parliamentarian, once in parliament and privy to information, resources and considerations not available before the election, to make their own independent decision on how to vote? While at first sight it might seem more democratic for a parliamentarian to declare, and be elected on the basis of, their voting intentions on every issue before being elected, this is not always possible. Parliamentarians face many issues once elected on which they may not have been given direction before an election. Also, keeping in mind the point that was made earlier about minorities needing representation, if the majority of voters instructed a representative to vote a certain way but to do so involved trampling on the rights of a minority, would it be more democratic not to abide by the majority of constituents' wishes? If a majority of constituents expressed the view that suspected terrorists should be able to be held in jail without charge for a lengthy period, a representative would need to weigh up the majority's views against the views of the minority opposing the policy (some of whom might have specialist knowledge in human rights or international law), and against the interests and rights of any individual who might be placed in jail under such a policy. If a threat to individual rights were severe, democratic theory would require that a representative preserved the interests of the minority over the majority. This scenario occurred with the introduction of anti-terrorism legislation in Australia after September 11, 2001.

Anti-terrorism laws, liberty and democracy

In March 2002 the federal government introduced draft anti-terrorism legislation into the Australian parliament. One of the important elements of this legislation was the ASIO Legislation Amendment (Terrorism) Bill 2002, which proposed giving the Australian Security and Intelligence Organisation (ASIO) the power to detain and question people who were suspected of being able to provide information related to terrorist activities. The draft provisions applied to people aged fourteen years and over, permitted indefinite detention subject to the securing of a warrant, and prevented people in detention from communicating with anyone else, including a lawyer (PJCAAD 2002, p. vii).

The proposed legislation was investigated by the Parliamentary Joint Committee on ASIO, ASIS (Australian Secret Intelligence Service) and DSD (Defence Signals Directorate), which recommended that the bill be amended to limit detention to seven days, to appoint a panel of senior lawyers to represent detainees, to require that ASIO must apply to a federal magistrate for a warrant to detain someone suspected of being able to provide information related to terrorist activities, and to include a 'sunset' clause so that the legislation would terminate in three years and the government would have to reintroduce it. It concluded that the ASIO legislation in the form initially proposed by the government would 'undermine key legal rights and erode the civil liberties that make Australia a leading democracy' (PJCAAD 2002, p. vii). After considerable public debate, the ASIO legislation was amended in line with some of the concerns expressed by the parliamentary committee and other critics, but many controversial aspects, including lack of legal representation and the possibility of indefinite detention, remained (Hocking 2004, pp. 213–30). The legislation was enacted in June 2003.

In 2005 similar tensions emerged when the *Anti-Terrorism Act* (No. 2) 2005 (Cwlth) was introduced. This legislation amended the *Criminal Code* (Cwlth) to allow for the issuing of preventative detention and control orders and to resurrect the crime of sedition. Despite the controversial nature of its provisions, the Senate Legal and Constitutional Legislation Committee had only a brief period in which to conduct its inquiry into this legislation (LCA 2005a; LCLC 2005), and the Law Council of Australia described the process as the government 'ramming these extraordinary laws through parliament' (LCA 2005b).

These events demonstrate the difficulty of the government implementing legislation to combat terrorism, which many people support on the ground of public safety, yet at the same time protecting the individual rights of citizens.

In modern democracies trustee and delegate models of representation have been supplemented by others. These include the idea of a representative being 'mandated' by the party to which they belong to vote in certain ways, on the basis that the party received support in order to elect that particular representative. Another is the idea that representatives may sometimes need to represent constituents who do not have a voice, such as environmental concerns, the needs of future generations or children. Finally, the model of 'mirror' representation has emerged; the idea that representatives should mirror demographic and other cleavages within the society they represent (Sawer 1998, pp. 31–6). This idea can be used to support quotas in parliament for women or other currently under-represented sectors of society, such as youth or indigenous people. It can be argued that women should make up 50 per cent of parliament since they make up 50 per cent of voters. All of these models have advantages and disadvantages from a democratic point of view. The position a person takes on which is the most democratic model of representation is intrinsically related to their overall outlook on democratic theory. Those who support a more liberal version of democratic theory are likely to support greater scope for individual discretion in decision-making. Those who support a more collectivist or majoritarian version of democratic theory are likely to support ideas of delegation and duty-bound representatives.

There is a range of institutional features of the Australian political system that can be characterised as democratic because they emphasise the role of the people in decision-making. Some of the most important include:

- the Australian Constitution, which establishes parliament as 'directly chosen by the people'
- regularly occurring elections for members of parliament, at which candidates compete for office. The elections are held by secret ballot, which means that nobody knows who you have voted for. Australia was the first country in the

world to introduce voting by secret ballot, which was initially called the 'Australian ballot' (Maddox 2000, p. 144)
- the institutionalisation of the role of the major opposition party in parliament, so when an election is held it is easy for the Opposition to assume government
- requiring legislation to pass through parliament in order to be enacted, so it cannot be enacted at the whim of a single person or party
- maintaining conditions so that people are generally free to express dissent and criticise government institutions and representatives.

Tensions in liberal democracies

Liberal democracy, then, is a complex system within which a tension exists between the ideals of mass representative democracy and liberals who favour individual freedom, effort and merit. Where liberals emphasise the individual pursuit of interest, the ideas of participatory decision-making were developed by those with a more collective consciousness. In a democracy, the majority can impose their will in ways that influence individuals' choices and can mediate outcomes to enhance equality, yet liberals believe in reward on the basis of individual endeavour. When the perspective of economic liberalism is applied, the tension between liberalism and democracy is more obvious. This is because the pursuit of wealth and growth via a free market and individual endeavour could jeopardise the standing of some people in society, by entrenching a permanent stratum of the poor who are unable to benefit from economic growth and whose voices are not heard in decision-making. This means that the pursuit of liberal and democratic values can be inconsistent with one another (Emy & Hughes 1993, pp. 232–4).

Although tensions are inherent to a liberal democratic framework, the values underlying liberal democracies are also interdependent because to a significant extent the provision of liberal values, like freedom, is best made possible via democratic frameworks. Freedom is in fact a necessary condition for democracy and not only a liberal ideal (Arblaster 1994, p. 90). Conversely the provision of democratic decision-making requires and is greatly enhanced by the participation of engaged and informed individuals who are able to identify and pursue their own interests.

The specific values discussed here are reflected in the snapshot at the beginning of this chapter. These include understanding individuals as rational self-maximisers in the sense that community members wish to protect their safety and security. Second, the snapshot raises the question of the appropriate role for government: how much scope should the government have to regulate the behaviour of individuals who have not committed a criminal or violent act. The issue of decision-making by the people is raised in the sense that government is claiming to act in response to people's demand for security and safety. The government has engaged specific organisations to assist in anti-terrorist procedures, and the courts often have the power to decide whether and when to violate an individual's liberty. The question of the general interest is also not straightforward, since in this instance the general interest may be calculated in terms of safety or in terms of freedom. We can see the interdependence and complications involved in translating these principles into practice in policy-making. It might help to consider another example as well.

Having established some of the core elements of a liberal democracy and the interactions between them, we will turn now to a consideration of how liberal democracy developed in Australia. In particular we will ask whether there is a distinctively Australian form of liberal democracy.

Farming genetically modified crops

In late 2007 Victoria and New South Wales for the first time granted farmers permission to grow genetically modified (GM) crops (Brown 2007). GM crops are regarded by some farmers as a potentially valuable addition to agricultural production because they can help by increasing resistance to diseases and drought and rates of production (NFF 2003, p. 2). In 2003 the Australian Bureau of Agricultural and Resource Economics predicted that 'agricultural biotechnology could generate substantial economic gains in the regions where it is introduced', and that if Australia did not adopt GM crops and other countries did, it would incur substantial economic losses amounting to more than a billion dollars a year (ABARE 2003).

But a survey of farmers' attitudes to GM crops in 2003 showed that farmers were cautious about the perceived problems associated with GM crops, which were unproven crop performance, a limited market for the produce and consumer concerns. Almost half of the farmers surveyed said they still opposed GM crops, and a large majority wanted more information to be provided (Biotechnology Australia 2003). These concerns are reflected in comments made by the Network of Concerned Farmers, whose spokesperson cautioned Australia against hastily adopting GM crops (Bolt 2004).

A 2007 Roy Morgan poll showed that 51 per cent of Australians would not buy GM food if they could help it, although this figure had decreased from 55 per cent in 2001 (Roy Morgan 2007a). A 2004 survey of public attitudes showed an increased perception that GM crops presented a potential public health risk but also an increase in support for the use and application of gene technology, especially in medicine (Biotechnology Australia 2004).

The farming of GM raises concerns to do with individual choice and government regulation. The government is expected to weigh up potential individual economic benefits to farmers and potential national economic interests against public concerns about the associated risks. Individual farmers want to be able to make an informed choice about whether to grow GM crops. Members of the general public are concerned about potential risks, including the transmission of GM genes to other crops, its effects on other wildlife, and potential and as yet unknown health problems.

The regulation of this newly emerging economic environment, therefore, raises issues of individual farmers' choices of what to produce against collective public concerns about safety and health, and collective needs for productive yields and drought-resistant crops.

Australian liberal democracy

Following white settlement in Australia, each colony developed its own system of government and laws by the 1850s based on Westminster traditions inherited from the United Kingdom. These systems of government embodied the liberal and democratic values we have discussed but implemented them in a particular way. For most of its post-settlement development, Australia has adhered to some of the principles of liberalism while simultaneously relying heavily on the state as a supporter of national development (Emy & Hughes 1993, p. 230). Particularly after the adoption of the Constitution in 1901, the Australian state and economy developed in a dependent relationship with one another. The government adopted such policies as regulation of industrial affairs to ensure needs-based wages and the protection of domestic industry from exports via the use of tariffs. These policy directions were in opposition to the principles of economic liberalism, and were designed to protect white Australian workers' jobs and standard of living. The state's involvement in national development involved the regulation, subsidisation, support and protection of emerging industry in order to enhance economic growth and to foster a particular type of (white) citizenship (Marsh 1995, pp. 17–24), which was committed to this version of national interest as national development.

Marsh describes the principles established by 1909, when the two major party groupings of Labor and non-labour had emerged, as liberal–egalitarian, describing the liberal component of the principles as 'advanced' liberalism. He argues that Australia did not adopt a reliance upon the free market to provide for individuals' interests and needs, but instead emphasised the role of government in providing for people's needs (1995, pp. 24–5). Thus, egalitarianism became an appropriate goal for government to pursue and maintain. Australia's version of liberal democracy has been described as 'Deakinite' (Cook 1999, p. viii) after Alfred Deakin, who was an architect of the Constitution and Prime Minister three times between 1903 and 1910, and who advocated government support to enable entrepreneurship to flourish, including government regulation of industrial policy and income security (Marsh 1995, pp. 25–6). This idea has also been referred to as 'Australian settlement' (Kelly 1992; see also the critique in Stokes 2004). Emy and Hughes agree that the state, since colonisation, played an active role in Australia's economic development and that the ideals of nineteenth-century economic liberalism, in terms of restrained government and a market developing freely without government intervention, did not exist (1993, p. 89). Historically, then, liberal democracy in Australia has taken a particular form that has emphasised an interventionist government and the pursuit of socially beneficial and democratically agreed goals.

In the contemporary era that is the primary focus of this book, Australian liberal democracy has changed and these ideas have been dismantled. The most important change has been the embracing of a doctrinaire type of economic liberalism that has informed and led to significant changes in the structure of government provision of services.

> The terms 'economic liberalism', 'economic rationalism' and 'neo-liberalism' have been used to describe the contemporary application of liberal principles of non-interference and maximum freedom to the operation of the economy, or market. These terms are used in this way here, and are used interchangeably.

In the contemporary era, both major political parties support the imposition of economic liberal principles in the marketplace and have adopted a common belief in the ability of a more unrestrained market to deliver goods and services best (Marsh 2002, p. 23). This shift has involved a reduction in the size and scope of government activities. These ideas are derived from economic liberalism and are not new, but their pre-eminence in determining the policy choices of governments has been particularly successful in Australia since the 1980s. Policy-makers here have increasingly pursued the ideas of economic liberalism in their contemporary free market form (Bell, S. 1997, p. 1; Beresford 2000, p. 78).

This development has happened in line with similar developments internationally. Globally, liberal democracies have been advocating reduced government regulation of the marketplace and promoting the liberal economic ideals of non-intervention, competition and smaller government. Increasingly there has been an emphasis on organising society around principles of economic liberalism, including freedom for markets from regulation and the pursuit of self-interest. This trend has equated free markets with the removal of centralised controls on wages and the freeing up of trade from regulations and tariffs (Gray 1998, pp. 11, 12). However, these economic policies also have considerable social implications such as increasing inequality, social dislocation due to the often rapid transfer of investment between industries, regions and countries, price fluctuations, job insecurity and unemployment.

'Globalisation' refers to the increasing global integration and interconnectedness of people, societies and economies. Some definitions of globalisation emphasise economic liberalism. For example, globalisation has been defined as 'a global phenomenon characterised by mobile capital and deregulated trade' (Gray 1998, pp. 6–7) and as liberalisation, meaning the removal of government restrictions on the movement of goods in trade (Scholte 2000, pp. 15–16). However, other definitions emphasise different aspects of global interconnectedness, including by arguing that Western cultural norms are increasingly prevailing over indigenous practices, or that states' decision-making powers are being reduced in a globalised world (Beresford 2000, pp. 61, 90; see also Firth 1999, pp. 271–84; Sheil 2001, pp. 1–10). Globalisation is a contested concept.

Emy and Hughes argue that the contemporary emphasis on economic liberalism within liberal democracies amounts to an overturning of the twentieth-century consensus in Australia that welfare liberalism was essential to national development. They point out that the pursuit of economic growth at all costs may erode democratic norms and procedures and that effort may be required to preserve these norms (1993, pp. 2, 92–4). Gray agrees, arguing that it is wrong to equate liberal democracy with the free market, because an unfettered market is 'incompatible' with democracy (Gray 1998, p. 8) because it imposes high human costs. Nevertheless, the free market is regarded by many as 'inexorable' (Gray 1998, p. 3) and unchallengeable. This has meant that in many of today's liberal democracies, economic liberalism and the free market prevail, and this outlook has even come to be equated with democracy. Gray calls this the idea of 'democratic capitalism' (1998, p. 4).

However, within contemporary economic liberalism lies a paradox. In calling for a freer market, economic liberals recognise that previous systems of market regulation, such as the imposition of tariffs on imports and the regulation of immigration in relation to perceived needs in the labour force, were systems created by government. They imply therefore that removing regulations of this kind creates a freer market, in which government plays less of a role. But the free market is itself a creation of people and laws. A free market requires regulation, but regulation of a different kind. In this sense, the idea of *laissez-faire* is a fiction (Sunstein 1995, p. 31; Gray 1998, p. 5ff). The free market is an artefact, a creation of human society.

If the free market is an artefact then it can be challenged, and contemporary economic rationalism can be mediated. Alternative models for economic and social organisation can be proposed, even in this contemporary era. Liberal democracy does not have to mean only, or even primarily, economic liberalism. There has recently been a range of scholarly work published that engages with the question of how to improve liberal democracies. Important writers in this field include Carole Pateman (1988), John Dryzek (2000), Phillip Pettit (1999), John Uhr (1998) and Duncan Ivison (2002). We will examine some of these works in order to sustain the normative argument that liberal democracy in the contemporary era amounts to much more than economic liberalism and to provide some direction as to how liberal democracies might be revitalised. Such revitalisation can open up new opportunities for democratic participation in both formal and informal institutions of power, opportunities that form the basis for many of the chapters in this book.

Strengthening liberal democracy

The first idea in the reinvigoration of liberal democracy that we will investigate is deliberative democracy. Theories of deliberative democracy rest on the idea that deliberation, or informed discussion, is an essential component of a good democracy. For democracy to work well individuals should be able to discuss and debate political affairs. This theory of democracy aims to enhance the involvement of all members of the public in decision-making and to enhance the quality of that involvement by ensuring higher levels of information and discussion.

John Uhr argues that Australian politics today is understood largely in terms of popular sovereignty (1998, p. xii), which is the idea that the system of government obtains its legitimacy and its power directly from the people. But popular sovereignty refers to more than elections. It means that without the ongoing consent of the people to be governed, and to be governed in a particular way, a government is illegitimate and should be removed. The people have the ultimate power to decide the direction of the system of government. He argues that if popular sovereignty is important to Australian democracy, one way of ensuring that it happens is by reforming political institutions to ensure that people are able to discuss affairs of government. This would mean a move towards a more 'deliberative' form of democracy. The crucial point of deliberation is not just to have debates or discussions but also that, in the process of doing so, people's opinions and policy preferences can be changed. Preferences are changed not by force or deceit but by the discussion itself. John Dryzek agrees, arguing that 'the essence of democracy itself is now widely taken to be deliberation, as opposed to voting, interest aggregation, constitutional rights, or even self-government' (2000, p. 1).

This view of the importance of deliberation has been exerting considerable influence on understandings of the Australian system of government since about 1990. Evidence of this is an enhanced concern with community participation. Federal, State/Territory and local governments are increasingly putting mechanisms in place to improve opportunities for community consultation in decision-making (see for example Head 2007; Carson & Gelber 2001; Hendriks 2002). The idea of deliberative democracy also has close links with the idea of participatory democracy—the normative argument that a democratic system of government should seek to promote and enable the maximum level of participation from its citizens (see Pateman 1979).

A second argument we will consider briefly in the contemporary revival of liberal democracy is that of post-colonial liberalism. Duncan Ivison argues for an invigorated, responsive and adaptive form of liberalism that recognises and engages with the historical experiences of those who have long suffered injustice at the hands of liberal democratic states: specifically indigenous peoples. Although his central argument is concerned with reconstituting and legitimising liberalism, there is a strong democratic element to it. He argues that in order to be just, liberal values need to engage with a diversity of local forces and contexts. For liberal values such as individual rights to be meaningful to indigenous people, they cannot be imposed as abstract concepts in ways that shore up existing inequalities. Instead, principles such as equality and freedom need to be recast in an engagement with indigenous people's experiences. In order to make this possible, he argues, deliberation and disagreement are crucial. A diversity of indigenous and non-indigenous voices must be heard in the formation and shaping of public debate and policy (2002, pp. 1–2, 7–8). These ideas resonate somewhat with the type of egalitarian liberalism that has historically been a strong part of Australia's post-colonial history, and strengthens that idea by explicitly drawing attention to the issue of indigenous participation. This is crucial because, as we discussed earlier, indigenous people have been effectively excluded from engagement in Australian liberal democracy since colonisation. Although initially this exclusion occurred through overt forms of decision-making and power, more recently it has continued through more covert and three-dimensional forms of power. Ivison's work seeks to try to redress the democratic deficit in Australia that is reflected in the state of our indigenous people. Like Uhr, Ivison also emphasises engagement, deliberation and disagreement and argues that they are important in establishing legitimacy. Protecting the interests of indigenous people, a numerical minority, requires that democratic forms do more than just reflect majority wishes.

We can see here some important and interesting ideas for the reinvigoration of liberal democracies in the contemporary era. These ideas not only challenge the dominance of economic liberalism in Australian society but also display a willingness to reconsider the interdependence between liberal and democratic values in innovative ways. It seems increasingly clear that this interdependence is crucial to understanding liberal democracy in Australia. In other words, Australia will become more democratic (in the sense of engaging all people actively in participating in decision-making at all levels) by being more liberal (in the broadest sense of protecting and enhancing individuals' rights and interests). Conversely, it will become more liberal by being more democratic.

Summary

- Liberal and democratic values interact and are interdependent in liberal democracies.
- Liberalism is concerned with individual freedom and democracy is concerned with decision-making by the people.
- Australian liberal democracy developed with an emphasis on the role of government in national development and in preserving standards of living.
- In the contemporary era policy-making in liberal democracies has become dominated by the concerns of economic liberalism.
- In this context, opportunities for public participation in decision-making and individual freedom can best be enhanced and protected by realising the interdependence of democratic and liberal values.

Further reading

Arblaster, Anthony 1994, *Democracy,* 2nd edn, Open University Press, Buckingham.

Brett, Judith 2003, *Australian Liberals and the Moral Middle Class,* Cambridge University Press, Melbourne.

Cook, Ian 1999, *Liberalism in Australia,* Oxford University Press, Melbourne.

Hocking, Jenny 2004, *Terror Laws: ASIO, Counter-Terrorism and the Threat to Democracy,* UNSW Press, Sydney.

Sawer, Marian 2003a, *The Ethical State? Social Liberalism in Australia,* Melbourne University Press, Melbourne.

Useful websites

- Democratic Audit of Australia: <www.democratic.audit.anu.edu.au>. This site provides information on a research project based at the Australian National University and the Institute for Social Research at Swinburne University, assessing how democratic Australia is.

- International Institute for Democracy and Electoral Assistance: <www.idea.int/about>. This intergovernmental organisation based in Sweden was created in 1995, and has member states from all continents. Its mandate is to support sustainable democracy worldwide. Its website contains information on a range of issues relevant to democratic practice including state reports, and democratic questionnaires.
- John Stuart Mill's *On Liberty* is available at <www.constitution.org/jsm/liberty.htm>. It was first published in 1859.
- Abraham Lincoln's Gettysburg Address is available at the Library of Congress at <www.loc.gov/exhibits/gadd/images/Gettysburg–2.jpg>.

CHAPTER 3
FRAMEWORKS FOR GOVERNING

BIRTH OF A NATION...
A FEDERATION PROPERLY CONSTITUTED – ON BROAD AND DEMOCRATIC LINES – WOULD BE ENABLED TO WORK OUT ITS OWN DESTINY....
Constitution

In this chapter we outline the Australian constitutional and governmental framework, and argue that it acts as a dynamic and adaptable system. Understanding the institutional framework for governing is important for understanding the framework within which decisions are made and implemented in Australian politics and how people can interact with and participate in the political system. Developing an in-depth understanding of the system of government as a whole requires understanding the text of the constitutional document, as well as implied elements, changing interpretations and expectations of government and political interactions.

In this chapter, we will first explain the three levels of government in Australia: federal, State/Territory and local. We will then outline how the Australian constitutional document was written and consider formal change to the constitutional text via referendum and the question of a preamble. We will examine some of the important components of the written and unwritten aspects of the Constitution, with particular attention to Westminster conventions and the doctrine of separation of powers. We will discuss the role of the judiciary and outline debates about judicial review. We conclude with the question of whether Australia should adopt a bill of rights. We argue that understanding how a constitutional system of government works is more complicated than reading the text of the Constitution. A constitution is interpreted, enforced and enacted within constantly changing political circumstances, expectations and opportunities. Developing an understanding of the entire constitutional system involves looking at the mechanisms by which our governmental institutions were established as well as examining the interaction and contestability between those institutions and the issues, expectations and players within any given era. This means the frameworks for governing are adaptable and subject to interpretation and change.

Topics covered in this chapter include:

- an explanation of the three levels of government in Australia: federal, State/Territory and local
- how the Australian Constitution was drafted and voted on by the Australian people
- an explanation of referendums as a mechanism for achieving formal constitutional change
- debate over a preamble to the Constitution

- discussion of the importance of the non-written aspects of our constitutional framework
- a discussion of the High Court of Australia as the judicial branch of the Australian system of government and its powers of judicial review
- an overview of debates about a bill of rights.

SNAPSHOT Judges vs legislators: individual rights and government power

The separation of powers doctrine suggests that powers should be separated in order to prevent any one branch of government becoming excessive or arbitrary. An important part of this idea is that the power to impose punishment is generally reserved to the judiciary, the courts. This is because the courts are seen as immune from political pressures and are therefore best equipped to be fair and impartial in imposing sentences that may include imprisonment or other restrictions on personal liberty. Punitive powers are restricted to the judiciary.

The implementation of this idea, however, is not always clear cut. In 2004 this issue was raised by an asylum seeker who was being detained indefinitely as a result of actions taken by the legislature and the executive.

Ahmed Al-Kateb arrived in Australia by boat in December 2000. He did not have an appropriate visa and was therefore placed in immigration detention. The *Migration Act 1958* requires that 'unlawful non-citizens' be kept in immigration detention until they are either granted a visa to remain or removed from Australia (section 196(1)).

Al-Kateb applied to be granted a visa to enter Australia, but was unsuccessful. This meant the Australian government tried to deport him to his country of origin. But this proved impossible because no country was prepared to take him. Al-Kateb had been born in Kuwait to Palestinian parents, had no citizenship rights and was effectively 'stateless'. This meant that Al-Kateb faced the prospect of being detained indefinitely, perhaps for the rest of his life.

No court had authorised Al-Kateb's detention. Instead, his detention arose from the parliament passing legislation that permitted the executive (that is, the minister responsible for immigration) to detain unlawful non-citizens until they are removed.

The fact that he could not be removed for practical reasons raised serious questions about the scope of governmental powers. Were the legislature and executive acting outside the bounds of their powers? Was Al-Kateb's detention punitive and therefore in breach of the separation of powers? These questions were taken to the High Court of Australia.

In 2004 the High Court ruled that the continued detention of Al-Kateb was legal, even if it was indefinite (*Al-Kateb v Godwin* (2004) 219 CLR 562). The Court said that the detention of 'unlawful non-citizens' was not a form of punishment because the purpose of the detention was to facilitate the removal of non-citizens, not to punish them (Gelber 2005, pp. 312–13). The legislature and executive, therefore, had not encroached on the powers of the judicial branch of government and had not violated the separation of powers.

In making this decision one of the judges, Justice McHugh, described the situation as 'tragic' but said nothing could be done. He said that it was not the job of the courts 'to determine whether the course taken by Parliament is unjust or contrary to basic human rights'.

The decision sparked a great deal of controversy. Critics noted that the High Court was out of step with courts in the United States and the United Kingdom, which had ruled indefinite detention to be unlawful (Marr 2005). Amnesty International (2005, p. 20) argued that the Court's ruling put Australia in breach of its international human rights obligations, particularly the prohibition against arbitrary detention in Article 9(1) of the *International Covenant on Civil and Political Rights* (ICCPR).

The decision also led to increased calls for Australia to introduce a bill of rights. Some pointed to the decision as evidence of continued potential for serious human rights violations in Australia and noted that such abuses commonly affect the most vulnerable of citizens (Williams 2007a, pp. 10–12). Shortly before his retirement Justice McHugh said that he favoured a bill of rights because, without one, judges have a limited capacity to strike down legislation that unambiguously impinges on individual freedom (2005, pp. 21–2).

In the end, political pressure from these critics, as well as refugee advocacy groups and human rights organisations, forced the government to intervene to resolve Al-Kateb's seemingly impossible predicament. The then immigration minister, Amanda Vanstone, granted Al-Kateb a bridging visa that entitled him to live in the community, albeit without the right to work, study or obtain social security benefits. In October 2007 Al-Kateb was granted a humanitarian visa, giving him the right to live permanently in Australia.

The Al-Kateb case raises several important questions about our system of government. Is it the role of the judiciary to place a check on legislative and executive power? How effective is the separation of powers in preventing abuses of governmental power in Australia? What safeguards exist in our constitutional and governmental framework to prevent abuses of human rights?

Three levels of government

The Constitution establishes two levels of government in Australia: federal and State. The seat of federal government is Canberra. Further discussion on this level of government is undertaken in Chapter 11.

In Australia, the national government is also called the 'federal government', the 'Commonwealth' or the 'central government'. These terms are used interchangeably in this book.

States

The six States that make up the Australian federation were originally independent colonies that agreed to unite to form a single nation. The framers recognised that the vast size of the country coupled with a small population made unitary central government—a system with only a national government and no regional level of government—impractical (Gillespie 1994, p. 61). In opting for a federal system of government, the drafters of the Constitution were also conceding to colonial demands for retention of their autonomy. Previously independent colonies wished to join in a single nation for some specific reasons, including the need to facilitate inter-State trade and commerce. However, the colonies were simultaneously jealous of their powers and did not wish to give too many away. The federal compact that resulted from the constitutional discussions was a compromise document, which recognised State autonomy and at the same time tried to limit the powers of the new national government by setting them out in section 51.

The States retained 'residual powers'—those powers that had not specifically been granted to the Commonwealth. The States are responsible for many areas crucial to our everyday lives. States have their own criminal justice systems, are responsible for urban development and planning, administer hospitals, run primary and secondary schools, and allocate resources to transport infrastructure including railways, roads and bus services. The States oversee housing services and collect revenue from the sale of commercial and residential properties. In other words, States direct policy and manage resources in a huge range of areas of day-to-day relevance.

States are also protected from federal interference in their affairs in important ways. The Constitution protects their existence and powers (in sections 106 and 107), and the High Court has interpreted these provisions to mean that the federal government may not place a special burden or disability on States which is not applied generally, and that the Commonwealth cannot destroy a State or curtail States' ability to function. This 'state immunity' principle was outlined in 1947 in the *Melbourne Corporation* case, and was more recently reaffirmed in 2003 in the *Austin* case. Also, the federal government cannot pass a law that directly overrides a single State if it disagrees with the State's policy. For example, if Victoria were to introduce a law legalising euthanasia and the federal government disagreed with this, it could not pass its own law saying that Victoria may not legalise euthanasia and try to enforce it under section 109 of the Constitution. This is because the States possess residual powers, and the prohibition of euthanasia under criminal law is a State prerogative. If the federal government wanted to override a State's euthanasia laws, it could do so only if it passed a law that applied to the entire country and if the law it passed fell within its constitutional jurisdiction under section 51. Since euthanasia is prohibited under criminal law, and criminal law is predominantly the jurisdiction of the States, this would be very difficult to achieve. But in 1997, after the Northern Territory had enacted a law to permit voluntary euthanasia, the federal government was able to prevent it from doing so by removing the Territories' ability to legislate in relation to that issue (Kline 2002, pp. 50–2). This was in relation to a Territory, not a State. Why this was able to happen is explained below.

Each State has its own Governor and enacts its own laws and policies. This is why laws and policies can, and often do, differ between States. Often the States cooperate on policy-making in order to develop nationally consistent rules and regulations. For example most road transport laws are controlled by the States and Territories, and these governments have cooperated with the National Transport Commission, a federal government body, to try to develop and coordinate nationally consistent road rules (see <www.ntc.gov.au>), which will apply in every State and Territory.

Territories

Territories do not have the same powers as States. They are created by a law of the federal parliament (according to section 122 of the Constitution), and did not exist as separate colonies before Federation. Territories that have been created in this way include the Territory of Cocos (Keeling) Islands, the Territory of Christmas Island and the Territory of Ashmore and Cartier Islands. The two best known, self-governing territories are the Australian Capital Territory (ACT) and the Northern Territory (NT).

ACT: The seat of government

The ACT was declared the future seat of government in 1909 and came into existence on 1 January 1911. It was governed under federal law with an administrator until it became self-governing, with its own parliament, in 1988. (For a history of the process by which the ACT was selected as the site for the federal government see <www.nationalcapital.gov.au/education_and_understanding/history>). The ACT parliament is unicameral, and has a Legislative Assembly made up of seventeen parliamentarians. The ACT government looks after both State-level and local-level functions within the territory.

Northern Territory

At Federation the Northern Territory was part of South Australia, and in 1911 control over the land belonging to the Northern Territory was ceded to the Commonwealth under a local administrator. The Northern Territory was granted legislative self-government in 1978 (see <www.nt.gov.au/lant/parliament/nt.shtml>). Its parliament is unicameral, with a Legislative Assembly of twenty-five members. In 1998 a Territory referendum on the question of becoming a State was defeated.

Because Territories are granted their powers by an Act of federal parliament, they all operate slightly differently (for a breakdown of the differences, see Singleton et al. 2006, pp. 91–4). They do not possess the same constitutional jurisdiction as States and, therefore, protection from interference by the federal government. A Territory's powers of government are provided to it in federal legislation. This means that the federal government can either amend its legislation granting the Territory its powers so as to delimit those powers, or override or terminate a law passed by the government of a Territory. This affects the ability of a Territory to legislate. It helps to understand this by providing an example.

In 2006 the ACT enacted a *Civil Unions Act* that conferred legal recognition under ACT law to same-sex relationships in which the couples had undergone a civil ceremony. The recognition accorded was the same as that granted to married couples. The federal government disagreed with the move, arguing that marriage is a fundamental institution and that (in concert with amendments to the Commonwealth *Marriage Act* passed in 2004) marriage should be a union between a man and a woman to the exclusion of all others. As a result the federal government exercised its powers under section 35 of the *Australian Capital Territory (Self-Government) Act* and requested the Governor-General to disallow the legislation. This occurred a month after the ACT legislation had been passed, an action that terminated the legislation (Zanghellini 2007, pp. 265–9).

Six months later, in December 2006, the ACT tried to recognise same-sex relationships again by introducing the *Civil Partnerships Bill*. This legislation tried to overcome the problems of its predecessor by specifying that civil partnerships be treated like de facto relationships and not like marriages. However, the federal government promised that if this legislation were passed it would disallow it, just as it had disallowed its predecessor (Zanghellini 2007, p. 298). Then in May 2008 the ACT government faced opposition from the new federal Labor government in yet another attempt to grant same-sex couples the right to a civil union, and instead implemented a watered down form of registration of same-sex relationships (Johnson 2008; Rudra 2008b).

The Territories have a relative lack of sovereignty compared with the States. This may be the reason why the Territories are often overlooked in studies of Australian federalism.

Local government

Yet another level of government, local government, is not mentioned in the Constitution. Local governments are set up by laws made by the parliaments of the States or Territory in which they are located, and they do not have any direct constitutional powers. For example, local governments in New South Wales operate under the State *Local Government Act 1933*. Local governments tend to be responsible for land use and zoning, rubbish, recycling and waste collection, local environmental projects, local libraries, suburban streetscaping, car parking and regional development. Local governments are also called councils.

According to the *Local Government National Report 2005–2006*, local government expenditure in 2004–05 amounted to $19.43 billion, which represented more than 2 per cent of GDP, and in May 2006 local government employed 167,400 people (DOTARS 2006, p. 3). Local governments are thus an important component of the national economy.

In 2006 a total of 701 local governments received federal funding. A breakdown of how many local governments exist in each State and in the Northern Territory derived from these data is shown in Table 3.1.

The number of local governments is subject to change. For example, in Queensland local governments were amalgamated to form half of their original number, and elections for the new councils were held in March 2008 (Connolly 2008; see also Queensland government information at <www.strongercouncils.qld.gov.au>). With all three levels of government clarified, we can consider other aspects of the constitutional framework for governing.

TABLE 3.1 Local governments by State/Territory

NSW	Vic	Qld	WA	SA	Tas	NT
155	80	73	142	74	29	64

Source: DOTARS 2006, p. 5.

Writing the Australian Constitution

A 'constitution' is a document containing a set of rules by which a group of people, in this case a nation, has agreed to be governed. Although most countries around the world have a written constitution, not all do. Indeed, a country with one of the most important influences on the Australian system of government, the United Kingdom, does not. Instead, it relies on rules and procedures that have developed and become accepted over time, as well as some explicit laws passed by the parliament, court precedent and international influences (Saunders 1998, pp. 2–4).

Following white settlement in Australia, each colony developed its own system of government and laws inherited from the United Kingdom. Economic development took place independently within each colony, and customs duties were typically imposed on inter-colonial trade. Helen Irving has written a fascinating cultural account of the metamorphosis of these independent colonies into entities that saw themselves as part of a greater whole. Irving describes how the Constitution was drafted during the last decade of the nineteenth century in a complex and time-consuming procedure (1997, pp. 27–31). As evidence of the need for this in constitution writing, she cites Edmund Barton's declaration that 'a constitution is not a dog licence' (1997, p. 27). A document of the import and significance of a constitution is neither lightly to be entered into nor easily composed. As sentiment towards nationhood grew, so did other essential factors. These included the legal will to combine the colonies into a single nation, the political skills to draft a constitution and achieve agreement between the colonies on what the new national government would do, a growth in the population, the achievement of widespread literacy, and enhanced forms of communication and transport. It was believed that a national government was necessary to oversee specific policy areas such as defence and diplomacy.

There were initial misgivings by some about the need for a new national government. These included criticisms that it would create an expensive new 'layer of government' and that the colonies were too divided and competitive to unite. Despite this, efforts continued to create a new national government and constitution. Conventions were held in 1891, 1897 and 1898 (Irving 1997, pp. 52–4).

'Constitutional Conventions' (with a capital 'C') are meetings or conferences at which constitutional issues are deliberated.

In 1899 the draft constitution in the form of a Constitution Bill was approved by all the colonies except Western Australia (Irving 1997, p. 5). The bill was taken to London to receive parliamentary approval. After passage of the

Commonwealth of Australia Constitution Act through the British parliament, Western Australians agreed to join. The Australian Federation came into being on 1 January 1901. Thus, unlike constitutions such as that of the US, which was the product of a revolution against imperial rule, the Australian constitution was drawn up peacefully and enacted via popular vote and parliamentary ratification.

The new system of government derived in large part from the Westminster parliamentary traditions inherited from the United Kingdom that had been imported to the colonies before Federation. But important changes were made to the Westminster system in the final document by incorporating federalism. These will be discussed in more detail below and in Chapter 11.

Constitutional change and referendums

The constitutional framework is capable of changing in many ways, including via High Court interpretation, policy shifts and people's engagements between and within institutions. There is only one mechanism for achieving formal constitutional change, meaning changes to the text of the constitutional document, and that is a referendum, detailed in chapter VIII of the Constitution. In order to put a referendum to the people the proposal must be passed by both the lower and upper houses of the federal parliament. In order for a referendum to be passed, it must receive both a majority of votes overall *and* a majority of votes in a majority of States. This is called the 'double majority' provision.

The requirement for the double majority makes referendums difficult to pass. Out of a total of forty-four referendum questions put to the people since Federation, only eight have passed. Most of those passed either related to minor technical matters or granted the Commonwealth powers to provide social service benefits and to intervene in regard to States' debts. In 1977 a referendum added a clause to the Constitution mandating a previously unwritten Westminster convention—that appointments to Senate vacancies between elections should be of a person from the same political party as the senators they replaced. Referendums that have attempted to expand the Commonwealth's formal powers tend to fail (Singleton et al. 2006, pp. 57–61).

The referendum that received the highest 'yes' vote in Australian history was in 1967, and it was heralded as a popular vote on Aboriginal rights (Attwood & Markus 2007; Attwood & Markus 1998). The referendum received 90.77 per cent approval nationwide and a majority in every State and Territory. It approved changes to the Constitution to allow the Commonwealth to make laws with respect to Aboriginal people and to include indigenous people in the national census. The relatively minor textual changes to the Constitution were, however, interpreted by advocates of a 'yes' vote as ushering in a new era of rights for Aboriginal people, although the government of the day proved itself reluctant to implement significant changes to Aboriginal policy, and it fell to a later Whitlam-led government to introduce significant change (Attwood & Markus 2007, pp. 54–64).

In November 1999 the most recent referendum was held, and it was on the question of whether to become a republic. One of the questions raised by this referendum is whether a successful referendum is needed in order for Australia to be able to be considered a republic in practice. It has been strongly argued that it is not, since the operation of the Australian system of government is already republican in all the respects that matter (Galligan 1995). This is because the Australian system of government has already changed in substantial respects to become a republic without a change to the constitutional text. This includes the abolition of appeals of High Court decisions to the Privy Council in the United Kingdom in 1975 and the passage of the *Australia Act* in 1986. High Court Justice Michael Kirby has called Australia a 'crowned republic', meaning that it is a republic in every sense except that the legal figure of the Queen still resides in the Constitution (Kirby 1993, p. 73). George Winterton argues that if 'modern republicanism' means that heredity does not determine those considered fit for office, then Australia already operates as a republic (1992). The Queen does not interfere with political events in Australia, and the Governor-General plays a largely symbolic role.

In this context, a referendum for Australia to become a republic is important for symbolic reasons. The discussion in this chapter has made clear that the constitutional system is dynamic and capable of change, and that the text of the Constitution is only one component of the overall framework for governing. This is not to downplay the importance of amending the Constitution to become a republic—symbolism in constitutional change is crucial as part of the process of revitalising Australian democratic practice. However, many of the practical changes towards becoming a republic have already occurred. In much the same way, the 1967 referendum had both a symbolic and a textual importance.

Constitutional change is a ubiquitous feature of the Australian system of government, but this occurs only occasionally in the form of changes to the constitutional text via referendum. Much more often, it occurs in changes to interpretations of the meaning of the constitutional text and changes in the ways in which government operates, including through the introduction of new representatives, changes in expectations of government, and changes in the interpretation of the appropriate role for each branch of government. This means that the frameworks for governing in Australia are dynamic, flexible and adaptable.

Preamble

The Australian Constitution contains no lofty preamble or introductory passage of the kind known in other countries. For example, the US Constitution drawn up in 1787 declares:

> We the people of the United States, in order to form a more perfect union, establish justice, insure domestic tranquillity, provide for the common defense, promote the general welfare, and secure the blessings of liberty to ourselves and our posterity, do ordain and establish this Constitution for the United States of America.

The Constitution of the Republic of South Africa was finalised in 1996 following the abolition of apartheid, which heralded momentous political and social change. The preamble to that document states in part:

> We, the people of South Africa, recognise the injustices of our past; honour those who suffered for justice and freedom in our land; respect those who have worked to build and develop our country; and believe that South Africa belongs to all who live in it, united in our diversity.

The Australian Constitution does not contain a preamble, but rather contains the introductory passages to the *Constitution Act* passed by the British parliament. It is much more sombre and dry than the two examples already provided, and announces only that: 'Whereas the people of New South Wales, Victoria, South Australia, Queensland, and Tasmania, humbly relying on the blessing of Almighty God, have agreed to unite in one indissoluble Federal Commonwealth ...'

In the 1999 referendum, a question was also asked on whether a preamble should be added to the Constitution. The precise wording of the question is available on the Australian Electoral Commission's website at <www.aec.gov.au/Elections/referendums/1999_Referendum_Reports_Statistics/1999.htm>. Advocates of a preamble argued that it was time to include a statement in the Constitution that would celebrate the values and aspirations of Australians and contribute to reconciliation between indigenous and non-indigenous Australians.

The preamble proposed at the referendum was drafted by the then Prime Minister John Howard with the poet Les Murray in August 1999, and amended before being agreed to by the federal parliament and then put to a popular vote. It included statements in support of Australia's multicultural heritage and a commitment to upholding freedom, tolerance, human dignity and the rule of law. However, its wording generated a great deal of controversy, especially over the wording relating to indigenous people. Many people felt it should include an explicit acknowledgement of indigenous 'custodianship' of the land, but the final version put to referendum instead recognised indigenous peoples' 'deep kinship' with their lands. Another debate emerged over Prime Minister John Howard's suggestion in his draft preamble that the word 'mateship' be incorporated into the document. This was criticised for its masculinist and Anglocentric overtones (Kingston 1999, p. 13), and the word was dropped from the preamble put to referendum. The referendum was lost and the constitutional text remained unchanged.

Just before calling the 2007 federal election, the then Prime Minister John Howard reinvigorated the idea of holding a referendum to change the preamble to the Constitution, to recognise indigenous people as Australia's first inhabitants (ABC News 2007a). In contrast to the 1999 process, Howard suggested he would consult indigenous leaders on the specific wording of any such referendum (Gordon 2007), although this was met with some cynicism by indigenous leaders (Cave 2007). The proposal lapsed when a new federal government was elected in November 2007.

Westminster conventions and separation of powers

A feature of the Australian Constitution is that its function is reliant on a number of unwritten rules of government, which were so well known and understood at the time of drafting the Constitution that it was felt they did not need to be written down. These are known as Westminster conventions of government.

'Westminster' or 'constitutional' conventions are unwritten rules of government. They are an essential part of our constitutional framework.

The reliance on Westminster conventions explains why the Australian Constitution does not explicitly mention some of the key characteristics of our system of government, such as the Prime Minister and the Cabinet. Many important mechanisms and practices of our system of government are not expressly or explicitly included in the Constitution. One is that the Governor-General acts on the advice of elected ministers, especially the Prime Minister. Although the Constitution grants the Governor-General important executive powers, in practice these have tended to be exercised in consultation with the Prime Minister. Ambiguity resides in the fact that the Governor-General's specific powers are not written down, an ambiguity that was raised starkly by the Governor-General's dismissal of Prime Minister Gough Whitlam on 11 November 1975 (which is discussed in more detail in Chapter 11). The fact that Westminster conventions are not written down has led to considerable differences of opinion over their enforceability, but it does not make them a less powerful component of the system of governing.

Additionally, the Constitution institutionalises the separation of powers in Australia. It does this by establishing three branches of government: the parliament, the executive and the judiciary. Modern liberal democratic governments are informed by the doctrine of the separation of powers: the idea that governmental power needs to be separated between separate institutions in order to promote good government, in the sense of preventing any single branch from becoming too powerful and thus being capable of acting in an authoritarian or dictatorial manner. A theorist who famously put forward this idea was Montesquieu, who argued that it would ensure a balance of powers and thus secure individual liberty (Patapan 2000, p. 152). But in Australia the institutional powers of government have been only partially separated. This is because although the judiciary is entirely independent, the executive is drawn from members of the legislature. The executive is drawn from the legislature on the basis of Westminster principles of parliamentary accountability—allowing the executive to be part of the legislature means that it can be called to account in the parliamentary chamber (see further discussion in Chapter 4). Thus, Westminster principles have interacted with the separation of powers idea to produce Australia's institutional framework.

The judiciary

The third chapter of the Constitution is titled 'The Judicature'. The setting up of an independent judiciary in the High Court does entrench a separation of powers between judicial powers on the one hand and legislative and executive powers on the other. The Constitution provides for judicial power to be vested in the High Court of Australia (section 71). Since a successful referendum in 1977, the Constitution has stipulated that judges must retire at the age of 70 (section 72); previously judges used to hold tenure for life. There are seven justices of the High Court bench. When the Court was first established in 1903 there were three, but the numbers were expanded in 1906 to five and in 1912 to seven. The High Court of Australia has two jurisdictions:

- appellate jurisdiction, which means the High Court is the highest court of appeal in the country, and
- original jurisdiction, which means the High Court is empowered to interpret the Constitution and to decide disputes between the Commonwealth and States.

Judicial review

The jurisdiction granted to the High Court allows it to mediate and decide upon disputes between the Commonwealth and the States, to interpret the meaning of the Constitution, and to be the highest decision-maker in interpreting law. This is called the power of 'judicial review'. Any written legal document, including the Constitution, is subject to differing interpretations of meaning and application. There are many reasons for the need for continuous interpretation of the constitutional document, including the imprecision of written language, changes in the meaning of terms since the Constitution was drafted more than a century ago, changing expectations of government responsibilities over time, and the inability of any written document to predict the future.

In exercising its interpretive capacity, the High Court is expected to be mindful of its constitutional mandate. The judges are appointed by the government, not elected. The High Court's role is to interpret existing law, not to make new law. The branch of government charged with the power to make laws is the legislature—the elected parliament, which debates and agrees upon new statutes, also called Acts of parliament.

The High Court

Much of the High Court's work relates to the hearing of appeals against decisions of the Supreme Courts of the States and Territories, the Federal Court of Australia and the Family Court of Australia. There is no automatic right to have an appeal heard by the High Court, and parties who wish to appeal must persuade the Court that there are special reasons for hearing the appeal. Decisions of the High Court on appeals are final. There are no further appeals once a matter has been decided by the High Court, and the decision is binding on all other courts throughout Australia.

Cases that involve interpretation of the Constitution, or in which the Court may be invited to depart from one of its previous decisions, or in which the Court considers the principle of law involved to be one of major public importance, are normally determined by a full bench comprising two or more justices.

The Court usually 'reserves' its decision at the end of a hearing and presents the judgment later in writing. Each justice makes their own decision on cases, and where decisions are not unanimous the decision of the majority prevails.

Sources: <www.hcourt.gov.au/about_01.html>; <www.hcourt.gov.au/about_03.html>.

Judicial 'activism'

Concern about the appropriate role of the High Court has been reflected in debates about 'judicial activism'—the accusation that the High Court has engaged not just in interpreting law but also in making law. This debate was most prominent in the 1990s. The High Court's activism was considered by some to mark a departure from previous trends in decision-making by the High Court. In the first two decades after Federation the High Court tended to interpret the Constitution to protect the States' powers and limit the powers of the Commonwealth. Then over the next two decades the reverse was true and the Commonwealth's intervention in policy areas previously regarded as belonging exclusively to the States tended to be upheld. An example of this was the celebrated *Engineers* case of 1920, in which it was found that States could be subject to federal industrial arbitration. In a third phase from World War II until approximately 1980 the High Court tended to maintain the status quo (Selway & Williams 2005, pp. 478–83; Singleton et al. 2006, pp. 49–54; Galligan 1995, pp. 170–4; Hall 2000). From about 1980 until the early twenty-first century the High Court entered a new, fourth, phase of decision-making which was described as 'activist'. Since that time it has returned to a more conservative phase of decision-making in which the Court has tended to interpret the Constitution as providing few limitations on executive decision-making, and it is now arguable that the activist phase of the High Court has declined (Kildea & Gelber 2007, p. 660).

The 'activist' phase of the High Court stood in contrast to the jurisprudence, or legal philosophy, underpinning the previous phases. In order to understand the differences it is necessary to understand some of the principles underlying legal interpretation.

- **Originalism:** the idea that it is the founders' intentions in writing the constitutional document that should be taken into consideration when determining the Constitution's meaning. This allows the original purpose of the text to be construed (Goldsworthy 1997, p. 14). This idea has been promoted in the context of constitutional cases.
- **Legalism:** the idea that the judiciary's role is a purely technical one of deciding what the law is and applying it to facts. In this view, legal interpretation of the Constitution or other laws should not depend in any way upon moral considerations of whether the law is right or wrong. Sir Owen Dixon, in his swearing in as Chief Justice of the High Court in 1952, advocated legalism and argued it was a 'safe guide in judicial decisions' (Galligan 1995, pp. 182–3).
- **Literalism:** the entire meaning of a constitution or a law is regarded as residing in the text (Goldsworthy 1997, pp. 35, 37). Since this chapter argues that understanding Australia's constitutional framework involves understanding a great deal more than reading its text, we regard literalism as deficient as a method for deciding constitutional interpretation.
- **Activism:** 'judicial activism' has also been called 'realism', and it is equated with the idea that a purely technical reading of the law is in fact not possible and that judges inevitably apply individual discretion in decision-making (Galligan 1995, pp. 184–5). In practice, realism has led to the High Court

> taking a more active role in interpreting constitutional, statutory and common law in accordance with contemporary norms, standards and expectations and even overriding long-established precedent.

In the context of the argument underlying this book—that power permeates decision-making at all times and in often invisible ways—we argue that it is not appropriate for judges to try to interpret the Constitution in terms of the intentions of its founders more than a hundred years ago. It is also not possible to interpret constitutional, statutory or common law according to legalist principles, because it is not possible to interpret the meaning and effects of all these types of laws in the present day without also having regard to external principles and beliefs in appropriate law-making. We argue that what has been described as 'judicial activism' is the appropriate way of interpreting and implementing the law, because it is important to recognise and give value to contemporary expectations of governance.

This argument can be illustrated by looking at judgments from the High Court. An example of a controversial area of decision-making is native title law. We will focus here on the outcomes of a series of important native title decisions in the High Court. In 1982 three Murray Islanders from Far North Queensland brought an action to the High Court claiming native title. The Court agreed to hear the *Mabo* case (*Mabo v Queensland* [No. 2] (1992) 175 CLR 1) because it provided an important opportunity to reconsider the state of play on native title, an evolving area of common law. Indeed, they described the case as 'far from ... ordinary', saying that the acts by which the 'dispossession of the Aboriginal peoples of most of their traditional lands' were carried out:

> constitute the darkest aspect of the history of this nation. The nation as a whole must remain diminished unless and until there is an acknowledgment of, and retreat from, those past injustices. In these circumstances, the Court is under a clear duty to re-examine the [law].

The High Court's judgment was handed down in 1992, ten years after the action was first brought. The Murray Islanders' claims to native title over their land were upheld by a majority of six to one (Patapan 2000, pp. 111–12).

The decision was momentous. It was the first time that indigenous peoples' entitlement to native title was recognised by the courts, which meant that the long-established common law doctrine of *terra nullius* was overturned. *Terra nullius* is a Latin term whose literal meaning is land that belongs to nobody, and it was the doctrine under which British settlement in Australia had been regarded as overriding and extinguishing native title. The *Mabo* decision overturned this precedent (Brennan et al. 2005, pp. 103–4).

Because the decision was so far-reaching, accusations were levelled at the High Court that it had breached the separation of powers doctrine and had made new law (Kirby 1994). The Tasmanian Premier, Mr Groom, called the decision 'extraordinary' (Kirby 1994, p. 67). The decision also created legal confusion over how native title could be claimed and what its implications would be for other areas of land (for more information, see the discussion in Butt et al. 2001, pp. 95–8). Because of this confusion, the legislature moved to clarify the law on native title with legislation. The federal parliament passed the *Native Title Act 1993*, which confirmed that native title could exist in Australia and established procedures and mechanisms for assessing native title claims (Brennan et al. 2005, pp. 105–6; Patapan 2000, p. 134).

Three years later the High Court was asked to adjudicate another case concerning native title. The Wik people had commenced their High Court action in 1993, claiming native title over land and waters in Far North Queensland. The *Wik* decision (*Wik Peoples v Queensland* (1996) 187 CLR 1) created even more controversy than *Mabo* had. The case asked the question whether 'leases' granted over cattle stations in Queensland for 'pastoral' (that is, farming) purposes gave the lessees exclusive rights to the land or whether in principle the lessees' possession could operate in conjunction with native title. In other words, the central question was whether under common law pastoral leases extinguished native title. A small majority of the High Court decided that pastoral leases did not automatically extinguish native title, but that if there were an inconsistency between the lessees' rights to use the land and native title, the pastoral leases would prevail (Brennan et al. 2005, p. 106; Patapan 2000, p. 137). Again, the Court had made a decision with far-reaching consequences and which overturned previously held understandings of the common law. Accusations were again made that the High Court had breached the separation of powers. The Premier of Queensland, Rob Borbidge, described the Court as an 'embarrassment'. The Prime Minister criticised the Court for adopting a law-making role. Again the federal parliament stepped in to clarify the confusion legislatively. The *Native Title Amendment Act 1998* delimited native title rights in a number of ways, including by spelling out the circumstances under which grants to land could extinguish native title and making it more difficult for native title holders to have the 'right to negotiate' (Butt et al. 2001, pp. 109–13).

These cases demonstrate the importance of the interpretive approach taken by the High Court. Under previously existing common law, Australian territory had been held to belong to no one when white settlement occurred. Yet in the contemporary era many people recognised that indigenous people were custodians of the land before white settlement and that they were forcibly dispossessed of their land. If the justices had not interpreted the common law in light of contemporary values and standards and adopted an activist stance, then this change in recognition of indigenous land entitlements would have taken even longer to develop. It was important that the law catch up with contemporary expectations and understandings of indigenous people's place in Australian politics.

Nevertheless, because the High Court had led change in a highly controversial area of policy-making, the initial decisions recognising native title were followed by legislative clarification of the state of play. Later judgments in the High Court demonstrated that the High Court's views had changed again and that they became much more likely to accept the executive government's policy approach on native title, with decisions including *Fejo* (*Fejo v Northern Territory* (1998) 195 CLR 96), *Anderson* (*Wilson v Anderson* (2002) 213 CLR 401), *Ward* (*Western Australia v Ward* (2002) 213 CLR 1) and *Yorta Yorta* (*Members of the Yorta Yorta Aboriginal Community v Victoria* (2002) 214 CLR 422). In these judgments an increasingly restrictive interpretation of opportunities for successful native title claims was developed (Brennan et al. 2005, pp. 106–7). This means that the impact of the earlier *Mabo* and *Wik* decisions was lessened.

Nevertheless, the High Court's interventions in native title in both the 1990s and the first decade of the twenty-first century demonstrate that it is not possible to separate completely the processes by which law is made and interpreted in contemporary politics. The distinction between making and interpreting law is 'deeply problematic' because both are inevitably involved in legal interpretation (Perry 1994, p. 7). The High Court is also an intrinsically political institution that forms part of the complex and dynamic system that makes up the Australian constitutional framework (Galligan 1987) and, as such, it has a political and not just a legal role to play. It is political because it is an institution that mediates power. As such, the High Court's intervention in political decisions is 'inevitable' (Patapan 2000, p. 3), although it will continue to be controversial.

Judicial appointments

A further aspect of the controversial nature of the High Court is the question of judicial appointments. When a vacancy arises, the Prime Minister appoints a replacement on the recommendation of the Attorney-General, a minister who provides legal advice and support to the government, and in consultation with the State Attorneys-General. This is in accordance with the requirements of the *High Court of Australia Act 1979* (Cwlth).

The appointment of justices by the government of the day can be controversial, especially in light of the argument supported here that it is inevitable that the High Court will be involved in making decisions with political and policy consequences. It raises two clear questions. First, to what extent do the justices make decisions that reflect the political views of the government that appointed them? Second, how representative are the views of the judges themselves?

In the United States the process of appointing new judges is an open contest between conflicting ideological positions and party affiliations (Segal, Timpone & Howard 2000, pp. 557–8). Nominations are made by the President but must be sanctioned by the Senate, which conducts hearings and questions nominees to determine their suitability. In Australia the process is less overtly partisan, but there have been indications that appointments can make a difference to judicial decision-making. Some commentators suggest that changes in the composition of the bench provide an insufficient basis for overriding precedent (Williams 2002, p. 188 citing Justices Barton, Gibbs, Stephen and McHugh), but to others such changes can have a 'major effect' on the High Court's direction (Patapan 2000, p. 61) and provide a practical means of exercising control over the executive branch of government (Galligan 1987, p. 188).

In 2003 the conservative Coalition government of 1996–2007 appointed its fourth justice and therefore a majority of the seven-member bench. Since that time two further justices have been appointed by the Coalition government, totalling five out of the seven current justices. A majority of justices currently tends to adopt a legalistic approach to constitutional interpretation and to avoid explicitly curbing executive governmental powers (Gelber 2006, pp. 450–1). For example, one commentator noted the continuation of the implied freedom of political speech 'despite' a change in composition of the High Court bench (Lee 2005, p. 80). Also, a study of dissent rates pointed out that one of the two remaining Labor government appointees, Justice Michael Kirby, who was appointed in 1996, is the 'great dissenter' with the highest dissent rate of any judge in the Court's history (Yallop 2003, citing Smyth 2003). George Winterton has suggested that Kirby's dissent rates are a product of a conservative court, and if it were differently constituted he would be unlikely to dissent so often (cited by Yallop 2003). Legalism is likely to be the prevailing majority approach of the court for the foreseeable future in constitutional cases. Thus, there is some evidence that the previous federal government was able to affect the tenor of decision-making by appointing a majority of justices.

Additionally, there is the question of representation. The majority of justices are white, middle-aged, upper-middle-class males. Only three women have been appointed to the High Court in its history: Justice Mary Gaudron (1987–2003), Justice Susan Crennan (appointed in 2005) and Justice Susan Kiefel (appointed in 2007). If the justices do not reflect the constituent groupings in society, does this affect the legitimacy of their decision-making when interpreting the law in relation to contemporary political realities? More in-depth study of actual decisions is required to answer this question, but the question itself is valid.

Bills of rights

In the contemporary era, a final important omission from the Australian Constitution should be considered. That is the omission of an explicit list of individual rights. At the time of drafting, the framers knew of the US Bill of Rights, which was constituted by the first ten amendments to the US Constitution in 1791. However, the Australian framers decided not to include similar provisions in the Australian Constitution. Only a few minor mentions of rights survived the debates, such as non-discrimination between States and the right to vote in federal elections once registered to do so at State level, but explicit rights protection in the Constitution is very weak (Williams 2002, pp. 47–8). Differing reasons are cited for this, including a belief that the Westminster model of responsible government was sufficient to prevent gross abuses of human rights from occurring, and conversely an argument that a bill of rights was excluded in order to allow governments to continue to discriminate as they had during colonial times, especially against indigenous peoples and Chinese immigrants to the gold fields (Williams 1995).

For information about the debates over what was left out of the Constitution at drafting, it is useful to read the account by Helen Irving of the Constitution's formation (1997, pp. 162–70), George Williams' detailed description of consideration of individual rights clauses (2002, pp. 33–45) or Hilary Charlesworth's concise and highly informative overview of the rights debates at the Conventions (2002, pp. 17–27).

Many other countries have adopted bills of rights, including the United Kingdom and Canada.

> **Canada's Bill of Rights**
>
> Canada adopted a Charter of Rights and Freedoms in 1982, which set out a range of rights including the freedoms of conscience, religion, expression and association as well as democratic rights such as the right to vote. Courts were granted the power to enforce the Charter, by granting remedies for the infringement of rights. Other laws must be consistent with the Charter; however, there is provision for 'reasonable limits' on the rights and freedoms contained within it.
>
> *Source*: Charlesworth 2002, p. 66.

Today, there is considerable debate within Australia about whether to adopt a bill of rights. Other mechanisms are used to protect rights in Australia, such as the High Court's interpretation of the Constitution, including its recognition of 'implied' rights in the constitutional framework, the common law, ratifying international multilateral human rights treaties, and passing domestic legislation at both federal and State/Territory level to protect specific rights, for example the *Sex Discrimination Act 1984* (Cwlth), *Racial Discrimination Act 1975* (Cwlth) and *Disability Discrimination Act 1992* (Cwlth). The Human Rights and Equal Opportunity Commission, which was originally established as the Human Rights Commission in 1981 and renamed in 1986, undertakes public education and mediates complaints under relevant legislation (see <www.hreoc.gov.au>). Also all States and Territories have their own anti-discrimination authorities, which undertake similar work to the HREOC and operate under laws enacted by the State parliaments. However, in the absence of a national bill of rights it is often argued that the existing mechanisms for the protection of rights are piecemeal and insufficient, and that a comprehensive bill of rights would achieve more comprehensive rights protection in the contemporary era. These arguments were prominent during media coverage of the enactment of anti-terrorism legislation, including provisions for control orders as discussed in the snapshot at the beginning of this chapter.

Australia has a potted and unsuccessful history of attempting to introduce a federal bill of rights. Attempts were made in 1944 and 1988 to insert explicit rights protection into the Constitution via referendum, but both were defeated. Additionally, there were attempts in 1973–74, 1983–84 and 1985–86 to introduce statutory rights protection at a federal level, but these were abandoned or withdrawn (Kildea 2003, p. 66).

There are two kinds of bills of rights. One is constitutional, also called 'entrenched', which means the Constitution is amended by popular vote in a referendum to include the bill of rights and it has the status of constitutional text. This means it is hard to amend—only another referendum can change it. The second is statutory, which means legislation is passed by the parliament bringing one into being. This means the legislation can be changed again in the future, should the parliament decide to do so and should it be willing and able to carry out such change.

There have been significant new developments in rights protection in recent years. The first way this has occurred is through the recognition by the High Court of 'implied' rights in the constitutional framework. The most important of these is the development since 1992 of an implied constitutional freedom of political speech (Gelber 2006, pp. 441–4; Gelber 2007, p. 3). This is the idea that, although the Constitution does not mention free speech explicitly, the system of representative and responsible government established by the Constitution assumes a freedom of communication on political matters in order to be meaningful.

Second, explicit forms of rights protection have emerged. Since the 1990s the federal government's active hostility to the codification of rights and mechanisms which could interfere in parliamentary decision-making (Baldino 2005, pp. 194–6; see also Chapter 14) and opposition to a national bill of rights (Ruddock 2007) have led human rights advocates to pursue change at other levels of government.

Australia's first bill of rights was introduced by the Hume City Council in Victoria, when it adopted a Social Justice Charter 2004 containing a Citizens' Bill of Rights (HCC 2005). Rights include both civil and political rights, such as the right to liberty, and economic and social rights, such as the right to work. The Bill of Rights was reviewed in 2007 as part of a continuous process of community engagement by the council (HCC 2007). However, the status of this bill as a document relevant only at local government level limits its ability to effect significant improvements to rights protection.

States and Territories have also moved towards stronger, more explicit rights protection. In 2004, after extensive community consultation, including the holding of a deliberative poll (ACTBoRCC 2003), the Australian Capital Territory parliament enacted a statutory bill of rights in the form of the *Human Rights Act*, which incorporates much of the International Covenant on Civil and Political Rights (ICCPR) into ACT law. The Act operates to try to increase rights protection through a variety of mechanisms, but without the ability for courts to strike legislation down as invalid. It requires other legislation to be interpreted and applied in a way that is consistent with it, and it requires that the Attorney-General assess each piece of draft legislation presented to parliament to ascertain its compatibility with the Act. If the draft legislation is incompatible, it can still be passed as long as the parliament demonstrates that it is justified in doing so (McKinnon 2005, pp. 5–6; Burke & Gelber 2005–06, p. 44). The Act is intended to influence policy makers to consider human rights issues when drafting proposals to put to parliament and to encourage public officials to apply public policy in a way that is consistent with rights protection (Stanhope 2005).

In 2006 Victoria followed suit, enacting a *Charter of Human Rights and Responsibilities Act 2006* (Vic). This Act works in a similar way to the ACT one. It does not permit the courts to declare a law invalid on the ground that it is incompatible with the charter of rights. Rather, it is designed to encourage parliaments and public authorities to act in a way that is compatible with human rights protection (Williams 2006). In Western Australia (McGinty 2007) and Tasmania (TLRI 2007) the implementation of a statutory charter of rights has also been considered. At the national level a bills of rights campaign under the slogan 'A Human Rights Act for Australia' was initiated in 2005 by online magazine and policy portal *New Matilda*, and since 2008 it operates as an independent campaign (<www.humanrightsact.com.au>).

Summary

- The Australian Constitution sets up two levels of government: federal and State. Territories and local governments derive their powers and jursdiction from the legislation that establishes them.

- The Australian Constitution was written to assist the unification of distinct colonies into one national framework, and it was enacted peacefully via popular vote and parliamentary ratification.
- The Constitution's text can be changed only by a referendum, which requires a double majority and is difficult to pass.
- The Constitution contains important information on key institutions of government, including the parliament, the executive and the judiciary. But many components that are not included in the written text are also essential parts of the overall frameworks for governing.
- The Constitution provides for a High Court with the power of judicial review. The High Court plays a crucial role in the political system by making decisions that mediate power.

Further reading

Galligan, Brian 1995, *A Federal Republic: Australia's Constitutional System of Government*, Cambridge University Press, Melbourne.

Irving, Helen 1997, *To Constitute a Nation: A Cultural History of Australia's Constitution*, Cambridge University Press, Melbourne.

Patapan, Haig 2000, *Judging Democracy: The New Politics of the High Court of Australia*, Cambridge University Press, Melbourne.

Uhr, John 1998, *Deliberative Democracy in Australia: The Changing Place of Parliament*, Cambridge University Press, Melbourne.

Useful websites

- Australian Parliament House: <www.aph.gov.au>. This website is a good starting point for learning about the federal parliamentary system.
- The High Court of Australia: <www.hcourt.gov.au>. This website contains historical information on the High Court and its justices, and it also lists and publishes judgments of cases heard by the High Court.
- Australian Electoral Commission's website on referendums: <www.aec.gov.au/Elections/referendums/index.htm>. The AEC provides information and statistics on all referendums held since Federation.

CHAPTER 4
PARLIAMENTS

To this point in Part I, we have looked at the elements of liberal democracy in Australia and the constitutional design of our system of government. In this chapter we explore how the formal rules set down in such documents as constitutions interplay with the ideas of liberal democracy and the actual practice of politics—the exercise of power—within one of the most important institutions in contemporary democracies: parliaments.

As federalism is a paramount feature of Australia's system of government, it is important to acknowledge that parliaments exist in all Australian States and Territories. The design and operation of these parliaments tend to be overlooked in many introductory Australian politics texts that focus predominantly, if not exclusively, on the Commonwealth Parliament. Therefore it is our intention in this chapter to counter this emphasis by discussing the features and function of parliaments in Australia more generally and by providing a theoretical framework that can be used to analyse the operation of parliaments both at the federal and State levels, illustrated with examples from both arenas. We compare the design of the various Australian parliaments, the way they function to give an institutional and practical expression to some of the normative principles of representative democracy, and the challenges they face in doing so. Finally, we analyse the work of individual parliamentarians and how they view their representative and legislative duties.

The topics covered in this chapter include:

- an introduction to the Australian parliaments, their origins and their structural characteristics
- an analysis of the ways in which parliaments put the principles of representative democracy into practice
- the relationship between parliaments and governments, in the context of accountability and the dominance of political parties
- an evaluation of the decline of parliament thesis
- the different representational roles of parliamentarians.

SNAPSHOT Deliberating the difficult issues—the RU486 debate

RU486 is a drug used in medical procedures to terminate pregnancy. In 2005, against the backdrop of a broader community debate concerning abortion, a controversial bill was introduced into the federal parliament that sought to alter the procedure for approving the use of RU486 in Australia. Unlike other drugs, the use of which is approved by a specialist body known as the Therapeutic Goods Administration (TGA), at that time responsibility for approving the use of RU486 was held by the federal Health Minister. One of the key issues involved was whether responsibility for approving the use of drugs with ethical implications, like RU486, should reside with politicians such as the Health Minister or with a body of experts such as the TGA.

A catalyst for the debate was the well-publicised view of the Health Minister at the time, Tony Abbott, that 'abortion is a stain on our national character' (Oakes 2006). These views coincided with calls from other Coalition MPs to reduce the funding of abortions under Medicare, and it was in this context that, on 8 December 2005, Senator Fiona Nash of the National Party introduced a bill into the Senate to remove the Health Minister's ability to decide on the use of RU486—the Therapeutic Goods Amendment (Repeal of Ministerial Responsibility for Approval of RU486) Bill 2005. The bill was co-sponsored by Senators Lyn Allison (Democrats), Judith Troeth (Liberal Party) and Claire Moore (ALP). It is the only piece of legislation in Australian history that has been initiated by four MPs from four different parties, let alone four women. As a co-sponsor of the bill, Senator Lyn Allison (2007) explained that she and the other senators wanted to:

> push for a vote on women's reproductive health because we had all that anti-abortion stuff going on. We had the minister himself saying it's a tragedy, women were feeling more and more vulnerable, more and more guilty, being made to feel like it's all their fault. I said we've got to stop this—we've got to do something that demonstrates our place in the parliament and how we will protect women—we will not allow this to happen.

The same day the bill was introduced into parliament it was referred to the Senate Community Affairs Legislation Committee, consisting of six senators from four different parties, for an in-depth examination of the issues. The committee gathered expert evidence and held public hearings over three days in Canberra, Melbourne and Sydney. It received 4788 submissions and public contributions expressing opinions on the regulation of RU486 and abortion (Senate Standing Committee on Community Affairs 2006). In its report published in February 2006, the committee regarded its primary purpose as gathering information to assist MPs to make an informed decision on the bill, and the final document contained a description of the pharmaceutical approval process, an outline of the issues involved and the arguments raised by those supporting and opposing the bill. In addition to the large volume of correspondence received by the committee, individual MPs also reported being inundated with letters and emails from both abortion supporters and pro-life groups urging them to vote a particular way.

The bill was debated for fourteen hours in the Senate and a further ten hours in the House of Representatives. It is rare in Australian politics for a bill not initiated by the governing party to be given time for a full debate, but the government agreed to this owing to the intense political pressure that had built up around the issue. Debate in both houses of parliament was often fiery and at times emotional, with many MPs and ministers revealing their own personal experiences with abortion.

Due to the underlying moral and religious dimensions of the legislation, when it came to vote on the bill, leaders of all the parties agreed to allow their parliamentarians to vote according to their conscience and individual view, rather than following the pre-agreed directions of their party. This practice is known as a 'conscience vote' and is rare in Australian federal politics, having occurred in only two other debates since 1996: overturning the Northern Territory's euthanasia laws (1996) and embryonic stem cell research (2002). Parliamentary voting overwhelmingly takes place along party lines. However, as Warhurst (2006, p. 2) notes:

> Many parliamentarians sing the praises of conscience voting ... references to the very high quality and thoughtfulness of such debates are common. Some MPs stress the value of parliament being free from executive control. Others stress the extra individual research that MPs undertake when free from the constraints of party policy.

For example, Prime Minister Howard said of the debate:

> I want to say at the outset that I think this has been a very good debate ... I think parliament rises to its greatest heights when we have debates of this kind. A free vote encourages people to examine their beliefs, to reflect upon their experiences, values and attitudes, and to deal sensitively with a difficult issue. (House of Representatives Hansard, 16 February 2006, p. 33; quoted in Warhurst 2006, p. 2)

Opposition leader Kim Beazley also expressed his approval of the parliamentary process in this instance:

> To be able to look up and see people struggling honestly to arrive at the right conclusions on this matter has been, frankly, inspirational. I have been in politics now for a very long time ... All too few occasions like this occur in the House. It is a wonderful thing when they do. They speak well of all of us. We are not simply identikit clones of some ad agency's decision as to what a politician ought to be; we in this place are much better people than that, and I am proud of my colleagues. On this occasion I am not only proud of my colleagues on this side of the chamber; I am actually quite proud of my colleagues on the other side of the chamber as well. (House of Representatives Hansard, 16 February 2006, p. 36; quoted in Warhurst 2006, p. 2)

The bill passed with clear support in both houses of parliament: 45 votes to 28 in the Senate and by 95 to 50 (second reading) votes in the House of Representatives. As a result, applications for the use of RU486 will now be processed by the TGA rather than by the federal Health Minister.

The cooperation and reasoned discussion undertaken during the passage of the bill is an example of parliament's potential to function as a deliberative and representative institution. It also highlights the potential of parliament to scrutinise government activity. If parliament can function in this way, why doesn't it happen more often?

The design of Australian parliaments

Parliaments, as political institutions, are only a few hundred years old. Before they existed, rule was carried out by an hereditary sovereign—a King or a Queen—who was not directly accountable to the people via parliamentary or representative mechanisms, but who could impose their will arbitrarily. The first use of the word 'parliament' dates to the mid-thirteenth century and comes from the word 'parley', meaning a public disputation. In other words, a parliament is an act of speaking; discussing and conversing in public, a place where antagonists may talk over their differences and come to agreement. Ideally, it is a place where opponents lay down their arms and agree to differ verbally instead of violently. Parliament has been described as a 'routinisation of conflict' (Maddox 2005). The terms 'parliament' and 'legislature' are used interchangeably.

When we speak of 'parliament' in Australia, it is common to assume that we are talking about the federal parliament. However, as we learned in the previous chapter, the Constitution establishes two levels of government—federal and State—with powers and responsibilities divided between them. Consequently, the Australian system of representative democracy actually comprises no less than nine discrete parliaments: one federal parliament, six State parliaments and two Territory parliaments, each with distinctive political cultures and responsibilities for legislating within the boundaries of their designated constitutional powers and geographic territories (Sharman & Moon 2003). In this section we provide an overview of some of the structural characteristics common to parliaments in Australia.

Table 4.1 presents a comparison of the basic features of the Australian parliaments. The Commonwealth Parliament was established in 1901 by the Constitution. The State parliaments are older, having been created in the process of transformation from authoritarian penal colonies to self-governing representative democracies. Previously administered by the Commonwealth, the Territory parliaments are relatively recent institutions. All these parliaments share a common history in the sense that they were created by legislation that was passed by another parliament: either the UK Parliament (in the case of the States and the Commonwealth) or the Commonwealth Parliament (in the case of the Territories). The key point to note here is that parliaments are institutions that are deliberately created, and their structure reflects the assumptions and preferences their makers held as to how democracy ought to operate in practice.

TABLE 4.1 Australian parliaments

Parliament	Year formed	Structure	No. of members	Term (years)
Commonwealth	1901	Senate	76	3 (Territory)
		House of Representatives	150	6 (State)
				3
New South Wales	1823	Legislative Council	42	8
		Legislative Assembly	93	4
Queensland	1860	Legislative Assembly	89	3
South Australia	1842	Legislative Council	22	8
		House of Assembly	47	4
Tasmania	1828	Legislative Council	15	6
		House of Assembly	25	4
Victoria	1851	Legislative Council	40	4
		Legislative Assembly	88	4
Western Australia	1832	Legislative Council	34	4
		Legislative Assembly	57	4
Australian Capital Territory	1989	Legislative Assembly	17	4
Northern Territory	1974	Legislative Assembly	25	4

The design of the Australian parliaments therefore imitates the traditions and practices of government in the United Kingdom, with modifications for the Australian context. However, it is also important to note that parliaments are dynamic, constantly evolving institutions. Within constitutional limits, they have the power to amend their own rules and procedures. Many of these rules are not codified, and hence the day-to-day operation of the parliament will depend to a significant extent on political practice, both established and pragmatic, and the parliament's composition: which parties and politicians have been elected to the chamber.

Table 4.1 also compares the structure of the various Australian parliaments. One feature inherited from the United Kingdom is bicameralism; that is, most parliaments in Australia consist of two independent houses. The Australian

Federal Parliament comprises a lower house, the House of Representatives, and an upper house called the Senate. All the State parliaments in Australia with the exception of Queensland consist of a lower house, called a Legislative Assembly or a House of Assembly (South Australia and Tasmania) and an upper house called the Legislative Council. This structure mirrors the division in the British parliament (also known as Westminster) between the House of Commons, the lower house designed to represent 'the people', and the upper house—the House of Lords. The traditional function of the upper house is to act as a 'house of review' to mitigate and protect against the 'democratic excesses' and potentially populist tendencies of the lower house (Singleton et al. 2006, p. 133). We discuss this function in more detail later in the chapter.

The Queensland and Territory parliaments are unicameral, with only one house called the Legislative Assembly. The Territory parliaments were intentionally created this way, whereas Queensland existed as a bicameral parliament until 1922. It was able to abolish its unelected Legislative Council despite the failure of a referendum on the issue due to a successful campaign by a Labor government in appointing Labor councillors sympathetic to this cause. The 'suicide club', as it was known, essentially voted itself out of existence and, in the absence of agreement on the organisation and structure of an elected Legislative Council, Queensland has remained a unicameral parliament ever since (Wanna 2003, pp. 80–1). A similar attempt by the Lang Labor government to abolish the New South Wales Legislative Council in 1925–26 failed when several of the Labor councillors appointed to vote for the abolition of the council either voted against it or abstained (Twomey 2004, pp. 367–8; Smith 2003, p. 47).

The size of the Australian parliaments ranges from seventeen MPs in the unicameral Northern Territory parliament to 226 MPs in the Commonwealth Parliament. The overall size of a parliament is determined according to the number of electors that need to be represented. As the people's house, the number of parliamentarians elected to the lower house of parliament varies according to the size of the State or Territory's population. The number of representatives elected to the upper house is calculated on the basis of the nexus provision (Australian Constitution section 24), which requires that the size of the lower house be roughly twice that of the upper house. This nexus is designed to ensure that the size of the chambers reflects an appropriate balance between their representational roles (see Evans 2004).

The typical length of a parliamentarian's term—that is, the length of time they can hold office without facing election—ranges from three to eight years. In order to reflect the current political opinion of the nation, elections for the lower house are generally held more frequently than those for the upper houses. Too long a term means that governments are held accountable less frequently (McMinn 1979, pp. 64–5). Too short a term can be criticised on the ground that it encourages an almost constant process of electioneering and campaigning, and that it does not leave enough time for voters to properly judge the competence of the government and the policies it has implemented (Jackson 2006, p. 170; Maddox 1996, p. 228). Consequently, governments may be tempted to introduce policies that are electorally popular rather than in the long-term interests of the nation.

Except in the event that a parliament is dissolved, elections for the upper houses of the Commonwealth, New South Wales, South Australian and Tasmanian parliaments are staggered. The term for upper house MPs in these parliaments is typically twice as long as their lower house counterparts, and at any ordinary election only a percentage of the upper house (usually half) will face election. Those MPs who are not forced to contest their seat at one election will do so at the next, and so the pattern continues. This provision is designed to ensure that while the lower house responds to the mood of the electorate, the upper house retains some continuity and hence stability (Evans 2004; Jaensch 1986, pp. 170–2). Nonetheless, the length of these terms has not escaped criticism, as the example of electoral reform in Victoria illustrates. Before 2006, members of the Legislative Council were elected for staggered eight-year terms. However, following concerns that these MPs were unaccountable and unrepresentative, the Bracks Labor government legislated to establish fixed, four-year terms for Legislative Council MPs (Bracks 2003).

The unique design of the federal parliament

The parliament of the Commonwealth of Australia consists of three elements: the House of Representatives, the Senate and the Head of State, which reflect Australia's position as a constitutional monarchy, a parliamentary democracy and a federation (Harris 2005, p. 1). In attempting to accommodate both the principles of American federalism and those of a Westminster parliamentary democracy, the Australian hybrid is often referred to as a 'Washminster' system (see Chapter 11).

Like many of the State parliaments, the Commonwealth Parliament is bicameral. The House of Representatives assumes the traditional role of the 'people's house' in which parliamentarians are elected to represent their local electorate. However, unlike the upper houses of the State parliaments and Westminster, which traditionally functioned to accommodate the interests of the aristocracy and property owners, the Senate was intended to function as the 'States' house'—to preserve the interests of the former colonies in a newly federated nation against domination by the Commonwealth (see Bach 2003, pp. 120–39). This protection was to be achieved by giving the Senate co-equal legislative powers to the House (except supply) and by allocating to the States an equal number of representatives in the Senate, to be elected by the people of each State regardless of their population size. Originally the Senate consisted of six senators—one representative from each State. Over the years the size of the Senate has been enlarged and now consists of twelve senators from each State. In 1975, each of the Territories was also allocated two senators.

Regardless of the intentions of those drafting the constitution, the Senate has never really functioned as a States' house. Soon after federation, strong political parties became a dominant feature of Australian parliamentary and electoral politics. Illustrating the importance of practical politics in shaping the workings of parliaments, senators routinely voted with the interests of their party rather than their State, and the Senate very quickly became divided along party lines. Nonetheless, as we shall discuss later in this chapter, like many of the upper houses of the State parliaments the Australian Senate performs an important function as a house of review.

Parliaments and representative democracy

There is no coherent 'theory' of parliament. Parliaments are not the products of democratic theory; rather they have evolved through a process of normative institutional engineering, by adopting and borrowing certain features of parliaments from other representative democracies around the world; and through actual political practice. They continue to evolve today. Despite some organisational differences among the various Australian parliaments that reflect their unique contexts, certain features common to these institutions seek to give expression to the principles of representative democracy, which we will examine in more detail; namely, that:

- parliament is elected by the people
- parliament is the supreme law-making body
- parliament is the source of government
- parliament holds the government accountable for its actions.

Elected by the people

The fundamental tenet underlying the principle of representative democracy is that parliament is elected by the people. For the federal parliament this is guaranteed in sections 7 and 24 of the Constitution, and State constitutions make similar provisions for their parliaments. For example, section 10 of the *Constitution of Queensland 2001* requires the State's Legislative Assembly to 'consist of directly elected members who are eligible to be elected by the inhabitants of the State who are eligible to elect members'. The idea that parliament must be 'directly chosen by the people' is a cornerstone of democracy because it responds directly to the democratic ideals of popular rule and the accountability of elected representatives. Although parliaments have been around for centuries, the idea that all citizens of a particular polity should be able to elect their representatives is a more recent (and still contested) practice.

The early colonial parliaments were wholly unelected—their members were appointed by the Governor. When the first parliament was established in Tasmania, parliamentarians were 'fairly selected from the more intelligent, wealthy and respectable members of the commercial, agricultural and professional bodies of the colony' (Townsley 1991, p. 42). The requirement that voters and candidates for Victoria's Legislative Council had to own property was removed only in 1950, at which time half the council still held pastoral interests. Similar qualifications were removed in Western Australia in 1964. Finally, it was only in 1978 that the New South Wales Legislative Council became directly elected by the people of that State. At the time of federation, women could vote for the election of members of parliament in only two States: South Australia and Western Australia. The first election for the federal parliament, conducted under the provisions of the *Commonwealth Franchise Act 1902* (Cwlth), marked a significant step forward in creating an inclusive political franchise and a representative parliament, extending the vote to women. However, indigenous Australians were not included in this conception of 'the people' and were excluded from participating in parliamentary elections on unqualified terms until 1962 (Norberry 2003, pp. 83–6). Even today, the term 'the people' is under constant debate. The law continues to exclude a number of groups from participating in federal parliamentary elections: prisoners serving a sentence of more than three years, unlawful non-citizens, holders of temporary visas, certain Australians living overseas and men and women under 18.

Although it is a prerequisite, having the right to vote and stand for election does not necessarily guarantee parliamentary representation proportionate to the size of a group in society. Even though women (who form 50.3 per cent of the population) have been able to vote and stand for election from 1902, they have historically been constrained by the opportunities for candidacy presented by the major political parties and are still a minority in all Australian parliaments (Smith 2007, p. 4; Sainsbury 2001, pp. 73, 76). In 2007, there were twenty-seven female senators and thirty-seven female members of the House of Representatives. Only two indigenous Australians have been elected to the federal parliament, and the average age of an MP is 50.6 years. Australian parliamentarians are typically middle aged, well-educated and mostly male (Miskin & Lumb 2006).

Parliament as a law-making body

All laws in Australia originate as bills before parliament. In the vast majority of instances, bills will be introduced into the parliament by a member of the governing party, usually a minister, although they may also be initiated by non-government members. These are known as private members bills. All bills, except for those involving financial matters (also called supply), can originate in either house of bicameral parliaments in Australia, but because most government MPs come from the lower house, this is where the majority of bills (around 90 per cent) are introduced. On average about 200 bills are introduced into the federal parliament each year, 70 per cent of which will become acts (Harris 2005, p. 337).

A 'bill' is a proposed piece of legislation presented to the parliament for a vote. After a bill has been passed by parliament and has received the royal assent (given by the Governor-General as the Queen's representative in Australia, or by a Governor in the States) it becomes a statute, and is then called an Act of parliament.

In order to become law, a bill must be passed by a majority of members in both houses of a bicameral parliament, or by a majority of the parliamentarians in a unicameral parliament. Depending on the number of seats a governing party has won, and the character and composition of each parliament, this passage will usually involve some degree of negotiation and compromise among the MPs. A governing majority in the lower house usually means the government's bills pass through this chamber unimpeded. However, the requirement that legislation pass through both houses in bicameral parliaments ensures that when the government does not hold a majority in the upper as well as in the lower house, the government must reach agreement with some of the other parliamentary representatives in the upper house in order to have its bills passed.

There are constitutional and legislative provisions to resolve stalemates between the two houses of bicameral parliaments. In the federal parliament, for example, if a bill is passed by the House of Representatives but rejected by the Senate, it can be reintroduced to the parliament after a wait of three months. If it is again passed by the House and rejected by the Senate, the government can advise the Governor-General to dissolve parliament. The general election that follows is called a 'double dissolution' election, at which both the House of Representatives and the whole Senate are elected simultaneously. If there is still a stalemate after the election, section 57 of the Constitution provides that both houses may sit as one body for the purpose of voting on the bill in question.

The legislative process—what we see and what we don't

As parliament is designed as an open arena for the resolution of political conflict, the formal passage of bills through parliament reflects this transparency. This passage occurs in several stages, descriptions of which (like the one below) can be found on the websites of all Australian parliaments.

- *Giving notice*: an MP (usually a minister) introducing the bill will notify the Clerk of the House in writing of their intention to introduce a bill into parliament. The Clerk is a non-elected official responsible for the day-to-day running of parliamentary business.
- *First reading*: this is a formal stage only—the long title of the bill is read by the Clerk.
- *Second reading*: debate on the legislative proposal, which is not limited to the exact contents of the bill and can include alternatives and

discussion of the necessity of the bill's provisions. Debates can also take place on amendments to the bill.

- *Report stage*: the chamber will receive the report of any committee that has been requested to examine a bill, and the report will be discussed and voted on.
- *Third reading*: a final review of the bill after any amendments have been made during the second reading. Discussion here is limited to the exact contents of the bill, and is not as wide ranging as in the second reading. Once a bill has been read a third time, it has passed the house.
- *Consideration by the other chamber*: in bicameral parliaments the bill is then sent to the other house for the same process of consideration.
- *Royal Assent*: if approved by the parliament, the bill is sent to the Governor-General or Governor (in the case of State parliaments) to be given Royal Assent.

However, this process just presents the public face in the creation of laws. Parliaments sit for only several weeks in a year. Since 2006 the federal House of Representatives has sat for an average of sixty-seven days and the Senate forty-nine days (<www.aph.gov.au/house/info/sittings>). Therefore, as Labor MP Tanya Plibersek (2007) explains, 'most of the [policy] discussion happens long before the debate in Parliament happens'. The details of a proposed piece of legislation will usually have been debated either within government departments or within political parties when they formulate party policy. How a party formulates the policy agenda it will pursue if elected to office differs from party to party, with varying degrees of consultation and debate (see Chapter 6). Government bills may also originate from a minister on the advice of their department that legislation is necessary. Typically, draft bills and all associated materials initiated by the government are confidential and may not be made public before their introduction to the parliament, unless disclosure is authorised by the ministers or the Prime Minister (Harris 2005, p. 342).

In addition to the deliberation taking place in the parliamentary chambers, both government and opposition parties hold their own debates and meetings during the passage of a bill. Backbench committees are formed by MPs with a particular interest in a policy area, and present an opportunity for party MPs to discuss and debate matters of policy importance to the party and the members' electorates. Formal meetings of parliamentary party groups are held regularly (usually weekly) when parliament is sitting. In these private meetings party MPs can discuss policy and tactics, voice their opinion and attempt to influence the party leadership. Many deals and negotiations (within parties and between them) take place behind closed doors: in the offices and corridors of the parliament as opposed to the floor of the chamber (Uhr & Wanna 2000, p. 16).

Parliament is the source of government

The relationship between the parliament and the government is often not clear or easy to understand because it is not expressly addressed in the Constitution. Rather, it is based on unwritten constitutional conventions, discussed in the previous chapter. Technically, governments in Australia (*as opposed to parliaments*) are not directly elected by the people. When citizens vote in general elections they vote to elect an MP to represent their electorate, rather than a government. The government is then formed by the party or coalition of parties that holds the majority of seats in the lower house. This ensures that the government has won a majority of seats in an election, so it has popular legitimacy. The party or coalition with the largest minority of seats becomes the Opposition.

Parliament and government

The relationship between the government and the parliament is shaped through constitutional provisions, conventions and political practice. The key elements of this relationship can be summarised as follows:

- MPs are elected to represent their constituents, and collectively form the upper and lower houses of parliament.
- These MPs will, in the vast majority of cases, either belong to or support a particular political party.
- The party (or coalition) with the support of most members in the lower house becomes the government party, while the party (or coalition) opposed to the government becomes the 'official' Opposition.
- The party with the support of most MPs will select a leader from the lower house, who is then commissioned by the Governor-General as the Prime Minister (federal), or by the Governor as the Premier (State).

- The Prime Minister or Premier may appoint, or the governing party may elect, several of its MPs to become ministers. The full ministry, or a selected group from within it, becomes the principal policy and decision-making group of the government, commonly known as the cabinet.

Source: adopted from Harris 2005, p. 41.

The key positions in the government are those of the ministers and the Prime Minister (or Premier in the States and Chief Minister in the Territories). The party that forms government selects its own leader, and this leader becomes the Prime Minister or Premier. This means the Prime Minister is not directly elected by the people but is indirectly elected, which clearly differentiates the Australian system of government from a US-style presidential one. The Prime Minister or Premier is supported by a group of MPs from their party or the governing coalition (ministers) who individually assume responsibility for the coordination and oversight of a particular policy area (or portfolio) and usually a government department.

While ministers are formally commissioned by the Governor-General (or the Governor at State level), in practice they are chosen by the governing party or coalition. Liberal prime ministers select their ministries, and although Labor ministers have historically been elected by the Labor parliamentarians (also known as the Caucus), this tradition was overturned by Kevin Rudd after his election in 2007 when he individually chose his ministry (Tadros & Davis 2007).

Those MPs who hold ministerial portfolios are collectively referred to as the government's 'frontbench', whereas MPs who are members of the governing party but who are not ministers are known as 'backbenchers'. These terms can also be used to refer to the division of labour within the Opposition. A 'crossbencher' is the term given to an MP not aligned to the government or Opposition, including independents and MPs belonging to the minor parties.

Individual ministers holding portfolios are collectively known as the ministry, while the most senior of these ministers form the Cabinet. The Cabinet is the key decision-making body within any government, and it meets regularly with the

Prime Minister to make important decisions regarding the implementation of the governing party's policy and the future political direction of the country. In overseeing the implementation of laws within their portfolio areas, the Prime Minister and the Cabinet fulfil an important constitutional role as the executive arm of government.

Ministers are also responsible for the implementation of public policy within their respective portfolio areas, and because they are also elected representatives, this forms a 'supposed chain of accountability' (Ward 1999, p. 14) between the people and the public service. In this chain, public servants are accountable to a Cabinet of ministers, who are in turn responsible to the parliament. As parliament is answerable to, and directly elected by, the people, if the people do not approve of the conduct of the government they can vote it out of office. This is known as the convention of 'collective ministerial responsibility' (Hughes 1998, p. 298), and is further supported by the doctrine of 'individual ministerial responsibility', which requires that ministers are individually responsible to parliament for the actions of their departments and should resign in cases of public maladministration. Together, these conventions are also referred to as 'responsible government'.

However, as Ward (1999, p. 14) argues, these conventions do not accurately reflect the way government in Australia actually works. It is extremely rare for ministers to resign in instances of public service failure, and they will tend to do so only when their actions embarrass the government and thwart its re-election prospects. Given the dominance of parties as the organising force in Australian parliaments, scholars have suggested that our system of responsible government should be more accurately described as responsible party government (Ward & Stewart 2006, pp. 83–5; Summers 2006, p. 71; Lucy 1985, pp. 6–10). In this model, the chain of accountability from the executive government (Cabinet) to the parliament is less significant than that between the governing party and the people, being enforced principally through general elections.

Furthermore, the nature of the public service and the legislative process has become increasingly complex in recent years such that there are ample opportunities for a 'breakdown' in the chain of accountability to occur. For example, ministers may not reasonably be aware of all activities within their departments. As we shall see throughout this book, other political actors such as senior public servants, special advisers and lobby groups may intervene in the legislative process, influencing the decisions of parliamentarians to the extent that their actions may no longer directly represent the 'will of the people'.

Finally, the media may also play a part in distorting the process of accountability, by controlling the flow of information about governments and shaping voters' attitudes towards parties, governments and political leaders (see Ward 1999, p. 32).

In recent years an argument has emerged that the executive in the Australian system is becoming more 'presidential', in the sense that the Prime Minister is increasingly deciding policy directions instead of the Cabinet as a whole. This argument can also be applied to the State premiers, a notable example being the leadership style of former Queensland Premier Peter Beattie, who was described as having been involved in every issue, dominating press releases across all portfolios and seeking every photo opportunity (Prasser 2007).

Sometimes this shift is attributed to the growing complexity of government, which increases pressure on the executive to 'perform' in relation to community expectations. Other reasons include media pressures and the demand for policy coherence and consistency across different areas, requiring a single person to oversee and direct the policy process for it to work efficiently and effectively (Keating & Weller 2000, pp. 51–2, 57–8). There is some evidence that the roles and responsibilities of the Department of Prime Minister and Cabinet, the department that provides policy advice directly to the Prime Minister on a range of portfolio areas, have increased over time (Keating & Weller 2000, pp. 62–3). Moreover, the presidential idea is very popular in media commentary. However, comprehensive evidence that the Prime Minister is increasingly directing the work of the executive in ways that are alien to the Westminster system is difficult to find. Although the Prime Minister can potentially dominate Cabinet, much depends on the Prime Minister's leadership style and individual personality. Weller (2007, p. 285) argues that the most effective prime ministers will work through this institution because of the collective support it offers.

More recently, such scandals as the Australian Wheat Board (see Chapter 14) and children overboard (Chapter 11) have drawn attention to the role and accountability of staff employed by the Prime Minister and the government, known as 'ministerial advisers'. Anne Tiernan (2007, p. 8) argues that the number, power and influence of these personal ministerial staff have grown significantly since the 1970s. In 2006 the Howard ministry employed 445 such staff, with forty-seven supporting the Prime Minister alone. According to Tiernan, ministerial staff:

> are a diverse group, providing political, policy, administrative, media and communications advice, and personal support to ministers. Unlike the non-partisan advice they receive from public service departments, ministers receive support that is explicitly partisan from their staff, whom they personally select. It is also highly personalised; tailored to the personality and working style of the individual incumbent. (2007, p. 4)

Ministerial staffers appear to be supplementing, if not gradually replacing, the traditional role of the public service in providing policy advice to ministers. However, they present an awkward fit in a Westminster system as they are not subject to the same accountability for their actions as public servants (see Chapter 13). The conduct and behaviour of certain staffers was brought into question during the children overboard and Australian Wheat Board scandals, revealing that disciplinary mechanisms are suboptimal, as responsibility for the supervision of their activities rests with the minister alone. Consequently, Tiernan (2007, pp. 234, 238–9) argues that, to provide adequate accountability, the ministerial staffing system is in need of urgent reform, which could begin by drafting an appropriate code of conduct.

Parliament holds governments accountable

As we have seen, the notion of responsible government creates a supposed chain of accountability between those delivering public services and those receiving them. Although this chain can be compromised, the government's accountability to its voters through regular elections is supplemented by the structures and procedures of parliament, which function between elections to scrutinise governments. In this section we will discuss the role of:

- the Opposition
- parliamentary questions and debates
- committees
- the upper house.

The first of these institutional safeguards is the formalised function of the Opposition. It is recognised as the 'alternative government': this means that the organisation of the Opposition mirrors that of the government, with a shadow ministry that specialises in the same portfolio areas that government ministers oversee, so that it is ready to govern at any moment should an election be called. The functions of the Opposition revolve around constantly challenging and seeking to defeat a government. The Opposition scrutinises and suggests amendments to legislation, expenditure and public accounts, asking questions of the government and seeking information on its activities. Although government business may dominate the agenda of the lower house, the Opposition is given opportunity to express its views on issues debated, having claim to an equal speaking time. It can initiate its own topics for discussion—in fact 'most discussions of matters of public importance are on topics proposed by the Opposition'—and outside the chambers of parliament opposition MPs serve as valuable and critical members of parliamentary committees, their views being taken into account in committee reports (Harris 2005, p. 80).

All parliaments in Australia make provision for some kind of 'question time'. This gives MPs an opportunity to submit questions either on notice or without notice to ministers, which must be answered within a fixed time. Other opportunities for questioning the government's activities occur during parliamentary debates and within committee inquiries. The aim of parliamentary questioning is to 'seek information, and to bring the Government to account for its actions, and to bring into public view possible errors or failings or areas of incompetence or maladministration' (Harris 2005, p. 37). All discussion in parliament takes place under parliamentary privilege, meaning that parliamentarians' comments in parliament are outside the ambit of defamation or other speech-restrictive laws, and immune from prosecution.

> 'Hansard' is the name given to official transcripts of State and federal parliamentary proceedings. It is provided on the internet for both houses of parliament within one day of the parliamentary session. Hansard is also usually provided for the committees of parliament. To access it, go to the website of any Australian parliament and click on the link to 'Hansard'.

However, the content and origin of many questions asked during question time often fall well short of providing a robust opportunity to hold the government answerable (Rasiah 2006). Ministers are often able to evade answering questions, or do not have the necessary information at hand to answer them fully. Half the questions to ministers will come from the governing party's backbenchers. Called

'Dorothy Dixers', these are essentially friendly questions and are asked in such a way as to allow government ministers to advertise their activities. An example of the character of a Dorothy Dixer is contained in the following extract of a question on the economy asked by a Liberal Party backbencher to Prime Minister John Howard during House of Representatives question time in 2007:

> Mr Bartlett: My question is addressed to the Prime Minister. Can the Prime Minister confirm that real wages are continuing to grow? How much have they grown since 1996? …
>
> Mr Howard: In reply to the Member for Macquarie, I can inform the House that, because of the successful economic policies of this government, real wages for Australians have continued to rise …

Many questions from the Opposition are also unconstructive, designed to embarrass the government or score political points rather than encourage transparency or reasoned debate. The adversarial nature of Australian parliamentary debates is often criticised for this reason (see Ward & Stewart 2006, p. 75; Cook 2004, pp. 7–8). Nonetheless, it is an inherent feature of the Westminster system, as 'the efficiency and effectiveness of a parliamentary democracy is in some measure dependent on the effectiveness of the Opposition; the more effective the Opposition, the more responsible and thorough the Government must become in its decision-making' (Harris 2005, p. 34).

As we saw in the snapshot, parliamentary committees conduct inquiries into specified matters and scrutinise government activity. They often undertake detailed examinations of controversial bills and conduct general reviews of policy areas and specific issues of public concern. Committees may oversee the expenditure of public money, and they may call the government or the public service to account for their actions and ask them to explain or justify administrative decisions. Committees consist of members of parliament appointed by one or both houses of parliament. Standing committees continue throughout the life of a parliament and often into subsequent parliaments, whereas select committees are more transitory—they are formed to deal with a specific issue or piece of legislation.

The outcome of a committee inquiry will be a report to parliament and, although it might be persuasive, it cannot bind the government or MPs to follow its recommendations. The effectiveness of committees acting as mechanisms of governmental accountability and in providing a balanced report will often directly reflect their composition: 'upper house committees in which non-government members often have a majority of places are generally more effective than their lower house counterparts, which are dominated by government members' (Smith et al. 2006, p. 26). Committees hold public hearings that take evidence from experts and interested parties and from members of the general public under parliamentary privilege. They provide an access point for concerned citizens to participate in the parliamentary process. Anyone can make a written submission to a committee or attend a public hearing, and the work of current committees is advertised online and in the major Australian newspapers.

Finally, the upper houses of the bicameral State parliaments and the federal Senate provide another check and balance on government activity. In recent decades, it has become usual for governments not to have control of the upper houses of Australian parliaments. Currently, the governing party does not have a majority of seats in any of the State upper houses and must rely on the support of minor parties and independent MPs to govern. This is due to the differential systems of electing upper and lower house MPs in the various parliaments, which facilitate the election of minor party and independent candidates to the upper houses (see Chapter 5). A government minority has also been the norm in the Senate since 1981, except for the period between July 2005 and July 2008 (Evans 2007, p. 199; Young 1999, p. 10). During its first three terms the Howard government had to negotiate with the Democrats to have its GST legislation passed (1998–2001); it negotiated with the Opposition to secure the passage of anti-terrorism and security legislation (2001–04); and a Medicare package was negotiated with independent MPs (see Evans 2005, p. 45; Bach 2003, pp. 161–79).

This composition has caused, and continues to cause, significant tensions between the two houses, both in State and federal arenas. For example, in South Australia, the upper house has frustrated successive Liberal and Labor governments. In 1998–99 the Olsen government's controversial campaign to privatise electricity faced great difficulties in passing the Legislative Council (Parkin 2003, p. 114). Opposed by the Australian Democrats and independent Nick Xenophon, the Liberal government had to rely on the support of two Labor MPs who crossed the floor to vote with the Liberals. It does not seem to matter which party is in government; major party attitudes to upper houses remain the same. South Australia's Labor Premier, Mike Rann, has called for a referendum on the abolition of the Legislative Council in 2010, describing it as a 'circus for political point scoring' and 'road blocking the state' (Rann 2005).

Therefore, the main argument for an upper house is that it has the potential to act as a check on government and the possibility of an overbearing majority in the lower house. Those opposed to an upper house see it as an unnecessary overlap and waste of resources if it agrees with the lower house, and an obstruction to the efficient working of government if it does not. It is a debate that reflects the continuing tensions between the executive and the legislature in the Australian 'Washminster' system; between efficient governance and the need to consider the interests of those not adequately represented by the majoritarian lower house. Interestingly, comparative evidence suggests that bicameralism, throughout the world, is in decline (Massicotte 2000, p. 282).

Australians' attitudes to the role of the Senate

Although successive governments have expressed their frustration with the Senate when legislative programs have been thwarted or, at the very least, delayed, Australians do not share the attitude of former Prime Minister Paul Keating that the Senate is 'unrepresentative swill', or that it has become a 'house of obstruction' (Howard 2003). When asked 'Which do you think is better—when the federal government has a majority in both the House of Representatives and the Senate, or when the federal government in the House of Representatives does not control the Senate?', almost half of the respondents in the 2001 Australian Election Study (44 per cent) preferred that the Senate was not controlled by the governing party in the lower house, whereas only a third did (Wilson 2003). In July 2005, the government regained control of the Senate, sparking criticism from commentators that the 'Senate's capacity for scrutiny, accountability and review' has been systematically eroded (Evans 2006) and suggestions that the decline in support for the Coalition since 2004 has partly been a result of the public's belief that the Coalition has abused its Senate majority (Hawker 2007). Indeed, rather than seeing an acquiescence in public attitudes towards government control of the Senate, the 2005 Australian Survey of Social Attitudes found that even more Australians (57 per cent) perceived this control as a 'bad thing' (Denemark et al. 2007, p. 25).

The 'decline of parliament' thesis

Some critics question whether parliament really does provide a forum for debate that has the potential to change parliamentarians' opinions and to ensure accountability. Hughes has argued that the accountability mechanisms within parliament are weak. One reason for this is that they rely on unwritten conventions that are difficult to enforce. Another is that real decision-making does not happen within the parliament at all but within the executive instead (Hughes 1998, pp. 298–9; Turner 1990, p. 69).

There is considerable evidence in support of this argument. For example, Ward and Stewart cite three reasons why the responsible government model has become a 'supposed chain of accountability'. These reasons can be contrasted with the example of the passage of the Therapeutic Goods Amendment Bill shown in the snapshot. First, they argue that party discipline ensures that members of parliament vote with their party rather than on the basis of an open and frank discussion. Since the government has a majority of seats in the lower house, this ensures that government bills are passed through this house with no real discussion or debate. Second, they argue that parliament passes too much legislation to allow for adequate scrutiny of each bill because there simply is not enough time to debate each proposal fully. Further evidence for the idea that the parliament cannot adequately scrutinise the executive is the government's use of the gag and the guillotine. A 'gag' is a motion put to parliament that 'the question now be put', which ends debate immediately. A 'guillotine' is the setting of a time limit in advance for debate of a bill (see Harris 2005, p. 518). Third, the tasks of government have grown too complex for parliament to act as an effective check on the government because parliamentarians do not always have enough information to understand the different options available (Ward & Stewart 2006).

These criticisms have led to what is known as the 'decline of parliament' thesis, an argument that parliament is in decline as an institution and is no longer able to fulfil its democratic decision-making function. The idea of parliamentary decline is not a recent phenomenon. It has been cited in publications as early as 1888 and 1896 (Herman & Lodge 1978, pp. 5, 24). Rodney Smith (1994) reminds us that there was never a 'golden age' from which Australian parliaments have declined. Rather, the procedures and mechanisms of parliament that limited scrutiny of the executive were established as early as two decades after federation and resulted from the emergence and stabilisation of a two-party system.

There is some evidence to suggest that Australian parliaments are achieving greater scrutiny of government activities, legislation and improved administrative accountability, due in part to the influx of minor parties and independents into parliament (Smith 1994, pp. 106–9; 2006). However, some of the reforms and legislation passed by the Commonwealth Parliament in recent years illustrate just how tenuous parliamentary democracy can be. Many of the federal accountability mechanisms that have been established in the past, including for example the Scrutiny of Bills Committee, have been possible only because of a lack of government control of the Senate. Evans (2007, p. 202) argues that once a government has control of the upper chamber, it can simply abolish accountability measures or use its majority to ensure that they do not operate.

From July 2005 when the Howard government gained control of the Senate until its electoral defeat in November 2007, it passed several pieces of contentious legislation on terrorism and industrial relations without the agreement of minor party and independent senators and with limited debate (see Gelber 2006, p. 438). Evans (2007, pp. 202–6) catalogues a number of examples:

- the rejection of all non-government amendments to the Telecommunications Interception Amendment Bill 2006
- many concerns raised by the committee inquiring into the Anti-Terrorism Bill (No. 2) 2005 were ignored
- the time available to committees to examine bills was reduced from forty to twenty-eight days
- from 1 July 2005 to 30 June 2006 sixteen gag motions and five guillotines were used, compared to no gag motions and only one guillotine in the previous year
- the time to debate contentious bills was shortened. The Anti-Terrorism Bill was allocated six hours and the Work to Welfare legislation given seven hours. Comparatively, the Native Title legislation passed in 1993 was debated for fifty hours and the Workplace Relations Bill 1996 for forty-nine hours.

Instances of governments using their majorities to circumvent accountability mechanisms and curtail debate are not unique to the Howard government—the Kennett era in Victoria was also similarly criticised. As we have also seen, State Labor governments have acted to abolish and continue to advocate the abolition of upper houses altogether. These examples serve to illustrate the point made early on in the chapter that parliaments are only as democratic as their rules, practices and composition provide. In the absence of any detailed constitutional provisions safeguarding the operation of a particular model of parliamentary democracy, successive governments are free to add, amend or remove any accountability mechanisms they see fit, provided they accept the electoral consequences.

The role of a parliamentarian

In the snapshot we saw parliamentarians provided with the opportunity to debate and vote on the passage of the RU486 legislation according to their conscience, an opportunity that is very rare in Australian politics as the majority of votes in parliament take place along party lines. While most parliamentarians belong to and are elected under the label of a particular political party and the party is a major influence upon their attitudes and behaviour, in their everyday working life members of parliament have three roles that they need to balance:

- parliamentarian
- electorate representative
- party member.

As parliamentarians, members participate in debates on legislation and public policy, question the government and seek information on its activities. Although it varies according to the individual, much of an MP's time is taken up with committee work as the detailed nature of the inquiry process necessitates a member becoming very familiar with their subject matter. As Democrats Senator Lyn Allison (2007) explained, 'we're in this environment where we're pretty much given a university fast tracked degree ... because the information comes to you, it's debated, there's the committee work—all of that. So we're pretty well informed.' Often MPs will specialise in one or several areas of policy interest in the course of their parliamentary career.

As a constituency representative, depending on how they are elected and which electorate they represent, an MP will seek to advocate and represent the interests of many thousands of people. For a member of the House of Representatives, this is about 120,000. An MP is a direct link between the constituency and the federal or State administration. Constituents may seek the help of their local member in individual matters such as immigration, social welfare and taxation, or in community campaigns and issues specific to the electorate such as the construction of an airport as:

> A member has influence and standing outside parliament and typically has a wide range of contacts with government bodies, political parties, and the community as a whole. Personal intervention by a member traditionally commands priority attention by departments. In many cases the member or the member's assistants will contact the department or authority concerned, where the case will be dealt with by the relevant section. In other cases, the member may approach the minister direct. (Harris 2005, p. 132)

In representing the interests of their electorate, a parliamentarian may act as a trustee, a delegate or a mirror of their constituents (see Chapter 2).

As a party member, it is expected that the MP adhere to the policies of their party and demonstrate loyalty and support in parliament. Before entering parliament, all Labor MPs take a pledge to vote in accordance with the majority decision of the Caucus and are bound to this by the party's constitution (ALP Constitution Part B, Art 5dii). The Liberal and National parties do not require a similar undertaking from their MPs, but are historically just as disciplined as their Labor counterparts. While agreements of this type are not legally enforceable, as Summers (2006, p. 71) argues, 'election to parliament depends on party endorsement, and it is a rare Parliamentarian who risks his or her endorsement by voting against a party decision'.

Such rigid party discipline is often cited as one of the reasons for the decline of parliament, concentrating power within the Cabinet and Shadow Cabinet and stifling independent thought and debate. However, the extent of party discipline and uniform voting practices tend to obscure the potential for members of parliament to produce changes to proposals originating from their own parties. As Labor MP Anthony Albanese (2007) commented:

> I'm part of a political party, I'm bound by that political party, I support that political party and I don't decry from that. Because of that I have an opportunity to influence government rather than just be an individual shouting out things.

Lobbying the leadership from within their own party is one of the many ways MPs balance their responsibilities to parliament, the electorate and their party. However, different parliamentarians will have widely varying views on how they conceive of their roles as legislators. For example, in qualitative research undertaken on the Greens party, parliamentarians were asked, 'There are many competing demands on MPs. How do you manage your time, as a representative of the parliament, the party, and the electorate?' Two quite different answers that prioritise different parts of an MP's work are given below.

> The majority of my work is about the work of the parliament, and the constituency. I'd say less of my time is with the party. I go to the meetings; I take calls; I talk to people. I went to a Greens women's event on Saturday. I will support things that the party asks me to support, but if you look at my overall work, that would not be very much compared to my parliamentary work. (Tucker 2003)

> I see myself primarily as a representative of the party. It's the way I was elected, as a Green. In terms of prioritising my time, and what I'm doing, a lot of that is prioritised around the goals that we, as an office, have set for ourselves, and then the specific campaigns that we've chosen to focus on, in terms of achieving those overall goals. (Nettle 2003)

Parliamentarians' roles, then, can be conceptualised in different and even competing ways. The way the practice of these roles is prioritised is important to the way we understand representation in Australian politics today. These roles also shape our expectations of parliamentarians: on whose behalf they speak and what they stand for.

Summary

- The Australian system of representative democracy comprises nine discrete parliaments. Although they have distinctive features, each has been designed to implement the principles of representative democracy: the people elect them, they are supreme law-making bodies and they are the source of governments.
- Parliaments function to hold governments accountable through such mechanisms as question time and committees, and such institutions as upper houses.

However, the chain of accountability is often compromised by the complexity of government and who is in power.
- The representative role of a parliamentarian is not straightforward. In fulfilling their legislative duties parliamentarians need to balance their roles as party members, electoral representatives and parliamentarians.

Further reading

Two of the most comprehensive and authoritative guides to the functioning of the federal parliament are published and updated online:

Evans, Harry 2004, *Odgers' Australian Senate Practice*, 11th edn, Department of the Senate, Canberra, available at <www.aph.gov.au/senate/pubs/odgers/index.htm>.

Harris, Ian 2005, *House of Representatives Practice*, 5th edn, Department of the House of Representatives, Canberra, available at <http://202.14.81.230/house/pubs/ PRACTICE/index.htm>.

A good introduction to the parliaments, governments and electoral systems of the Territories and States is:

Sharman, Campbell and Moon, Jeremy (eds) 2003, *Australian Politics and Government: The Commonwealth, the States and the Territories*, Cambridge University Press, Melbourne.

Useful websites

Each parliament in Australia has its own web page, which contains useful information on the parliament's history and operation, as well as profiles of all MPs and their contact details, a calendar of sitting dates and the parliamentary *Hansard*.

- Parliament of Australia: <www.aph.gov.au>.
- Parliament of New South Wales: <www.parliament.nsw.gov.au>.
- Parliament of Queensland: <www.parliament.qld.gov.au>.

- Parliament of South Australia: <www.parliament.sa.gov.au>.
- Parliament of Tasmania: <www.parliament.tas.gov.au>.
- Parliament of Victoria: <www.parliament.vic.gov.au>.
- Parliament of Western Australia: <www.parliament.wa.gov.au>.
- Australian Capital Territory Legislative Assembly: <www.legassembly.act.gov.au>.
- Legislative Assembly of the Northern Territory: <www.nt.gov.au/lant>.

CHAPTER 5
ELECTORAL SYSTEMS

This chapter presents an overview of the electoral systems used to elect parliaments in Australia. Australia has a progressive system compared to many other countries in the world, and provides opportunities for representation of different political parties. However, these opportunities are only occasionally realised. There is much debate about our two-party system whereby majoritarian, voting and democratic practices prevail over proportional, consensus-based electoral approaches.

Electoral systems are dynamic and can be changed through parliamentary means to reflect population changes or changing priorities given to representation of the people. There are also controversies about how elections are funded, such as through donations, and whether citizens' allegiance to the two major parties in Australia has diminished over time.

The topics covered in this chapter include:

- an overview of the democratic elements in the electoral system that bring political parties to government
- an explanation of the different ways votes are counted, with a focus on the contrast between preferential voting and proportional representation
- an interpretation of results in recent elections, including the 2007 federal election
- a focus on recent controversies about funding and advertising of election campaigns
- a look at how stability in the way Australians vote has decreased, leading to claims of a 'volatile electorate'.

SNAPSHOT One vote, one value? Electoral reform in Western Australia

Western Australia has a distinctive political culture due to both its sheer geographic size and its distance from the Sydney–Melbourne–Canberra political centres (see Moon & Sharman 2003). Until recently it had one of Australia's more idiosyncratic electoral systems. One facet of this electoral system was the 'malapportionment' that characterised electorates for both lower and upper houses. This meant that the number of voters in non-urban, mostly rural and remote electorates was much less than in the urban electorates around Perth. The democratic principle of 'one vote one value' did not exist in either the Western Australian Legislative Assembly or the Legislative Council. Voting was in favour of rural seats by 2:1 and 3:1 respectively. Western Australia was the only State in Australia without 'one vote, one value' principles applied to the government forming lower house (van Onselen 2005, p. 3). A justification for this was the desire to have wide-ranging community and regional representation in parliament.

The Western Australian Legislative Council's malapportionment had six multi-member electorates (with five or seven members) based on geographic areas, elected using proportional representation; that is, an area like Mining and Pastoral, which is one of the largest electorates in the world covering most of outback Western Australia, has similar representation to a smaller urban electorate such as North Metropolitan. This system in Western Australia was similar to the clear malapportionment in the Senate, which is based on the need to have equal representation of the six Australian States, all of which are entitled to elect twelve senators each.

There has long been debate about reforming the Western Australian electoral system to have a parliament in which electorates are equal in the populations they represent. An Electoral Amendment Bill in 2001 failed to gain a majority of parliamentarians' support in both houses of the Western Australian parliament. It was not until after the ALP won another State election in 2005 that they could successfully move to reform the electoral system.

The successful 2005 'one vote, one value' reforms led to an electoral system in which each lower house seat now has roughly the same population. From the next State election, due in late 2008 or early 2009, six seats will be removed from regional Western Australia and eight added to the city, while up to seven sparsely populated regional electorates will be made special cases (AAP 2005). Overall, there will be two extra MPs in both houses of parliament.

Arguments were presented from both sides. The argument in support of electoral reform was based on changing the system to reflect 'one vote, one value' and remove the effective gerrymandering whereby the parties that were successful in rural and regional seats, usually the Liberal–National Coalition, benefited in having increased parliamentary representation (see Davies & Tonts 2007). A 'gerrymander' is a pejorative charge against legislators who are accused of manipulating or changing electoral boundaries to suit themselves and increase their vote.

Attorney-General Jim McGinty says the new electoral deal is about ending a 150-year gerrymander. 'This [deal] takes away unfair vote weighting which has previously been enjoyed by the conservative parties in this state,' McGinty said. 'It puts Western Australia in exactly the same position as the federal parliament and every other state and territory parliament in Australia.' (Dodd 2005)

The alternative argument was to keep the status quo with the regional focus that could reflect a wider range of interests than the mainly urban population around Perth. Some, such as Liberal Member for Roe Dr Graham Jacobs, also suggested in parliamentary debate that creating such large geographical electorates based on sparse population was discriminatory:

> The bill will place the seats of Merredin and Roe in the same electorate covering over 100,000 or possibly 110,000 square kilometres. Nevertheless, that electorate still will not get a large-area allowance. My constituents have been disadvantaged; in fact, I go so far as to say that they have been discriminated against. People opposite may say that I am only looking after my career or my electorate or that I am worried that I may be up against the member for Merredin at the next election. I do not give a toss about that! I care about the representation of my constituents. To spread a representative so thinly throughout an electorate that he is ineffective for his constituents is a sad day for Western Australia, and particularly a sad day for my constituents who put me here. As I have said, this is an *Animal Farm* bill that states that everybody is equal, but some people are more equal than others. (WA Legislative Assembly 2005)

The electoral reform was portrayed as increasing fairness in the distribution of electorates, but was also interpreted as the ALP government in Western Australia changing the system to the detriment of the Liberal–National Coalition:

> 'I am red-hot angry,' shouted Nationals leader Max Trenorden, whose party now faces political extinction. 'This is not about electoral fairness—this is about the Labor Party winning the next election,' said prominent

Liberal and former Court government minister Paul Omodei.
(Dodd 2005)

This recent example of electoral reform in Western Australia shows that many political factors influence the way an electoral system is structured and ultimately reformed. How do electoral systems take into consideration the representation of smaller communities? How are both geography and shared values and identity important? How are electoral systems adapted to make them more representative and less majoritarian? How does the way people vote and identify with a political party entrench the Australian two-party system?

Australia's electoral system

Australia has a mainly majoritarian, Westminster parliamentary system of government imported from the United Kingdom, as highlighted in Chapter 4. A recent debate about representation and electoral systems asks whether it is best to have a single member, or representative, for each electorate or whether it is better to have electorates with multiple representatives. This argument is a trade-off between the virtues of two different theoretical approaches to representation: majoritarian theories, usually associated with the Westminster approach, and consensus theories, based on the principles of proportionality.

Arend Lijphart distinguishes between majoritarian and consensus (proportional) experiences of democracy. Majoritarianism is typically characterised by:

- concentration of executive power in one party only
- executive–parliamentary relationships in which the executive is dominant
- two-party systems
- majoritarian, disproportional electoral systems
- a pluralist system of pressure groups.

Consensus systems are characterised by:

- power-sharing executives in multiparty coalitions, or minority governments that have to bargain to stay in power and to pass laws
- balance of power between the executive and the parliament

- multiparty systems
- proportional representation
- a corporatist pressure groups system (Lijphart 2001, p. 190).

The type of democracy—either majoritarian or consensus—and the subsequent electoral system used—either disproportional or proportional—have major consequences for the types of representatives elected, the mix of political parties within parliament and the make-up of a government, such as whether it is more likely to be formed by a single political party or by a coalition of political parties. Majoritarian systems are favoured by those who believe there ought to be a single-party government that is able to pass its legislation without major compromise and subsequently be evaluated and held accountable on its performance at election time. In contrast, the consensus model is favoured by those who like to see broad participation in government, and tends to emphasise 'inclusiveness, bargaining and compromise' in government policy-making (Norris 2001, p. 880).

Of the sixty-eight countries in the world labelled as 'established democracies' (that is, those countries that have had free elections for more than twenty years and a population greater than 250,000), thirty-five have a predominantly majoritarian electoral system, including the United States, United Kingdom, Canada and India. The remaining thirty-three are structured around proportional considerations; examples are Israel, Germany, New Zealand and Mexico (Reynolds et al. 2005, p. 30).

Now we will examine some of the formal aspects of Australia's electoral system to learn how, in practice, it is influenced by both majoritarian and consensus approaches.

Compulsory voting

Voting in an election is considered to be a basic political right for Australian citizens. This right is put into practice regularly, with elections held at all three levels of government. Federal elections for the House of Representatives have to take place at least every three years; the average federal government term is two years and six months (Newman 2002, p. 3). In Australia to be eligible to vote you have to be:

- an Australian citizen

- older than 18
- registered on the Australian electoral roll.

There are a number of exceptions to these conditions. British subjects who were living in Australia before January 1984 and were enrolled to vote here remain eligible to vote. Those who are excluded from voting include: people who are permanent residents but not citizens, people considered to be of unsound mind and not capable of understanding the significance of voting, and homeless people not registered as an 'itinerant voter' (Smith 2001a, p. 4). There was debate recently about changes made to the electoral roll and prisoners' entitlement to the vote (see Orr 2007).

Compulsory voting was first adopted in Queensland in 1915. It was introduced in federal elections in 1924, and all the States gradually introduced it in the twenty years following federal adoption. This practice is distinctive because very few other countries enforce compulsory voting as strictly as we do. The only other countries that enforce compulsory voting by fining individuals and/or asking for an explanation from those who do not comply include Belgium, Cyprus, Fiji, Luxembourg, Nauru, Singapore and Uruguay (see the International Institute for Democracy and Electoral Assistance (IDEA) website <www.idea.int/vt/compulsory_voting.cfm#compulsory>).

Occasionally there are public debates about Australia's retention of compulsory voting. The debates for and against compulsory voting occur around positions on the rights and responsibilities of Australian citizens. For example, some believe that voting is a right shared by all but that citizens should have the freedom to choose to participate or to not participate, and ought not be forced into choosing a candidate if none are to their liking. Other arguments range from suggesting that compulsory voting has made life easier for political parties in that they do not need to appeal to people to participate, to arguments that compulsory voting leads to the politically apathetic and less informed electors being forced to make a choice (see Bennett 2005, pp. 7–9).

Alternatively, arguments are made that compulsory voting should be retained because it ensures the civic responsibility of all Australians, to actively shape and participate in democracy, is met. This responsibility argument is also used to demonstrate that voters benefit from the experience by learning more about their system of government through participation, and that it legitimates the electoral system itself because everyone is an active participant. Australian voters themselves tend to support compulsory voting. For example, in the 2004 Australian Election Study 74 per cent of respondents supported the retention of compulsory voting (Bean et al. 2004).

The federal electoral system

At the federal level Australians vote for their parliamentary representatives in both the upper house—the Senate—and in the lower house—the House of Representatives (see Chapter 4). The methods of selecting the representatives of these two houses are quite different, and are based on the different principles of majoritarianism and proportionality already discussed. This is another area where the Australian electoral system is distinctive in that we use multiple methods to select representatives. Furthermore, the precise way votes are counted to elect members of the House of Representatives, called preferential voting, has been widely used only in Australia. Although preferential voting is now also used at the national level in Fiji and Papua New Guinea (Bennett & Lundie 2007), other countries tend to rely on different methods of counting votes.

Australian Electoral Commission

The Australian Electoral Commission is an independent statutory authority established under the provisions of the *Commonwealth Electoral Act 1918.*

It is responsible for:

- conducting federal elections and by-elections
- maintaining the Commonwealth Electoral Roll, in accordance with Joint Roll Arrangements with the States and Territories
- administering compulsory enrolment and compulsory voting
- determining State and Territory representation in the House of Representatives in accordance with the latest population statistics, and administering redistributions
- administering election funding and financial disclosure
- conducting electoral information and education programs to promote public awareness of electoral and parliamentary matters
- providing information and advice on electoral matters to the federal parliament, the federal government and federal government departments and agencies

- conducting and promoting research into electoral matters and publishing relevant material
- conducting national referendums to amend the Constitution
- conducting elections for registered industrial organisations.

Source: adapted from 'AEC functions', <www.aec.gov.au/About_AEC/functions.htm>.

In 2008 there were 150 federal electorates around the country. They are intended to be roughly equal in size in terms of the population they contain, and the quota set by the AEC is currently at 137,000 people, which amounts to an average of about 86,000 voters per electorate. The total population in the electorate include those who cannot vote such as those younger than 18, most permanent residents and immigrants. Regular redistributions happen when the population in electorates change. Electorates based on population quotas means that they can vary dramatically in their geographic size as Australia's population is extremely sparse in some locations. For example, the electorate of Kalgoorlie covers the majority of Western Australia with its 2,295,400 square kilometres, as compared to a small inner-city electorate such as Melbourne, which covers only 53 square kilometres. The differences in electorates' geographical size, coupled with the vast distance most electorates are from Canberra, can make the practice of being a local representative, in touch with local people and issues, a difficult task.

As electorates are based on population quotas and not on geographical size, this means that more electorates are located in the more populous States. Table 5.1 shows the distribution of electorates among States and political parties, and demonstrates that the House of Representatives is dominated by the populous but geographically smaller States of New South Wales and Victoria.

When we vote in elections for the House of Representatives, we vote for a local representative who becomes the member for our local electorate. The political party, or coalition of parties, that wins the majority of House of Representatives electorates forms government. As you can see in Table 5.1, the Australian Labor Party won a clear majority of electorates—eighty-three—in the 2007 federal election. It formed government and its leader, Kevin Rudd, became Prime Minister. This means that we do not directly elect the head of government as voters in the US do when they vote for the President.

By contrast, when we vote for the Senate, we vote for State- or Territory-based representatives. Each State has twelve representatives in the Senate, and each of the two Territories has two representatives. This allocation of senators is not

TABLE 5.1 House of Representatives after 2007 election

Party	NSW	VIC	QLD	WA	SA	TAS	ACT	NT	TOTAL
ALP	28	21	15	4	6	5	2	2	83
Liberal Party	15	14	10	11	5	–	–	–	55
National Party	5	2	3	–	–	–	–	–	10
Independent	1	–	1	–	–	–	–	–	2
TOTAL	49	37	29	15	11	5	2	2	150

Source: Australian Electoral Commission, <www.aec.gov.au>.

proportionate to the population within States and Territories. For example, as is reflected in Table 5.2, although the number of designated Senate representatives remains the same for the two Territories as it is in the House of Representatives, it differs dramatically for several States. Tasmania has many more representatives in the Senate than it has in the House of Representatives (twelve compared to five), while New South Wales and Victoria's proportion of representatives has diminished dramatically (i.e. combined they only have 32 per cent of senators, dropping from their 57 per cent share of members of the House of Representatives).

TABLE 5.2 State of the full Senate from 1 July 2008

Party	NSW	VIC	QLD	WA	SA	TAS	ACT	NT	TOTAL
ALP	6	5	5	4	5	5	1	1	32
Liberal	4	5	5	6	5	5	1	–	31
National	2	1	2	–	–	–	–	–	5
Country Liberal	–	–	–	–	–	–	–	1	1
Green	–	–	–	2	1	2	–	–	5
Family First	–	1	–	–	–	–	–	–	1
Independent	–	–	–	–	1	–	–	–	1
TOTAL	12	12	12	12	12	12	2	2	76

Source: Australian Electoral Commission, <www.aec.gov.au>.

The Senate also differs from the lower house in that only half its members stand for election at each federal election whereas all House of Representatives members must compete for their seat at every federal election. This means that senators are elected for six-year terms. There are two exceptions to this rule. The first exception is that the four senators representing the two Territories compete at every federal election for their spot. The second exception is when there is a double dissolution election. The government can opt for a double dissolution election, at which all members must compete for their parliamentary seat, when there are lengthy or unresolvable differences on whether a proposed bill becomes a law. There have been only six double dissolution federal elections since Federation (Smith 2001a, p. 2). Table 5.2 also reveals that no one party or coalition of parties has a majority of senators after the 2007 election. This is mainly because the Liberal–National Coalition gained a historic majority in the Senate after the 2004 election (for more on this see Economou 2006). This means that from mid–2008 the government party, the ALP, will need to cooperate with minor parties, such as the Greens, Family First and/or Nick Xenophon, the South Australian independent, to have new legislation passed through the Senate.

Electing representatives

Three main methods are used to elect representatives, and they provide three different outcomes for representation in parliaments:

- first past the post
- preferential voting
- proportional representation.

In the first-past-the-post method voters simply mark their single preferred candidate, and whoever gets the most votes is elected regardless of whether they obtain an overall majority of the votes. This means the more candidates standing in an election, the fewer votes an individual candidate may need to get the highest number of votes. First past the post is not used to elect representatives in Australia, but it is still used in most elections in the United Kingdom and in the United States. We will focus on the latter two systems for electing representatives.

Preferential voting

The preferential voting method has at its core the idea that the winner needs to have obtained the *majority* of votes. The distribution of preferences comes into play when there are more than two candidates and no candidate has won an outright majority. In the 2007 election seventy-five electorates, or seats, were decided simply as the winner won a majority of first preference votes. The remaining seventy-five seats needed to have preferences distributed to determine the winner. It is quite common, however, for the party that is first past the post still to win after preferences are distributed.

For example, in the 2007 election preferences changed the winner from the candidate who initially had the most first preference votes to the candidate who was second in only nine electorates. In most of these electorates the contest was very strong between the two major party candidates, who between them gained at least 90 per cent of the overall vote. For example, in the New South Wales seat of Bennelong, which the sitting Prime Minister John Howard lost, the Liberal Party gained 45.5 per cent of first preferences and the ALP gained 45.3 per cent. Preferences were distributed from minor parties, such as the Greens, to win the seat for Maxine McKew, the ALP candidate. However, preferences sometimes change the outcome when there is a strong showing for a third party behind the two major parties. An example from the 2007 election is the Tasmanian seat of Bass, where the ALP had 37.2 per cent of the first preferences and were well behind the Liberal candidate on 43.5 per cent. The Greens received 15.3 per cent of first preferences and, as the majority of Green voters preferenced the ALP second, the ALP was able to win the seat (all data from <http://vtr.aec.gov.au/HouseResultsMenu–13745.htm>).

The 2007 election was important because it was the first time that government had changed hands since 1996, or for more than four elections. This is reflected in Table 5.3, which shows the political party distribution of House of Representatives seats since 1972. Examples of elections where a government changes (1972, 1975, 1983, 1996 and 2007) can be seen in Table 5.3, and each of these elections produced a major change in overall party-based electorate representation. Also note that during the last thirty years independents have secured seats in the federal parliament's House of Representatives only in the 1990s.

Despite occasional governmental change, the majority of electorates in the Australian electoral system have predictable outcomes, or are what we consider to be 'safe seats', as opposed to marginal electorates, where the electoral outcome is more transient. The AEC suggests that when a party receives less than 56 per cent of the two-party-preferred vote the electorate is classified as marginal, 56 to

59 per cent is classified as fairly safe, and more than 60 per cent is considered safe (AEC 2007). On the basis of these arbitrary considerations, about fifty out of 150 electorates are considered marginal, yet it would be more instructive to examine how often electorates have actually changed party representation during recent federal elections to judge their vulnerability to representational change. For example, in the 2007 election twenty-seven seats changed party, most from the Liberal–Coalition to the ALP; however, several seats went the other way in Western Australia. Similarly, after the 1998 federal election, party representation changed in twenty-three electorates. However, the 2001 and 2004 elections saw less change, with only twelve seats changing hands in 2004.

TABLE 5.3 Party representation in the House of Representatives, 1972–2007 elections

Year	ALP	LP	NP	IND	Total	Government
2007	83	55	10	2	150	ALP
2004	60	74	13	3	150	Liberal/NP
2001	64	68	14	4	150	Liberal/NP
1998	67	64	16	1	148	Liberal/NP
1996	49	75	19	5	148	Liberal/NP
1993	80	49	16	2	147	ALP
1990	78	55	14	1	148	ALP
1987	86	43	19	0	148	ALP
1984	82	45	21	0	148	ALP
1983	75	33	17	0	125	ALP
1980	51	54	20	0	125	Liberal/NP
1977	38	67	19	0	124	Liberal/NP
1975	36	68	23	0	127	Liberal/NP
1974	66	40	21	0	127	ALP
1972	67	38	20	0	125	ALP

Note: Years when the government changes are italicised. Due to redistributions of electorates based on population change, the total number of seats has changed.

Source: adapted from Australian Electoral Commission, <www.aec.gov.au/Elections/federal_elections/index.htm>.

Preferential voting—in practice

To understand the distinctiveness of preferential vote counting in the Australian political system we need to understand how preference distribution works in practice. A fictitious example of a ballot paper for the electorate of Chocolatariana is shown in Figure 5.1, followed by equally fictitious election results to demonstrate how the distribution of preferences works in practice. First, note that in electoral systems where preference distribution is compulsory, all boxes must be numbered; that is, all candidates need to be ranked in order of preference. Any boxes missed, or the same numbers used more than once, means that the vote is considered informal and cannot be counted.

When the votes are first counted five piles of first preference votes, one for each candidate, will be formed. In the example no single candidate has a majority of the votes, therefore the preferences of the smaller parties need to be distributed to the major parties: the Milk Chocolate Party and the Dark Chocolate Party. The first candidate to be eliminated from the count is the one with the least votes—in this example it is the candidate for the Chocolate Ginger Party. His votes are examined and then redirected to the second preferences of these voters. In the example 2 per cent went to the Chocolate Liquorice candidate and 1 per cent went to the Milk Chocolate Party. Then the White Chocolate Party redistributes votes, which maintain the lead of the Dark Chocolate Party. It is not until the last smaller party candidate is eliminated that the lead changes as most of the Chocolate Liquorice preferences go to the Milk Chocolate Party, resulting in the electorate being won by this party. The example clearly shows that preferences from smaller party voters can play an important role in determining the winners of elections.

As preferential voting makes it possible for results to change in this way, it has been argued that preferential voting is not a simple indicator of a majoritarian system. Rather, it is argued that it should be considered to have consensus elements because of the 'extra information that it elicits from voters. Allowing voters to indicate a preference ... creates incentives for political actors to reach out for secondary preference votes and thus to bargain, cooperate and compromise in search of electoral victory' (Reilly 2001, p. 94). Most elections involving preferences are really a contest between the two major parties; hence it is difficult to be persuaded that consensus principles are also utilised in parliamentary and formal decision-making settings. It is instead in our Senate, and most State upper houses, elections that proportionality and consensus elements are at work.

Proportional representation

Proportional representation systems were devised to ensure that parties could win parliamentary seats roughly in proportion to the size of their vote. Elections for the Australian Senate use proportional representation, also known as the single transferable vote, to count the votes cast. Proportional representation is used when multiple representatives are being elected in each electorate. In the case of the Senate the electorate is each State and Territory; and each State has a different list, or ballot paper, of candidates to choose from. To be elected, a candidate will have to achieve a quota, or a predetermined proportion of all votes cast.

For example, in regular elections for the Senate (often also called 'half-Senate' elections because only half the parliament's senators will be elected) when six representatives will be elected from each State, the quota needed by the candidate for election is 14.3 per cent of all votes cast. This lower threshold makes it easier for minor parties to win Senate spots than it is for them to win the majority of

FIGURE 5.1 Fictitious example of a ballot paper

Ballot Paper
House of Representatives
Electorate of Chocolatariana
24/11/2010

Please number all boxes, from 1 to 5, in the order of your choice

Jenny Jones
Chocolate Liquorice Party ☐

Stan Smith
Dark Chocolate Party ☐

Martin Ng
Milk Chocolate Party ☐

Steve Stanislavsky
Chocolate Ginger Party ☐

Jill Bloggs
White Chocolate Party ☐

TABLE 5.4 Election results in Chocolatariana

	First preference votes %	1st round elimination %	2nd round elimination %	3rd round elimination %	Final result %
Jenny Jones Chocolate Liquorice Party	8	10	10		Eliminated
Stan Smith Dark Chocolate Party	42	42	48	49	
Martin Ng Milk Chocolate Party	39	40	42	51	Winner
Steve Stanislavsky Chocolate Ginger Party	3				Eliminated
Jill Bloggs White Chocolate Party	8	8			Eliminated

votes in a House of Representatives seat. Nevertheless, while a growth in parliamentary representation of minor parties and independents over the last thirty years has been noted (see Newman 2005), the vast majority of Senate seats are still shared between the two major party groups.

Counting votes for the Senate is not straightforward. The proportional representation system of counting votes is based on voters directing where their preferences will go; that is, it is a 'quota-preferential' system (Smith 2001a, p. 24). Similarly the distribution of preferences comes into play when full quotas are not achieved by candidates; hence a quota can be obtained by candidates receiving preferences from supporters of other candidates. Furthermore, like preferential voting used in the House of Representatives, all candidates need to be given a ranking by individual voters. However, this is not as straightforward as the Chocolatariana example given above where voters needed to rank only five candidates (for more detail on how the votes are calculated see Singleton et al. 2006, pp. 289–92).

Voting for the Senate

In 1984 the Senate ballot form was changed to allow voters to vote by party. The names of each political party and all independents are placed along the top of the ballot form. Under this is ruled a line. Either voters can put a '1' in a single box above the line or they can number all of the boxes below the line, in order of their preference.

In Senate elections the vast majority of voters regularly choose to vote 'above the line' on their ballot paper for the single party of their choice. In the 2007 election only 3.2 per cent of Australian voters chose to rank all the candidates listed 'below the line', according to their own preference. This ranged from 1.8 per cent voting below the line in New South Wales to 15.8 per cent in Tasmania and 17.2 per cent in the ACT (see <http://vtr.aec.gov.au/SenateUseOfGvtByState–13745.htm>.

This pattern of voting above the line is understandable as many more parties and individuals compete in Senate elections. For example, in the 2007 federal half-Senate election there were 367 candidates, ranging from seventy-nine in New South Wales to twenty-eight in Tasmania and eleven in the Northern Territory (see <http://vtr.aec.gov.au/SenateNominationsByState–13745.htm>). The option for voters to rank all of these candidates against one another is time-consuming and requires an opinion of candidates whom many would not have heard of before.

For the vast majority who vote for the single party of their choice, their preferences are predetermined by a legal agreement, or preference registration, that the political party has lodged with the Australian Electoral Commission before the election. For an accessible overview of how parties preferenced one another for the 2007 Senate election, see elections expert Antony Green's web site <www.abc.net.au/elections/federal/2007/guide/groupvotingtickets.htm>. The power that parties have to determine preference exchanges and influence electoral outcomes has been controversial. See Antony Green's overview of this debate at: <http://blogs.abc.net.au/antonygreen/2007/11/senate-backgrou.html>.

Often in half-Senate elections it is the fifth and/or sixth Senate seat in each State that gains most interest as they often have the potential to be won by a minor party or independent rather than the two major parties, and these parties can play a balance-of-power role within the Senate (this role is discussed further in Chapter 6, especially when undertaken by the Australian Democrats). It is rare for minor parties or independents to gain the quota of first preference votes necessary to gain Senate representation. In the 2001 and 2004 elections none of the minor parties, such as the Democrats, One Nation, Family First or the Greens, were able to achieve the quota and needed to rely on the redirection of preferences from other minor party candidates, or surplus to quota votes received by major party candidates, to win seats. In the 2007 election two non-major party candidates won outright quotas: Bob Brown from the Australian Greens received 18.1 per cent of the Senate vote in Tasmania, and independent candidate Nick Xenophon received 14.9 per cent in South Australia.

State and Territory electoral systems

Sharman and Moon suggest that Australia is simultaneously both 'one and nine political systems' (2003, p. 241), and in terms of electoral systems we can see that this argument rings true. Table 5.5 shows that no State or Territory has exactly the same way of electing its representatives to their parliaments, and only two States, Victoria and Western Australia, use the same model and principles of counting votes as are used for federal parliament. Part of the difference between States is that electoral systems have evolved and changed over time as a result of State governments making different changes, whether in the guise of fairness or to further enhance the positions of the major parties, as was seen in the snapshot at the beginning of the chapter. States, as reflected in Chapter 3 on developing the framework for democracy in Australia and later in Chapter 11 on federalism, also like to see the evolution of their own political practices as unique.

Debates that happen at a State level often involve the prioritising of either a majoritarian- or consensus-based model for the electoral system, or even for one of the houses of parliament in particular. For example, New South Wales moved to optional preferential voting in the Legislative Assembly in 1979 (Smith 2003, p. 57). As this method of counting votes allows voters to nominate only one candidate, it is akin to first past the post and signals a stronger shift to a majoritarian system. Similarly, Queensland has no upper house and no elements of proportionality in its electoral system at all. The places most characterised by a consensus-based approach are Tasmania and the ACT, because the election of representatives and government formation are based on multimember electorates.

TABLE 5.5 Methods of counting votes in the States and Territories

State (party of government in 2008)	Lower house	Upper house
NSW (ALP)	Single-member electorates Optional preferential voting	Proportional representation (with optional preferences)
Queensland (ALP)	Single-member electorates Optional preferential voting	No upper house
South Australia (ALP)	Single member electorates Full preferential voting	Proportional representation (with full preferences)
Tasmania (ALP)	Multimember electorates Proportional representation	Single member electorates Preferential voting
Victoria (ALP)	Single member electorates Full preferential voting	Multimember electorates Proportional representation
Western Australia (ALP)	Single member electorates Full preferential voting	Multimember electorates Proportional representation
Australian Capital Territory (ALP minority)	Multimember electorates Proportional representation	No upper house
Northern Territory (ALP)	Single member electorates Full preferential voting	No upper house

Source: adapted from Bennett and Lundie (2007, p. 31); and State-based electoral commission websites.

A facet of electoral systems more likely to be experienced at State levels than in federal parliament is minority government. A minority government occurs when no major party wins the majority of seats in the lower house, which is necessary for them to form the government outright. In this situation a government needs to be formed through an agreement with minor parties or independents, who will support the minority government to actually govern. The agreement can be a formal one, whereby the minor party or independent actually forms a coalition with the major party to form government, or it can be a less formal agreement, whereby a minor party does not want to be part of the government but will vote with the government often in exchange for policies that meet the minor party's agenda. As coalitions generally are an indicator of a consensus approach to the electoral system it is no surprise that the two lower houses that use proportional representation, Tasmania and the ACT, are more likely to have had minority governments than anywhere else. In fact, since its parliament was formed in 1989 the ACT has mainly had minority government (Moon & Sharman 2003, pp. 253–4). The distinctive proportional systems used in Tasmania and the ACT to elect governments also socialise voters to a proportional approach. This can be seen when we look back at the figures mentioned earlier, which showed that voters in the ACT and Tasmania were much more likely to number all the boxes 'below the line' in a half-Senate election. For more detail see the box on the ACT below.

Government in the Australian Capital Territory since 1989

Canberra is divided into three electorates: Brindabella, Ginninderra and Molonglo. Brindabella and Ginninderra elect five members and Molonglo elects seven, making a seventeen-member Legislative Assembly as the government.

Members of the Assembly in the ACT are elected by a variant of proportional representation called Hare Clark (which is also used for the Legislative Assembly in Tasmania) whereby there is no option to vote 'above the line' for a party and at least five (or seven) boxes must be numbered. This number reflects the number of representatives to be elected for each electorate (Bennett & Lundie 2007, pp. 20–5). Elections are held every three years on the third Saturday in October; the next will occur in 2008.

The Chief Minister is elected by ballot on the first sitting day of a new Assembly. The Chief Minister, who is the leader of the government, appoints ministers, and together they make up the Executive. The number of ministers is not to exceed five. The members of the Executive usually come from the same political party. However, in 1998 an independent member was appointed to the Executive.

Before the 2008 election there were nine ALP, one Green, one independent and six Liberal Party members of the Assembly. Five members were women, twelve were men. This was the first majority government the ACT has had since 1989. For the 2002–05 government the ALP formed a minority government with the support of the Greens, but they were not a formal coalition. The previous two governments were formed by the Liberal Party in a formal coalition with independents.

Source: <www.elections.act.gov.au/education/factHC.html>; <www.parliament.act.gov.au>; Warhurst 2003.

Campaigns, advertising and election funding

Contemporary election campaigning features expensive, slick campaigns that focus heavily on television advertising and are coordinated on behalf of the party by media consultants. It is rare for individual candidates of major political parties to have significant funding to run their own specific and localised campaigns. Instead, campaigns are increasingly focused on the competition being waged between party leaders, mainly the Prime Minister, or Premier, versus the Leader of the Opposition.

In the past Australian election campaigns were locally constructed, targeting community members through street corner meetings and mobilising a relatively large party membership. Ward (2003a, p. 586) notes that the arrival of television had great political significance, with the ALP's 1972 federal election campaign's strong television focus demonstrating that modern electioneering had emerged in Australia. This campaign was also distinctive because it used a national campaign committee to coordinate the States and utilised opinion polling conducted by market researchers. By the mid-1980s these new political techniques were dominant in election campaigning.

Political parties use in-house opinion polling units to regularly test new campaign and policy ideas on the electorate. These polling units use randomly selected telephone interviews, as well as in-depth focus group discussion. The aim is to find out what political issues have resonance with a majority of the voting public, and results are used as a guide for parties on what issues to avoid debate on and which issues are electoral 'point-scorers'. This is not a new phenomenon in Australian politics as the major parties have enlisted pollsters since at least 1972, but it is technology that has developed and strengthened this shift in election campaigning. Information technology plays a diversified and important role in party-based campaigning. For example, all major parties now have well-designed websites to deliver information to those who seek it. Another element is the increasing use of database technology to engage in direct mail and targeted campaigns during election campaigns (see Van Onselen & Errington 2004). This approach to campaigning also owes a debt to election campaigning in the United States (see Mills 1986, pp. 11–42). In Chapters 7 and 8 we will further discuss the role of opinion manipulation and opinion polls in the Australian political process.

Another factor in the professionalisation of election campaigns is the increasing amount of money now being spent by political parties on advertising. Sally Young (2002, pp. 83, 90) found that during the 1996 federal election the two major parties spent $15 million on broadcast advertising alone, and that these broadcast advertising costs rose 900 per cent between 1974 and 1998. This demonstrates that the parties must believe that prolific election advertising produces favourable outcomes at elections. However, by charting the amounts spent by the two major parties over time Young (2002) also found that there is no clear electoral advantage from outspending an opponent on television advertising, in that the party that spends the most does not always win elections. For example, the ALP spent nearly $9 million compared to the Coalition's $6.5 million in the 1996 federal election, but the ALP still suffered a resounding defeat to the Coalition parties led by Prime Minister John Howard (Young 2002, p. 91). Election advertising outlays by the major parties continue to rise: after the 2004 federal election it was estimated that the two major parties spent $20 million each on advertising (Young & Tham 2006, p. 105). Furthermore, at the federal level, there are no legislative constraints on how much advertising parties produce, or on how much they can spend on campaign advertising and electioneering generally. There is also no formal mechanism to identify how much money is being spent by parties during campaigns.

The professionalisation of election campaigning, by the major parties in particular, through increased targeting of swinging or undecided voters has changed the way we analyse Australian politics. The increased focus on both advertising and specialised, individualised databases is about 'capturing' the votes of those who are less committed to and less likely to identify with a particular party. As will be shown later in this chapter, political scientists have found that there is a great range of motivations and reasons for a lack of party identification. Clearly political parties themselves have become increasingly adept at funding their own research and identifying the voters they need to target to win electorates and to win government.

Electoral funding

Election funding and financial disclosure was introduced at the federal level by the new ALP government in time for the 1984 election. The scheme has two main purposes:

- to publicly fund election campaigns
- to ensure disclosure of financial details by candidates and registered political parties. Disclosure is by means of returns that have to be submitted to the Australian Electoral Commission and subsequently become public documents.

Political parties that endorse candidates, and independent candidates, receive public election funding when candidates receive at least 4 per cent of the formal first preference vote in the federal election they contested. In 2008 the rate was approximately $2.14 per vote received (see <www.aec.gov.au/Parties_and_Representatives/Political_Disclosures/Current_Funding_Rate.htm>).

Why publicly fund elections? Part of the rationale of publicly funded elections is that it creates a more equitable situation whereby smaller parties and independents have access to resources for election campaigns. Furthermore, federal electoral funding regulations no longer influence how much money a party ought to have spent on an election campaign. In the past public funding came in the form of a reimbursement for outlays during an election. This is controversial, and some people within major parties argue for a reversion to reimbursement to stop small parties from profiting from election campaigns. It has been argued that some small parties gain a reasonable proportion of the vote but have minimal campaign expenditure. For example, the former leader of One Nation, Pauline Hanson, gained public funding from standing as a candidate in the 2004 and 2007 federal elections that was arguably in excess of her campaign outlay (Lewis 2007). Other suggestions are for a cap to be put on campaign expenditure at the federal level, similar to that which occurs in State elections in Victoria and Tasmania (see Cass & Burrows 2000, pp. 493–5).

However, the major parties also raise substantial funds from business interests and community-based organisations, such as trade unions. As part of the disclosure laws the details of these contributions are available from the Australian Electoral Commission website. The AEC regulates donations made to political parties, in that every financial year registered political parties, their State or Territory branches and associated entities (such as think tanks, registered clubs, service companies, trade unions and corporate members of political parties, which operate to benefit a party financially) are required to lodge a return with the AEC. The return provides information about amounts received and paid during the financial year, and outstanding debts. From 2007, third parties (including associated entities) that incur political expenditure in excess of the threshold were also required to lodge an annual return. In 2008 the threshold for the donor disclosure rate was $10,500 or more, and all donors have to annually disclose gifts and donations that they make to a registered political party. This threshold was increased in 2005 from the previous donation disclosure threshold of $1500. It has been estimated that, on the basis of recent returns, the change in threshold will mean that only 64 per cent of donations to parties will now be itemised, as opposed to about 75 per cent in the past (Miskin & Baker 2006). There are also debates about the loopholes in disclosing donations and whether the regulations in Australia are strict enough, especially compared to other systems such as in the United States (see Mayer 2006).

Political donations are an important dimension of both election campaigns and the ongoing upkeep of political parties. For example, in the 2004–05 financial year, which included the 2004 election, the national office of the ALP declared that it had received $30,082,000 in funds and that $16,783,000 of this came from the Australian Electoral Commission as public funding (see <http://fadar.aec.gov.au>). The remainder was a mixture of money received from associated entities, such as companies that hold assets for the party, investments and trust funds, fund-raising organisations, groups and clubs; and donations from other donors, such as business organisations, unions or individuals.

Some business organisations make large donations to both major parties. However, business funding overall continues to favour the Liberal Party at the expense of the ALP, while unions are consistently large donators to the ALP. It is important to keep in mind that most analysis of donations looks at the federal arena but significantly more money is also donated at the State and local levels and often by a broader range of organisations (see Young & Tham 2006, pp. 14–35).

Why do business organisations give money to political parties? One perception is that they donate money in exchange for political favour such as through legislation that benefits their company or industry. This perception prompted a controversy in 2003 after subsidies were given to the ethanol industry in its quest to develop an alternative to petrol. One company, Manildra, received more than $20 million a year through the subsidy scheme as it produces 87 per cent of the nation's ethanol. Manildra was also identified by the media as a major donor to Coalition election campaigns (Riley & Marriner 2003, p. 4). Other business organisations have become concerned by this perception and have declared that they will no longer make political donations, for example:

> Lend Lease spokesman Roger Burrows says the company 'used to donate to support the democratic process—not to buy influence'. But it was 'becoming concerned that people were starting to perceive that was what it was for' so it stopped the practice. (Pettafor 2003, p. T01)

Controversy over the purpose and expectations of business donations has led two minor parties to campaign for changes in electoral funding law. The Australian Democrats have argued for an annual cap of $100,000 to be placed on the amount of money any organisation can donate to a political party. They also argue that disclosure laws need to be tightened to ensure that businesses and unions are not slipping through loopholes in the law, and that these organisations ought to fully disclose to their shareholders and members the amounts they donate to parties (Joint Standing Committee on Electoral Matters 2006). The Australian Greens are also concerned about business donations to parties and unsuccessfully attempted in 2004 to introduce a Private Members Bill in New South Wales parliament to ban all donations from property developers. The Greens run a 'watchdog' website on political donations that is regularly used by the media as a source of information on this complex field of politics (see <www.democracy4sale.org>). Greens New South Wales representative Lee Rhiannon has claimed: 'Nobody believes that developers give something for nothing—nobody believes that developer donations are about altruism.' Property developers responded by arguing that they provide political donations to both major parties equally as it will bolster their competitiveness and create access to political decision-makers (Pettafor 2003, p. T01).

Voting and party identification

Understanding why people vote the way they do, how this changes over time and predicting which political parties will win, or how they will perform in elections, are all major concerns for commentators on Australian politics. Quantitative research approaches tend to dominate explanations of voting patterns in Australia. For example, the Australian Election Study (AES) provides Australian political science with its main source of information on the Australian public's attitudes towards politics and voting, detailed in the box below. The datasets from these studies (from the 1987 federal election onwards) are publicly available at the Social Sciences Data Archives website (see <http://assda.anu.edu.au>). The Australian Survey of Social Attitudes, which was first conducted in 2003 and every two years since, is an important additional data source.

Australian Election Study

The Australian Election Study is a series of surveys that began in 1987 and have been timed to coincide with federal elections. The series also builds on the 1967, 1969 and 1979 Australian Political Attitudes Surveys. The Australian Election Studies aim to provide a long-term perspective on stability and change in the political attitudes and behaviour of the electorate and to investigate the changing social bases of politics as the economy and society modernise and change character. In addition to these long-term goals the surveys examine the political issues prevalent in each election and assess their importance for the election result.

Sections include: the respondent's interest in the election campaign and politics, their past and present political affiliation, political involvements, evaluation of parties and candidates, alignment with parties on various election issues, evaluation of the current economic situation, attitudes to a range of election issues that have included: immigration, refugees and asylum seekers, terrorism, taxation, unemployment, and workers' entitlements, attitudes to issues relating to the environment and defence, assessment of the current level of racial prejudice in Australia today, and opinions on various social policy issues, including abortion, equal opportunities, sex discrimination and government assistance to Aboriginal Australians.

Individual background variables include level of education, employment status, occupation, type of employer, position at workplace, trade union membership, sex, age, own and parents' country of birth, parents' political preferences, religion, marital status, income and, where applicable, the occupation, trade union membership and political preference of the respondent's spouse.

The sample population is all Australians on the electoral roll at the close of rolls before the election, and a stratified systematic random sample process is used. Usually about two thousand people are included in the final sample. The method of data collection is a self-completion questionnaire, mail out, mail back, and it is sent out just after the election.

Electoral behaviour research, in Australia and in other English-speaking countries, is driven by a major preoccupation: explaining the level of vote received by each political party at a particular election (Catt 1996, p. 13). Hence, the AES is used after each election to obtain a series of attitudes and demographic details from individual voters to help explain why they voted the way they did. Charting how strongly attached people feel to the political party they voted for, or measuring their level of party identification, is an important element of this.

Party identification

A continuous debate is whether Australian elections are still predictably based on individual longstanding loyalties to political parties and to one of the two major parties in particular. Clive Bean and Ian McAllister (2005, p. 331) use AES data to argue that 'party identification continues to be the dominant influence in Australian political behaviour'; that is, they demonstrate that it is not campaign issues that determine the way individuals vote at each election; instead a longstanding loyalty to a particular party is the best predictor of people's vote. They do note, however, that individuals' opinions of party leaders also play an increasingly important role in the decision to vote one way or another (2005, pp. 326–33). Their analysis implies that the majority of individual voters develop or inherit a particular political outlook that is then sustained over time and over elections (see Leigh 2005).

After the 2007 election the AES data show that in response to the question 'Generally speaking, do you usually think of yourself as Liberal, Labor, National or what?', 77 per cent named the major parties (ALP, Liberal and National parties; see Table 5.6). In a subsequent question asked of those who identified with a party, 27 per cent of people agreed that they were not very strong supporters of the party (Bean et al. 2008). When this is considered with the 8 per cent who identified with a party other than the Coalition or the ALP, and the 15 per cent who did not identify with any party, it would imply that the way Australians feel about the major parties, and how this relates to their vote, is a lot more precarious than Bean and McAllister suggest.

TABLE 5.6 Party identification by age group in 2007 AES

Party	Total %	18–34	35–49	50–64	65+
Australian Labor Party	**37**	36	40	37	36
Liberal Party	**36**	28	34	37	42
National Party	**4**	1	3	4	5
Australian Greens	**6**	11	6	5	3
Other party	**2**	3	1	2	1
No party	**15**	21	16	15	13

Source: Bean et al. 2008.

There exists extensive critique of the 'electorate stability' approach of these authors. Rodney Smith offers a 'revisionist account of Australian partisanship', which argues that to understand the clear decline in party identification over time we need to discuss and analyse both the 'weak' (not very strong) party identifiers *and* those who have no party identification at all (2001b, p. 58). Smith also suggests that we ought not separate an understanding of party identification from the broader political context and the change in the outlook of political parties during the period (from the mid-1980s onwards) in which party identification has been in decline (2001b, p. 62; see also Catt 1996, pp. 80–3).

Returning to Table 5.6, it is also shown that there is a difference in party identification between younger and older Australian voters. Those aged 18–34 are more likely to identify with the Australian Greens than older Australians and much more likely to have no party identification at all. There are two possible explanations of this tendency: either some younger Australians are not yet fully socialised into Australia's political culture and will learn to identify with a party as they grow older, or some younger Australians have lost faith in political parties and are less likely to form a strong and sustainable allegiance to a major party. This second explanation would mean that there may be more volatility in future elections as younger voters will be motivated by leadership or election issues in determining their choice. Some argue that it was this younger voters bloc who did not strongly identify with the ALP but were mobilised into voting for Kevin Rudd in the 2007 federal election as they found his leadership appealing (Megalogenis 2007).

A large proportion of the population do, however, regularly vote for the major parties for a range of socialisation reasons that are often linked with individual characteristics of voters, such as socioeconomic status, age, sex and level of education (Bean & McAllister 2002, pp. 274–5). In Chapter 6 we will mention the continuing importance of the relationship between voter backgrounds, political party campaigning and ideological positions. Ideas of class and socioeconomic status are particularly important in interpreting Australian politics and elections (see McGregor 2001, pp. 86–109). However, not everyone fits into this pattern, as there are people who choose to 'swing' between major parties, vote strategically against major parties or vote depending on the political issues and leaders of the day.

Helena Catt (1996) points out that most mainstream, or orthodox, interpretations of the way people vote assume that a vote is a positive indicator of support for the particular political party and is based on rational self-interest. A rational self-interested choice would mean that individuals weigh up the policy platforms and ideological positions of each party, then choose the party that will act most in the individual voter's interests. Catt counters this view by suggesting that voting can also be based on negative feelings about, or even a protest against, particular political parties. The potential for negative voting seems only to increase in a period when parties themselves often run negative campaigns against their opposition (Catt 1996, pp. 42–9).

There are also voters who choose to vote for, or 'swing' between, different parties at different elections (see Smith 2001b, p. 63). One straightforward example is of voters who, at the same election, vote for one of the two major parties in the lower house but then vote for a minor party in the upper house, possibly as a protest against their usual party. This is called split ticket voting. This could be seen as a strategic way of approaching voting, in line with the approaches outlined above. Smith suggests that analysis of swinging, or 'softly committed', voters has tended to treat all non-major party voting behaviour as the same, when in practice there are several different types, including undecideds, protesting lower house voters, weak party identification split ticket voters, minor party identifiers, non-party identifiers, the politically aware and the uninterested (2001b, p. 65; see also Chaples 1997). Political parties themselves clearly recognise the diminished commitment to party identification among Australian voters, as is indicated by the way they run election campaigns that prioritise broad-based advertising and direct mailing methods.

This chapter has shown that there are several distinctive features to the Australian electoral system that creates parliamentary representation. An understanding of the roles and ideological foundations of the political parties of which our elected representatives are members provides an important foundation for analysis of the dynamics of the Australian system. An introduction to Australian political parties is presented in Chapter 6.

Summary

- The Australian electoral system is distinctive due to compulsory voting and the use of both preferential and proportional representation methods to count votes and elect governments.
- Theories of representation question the nature of electoral democracy today and can be used to highlight both the majoritarian and consensus elements in Australian politics. When preferential voting and proportional representation at both the federal and State levels are contrasted, we can see that Australia has elements of both approaches to democracy in its electoral systems.
- Election campaigns have professionalised and developed a focus on information collection, marginal seat campaigning and advertising. This professionalisation has been facilitated by generous State-based funding and the receipt of business and union political donations.
- Stability and predictability in the way Australians vote for the major parties have decreased, with more people being likely to vote for a minor party and/or to be not strongly committed to a party before each election.

Further reading

Catt, Helena 1996, *Voting Behaviour: A Radical Critique,* Leicester University Press, London.

Moon, Jeremy and Sharman, Campbell (eds) 2003, *Australian Politics and Government: The Commonwealth, the States and the Territories,* Cambridge University Press, Cambridge.

Sawer, Marian (ed.) 2001, *Elections: Full, Free and Fair,* Federation Press, Sydney.

Simms, Marian and Warhurst, John (eds) 2005, *Mortgage Nation: The 2004 Australian Election,* API Network, Perth.

Useful websites

- Australian Electoral Commission at <www.aec.gov.au>. This is a comprehensive website giving information on everything to do with recent Australian federal elections from detailed results to donations and party registration information.
- Institute for Democracy and Electoral Assistance at <www.idea.int/index.htm>. This organisation supports sustainable democracy in both new and long-established democracies, and contains extensive research comparing parties and election systems in countries around the world.

PART II
POLITICAL ACTORS

CHAPTER 6
POLITICAL PARTIES

In Chapter 5 we outlined the assumptions made by political scientists about the majoritarian tendencies of the Australian two-party system and the subsequent stability this provides for governments. We challenged this idea of stability by suggesting that consensual forms of democracy marked by multi-party systems broker deliberation and debate, not instability. Furthermore, the nature of the two-party system is necessarily changing as a significant minority of the electorate no longer provides the two major party groups with their first preference in elections in both lower and upper houses (see Bennett 1999; Sharman 1999; Bowler & Denemark 1993, p. 21). These shifts in voting patterns have an interdependent relationship with the changing organisational nature of political parties.

This chapter describes the political parties that operate federally and within the States. It highlights contemporary issues in the analysis of party systems and current understandings of the ideological positions of parties. This chapter is not a historical account. Rather, it explores the evolution of parties in what has been termed the 'cartel' age, characterised by electoral professional strategies that focus on campaigning, marketing and a new form of party organisation. We will continue the theme of representativeness by looking critically at party membership, mechanisms used to select candidates, as well as the continuing relevance of 'party' as a vehicle for group representation.

The topics covered in this chapter include:

- theoretical perspectives on parties as representative and participatory organisations, evolving from mass parties to cartel parties
- an introduction to the major features of Australian political parties, comparing their electorates and use of policy discourse
- a comparison of party organisations, with a focus on decreasing party membership
- independents in State and federal politics.

SNAPSHOT A tale of two parties—One Nation and the Australian Democrats

We have recently witnessed the decline of two parties that have played a significant role in Australian politics since the 1990s: One Nation and the Australian Democrats.

One Nation was formed in 1997 by the high-profile MP Pauline Hanson, appealing to Australians disillusioned with mainstream politics. Within twelve months of the party's creation it had attracted more than 25,000 members throughout Australia (Maddox 2000, p. 376). The party's vote peaked at the 1998 Queensland State election, in which it polled 22.7 per cent and won eleven of the eighty-nine seats in parliament. However, at the following State election both the number of seats won by One Nation and its vote share decreased dramatically. The party has since lost all of its parliamentary representatives and polled just 0.3 per cent in the 2007 federal election for the House of Representatives.

One Nation's downfall was regarded as chiefly organisational—the party's leadership had not established sustainable party structures that would be able to continue to contest Australian elections successfully. Ian Ward (2000, p. 89) writes that the party's 'unique corporate structure was purpose-built to prevent its rank and file from disturbing the complete control which its founders wished to preserve for themselves'. The consequence was that 'while large numbers flocked to One Nation in the anticipation that it would give them a political voice in a system [that] had long ignored them, the party's leadership was not interested in allowing its members a real say in its affairs' (Ward & Stewart 2006, p. 184).

One Nation was structured in such a way that Hanson and her co-directors, David Oldfield and David Ettridge, were able to exercise complete control of the party and its finances. The party was plagued by infighting caused in part by the authoritarian rules that the party had adopted to govern its operation. For example, One Nation candidates were required to lodge letters of resignation with the leadership that could be activated at any time; rebellious branches were promptly closed by the leadership; and party members did not have access to the names and addresses of other members to prevent the unauthorised formation of networks within the party (Ward & Stewart 2006, p. 185; Maddox 2000, p. 376; Ward 2000, pp. 102–4). In 2003 Hanson and Ettridge were convicted of electoral fraud relating to the way in which they had structured the party (*Hanson v Director of Public Prosecutions* [2003] QSC 277), but these convictions were later quashed on appeal.

The experience of One Nation suggests that parties without democratic internal structures so that members have an opportunity to participate in the party's activities are prone to failure. How does this compare to the decline of the Australian Democrats?

Unlike One Nation, the Australian Democrats embraced the principles and practices of internal party democracy. The Democrats were established in 1977 by Liberal Party defector Don Chipp as a party of the 'new politics' movement, and members have always been regarded as the driving force behind the party organisation: formulating policies, selecting office bearers, pre-selecting parliamentary candidates and determining the party leadership, all by postal ballot.

The Democrats were represented in the Senate from 1977 to 2008 and held the balance of power (either outright or with other minor parties) from 1981 to 2005. The party's federal election results peaked in 1990 under the leadership of Cheryl Kernot, when the party polled 12.6 per cent in the Senate. However, the Democrats' vote dropped significantly after the 2001 election, and in 2007 they polled just 1.29 per cent in the Senate and were unable to retain any seats. Although the Democrats' decline can be explained partly by the transience of their support base and the corresponding rise of the Greens, the party's democratic organisation and the internal tensions it created may also have contributed to the party's demise.

In contrast to One Nation's members, who joined the party seeking to influence policy but found that they couldn't, Democrat members rarely took up the participatory opportunities on offer to them. Participation in intra-party activities was very low throughout the life of the party, undermining the effectiveness of the Democrats' participatory structures and rendering them vulnerable to minority and elite control (Gauja 2005). The party membership had the right to select their party leaders and remove them by petition. However, this practice resulted in a high level of leadership churn (eleven leaders in thirty years) and installed leaders who, while popular with the membership, did not enjoy the support of their fellow parliamentarians. Members were able to formulate party policy by voting in postal ballots, but this proved to be a cumbersome process that did not allow the party enough flexibility to respond to topical issues quickly.

The strain on the party's organisation became most acute when the parliamentary party was forced to make difficult and contentious decisions in exercising its balance of power position. A key example was the party's negotiations over the new tax system (GST) legislation (1998–99). Disagreement as to whether the outcome of the negotiations by the Democrat senators actually reflected party policy and the views of members caused irreparable ructions both within the membership and the parliamentary party and resulted in two separate attempts to spill the leadership. The irony of the Democrats' decline lies in the fact that even though the party has been regarded as the most democratic party in Australian politics (Gauja 2005; Johns 2000; Warhurst 1997; Sugita 1995), as former leader Andrew Bartlett (2007) reflects, 'we didn't realise how high we were shooting and do enough to make sure we were capable of it'.

This snapshot raises important questions about the organisational nature of Australian political parties. Should members be able to participate in party decision-making processes, and to what extent? Who do party leaders need to listen to: their members or their voters? Is debate, disagreement and conflict within political parties a good or bad thing for representative democracy in Australia?

Three party models

Political parties in Australia are changing as representative forms. Once they were associated with cleavages—that is, distinct divisions in society—and the need for different groups of people to be represented in parliament. Now they have become centralised organisations, highly skilled in the policy language, campaigning techniques and the fund-raising efforts needed to win elections. Party scholars have charted similar changes occurring in both the electoral support for parties and their organisational form in other democratic countries, and have developed three party models—the mass party, the catch-all party and the cartel party—to explain this transformation. In this section we apply these three models to an analysis of the current incarnations of Australian political parties.

Katz and Mair have observed that 'a party is itself a political system' (1992, p. 6), comprising a number of different organisational facets (or faces) that interact with one another to shape the operation and policy directions of the party. Rather than looking at parties as a whole, it is useful to divide a party into three distinct faces: the 'party on the ground' (the general membership), the 'party in central office' (the permanent party bureaucracy and executive organs), and the 'party in public office' (the parliamentarians) (Katz & Mair 1993). The relationship between these different faces is not static and has changed significantly throughout the last century as political parties have evolved from mass to catch-all to cartel organisations.

'Mass party' is the term used by political scientists to describe the type of party that characterised electoral politics from the late nineteenth to the mid-twentieth centuries. Mass parties sought to recruit members and expand resources, develop policies to be implemented by elected officials and contest election campaigns (Ware 1996, p. 111). The mass party prioritised the party on the ground and had a large membership with many local branches, which contributed labour resources (for example, volunteering at elections) and funding to the party. It therefore needed a substantial party in central office to coordinate this membership base and a branch structure and to create national policy (Katz & Mair 2002, p. 117). While these two faces (the membership and the central office) are symbiotic, they are differentiated by the former being made up of volunteer members and the latter being staffed by paid party employees and elected officials (for example, the party president). The party in public office—that is, the members of parliament—were considered to be subordinate to the membership, bound to follow the party's directives and policies and supervised by the central party office.

The mass party arose to provide political represention to particular segments, or classes, in society. For example, in the United Kingdom and Australia, the emerging labour parties based their organisations on a very close relationship between members, electors and representatives through trade unions, shared class backgrounds and a common ideology—to protect and advance the interests of 'workers' (Judge 1999, pp. 75–6).

The lessening of class cleavages in the post-war period, a growing middle class and changes in campaign technology are generally considered to have encouraged the development of the 'catch-all' party. The political practice of catch-all parties differs significantly from the mass parties that preceded them; rather than representing a segment of society or a set of interests (for example, the working class), these parties turn their efforts to capturing the support of the 'median voter'; that is, producing policies to appeal to the electorate at large, often at the expense of ideological purity. This approach has been facilitated by improvements in campaigning technology that have emerged with the mass media. Rather than working through traditional channels and using party members as a resource for door-knocking and conducting public meetings, party leaders are able to reach an unprecedented percentage of the population through television, radio and printed publications.

This shift in practice has, in turn, affected the role of parties in modern democracies. As electoral pragmatism has replaced an ideologically driven agenda, parties have shifted from representing (and responding to) the views of their members and supporters to formulating policies perceived to be popular with the entire electorate. The function of parties as centres of participation is also downgraded, as members' roles in policy-making, fund-raising and campaigning are reduced and replaced by paid professionals. Therefore, in this model the party in public office attempts to become dominant over both the party on the ground and the central party office. The parliamentarians become a prominent 'face' of the party and work at winning elections, within the constraints of being in government. The central party office often acts as the buffer zone, mediating the inevitable conflict between the party membership and the parliamentarians. Conflict can be over such issues as leadership—is the leader in parliament or the party secretary in central office the leader of the party?—and over policy-making—is policy made by the group of parliamentarians or by the membership through the coordination of the central office?

The most recent evolution described by Katz and Mair, the cartel party, now arguably typifies the behaviour of many major political parties, particularly in Europe (Detterbeck 2005). In the cartel party model there is no longer real conflict between the different faces of the party because the party in public office has clearly won within the party structure, and it is the chief decision-maker and organiser. Fundamental to the 'new pattern in the internal balance of power' (Katz & Mair 2002, p. 123) is the distribution of financial resources. Table 6.1 illustrates the current sources of federal funding for parties and the face of the party that is now the primary beneficiary of these income streams.

Many political parties now receive state-based subventions, or electoral funding, directly related to their performance in elections. This means that parties no longer need to rely on a large membership for fund-raising or campaigning. However, if we examine the sources of funding on which political parties now rely, it is clear that the income derived from parliamentary duties clearly outweighs that received from donations and reimbursements for election expenses for all parties except the Greens. Australian federal MPs are entitled to uncapped phone, travel and photocopy allowances in addition to annual subsidies for printing

TABLE 6.1 Sources of party funding and their beneficiaries

Party	Funding source ($)			Primary beneficiary
	Donations	Election funding	Parliamentary duties	
Australian Democrats	3,017,909 (45.9 %)	8491 (0.1 %)	3,548,096 (54.0 %)	Party in public office
Greens	2,276,284 (24.9 %)	3,316,702 (36.3 %)	3,548,096 (38.8 %)	Party in central office
Labor Party	44,953,523 (32.1 %)	16,710,000 (12.0 %)	78,058,112 (55.9 %)	Party in public office
Liberal-National Coalition	53,431,433 (28.8 %)	20,923,000 (11.3 %)	110,878,000 (59.9 %)	Party in public office

Source: adapted from Young and Tham for the financial year 2004–05 (2006, p. 140).

($125,000), postal ($44,000) and electorate costs ($27,000). Estimates of the total value of parliamentary benefits available to Australian MPs are around $890,000 per annum (Young & Tham 2006, p. 58). Members of parliament are entitled to employ three staffers; a greater staff allocation is available for members of the ministry and shadow ministry (Holland 2002).

Previously, when donations to parties and other private sources of income constituted the bulk of parties' revenue, money was channelled into the party organisation, which was the primary employer of party staff, and it was this arm of the party that funded the development of party policy and election manifestos. However, as parties now gain the largest proportion of their income from parliamentary activities, this arm of the party is now the largest employer of staff. In 2002 the ALP had 1200 parliamentary staff at its disposal throughout Australia (Bramble & Kuhn 2007, p. 8). As Anthony Albanese (2007) reflects on the shift in policy-making within the ALP:

> Politics is now more driven by people who are full time members of parliament, members of staff . . . there's a negative in that it . . . previously I think the party was

> more vibrant at the rank and file level and there were more motions coming through and the party was more likely to be driven by that.

All of these elements led to the professionalisation of political parties, which now focus primarily on 'the demands of the party leadership in parliament and in government' (Katz & Mair 2002, p. 126). Katz and Mair suggest that it is the power of office that socialises and shapes the subsequent actions of parties, which focus mainly on retaining or regaining that source of power (2002, p. 124); that is, the major political parties construct policy battles and election campaigns with the goal of winning government, and they are less likely to be driven by ideological concerns.

Throughout the remainder of this chapter we will examine the application of the cartel party model to the Australian context. While there is some disagreement among Australian political scientists as to whether the cartel party thesis is a precise descriptor of the Australian party system (Woodward 2006, p. 185; Goot 2006), most regard the model as 'a useful prism through which to interpret current developments' (Marsh 2006, p. 19). In particular, we believe the cartel thesis provides valuable theoretical insights for questioning the broader participatory and representative role of parties in Australian society: how this has changed from the past, and where it might be headed in the future.

In Table 6.2, we have historically and organisationally situated six of the parties that have played important roles in the Australian political system in recent years. These parties can be divided into the established 'major' parties (the ALP, the Liberal Party and the National Party) and the 'minor' parties: the Greens and Family First. Despite having lost representation in the federal parliament, the Australian Democrats continue to feature in this chapter due to their historical significance and the interesting comparison they provide with current challengers to the major parties, particularly the Greens. The major/minor distinction classifies the parties in terms of their parliamentary status and history, but tells us little about their organisational formation or their internal processes of change.

Political parties can also be compared by their publicly espoused principles or their ideological position. The principles upon which a party is based are important because they provide the broad context for the development of a party's policies and programs. They are also the beliefs by which the party generates support among both its membership and the electorate more generally. Thus,

TABLE 6.2 Australian political parties compared

Party	Australian Labor Party	Liberal Party	National Party	Australian Democrats	Australian Greens	Family First
Year founded	1891	1944	1919 (as Country Party)	1977	1992	2002
Principles	Fairness, compassion, individual freedom, labour rights, responsibility, democracy, community	Stands up for interests of the individual, families and free enterprise	Security, individual achievement, strong representation for local communities	Representative, democratic, independent, focused on employment and economy, planet survival, foreign control, opportunity for women	Economic justice and social equality, grassroots democracy, peace and non-violence and ecological sustainability	Family as the most important social unit, 'commonsense, mainstream values'; affordable health, education and housing; opposes same-sex marriage, abortion and euthanasia
Year won first seat in federal parliament	1901	1946	1919	1977	1996	2004
National or State structure	State	State	State	National	State	State
Membership	Est. 40,000	Claimed 80,000	Est. 100,000	Est. 2500	Est. 8700	Est. 2500
Local branches	Yes	Yes	Yes	Few	Yes	Few
Official affiliations	Trade unions	–	–	–	–	Links to the Assemblies of God Church have been suggested, but denied by the party
Website	<www.alp.org.au>	<www.liberal.org.au>	<www.nationals.org.au>	<www.democrats.org.au>	<www.greens.org.au>	<www.familyfirst.org.au>

Sources: <www.alp.org.au>; <www.liberal.org.au>; <www.nationals.org.au>; <www.democrats.org.au>; <www.greens.org.au>; <www.familyfirst.org.au>; Family First (2004); Debelle & Schmidtke (2004).

'Major parties' are those that regularly form all or part of the government of the day. 'Minor parties' contest elections for public office but are consistently unable to form government or to participate in governing coalitions. They may fail to contest or win any seats in an election, or gain parliamentary representation but win too few seats to govern alone, or be excluded from coalition government (Smith 2006, p. 13).

party-based politics can be about values and finding the best way to represent particular value positions in an appealing way. For example, Table 6.2 demonstrates that the value positions of the two major parties—the ALP and Liberal Party—have quite different foundations. While both mention the importance of the individual they present different stances: one based on collectivist ideas of justice, community and responsibility (ALP) and the other on freedom and rights to improve one's position in the world (Liberal). These ideas seem somewhat abstract, but it is possible to see how these ideological values permeate opposing positions to policy-making.

The structures or organisational dimensions of the political parties are broadly similar in that all, except the Australian Democrats, are based around State divisions of the party. This means that the national organisation often acts as the peak for this federalist structure. Financial matters and the preselection of candidates still happen at the State level for most parties, and each State division may have distinctive processes and rules. The Liberal Party's organisational structure is outlined below. There are clearly defined roles for the party in central office—the organisational wing—which has more of an advisory than a decision-making role. The main decisions are made by the party in public office—the parliamentary wing—and by the leader of the Liberal Party in particular. At the base of each party are the members, who are grouped into branches. The parties differ in the level of activity of their branches and clearly in the number of members they can attract and sustain. The falling membership of political parties in general, and the implications of this, will be discussed later.

Liberal Party structure

The organisational and parliamentary wings of the Liberal Party each have clearly defined and separate roles. In the Liberal Party, the organisational wing cannot dictate policy but consults with and advises the parliamentary wing, particularly on the development of longer-term policies.

The organisational wing is based on the party's paid membership of supporters, and across Australia the Liberal Party has more than two thousand branches, which are governed by their respective State Liberal Party structure—known as 'divisions'.

The organisational wing is responsible for:

- the party's 'platform'—the broad statement of Liberal fundamental beliefs and intentions
- pre-selection of the party's candidates for elections
- management and conduct of election campaigns, and
- fund-raising.

The parliamentary wing of the Liberal Party is made up of federal and State parliamentarians. The parliamentary wing is responsible for:

- the representation of electorates held by Liberal Party MPs
- the Liberal Party's policies, strategies and parliamentary priorities guided by the principles contained in the 'Party Platform'.

Source: <www.liberal.org.au/about/ourstructure.php>.

Party representation and demographic change

Katz and Mair (2002) suggest that parties no longer represent purely class-based cleavages, but instead represent more complicated cleavages because the nature of society has changed. This argument can be verified in the Australian context by an examination of whom the parties target through their policy and ideological positions and whom they now represent in particular electorates. Australia has experienced a series of social changes since the end of World War II that have facilitated diversity in the general population, for example:

- a shift in the labour market away from blue-collar work, such as in manufacturing and primary industry

- increased casualisation of work, especially for young people
- more women entering the workforce and higher education
- an increase in school retention rates and university degree completions
- an increase in immigration, leading to an increase in a non-Anglo-Celtic population
- a decrease in number of people living in rural Australia
- declining levels of church attendance.

It has been suggested that the major parties have not wholly adapted to these social changes and have managed them with 'a combination of reluctance and dexterity, competing for each new group of voters while attempting to retain the loyalties of their old support bases' (Smith 1998, p. 118); that is, the established governmental parties have tried to retain their original voter base while at the same time trying to make inroads into the constituency of their opposition. For example, from the late 1960s the ALP tried to generate support among public sector workers who were predominantly professional and tertiary-educated white-collar workers.

In general, the customary understanding of social class as based on the blue-collar/white-collar occupational classification has less relevance now to predicting how people vote (Manning 2002, pp. 250–2). However, this is not to suggest that conceptualisations of class and experiences of privilege no longer affect voter support for particular political parties; rather our understanding of this dimension needs to become more nuanced and to take into account a range of factors, including demographic characteristics such as occupation, status, gender, religion, ethnicity and where people live. Haydon Manning argues that 'social class in its basic underlying sense—as a measure of the distribution of advantage, life experience and life chances—continues to clearly relate to voting behaviour' (2002, p. 262). Therefore, those with less still tend to vote for the ALP, and those with more still tend to vote for the Liberal Party.

However, in recent elections parties have also been successful in creating new appeals to particular sections of the population. For example, it has been acknowledged that part of the Liberal Party's success in the 1996, 1998 and 2004 elections was its construction of the 'battler' vote among struggling white-collar workers (see Crosby 2000; Johnson 2005, p. 51; 2007, pp. 39–55). The quote below from a speech by Prime Minister John Howard reflects on the Liberal Party's substantial win in the 1996 election and the way it appealed to and, importantly, provided economic benefits to the Australian battlers.

> When we were elected in March of last year it was rightly said that there were many people who voted for us on that occasion who had never previously done so. And that one of our prime responsibilities was to keep faith with those people—commonly called, often called, the battlers of Australia.
>
> . . . once again we are keeping faith with the battlers. Delivering interest rate cuts which on an average housing loan have been worth $225 a month, that's over $50 a week—let me repeat—over $50 a week added to your disposable income, after tax, to the average wage and salary earner. I can't think of a greater delivery on the commitment we made to the battlers of Australia in March of last year than to be able to deliver that kind of reward—for their support, for their wage restraint, and for the fiscal policies of the Howard Government. (Howard 1997)

Nonetheless, not everyone votes for or identifies with the two major parties. Social change in Australia has also affected the fortunes of smaller parties as it influences their campaigns and general appeal to the electorate. For example, the electoral appeal of the National Party has been affected by shrinkage in its rural constituency (see Davis & Stimson 1998). Such parties as the Greens and the Australian Democrats have been commonly understood to be competing for similar sections of the electorate: voters who are highly educated and interested in new, post-material political issues, but who are geographically dispersed throughout electorates. Consequently, neither party has gained much success in winning lower house seats at federal elections, but has instead been assisted by the system of proportional representation used to elect upper houses in Australia. However, unlike other analysts of minor parties in Australia (see Jaensch & Mathieson 1998, p. 29), we think that it is necessary to draw a general distinction between the Greens and Democrats. The demise of the Democrats and rise of the Greens can be partly attributed to the fact that these parties have campaigned differently, have very different party organisations and appeal to different sections of the electorate.

> **The new 'third force' in Australian politics: the Greens**
>
> Although environmental activists have been in Australian State parliaments since the early 1980s, the first Australian Green Party was not formed until 1992. Despite the initial hesitancy, the Greens have consistently argued for the development of robust environmental legislation requiring them to

have a voice in federal parliament (Brown 2004, p. 71). The party retains a strong federal structure, and State divisions are responsible for policy development and pre-selections, despite a recent emphasis on consolidation of the national party apparatus (Miragliotta 2006, p. 592).

Most of the party's electoral successes have been at the State level, although Bob Brown has been an effective figurehead for the party in the Senate since 1996. In the 2007 federal election, the party consolidated its vote, polling 7.55 per cent in the House of Representatives and 9 per cent in the Senate, and the Greens are now regarded as the 'third force' in Australian federal politics behind the two major party groupings. In addition to the five federal senators, there are fifteen Green members sitting in State and Territory parliaments. Only once in the party's history has a Green been elected in a single-member electorate: Michael Organ in the 2002 Cunningham by-election for the federal House of Representatives.

The Greens' membership has increased in recent years. There are at least 150 active Greens local groups, or branches, throughout Australia, and in mid-2007 there were 8700 members of the Greens. Within the party there is an emphasis on strong party structures underpinned by active participation of the membership through local groups (Turnbull & Vromen 2006, pp. 459–60). All MPs are expected to participate in their local groups, and most do. The party provides local groups with considerable autonomy in pre-selecting local candidates and conducting independent campaigns in their region. Overall the membership tends to be female, highly educated professionals aged around 50 who have experience in environmental groups and protest politics (Vromen 2005).

No large-scale research specifically on voters for the Democrats and the Greens has been undertaken. However, research based on AES studies showed that Democrat voters were typified by a low degree of party identification, high education levels and no religious identification; women were more likely to vote for the Democrats, and the party tended to appeal to voters in the 30–50 age group (Bean 1997, p. 78). Less research exists on voters for the Greens; however, it has been assumed that their vote has grown from those no longer choosing to vote Democrat, and especially from progressive voters disillusioned with the ALP (Rhiannon 2003). The two parties are also clearly different in their ideology: while the more pragmatic Democrats 'occupied that small part of the political spectrum between Labor and the Coalition', the Greens hold a much stronger ideological position 'unambiguously to the left of Labor' (Green 2003).

The emergence of smaller parties that appeal only to small, specific parts of the electorate is emblematic of the shift away from major party politics. However, all Australian political parties have needed to find ways to maintain their links with the community and business sectors, including unions, business associations and new social movement organisations, for example, environment, feminist and indigenous groups. The ALP has many Australian trade unions formally affiliated with it, and they are still a major source of funds for the party. Union affiliates are currently entitled to 50 per cent of the voting places at the ALP's national conference, the party's supreme policy-making forum. However, there has been a longstanding argument within the ALP as to whether this level of influence is appropriate, given that only around 20 per cent of the workforce actually belongs to a union (Aarons 2008).

The Liberal and National parties rely on business groups and wealthy donors to generate financial and public support. Increasingly, the ALP also utilises the financial and public support of business. Yet support from the business and community sectors is not only of a financial nature, it can also be about perceptions of political alliances that are able to influence voting patterns. For example, the Greens do not have official affiliations with environmental organisations, but they clearly portray themselves as a participant in movements for social change, especially the environment movement, and rely on these groups for electoral support.

Policy positions

Having compared the different values parties publicly claim to uphold, it is also imperative to scrutinise the policy positions that parties take during political debates to gain an understanding of the differences between the parties, how they are pitching themselves to a changing electorate and changing party needs; that is, it is important to examine the values, ideas and beliefs espoused by parties and their leaders to understand the policy positions adopted during election campaigns. These analyses guide us to a focus on discourse in terms of what is said, and by whom, and develop a subsequent understanding of how powerful relationships are revealed in political speeches and debates. We discuss the concept of political discourse and its influence on policy development further in Chapter 12, 'Policy analysis'.

Carol Johnson argues that ideological considerations have become an important dimension of political analysis due to the influence of neo-liberal economic thought on recent ALP and Coalition federal governments (2002, p. 2). For example, throughout the speeches of former Prime Minister John Howard it can be seen that the emphasis is on how the government should facilitate choice for the electorate in diverse policy areas such as education, health, employment or in work and family arrangements (Johnson 2002, p. 6). In discussions of family policy generally, and maternity leave in particular, John Howard utilised ideas of individual choice (Johnson 2000, p. 77); that is, emphasis was placed on the choice of families to choose actions that suit them, and the argument was made that it is inappropriate for governments to intervene in how parents make caring arrangements. This can be seen in the following radio interview transcript:

> There's a range of families and there's a range of financial and particularly female aspirations in this area and we should have policies that fit the range, not say, 'you will accept paid maternity leave' or 'you will accept something else because that is our view as to how you should organise your life'. We don't do that. We exist as a government to facilitate and support choice, not tell people how to mould the nature of their family life. (Howard 2002)

Johnson suggests that the 'emphasis on "choice" acts as a device which enables the government to deny the operation of disadvantage or power relations' (2000, p. 77); that is, all families are simply able to make choices as to what suits them, and these choices are not constrained by their economic or social situation.

The ALP took a different view as to the future of family policy, and instead argued for increased government intervention into family policy linked to a broader critique of the Liberal Party's conception of neo-liberalism in Australia. Kevin Rudd has argued:

> Neo-liberalism's core philosophical dilemma is that it has no answer to the relentless march of market fundamentalism into the sanctum of the family itself... the impact of the quality and quantity of time that families have together as a direct consequence of Howard's industrial relations revolution is now a matter of great personal and therefore political importance. (Cited in Johnson 2007, p. 178)

The party formulated policy on the basis of these values, and during the 2007 federal election the ALP pledged to provide 260 new childcare centres, secure twelve months of unpaid leave to both parents after the birth of a baby and create an Office of Work and Family 'to ensure that the formulation of policies to get the balance right between work and family life takes place at the highest level and is central to all Rudd Labor Government policy decisions' (ALP 2007c, p. 3). In 2008 the Rudd government asked the Productivity Commission to conduct a report to assess the social and economic costs and benefits of paid maternity, paternity and parental leave (Swan 2008).

There are also clear policy differences between the Rudd Labor government and its predecessor in the areas of industrial relations (repealing WorkChoices), climate change (ratifying the Kyoto Protocol) and indigenous affairs (apologising to the Stolen Generations), giving effect to Labor's ideological commitments as to the position of the individual in society:

> Social democrats believe in the market but we don't believe in market fundamentalism . . . We believe passionately in public goods such as education and health. We accept the reality of market failure, as we have seen most recently and most spectacularly with the failure to respond to global climate change. We also believe in the instrinsic dignity of human beings. We don't therefore believe that human beings should be treated as any other economic commodity to be traded on the market . . . Above all, social democrats believe in a strong economy, but one where we still have a fair go for all, not just for some. (Kevin Rudd, quoted in Johnson 2007, pp. 176–7)

The policy divergence seen in the 2007 federal election casts some doubt over the cartel model's assertion that political parties are increasingly converging in their ideological and policy positions with the aim of winning and retaining government. Nonetheless, despite the rhetoric of party leaders, historically both major party groupings in Australian politics have moved to accept many neoliberal economic ideas. While denouncing Howard's vision of the state/market relationship, Rudd has adopted a similar position to the previous Liberal government in supporting free trade, increasing individuals' economic capacities through education as a means of achieving equity, and arguing the need for fiscal conservatism and balancing the budget (Johnson 2007, p. 177).

Further, analysts have argued that the prioritisation of economic policy and neo-liberal economic ideas actually commenced in Australia during the ALP's term in federal government (1983–96), when it started to retreat from core party policies of public ownership and government regulation of the finance and banking sectors (see Smith 1998, p. 121; Woodward 2002, pp. 426–32). Another interesting development that may signal policy convergence and co-operation for the sake of governance rather than representation and ideological purity was the decision by the federal Liberal–National Opposition in February 2008 not to block the Rudd government's repeal of the WorkChoices legislation, which had been introduced by the Howard government in 2005.

Party organisation

As the cartel model predicts, the organisation of Australian parties has clearly changed over the last century, and one particular element that has altered substantially is the party on the ground, its relationship to the party in central office and the clear dominance within the major parties of the party in public office. Several factors have contributed to the declining role and level of importance of the party on the ground. They are:

- decreases in party membership
- centralisation of party structures, particularly around party leaders
- the interventionist processes used to select party candidates in elections.

Party membership in most parties is in decline. On the basis of AES data, it is estimated that around 2 per cent of eligible Australians are currently members of a political party, a figure that has more than halved since the late 1960s (McAllister 2002, pp. 389–91). However, the exact numbers within parties are difficult to obtain as most parties are not obligated to reveal their membership numbers nor do they like to disclose them. Of all the parties examined in this chapter, only the Liberal Party publicly discloses its membership size on its website. Otherwise, information has been accessed unofficially or informed estimates have been made. The ALP is now thought to have about 40,000 members, which has declined from a peak of 370,000 in 1939 (Ray 2006). The Liberals' claimed membership of 80,000 also represents a significant decline from its high in the early 1950s of 220,000 members (Jaensch 2006, p. 28).

The Australian Greens is the only party that lays claim to membership growth in recent years. The party's membership is now estimated to stand at approximately 8700. It could be argued that the growth in the Greens' membership is partly attributable to the party's renewed electoral appeal in the recent State and federal elections, replacing the Democrats as the third force in Australian party politics, and partly to organisational practices and the opportunities for localised and grassroots group involvement in decision-making. The Greens' participatory processes stand in contrast to those of other minor parties that have achieved representation in the Australian Senate in recent years, such as the Australian Democrats and One Nation, which were unable to sustain members (see the snapshot at the beginning of this chapter).

It ought to be noted that decline in party membership is not characteristic only of Australia as many other democratic nations are also seeing their party organisations change as they face difficulty in attracting new members. Mair and van Biezen (2001) found that within thirteen long-established European democracies, party membership fell markedly between the beginning of the 1980s and the end of the 1990s, from an average of 9.8 per cent of the electorate to 5.7 per cent. The decline can be traced back even further, from an average of 14 per cent at the beginning of the 1960s (Mair 2005). At face value, these trends raise questions over the continuing democratic legitimacy of parties when we consider the declining levels of popular engagement.

Mair and van Biezen attribute this decline in party membership to the general population's increasing disenchantment with political institutions and traditional forms of participation (2001, p. 14), and we will place this discussion in an Australian context in Chapter 8. Katz and Mair (2002) see decreasing membership in a complex, interdependent relationship with the increasing centralisation of party organisation; power now is primarily located in the party in public office. Present-day parties need to be understood not in terms of the interplay between members and parliamentarians but rather in terms of the role of leaders because, in modern political parties, 'the leaders become the party; the party becomes the leaders' (Katz & Mair 2002, p. 126).

Earlier in this chapter we pointed out that the Liberal Party's organisational framework clearly prioritises the policy-making powers of the leader of the party (see Brett 2003, p. 30). In other parties it is less clear how the party operates in practice, as this may not necessarily reflect the formal structure outlined in publicly accessible party documents such as party rules and constitutions. For example, at face value the ALP's structure seems to be participatory as it is based on active local branches and party conferences as deliberative forums. However, it tends to be acknowledged by analysts of the ALP that 'in practice, the elected Members of Parliament enjoy considerable autonomy in the interpretation and even the determination of policies, especially while in government' (Warhurst & Parkin 2000, p. 29).

An internal review undertaken by former party leaders Bob Hawke and Neville Wran found that the membership generally felt detached from decision-making in the party and blamed this on the factions, party officials and party representatives (2002, p. 6). Their report also indicated disquiet about preselection processes within the party. Recommendations from this report to enhance membership involvement included increasing member representation at the national conference; exploring alternative branch structures, either based on policy issues or located where people work; consolidating existing branches; and establishing online branches. However, former Labor Party leader Mark Latham is far more sceptical of the possibility of organisational reform:

> Given that most people have no desire to attend party meetings and devote their time to organised politics, it is difficult to see how these changes could succeed... The factional system of command and control has gutted the effectiveness of grassroots participation in the Party. Most local branches are rorted and empty. Labor conferences and policy committees are tightly stage-managed, devoid of creativity and genuine debate. Party membership and activism are now in inexorable decline. (Latham 2005, pp. 7–8, 11)

Party preselection

Preselection is the name for the process used to select party candidates to stand in elections. It is complex and has become increasingly contentious. In the ALP, the Liberal Party and the Greens, preselection is underpinned by the general principle that the party membership has a right to choose their local candidate, although the exact practice varies between State branches (ALP Constitution, section 15; Liberal Party Constitution, section 103; Green Party Constitution, section 40.1).

Preselection constitutes a fundamental element of intra-party democracy by allowing members to have their say and shape the future directions of their party, as well as acting as a mechanism for holding the party's MPs to account or, in Australian Greens' Senator Christine Milne's words, the best 'controlling mechanism' by which members can influence the decisions of the party in public office. If members do not like the actions of a particular MP, they may choose simply not to endorse their candidature at the next election.

> It's up to that body [the federal executive] to determine if in the future you'll be preselected—whether that breach, or what they would see as a difference of opinion—not a breach—would warrant you being preselected or not. So it's not as if Green Members of Parliament can willy-nilly go off on a whim . . . (Australian Greens Senator Christine Milne 2007)

> If you're in the situation in the Parliament and a piece of legislation is presented or a package of reforms is presented, you simply wouldn't have the time or the resources to involve party members in making those sorts of decisions. That's why we have a preselection process. The people that elect you to be the Labor candidate for a particular area have to have some faith that you are able to make decisions on their behalf in areas like that. (ALP minister Tanya Plibersek, 2007)

However, many preselection processes have been subject to significant criticism, the most common being accusations of 'branch stacking'. To 'stack' a branch, a candidate will typically enrol (and pay for) the membership of multiple branch members, who then agree to vote for the candidate in the party's preselection process. The ABC TV program *Four Corners* raised allegations of branch stacking in the New South Wales Division of the Liberal Party in 2006, where it was claimed that people were offered cash to attend party meetings where their vote was needed (ABC 2006a). Similar concerns were raised in the Victorian Division of the Labor Party in 2005, when the Socialist Left faction of the party accused the Right of branch stacking before preselections for the 2007 federal election. Unless it involves the use of false identities, enrolments or electoral fraud, branch stacking is not illegal and is a matter for the internal rules of a party to regulate and control (see Gauja 2006).

Preselection also raises questions of gender equity and the prospective intervention of the party in central office in selection processes where the membership cannot achieve progress and change on its own. In 2002 the federal conference of the ALP adopted an affirmative action principle to govern the conduct of all party preselections, to be phased in by all State branches of the party by 2012. The intention of this rule is to produce an outcome whereby not less than 40 per cent of seats held by Labor will be filled by women and not less than 40 per cent by men (ALP 2007d, pp. 295–6). Affirmative action targets in party preselections have also been adopted by the Greens, but rejected by the Liberal Party (Ward & Stewart 2006, p. 148).

An example of using the principle to bring in an experienced, well-known female political candidate was the preselection of former Australian Council of Trade Unions President Jennie George to the federal seat of Throsby in 2001. This does not mean that all impositions of female candidates are beneficial to the ALP. In the 2002 Cunningham by-election the ALP central office intervened to preselect Sharon Bird. Bird was perceived not to be a local candidate, was not well linked in with the branches, and did not receive broad support from the local unions either. The ALP subsequently lost the seat, giving the Australian Greens their first seat ever in the House of Representatives.

The internal organisation of most Australian political parties accommodates factional subgroupings of some sort, but the ALP is the only party that has formalised factions. For example, the Liberal Party is judged to contain both economic and social liberals, or the 'drys' and the 'wets' respectively (Brett 2002, p. 180), and the Australian Greens often divide along State lines (Miragliotta 2006, p. 592). The ALP has Left, Right and Centre factions, and subgroups within these factions. The existence of these factions is usually seen negatively, as leading to deal-making instead of open debate, an emphasis on division rather than unity, and a tendency towards branch stacking in place of active participation by members. However, counterarguments suggest that open competition could be healthy for the party and that the involvement of opposing factions in policy debate 'may, in sharpening the focus of discussion, contribute to a more ideologically aware party membership' (Warhurst & Parkin 2000, pp. 37–8).

The decline of parties?

Political parties are generally regarded by political scientists as an indispensable element of modern democracy and a primary means of linking citizens with the state (Dalton & Wattenberg 2000, p. 275; Lawson 1988, p. 14). In 1994, Dean Jaensch argued:

> For Australia, parties and the party system are not just among the most important, they remain *the* critical components in the polity. There can be no argument about the ubiquity, pervasiveness and centrality of party in Australia. The forms, processes and content of politics—executive, parliament, pressure groups, bureaucracy, issues and policy making—are imbued with the influence of party, party rhetoric, party policy and party doctrine. Government is party government. Elections are essentially party contests . . . Politics in Australia, almost entirely, is party politics. (Jaensch 1994, pp. 1–2)

This sentiment is generally reiterated in public opinion. An international comparative analysis of survey data from thirteen democracies revealed that three-quarters of respondents thought that political parties were necessary for democracy (Dalton & Weldon 2005, p. 933).

However, as we have seen throughout this chapter, political parties are not what they used to be. Membership of parties is dropping as these organisations become increasingly centralised and focused on maintaining government rather than representing ideological cleavages and partisan interests. Technological developments, such as the electronic media, have restructured political campaigns as direct appeals from political leaders to citizens, privileging the personalities of party leaders over the presentation of ideology and policy, and reducing the utility of the mass membership as a vehicle for electoral mobilisation (Gunther & Diamond 2003, p. 168). Political campaigning is now undertaken by teams of professionals (Panebianco 1988), their activities increasingly directed by the party in public office and resourced by the state and public funds (Katz & Mair 1995; van Biezen 2003). As Bale and Roberts (2002) argue, society's acceptance of political parties as actors in the political process seems to be deteriorating to that of a 'necessary evil'.

What does this mean for the future of parties? It is unlikely that political parties will disappear as there has been no perceived decline in political parties in public office or parties in central office. However, as parties lose their appeal as membership organisations, international evidence suggests that the nature of political participation may be shifting (Mair 2005). Lifestyle changes over the last century as well as the availability of alternative forms of political participation mean that citizens are less willing to participate in party politics (see Scarrow 2000, p. 83). We will look at the different ways in which individuals participate in politics further in Chapter 8, 'Individual engagement'.

Independents in Australian politics

The majority of election candidates and MPs in Australian parliaments will be affiliated with a particular political party. The benefits of standing as a party candidate include access to organisational and campaign resources and the instant public recognition that comes with running under an established political 'brand'. Nonetheless, election candidates may also choose to declare themselves free of any party affiliation, such candidates being known as 'independents'.

Do independents present a significant challenge to the dominance of parties in Australian politics? There are currently twenty independent MPs serving in Australian lower houses, a figure that constitutes only 3.3 per cent of available seats. In 2007 two independents were relected to the federal House of Representatives: Bob Katter (Kennedy, Qld) and Tony Windsor (New England, NSW). The most successful of the independents elected in the postwar period was Peter Andren, who was elected in 1996 and re-elected in 1998, 2001 and 2004 with increasing majorities. Sadly, Andren died in 2007, and his seat of Calare in rural New South Wales returned to the National Party.

Although high-profile South Australian independent Nick Xenophon was elected to the Senate in 2007, independents have been relatively less successful in gaining representation in the federal upper house (see Costar & Curtin 2004, pp. 48–52). The most influential independent in recent decades was Tasmanian Senator Brian Harradine, who was elected to the Senate in the 1975 double dissolution election after having been expelled from the ALP. Harradine retained his seat until he decided not to contest the federal election in 2004. Along with Mal Colston (who resigned from the Labor Party in 1996), the two independents altered the balance of representation in the Senate and gained an unprecedented amount of political leverage over the Liberal government, obtaining concessions and benefits for their respective States in return for supporting the government on key issues. For example, Costar and Curtin (2004, p. 52) report that in return for supporting the partial sale of Telstra in 1996, Harradine secured $150 million in expenditure for environmental programs in Tasmania.

In order to achieve representation, independents require strong local support and commonly hold a high profile in their electorates or have a history of involvement in local government and community activities. Other independents, like Harradine, have had previous association with a political party. Independents share organisational characteristics with political parties in that they rely on 'groups of supporters that work to attempt to get them elected and, if successful, help independent parliamentarians carry out their representative functions' (Smith 2006, pp. 15, 188–91).

Costar and Curtin (2007, p. 3) argue that independent MPs have been most successful in the regional and rural electorates neglected by the National Party in recent decades. More than 50 per cent of the independents who have been elected since 1990 hold seats in rural or regional areas, and 80 per cent of currently serving independents do so. As a part of the Coalition government, the National Party has presided over the implementation of many neo-liberal policies that would have been contrary to the National Party's values in times past, and were seen in many country areas as producing economic uncertainty and having a detrimental effect on livelihood (Costar & Curtin 2007, p. 7).

Independents represent an attractive prospect in electorates where voters feel their MP has put the party's interests before those of the constituency. As Peter Andren argued, independents are free from the dictates of party discipline to focus exclusively on the needs of their constituents: 'an independent has not a baton in his haversack to be anything else but a good representative of that electorate' (quoted in Costar & Curtin 2004, p. 25). This conception of the role of an independent invokes the delegate model of representation (see Chapter 2). However, independent MPs can also act as trustees in the Burkean sense: pursuing policies for the good of the nation rather than the specific interests of their electorate. For example, Andren used his position in the parliament to champion the rights of asylum seekers and to advocate a republic—despite these issues being in conflict with the majority opinion of his electorate. While these representative roles were in conflict, Andren sought resolution by communicating the reasons for his position to his electorate in a deliberative manner, and appealed to them 'to view these issues as being of significant importance to Australia as a nation' (Costar & Curtin 2007, p. 9).

Like minor parties, independent politicians have played an important role in holding the major parties, particularly the government, to account. They have participated in minority governments and at various times negotiated charters designed to secure good governance in most Australian States and Territories. Although the effectiveness of many of these charters has been questioned (see Costar & Curtin 2007, pp. 10–16), the *Memorandum of Understanding* negotiated by three New South Wales independents and the Coalition in 1991 was able to achieve some reforms, including entrenching judicial independence and fixed-date elections in New South Wales (Smith 2006, pp. 155–9).

However, the pivotal positions that independent MPs have occupied in Australian parliaments (particularly when holding the balance of power) have, in turn, led to criticisms of their lack of accountability. Maddox (1992, p. 24) has suggested that agreements struck by independent MPs and governing parties are potentially threatening to democracy, as 'a small group of independents striking agreements in conclave and certainly beyond the public gaze, are now in a position to propose, and demand action upon policies which have never been presented in a coherent way to the . . . electorate'. Similarly, the *Sydney Morning Herald* argued that independents 'seek to change the behaviour of the government, not to govern. But because they want none of the responsibilities of government, they are usually a menace' (quoted in Smith 2006, p. 10). However, whether the role of independents in Australian politics is viewed positively or negatively depends upon the normative view of democracy that the analyst holds. Those advocating a majoritarian conception of democracy may caution independent MPs in positions of power from using their influence against the will of the majority of electors, whereas those who favour a consensus approach will welcome the deliberations and negotiated outcomes that independent MPs can potentially bring to parliamentary democracy in Australia.

Summary

- The cartel party model has resonance in the Australian context because power and decision-making capacities are increasingly centred on the party in public office. This is the case for all Australian political parties, with the exception of one of the youngest parties, the Australian Greens.

- Parties no longer mobilise a mass support base because the nature of society itself has changed, and major Australian parties have needed to broaden their appeal beyond traditional class bases. This has also allowed the emergence of new small parties and independents, not based on traditional social groupings.
- Independents have always occupied a small but crucial space in Australian politics. Many have held the balance of power in their respective chambers and have been able to secure benefits and concessions from the government in return for legislative support.

Further reading

Brett, Judith 2003, *Australian Liberals and the Moral Middle Class,* Cambridge University Press, Melbourne.

Costar, Brian and Curtin, Jennifer 2004, *Rebels with a Cause: Independents in Australian Politics,* UNSW Press, Sydney.

Leach, Michael, Stokes, Geoffrey and Ward, Ian (eds) 2000, *The Rise and Fall of One Nation,* University of Queensland Press, Brisbane.

Marsh, Ian (ed.) 2006, *Political Parties in Transition?*, Federation Press, Sydney.

Warhurst, John (ed.) 1997, *Keeping the Bastards Honest: The Australian Democrats' First Twenty Years,* Allen & Unwin, Sydney.

Warhurst, John and Parkin, Andrew (eds) 2000, *The Machine: Labor Confronts the Future,* Allen & Unwin, Sydney.

Useful websites

- The Australian Labor Party at <www.alp.org.au>. This is the website for the federal ALP, and it has links to the State divisions and, usefully, also includes most of the ALP media releases.
- The Liberal Party at <www.liberal.org.au>. This is the website for the federal Liberal Party. It includes contact details for all the federal Liberal Party members of parliament and also has a comprehensive media section that includes transcripts.
- The National Party at <www.nationals.org.au>. This website is for federal division of the National Party. It has links to the State divisions and includes policy documents.

- The Australian Democrats at <www.democrats.org.au>. The Australian Democrats' site has information on all the Democrats' policies, history and achievements.
- The Australian Greens at <www.greens.org.au>. The national Australian Greens site has links to the State divisions and includes the party's newsletter and policy documents.
- Family First at <www.familyfirst.org.au>. Family First's site contains a summary of the aims and objectives of the party, its policies, a database of media releases and links to State branches.

CHAPTER 7
NEWS AND MEDIA

The media, and their representation of issues and events, are ubiquitous in our understanding of Australian politics. The media provide us with information, but their crucial role is in the powerful *way* they shape and produce that information. Politicians shape the media through sophisticated public relations processes, at the same time as journalists choose what to present as newsworthy. Hence we need to understand the media's task, of communicating the Australian political landscape to the general public, as a complex process.

This chapter on the media is the third chapter discussing representational issues in Australian politics. The previous chapters on elections and political parties canvassed the institutional forms that facilitate representative politics. This chapter develops this perspective by labelling the media simultaneously as the window through which Australian politics is represented to the majority of the people, who utilise it for political knowledge, and as powerful political actors in the actual construction and realisation of representative and participatory politics (see Street 2001, pp. 231–49). The chapter will look at what media sources the general public use for information on news, politics and current affairs, followed by an analytical discussion of the relationship between the media and their audience. The chapter will then look closely at the construction of news through agenda-setting and discursive practices. In the last section of the chapter, contemporary players in the media will be analysed, including the Internet and talkback radio, which are both increasingly used by Australian politicians to deliver their messages.

The topics covered in this chapter include:

- how politics is represented in the main media of television and newspapers
- the relationship between the media and their audience, the importance of agenda-setting, media ownership and everyday media production
- the relationship between politicians and governments, and the media
- media construction of political discourse
- interactive forms of media: radio talkback, alternatives to the mainstream, and the Internet.

SNAPSHOT YouTube, earwax and blogs biting back: the Internet and election 2007

> The election may not have been decided in cyberspace, but it certainly changed the shape of the campaign. (Hills 2007)

During the 2007 federal election campaign the Internet finally took centre stage as a media platform for both politicians and citizens. In the United States the 2004 election was seen as the historic moment for the use of the Internet by political contenders and, while Australians have turned to the Internet for information for several years, it was not until recently that the interactive and political opportunities presented by the Internet have been fully explored.

Parties' adoption of well-funded websites and launching policy over the Internet through short video announcements led to the 2007 federal election also being dubbed the 'first YouTube election'. Leaders of both major parties used new media social networking sites to appeal to their potential voters, in essence trying to cut out the filters of journalists and traditional media in their bid to reach voters. Even the older generation Prime Minister, John Howard, was uploading his policy-related video messages on YouTube and MySpace. All parties made policy announcements via YouTube, often launching them early in the morning to set the day's campaign agenda. For minor parties the Internet became incredibly important because it provided much more affordable advertising space than television or major metropolitan newspapers. The Greens and the Democrats also did better than the main parties in using the interactive capabilities (see Rodrigues 2008).

What this tells us is that while the parties used the Internet during this election campaign, it was essentially relying on the more traditional media-oriented broadcast function of one-way communication. Most sites had capacity for voters to post messages, but there was very little two-way dialogue between politicians and citizens; that is, political parties prioritised information distribution and control over interactivity.

As a result it was not the party political advertisements being distributed through YouTube or the MySpace pages being set up for leaders that were the most popular and often visited Internet sites. For example, while Labor's most popular video ad received 100,000 hits on YouTube, it was the Kevin Rudd earwax event that had five times as many (Hartcher 2007). Therefore, this election really told us about citizen journalism and the power of user-generated content over the Internet. For example, one of the most popular YouTube clips of the election campaign was footage of ALP leader Kevin Rudd picking and eating his earwax. It wasn't recent footage as it was from a parliamentary Question Time about six years before, but it was a good example of how the Internet was used by Internet users to ridicule politicians while also promoting them.

Other examples were the more direct parodies of election advertising that appeared on YouTube. For example, most major party policy announcements were quickly followed by 'mash-ups' that attracted many more views than the routinised speaker facing the camera, making dry and detailed policy announcements. One further parody depicted Kevin Rudd as a Chairman Mao figure in a video styled on Chinese propaganda films and made its creator, Hugh Atkin, 23, a law student at the University of Sydney, a minor celebrity. Atkin was quoted as saying that 'he is not anti-Liberal, "but I'll be supporting Labor. I'd like to see Labor win the election, but I'd like to make fun of them in the process"' (Coultan 2007).

The Internet also turned out to be a courtroom, with Family First candidates Andrew Quah and Renee Sciberras instantly disendorsed after online pictures showed Quah clutching his genitals and Sciberras pole-dancing (Hartcher 2007).

This interest in people providing their own content and commentary on the Internet is driven by the recent increase in interactive social networking sites. About two million Australians are signed up to Facebook and three million to MySpace. More than 42 per cent of Australian children now have their own Facebook and MySpace accounts, according to the Australian Communications and Media Authority (see Walliker 2007).

The other facet of the Internet during the campaign was the sophistication and influence of many political blogs. These sites closely followed the campaign and often had broad-based and detailed opinion poll analysis not obtainable anywhere else. Usha Rodrigues points out that while some of the blogs were just a reflection of what was covered in the traditional media and party politics, there were others, including such sites as Possums Pollytics, Larvatus Prodeo, the PollBludger and Crikey.com, and sites run by journalists such as News.com.au's Blogocracy, the *Australian*'s Meganomics Blog and the ABC's Poll Vault, and Youdecide2007, which all closely analysed polls and electoral behaviour (Rodrigues 2008). The rivalry between traditional media and the new media was demonstrated by the contrasting positions taken by the *Australian* and the psephologist bloggers. The 'national newspaper kept expecting a "bounce" back by the ruling party, and a correction in people's voting intentions, whereas the psephologists demonstrated a long term decline in the Howard government's popularity' (Rodrigues 2008).

This snapshot raises questions about the contrast between traditional and new media, such as the Internet. Do new media change the way we see and understand contemporary politics? Do they also challenge the dominance of traditional media, such as television news and newspapers? Further, can user-generated content really have a broad political influence and move beyond the small number of active producers who blog or create YouTube posts?

Politics in the media: television and newspapers

> News on television has many of the qualities of entertainment. Political news is much less the reporting and analysing of issues; it is drama, pathos, tragedy and combat. (Windschuttle 1984, pp. 311–12)

It has been argued that the 'formula' for Australian news stories is celebrities, death and disaster, and deviance. It is inevitable that the reporting of political news will rarely enter into mundane territory; instead it will concentrate on issues that are exciting, rather than on the administrative details (Smith 1997b, pp. 345, 348). Leaders like prime ministers and premiers are treated as celebrities rather than as elected politicians; elections are constructed as battlegrounds with the potential for bloodletting and disastrous defeat; and political protest gets media coverage more for what it looks like than what it stands for.

It is important for us to think through this dilemma. For most people the media will remain their primary source of information, but the media are selective about the way they portray politics. The criteria for 'good news' may not be the same criteria that academic writers on politics apply to what Australians ought to know about their political system. In many respects political scientists and the media work in tandem to represent and analyse politics, but one has a much larger audience for its work than the other! This is why the media deserve analysis as ever-present and important players in representative politics in Australia.

In summary, media in liberal democracies need to serve three main functions:

1 to be a 'watchdog' on government and other powerful actors, and provide scrutiny of day-to-day political events
2 provide accurate and well-researched information on news to the public with which they can form opinions
3 contribute to the creation of a deliberative public sphere where citizens exchange views and engage in rational debate, to reach an ideal of the 'good society' (Errington & Miragliotta 2007, pp. 8–9).

Whether and how the media serve these functions is increasingly questioned. To begin with, we will first examine media consumption by the Australian public, and recognise that the media the newsmakers respect the most are rarely reflective of the content that audiences utilise the most. The Australian Broadcasting Authority (ABA), the predecessor to Australian Communications and Media Authority (ACMA), the regulator of broadcasting media in Australia, commissioned an extensive research report on news and current affairs media (ABA 2001). The report was based on twenty in-depth interviews and 100 interview questionnaires with news producers and journalists, as well as a survey of the audience of news and current affairs. This study recognised that in any well-rounded consideration of politics and the media we need to understand both angles: production and audience.

Table 7.1 lists the most *important* and *influential* news and current affairs types and services according to the producers and journalists. The news producers themselves clearly believe that newspapers and radio are the most important sources of information for news and politics, not television.

A majority (62 per cent) of Australians older than eighteen spend an hour or more every day consuming news and current affairs (ABA 2001, p. 319). Table 7.2 shows that when the general public thinks about news and current affairs coverage, both in terms of their own use and credibility, they tend to think of television as the medium of delivery. The journalists and news producers, like the general audience, believe that the most credible television news program is ABC News (ABA 2001, p. 48); but it is not the news that the general public watch. Channel Nine News continues to have a large share of the news and current affairs audience, but throughout most of 2007 it was surpassed by Channel Seven News, and then closely followed by *Sixty Minutes* and *Today Tonight* (see Oztam 2007a and 2007b).

TABLE 7.1 Media important to media makers

Type of medium	Services
Newspapers	All newspapers; but particularly the *Australian* and the *Daily Telegraph* in Sydney
ABC Radio	*AM*
Wire services	AAP
Talkback radio	Mainly 2UE in Sydney

Source: adapted from Australia Broadcasting Authority 2001, p. 15.

TABLE 7.2 Media important to media consumers

Item	First	Second	Third
Most used sources	National Nine News	ABC Radio News	ABC News
Most credible news program	ABC News	*A Current Affair*	*7.30 Report*

Source: adapted from Australia Broadcasting Authority 2001.

It is important to consider this nexus in use and influence between the main news deliverers of newspapers and television. While newspapers are recognised for providing quality journalism about politics, few people read them. It is the more convenient television news that most people consume for their political information. John Henningham (1999) charted Australian society's gradual shift from predominant usage of newspapers to television news by demonstrating the decline in daily newspaper circulation. In 1956, the year television was introduced, newspapers were bought daily by 576 per 1000 people (Henningham 1999, pp. 280–1). This fell to 322 by 1980, 305 in 1990 and by 2000 the number was 162—only 16.2 per cent of people buy a newspaper every day (Tiffen & Gittins 2004, p. 182). Tiffen and Gittins also show that this contemporary proportion of Australians reading newspapers is significantly less than the average (of 288 per 1000 people) when compared to eighteen other democratic countries (2004, p. 182). Tiffen (2006a, p. 98) attributes the Australian newspaper readership decline to the contraction in the number of newspapers available to read and the resulting concentrated media ownership in Australia (discussed further below).

Audit Bureau of Circulation figures for 2006, published in the *Australian* (Bodey 2007), indicate that most daily newspaper sales have continued to decline in absolute numbers. There are also stark differences in circulation numbers between different newspapers. In addition to the low-selling national daily newspapers, the *Australian* (134,600) and *Financial Review* (86,300), only two cities in Australia have access to two daily metropolitan newspapers: Sydney and Melbourne. For example, in Melbourne the *Age* has 202,000 daily readers. Compare this with the tabloid *Herald Sun*, which has an average daily readership of 535,000 readers. Overall the highest circulating newspaper in Australia is Sydney's *Sunday Telegraph* (684,100).

In light of falling circulation some argue that newspapers are in a 'transformational phase' as they adapt and learn both how to compete with the Internet and how to develop a presence on it (Australian Press Council 2006). The figures above also suggest that, when trying to understand the relationship between news media and their audience, we need to take into consideration the type of information people are choosing to purchase; that is, we ought to differentiate more specifically between different media sources as newspapers—indeed most media—differ in terms of their content and emphasis. Different media supplying news and current affairs also increasingly target different demographic sections of the population.

For most Australians (54 per cent) television is their main source of information on Australian news and current affairs, followed by newspapers (20 per cent), radio (16 per cent) and the Internet (10 per cent). There are some demographic differences: women are more likely than men to use television as their main source; and people younger than 50 are more likely than those older than 50 to use the Internet and much less likely to use newspapers as their main source (Roy Morgan 2007b). However, what we seem to know little about is how people integrate their news-gathering habits into their everyday lives. For example, do people tend to read newspapers at weekends when they have more free time, then during working or study days keep up to date with the radio in the shower, the TV news at night when they get home, and maybe the Internet during lunch breaks? When people's use of news sources is understood in this way, the decline in newspaper readership is not so dire; rather it is all about finding time and news itself fitting into people's lives.

Most liberal democracies maintain some form of commitment to publicly funded broadcasting, often both television and radio, to ensure that there are some sources of information that are not necessarily wholly dictated by commercial interest. There are two government-funded television networks: the Australian Broadcasting Corporation (ABC) and the Special Broadcasting Service (SBS). Since the introduction of television in the 1950s, the Australian government has been committed to maintaining at least one independent, non-commercial television network. SBS, originally funded wholly by government, now features a small amount of commercial advertising. Australia has three free-to-air commercial national television networks—Channels Nine, Seven and Ten—and a number of affiliated regional networks, mainly servicing regional and rural Australia.

Pay television, which was in 26 per cent of households in 2006 (ACMA 2007), is predominantly provided by Foxtel, which is owned by Telstra (50 per cent), News Corporation (25 per cent) and Publishing and Broadcasting Limited (25 per cent). Foxtel, as the most powerful player in the Australian pay TV landscape, controls the bulk of programming through ownership or distribution agreements. It also has the largest number of subscribers and the most extensive reach on its combined cable and satellite networks. Foxtel Digital was launched in March 2004, with new services including video-on-demand channels and some interactive services. The major news station available on Foxtel is Sky News. However, compared to the United States and the UK, subscription-only pay television has been less successful in Australia in attracting a broad-based audience (Australian Film Commission 2007).

The primary way of measuring everyday television and radio audiences is through the ratings system produced by market research organisations: AC Nielsen and OzTAM. The ratings research is conducted by the installation of meters in people's homes. These measure the amount of time television or radio are used and what people are watching or listening to. OzTAM's research is paid for by the commercial television stations. They use the research as a competitive measure but also to assess successful programming and to market themselves to potential advertisers (see Turnbull 2006, pp. 82–3). The research is rarely publicly available without paying fees, but you can access weekly figures on the top twenty shows on free-to-air television (see <www.oztam.com.au>). Perusal of this data shows that news and current affairs are rarely the most popular shows on television, which are more likely to be a major sports event, a light entertainment show such as *Kath & Kim*, a US-based drama series such as *CSI*, or the finale of a reality TV show such as *Dancing with the Stars* or *Australian Idol*.

Television and newspapers remain the big players in news and current affairs delivery in Australia, and it is worth examining the theoretical positions that have been developed to help us understand the delivery of information on politics through media sources.

Media power

Collectively, media undoubtedly constitute a powerful institution in Australian society. Commentators on the media discuss this application of power in two main ways: first through analysis of the relationship between the media and their audience, and second through an examination of the power of media owners and producers. This section will look at the first set of power relationships (see for example Smith 1997b, pp. 350–1; Windschuttle 1984; Errington & Miragliotta 2007, pp. 40–59):

- **Total media power:** in this approach people are viewed as uncritically taking on the views of the powerful and/or the status quo; that is, people's opinions are assessed as being determined by what they read, hear and watch in the news, and they are unlikely to look for opposing interpretations. This approach often emphasises the powerful role of wealthy media proprietors in society. A subcategory of this view examines the media as an active agent of socialisation in society that influences individuals by 'teaching' them how to conform to social norms and values.
- **Limited media power:** in this approach the power of the media over audiences lies in agenda-setting; that is, rather than news media changing attitudes over the short term, they are able to suggest to audiences what political events and issues are important and, in turn, respond to what the audience is interested in. Thus the newspaper may be successful in creating an agenda or suggesting what the topical issues are. Examples of topical issues in the media in recent years are crime, law and order, drugs and immigration. These are all controversial and debated issues, and are significantly different from the everyday issues that dominate Australian politics, such as employment, education and healthcare.

Many academic commentators advocate the limited media power approach when discussing the relationship between audience and the media (see Tiffen 2000). Ian Ward suggests that news does not *change* basic political attitudes but does *influence* some types of belief and attitudes. He argues that the news media may influence and shape individual opinion on what are believed to be significant problems in the nation or society (Ward 2002a, p. 404). Rod Tiffen also suggests that analysis of the media and audience relationship should focus on *how* the media set the agenda. For example, he argues that the ubiquitousness of the media has changed the process of contemporary election campaigns, in that the media have the power to set agendas and highlight important election issues (Tiffen 2000, p. 185). This argument is supported by the increasing amounts of money being spent on political advertising during election campaigns, highlighted in Chapters 5 and 6. The media's role as an agenda-setter is highlighted by understanding the privileged role they occupy as intermediaries between the politicians and the public. For example, the media have regular access to politicians, and politicians can influence news through their media releases and media advisers (Papadakis & Grant 2001, p. 295).

Media ownership and everyday media production

Most analyses of politics and the media in Australia describe the current situation by itemising media ownership. The Australian media are chiefly a business and profit-making enterprise, with the exception of the ABC, which does not accept advertising; that is, the media do not simply provide consumers with news and current affairs information; in fact these are far from being their most profitable functions. Therefore, in an analysis of any business formation it is important to reflect on who the owners and producers are to gain a more complete understanding of the power structures that that business represents. The 'Media ownership' box details the interests of the major players in Australian news media.

Media ownership

News Corporation (controlled by the Murdoch family): pay television (25 per cent of Foxtel); metropolitan newspapers (*Daily Telegraph*—Sydney; *Herald Sun*—Melbourne; the *Advertiser*—Adelaide; the *Courier Mail*—Brisbane; the *Mercury*—Hobart; the *Australian*—national); local newspapers (such as Cumberland Newspaper Group—twenty titles in Sydney suburbs); Leader Newspaper Group (thirty titles in Melbourne suburbs); Quest

Community Newspapers (seventeen titles in Brisbane suburbs); opinion polling (50 per cent of Newspoll); and Internet (MySpace).

John Fairfax Holdings: newspapers (*Sydney Morning Herald*, the *Canberra Times*, the *Age*—Melbourne, *Australian Financial Review*—national; more than 140 Rural Press titles in Australia, New Zealand and the US); and magazine publishing (*Business Review Weekly*).

Publishing and Broadcasting Limited (controlled by the Packer family): free-to-air television (Channel 9, in most capitals); pay television (25 per cent of Foxtel; SkyNews); magazine publishing (Australian Consolidated Press—*Australian Women's Weekly*, etc.) and Internet (ninemsn 50 per cent).

Southern Cross Broadcasting: radio (2UE—Sydney, 3AW—Melbourne, Magic 693—Melbourne, 4BC—Brisbane, 6PR—Perth, 96FM—Perth); and television (Channel 9 in Adelaide; Southern Cross Ten in regional areas of New South Wales, Victoria and Queensland).

Sources: Productivity Commission (2000), table 10.4, p. 347; Ketupa.Net media profiles.

This information sheds some light on the state of play in media ownership in Australia, principally in considering the three biggest players: Murdoch, Packer and Fairfax. Australian media are owned or controlled by relatively few players, and economic and regulatory barriers hinder an expansion of those who own media. For example, nearly all metropolitan daily newspapers Australia-wide are owned either by Murdoch's News Corporation or by Fairfax. The exception is the *West Australian*, which remains under the separate ownership of WA Newspapers Holdings.

Media ownership falls under the jurisdiction of the *Broadcasting Services Act 1992*, and the 'Media ownership' box shows that cross-media ownership is being regulated by government as no company owns news media across the main media of television, radio and newspapers. The Act contains provisions that shape cross-ownership and control of television, radio and newspapers, the foreign ownership and control of television licences and the audience reach of commercial, free-to-air television. Cross-media rules do not yet apply to some existing media, such as magazines and cinema, or to new media, such as the Internet or pay television (Gardiner-Garden & Chowns 2006). Current policy debate includes how many digital channels could be made newly available to media producers once all television is officially switched over from the analogue network to the digital network. There are also arguments suggesting that the current laws on cross-media ownership should be relaxed and that the sector could be treated the same as other areas of the economy subject to the Australian Competition and Consumer Commission (ACCC).

In consideration of ownership of the media, distribution of power is an important factor in understanding the production of news about Australian politics. There is a debate in the Australian literature on media and politics as to how much influence owners have and how much attention we should pay to this. Comparatively the concentration of Australia's media ownership stands out. For example 88 per cent of Australian newspaper ownership is shared by two major corporations, as compared to 58 per cent in the UK, 35 per cent in France and 16 per cent in the US (Tiffen 2006a, p. 100). Trevor Barr (2000) lists four types of statement made about the high level of concentration in Australia's media ownership:

- it is a potential abuse of power
- it leads to a loss of diversity of expression
- it constitutes a conflict of interest
- it contributes to a repressive journalistic culture.

All of these arguments assume that individuals within companies, especially owners, will use their power to control the agendas of news production; that is, media production in Australia is inherently about contestations of power, based in either economic or political domains. This viewpoint would argue that a concentration of media ownership impedes the media's democratic functions both to critically scrutinise political actors and to provide sufficiently accurate information to the audience. Another way of thinking about media ownership and power is seeing who the consumers of media news and current affairs consider to be the greatest source of influence on what they read, hear and see. Research found that the general public thinks media owners (67 per cent), followed by big business (53 per cent) then commercial sponsors (49 per cent) are very influential in the production of news and current affairs. The next two categories of group with influence are audiences (30 per cent) and politicians (26 per cent) (ABA 2001, p. 335).

On the other hand, it has been suggested that we should not assume media owners play an instrumental role in the day-to-day production of news stories.

Ward (2002a, p. 407) argues that it is a 'stereotypical caricature' to see the owner of a media outlet as all-powerful and dictating the political line of a daily newspaper or television or radio show. Others have suggested that it is not necessary for proprietors to be heavy-handed about editorial direction, as self-censorship by journalists who assume a particular line may achieve similar outcomes (Productivity Commission 2000). Either way, how can we best understand how news is written or produced? Several authors emphasise the bureaucratised nature of news reporting (for example, Smith 1997b; Ward 2002a, p. 408); that is, news production is a well-established everyday process. Very little differs in the everyday work of the news-maker as there is a set pattern to collection of sources and set timeframes for when news goes to print or to air. To understand the production of news we need to look at the institutionalised processes in gathering and presenting news. Tiffen (1989, p. 4) suggests that analyses of the media that focus on actual, everyday process will ensure we do not see news-making in basic terms either as the representation of an individual owner's ideology or as simply a 'mirror of reality'.

One of the determining factors in the production of news is time: time allotted to research a story, then produce it. Time affects the amount and thoroughness of research, the depth to which a topic is explored and the ability to access a range of views and commentary. The quote below, from a commercial radio producer on how news and current affairs stories are produced, demonstrates the importance of both time and the routine processes, of looking to other media for stories, in the creation of the news:

> I'd come in, say, at about three in the morning and have all the papers there—the first edition of the papers—and I'd start going through. The second edition of the papers come at 3.30, quarter to four. They're dropped off here and we just go through and see if there's any changes to front pages or any of the major stories and from that I'll sort of make a rundown list . . . The night before I've spoken with the host of the program after we've both watched the major TV bulletins and listened to some of the radio that's been around in the afternoon so we've sort of got a feel of what's around and what's happening from the night before and based on that we would have . . . organised some interviews because we have a number of interview slots that we have to fill.
>
> And so when I come in to work we'd already have one or two organised, based on what's been around the previous afternoon. We're going to take those stories a

> step further and talk to news makers and then we see what's in the papers, make up a list of all the major stories in the papers, then we'll have our editorial meeting. So based on what's been on the radio and the television and the newspapers up until that point, we decide how we're going to run the show.
>
> We have set times, our major interviews will be at 7.10, 7.40 and 8.10, so the big interviews of the day will go into those slots. But of course, being a radio show, if they're not pre-organised and if we had no idea about the story, if something has broken overnight, for example, some big issue ... that's when you have to think about ... calling up reporters, people on the scene, trying to get some background, experts and so on ... (ABA 2001, p. 140)

Traditionally at a major newspaper a news story is usually checked by at least six staff before it is published: the reporter, the chief of staff, the news editor, the chief subeditor, the subeditor and the proof subeditor (ABA 2001, p. 143). The multiple handling of each story allows corrections to be made, but it also increases the potential for the meaning of the story to change. Nevertheless, headlines, a powerful signal of meaning attached to the story, are often now viewed only by a single subeditor. It is assumed that the advent of twenty-four-hour news operations and placing stories almost instantaneously on the Internet has led to a bypassing of traditional mechanisms for checking news stories. The other issue raised by the process of news production is whether it is now the editor who plays a 'gate-keeping' role rather than the owner of the media. While the journalists interviewed see that it would be naive to not assume the editor, or the radio and television producer, does have the most power in shaping news production, they do not believe the editor unilaterally directs the tone or conclusions of news content (ABA 2001, pp. 149–50). Although it might not be individuals who construct the content of the media, certain stories become more 'media worthy' than other stories; and in the following sections on the relationship between political players and the news and on media discourse we will examine how political viewpoints are constructed. This can be through 'spin' or through words and pictures.

The relationship between political actors and news

Of recent interest to media analysts has been the nature of the relationship between political actors and the producers of political news. Who has more power: the Canberra Press Gallery journalist who can publish a scathing evaluation of the Prime Minister's performance on page 1, the backbenchers who act as sources for the story, or the Prime Minister's media advisers? The answers are not clear-cut. For example, Rod Tiffen suggests that the extent to which news is shaped by politicians themselves has been underestimated: 'the central product of news is the words and deeds of others. This gives those others—specifically, those who command newsworthy information—considerable scope to influence the news' (2002, p. 45).

Some argue that it is the media management and public relations staff of individual politicians who are allowing us access to some political stories rather than others, and are creating the 'spin' on political events. These are the political staffers who attempt to persuade journalists to write positive analyses of a politician's speeches and actions. These political staffers are known as 'spin doctors' and are rarely public figures themselves, but exist in the background, reanalysing an event to the advantage of their political employer (see Craig 2003, pp. 140–3). While media management, or 'spin', has been a fundamental feature of politics in the United States and the United Kingdom, it has increased significantly in importance in Australia. Others have suggested that 'impression management' has become of central importance to politicians and that spin doctors help to 'celebrity-ise' politicians to sell them to voters. This means that most public interactions between high-profile politicians and the public are often done with the televisual affect in mind. Often a spin doctor's focus is on constructing celebrity politicians to have 'ordinary' features that voters can identify with and find familiar (Louw 2005, pp. 172–6). For example, in Australia the previous Prime Minister, John Howard, was often portrayed as a 'cricket tragic' as part of his connection with 'ordinary Australians' (Ritter 2006) and has been extensively analysed for his use of spin in dealing with the media during his eleven-year period in office. Tiffen argues that we best understand Howard by focusing on his defensive spin strategies used to control media messages about his government (Tiffen 2006b). Following from this the increased focus on spin can be analysed to identify how politicians are keen to control the bad news stories even more than they try to promote good news and favourable coverage. For example, Savage and Tiffen (2007, p. 89) point out that politicians can control the spread of bad news by not offering televisual opportunities such as interviews, or they release contentious political information either close to media deadlines or in the middle of a period when another all-consuming story is dominating the airwaves, such as a disaster, war or external crisis. Thus the new information cannot be really looked at in-depth on nightly news.

Ian Ward (2003b) identifies that the spin that politicians and their staff create is an indicator of the institutionalisation of public relations in government in Australia today. For example, the number of ministerial media advisers in federal government has increased to the point where 10 per cent of all ministerial staff are now classified as media advisers; these are the people who write media releases, deal with journalists' inquiries, plan doorstops and generally keep tabs on media coverage of their politicians. Furthermore, government departments are also spending an increasing amount of money on their public affairs arms, such as the Department of Defence, which has 105 staff employed to work in public affairs (or public relations) at the cost of $11.6 million (Ward 2003b, pp. 29, 33). The Department of Defence's relationship with the media and accusations of 'spin' were featured in the 'children overboard' controversy just before the November 2001 federal election.

Spinning 'children overboard'

On 7 October 2001 the Minister for Immigration, Philip Ruddock, announced to the media that a number of children had been thrown overboard from a vessel suspected of being an 'illegal entry vessel'. Crew of the Australian Navy ship HMAS *Adelaide* subsequently rescued asylum seekers from the sinking *SIEV 4*. No children were actually thrown overboard from *SIEV 4*.

Peter Reith, the Minister for Defence, was informed by the Navy by 11 October that the photos already published in major newspapers were actually of the boat sinking, *not* of children having been thrown overboard.

The way this story was then relayed in the media and pictures from this event were used to suggest that the asylum seekers threw children overboard has been the subject of much debate both in formal political institutions, such as the Senate Select Committee on a Certain Maritime Incident, and in the media. Much of the debate centres on how the photos were used to suggest an event that did not happen and, more substantively, to question the role of the public affairs office and media advisers in both the Department of Defence and the Defence Minister's office. There are also questions about how much this controversy contributed to the Coalition winning government in the November 2001 federal election.

The Senate Committee found that 'Mr Reith deceived the Australian people during the 2001 Federal Election campaign concerning the state of the evidence for the claim that children had been thrown overboard from *SIEV 4*'.

The Senate Committee Report can be read at <www.aph.gov.au/Senate/committee/maritime_incident_ctte/report/contents.htm>.

Media discourse

To this point in the chapter we have discussed the power of the media to influence their audience through the information they choose to present and explored the power in ownership and production of Australian media. This section, as an accompaniment to the previous section on political 'spin', will look at how the media report issues. We will analyse the discursive practice of constructing news stories through words and pictures. The shift towards scrutiny of how media construct meanings through the words and pictures they use is an element of the cultural studies turn in media analysis.

'Discursive practices' are when text, such as a newspaper report, is used to generate debate, argument or discussion. Examples of different uses of words and images will be used to show different sides to an argument.

This approach assumes that language and images used by the media do not just describe the world but actually shape and build particular ways of thinking about the world we live in (McKee 2002, p. 62). In this chapter we do not argue that the media merely represent Australian politics by delivering us news and information; instead we have suggested that the media are active in shaping the way politics is analysed and discussed. In this view media power operates through the way it privileges particular discourses, or ideas, and constructs particular forms of reality and experience to be normal or 'common-sense'. This approach is clearly related to Luke's third dimension of power whereby there is no overt conflict or visible use of power. The media is able to shape people's political preferences, which may even be counter to what they would want if they were free agents, by building this idea of what is a normal understanding or reaction to a political issue (Street 2001, pp. 233–7). Other people explain this as the media's approach to 'framing' politics and say that dominant frames, or accepted ways of thinking, are used:

> to take cognitive shortcuts and quickly and routinely process large amounts of information into stories. They are convenient ways of pigeonholing information of situating events. That is, new events can be put into a framework which is already understood and anticipated. (Ward 1995, p. 112)

Existing frames are 'clamped over' or made to fit sets of events, and new details that cannot be accommodated within the frame will often be downplayed or entirely dispensed with in the final analysis. Frames are not ideologically neutral in what they portray as right or wrong or as politically acceptable (Ward 1995). It is important to investigate closely the way the media present politics in Australia. Two examples of articles, focusing on their headlines and lead paragraph, are presented in the box: one in which a protest group complains about its treatment in the media and another in which the Premier of Western Australia does likewise. We will also look at how the media itself is monitored to ensure accuracy and fairness in its representations of news and politics.

Chain gang chokes city

Daily Telegraph, 25 November 2006 (Carswell 2006)

Berks on bikes ruined last night for thousands of people—by causing maximum traffic gridlock in Sydney. Peak-hour motorists were delayed by more than an hour as several hundred cycling activists—dubbed Critical Mass—blocked the city's streets and cut off the Harbour Bridge northbound. The bizarre group—with police escort—pedalled sluggishly from Hyde Park to North Sydney to promote their plea to rid the CBD of cars, stop global warming and free imprisoned terror suspect David Hicks.

Global warming is good for WA, says Premier

West Australian, 4 November 2006 (Taylor 2006)

Western Australian Premier Alan Carpenter has commented on the economic impact of global warming. He noted that the move by nations around the world to combat greenhouse gas emissions would offer a great opportunity to WA, which can sell clean-burning gas from its offshore gas fields. Carpenter also wants WA to develop solar and wind power plants to complement the current reliance on gas and coal, but rejects the idea of carbon taxes. An emissions trading scheme would only be supported by the WA Government if also backed by the Australian Government, and if it factored in WA's gas exports.

In general, protests and non-institutionalised politics rarely obtain support in mainstream media in Australia. This is a quandary because protest-based events often rely on the media to generate publicity for their cause (see Scalmer 2002, p. 41). Nevertheless, the media rarely report protests in an uncontroversial manner, as the example in the *Daily Telegraph* clearly shows. The newspaper has discursively constructed the protest, by using typically derisive language ('berks on bikes'), and portrays the Critical Mass demonstration as an intrusive nuisance. The photo accompanying the story says: 'Protesters cause chaos on the Harbour Bridge last night.' The intended political message of the event is not taken seriously and is mentioned only towards the end of the article when one of the organisers is quoted. The newspaper then took the step of publishing the organiser's private mobile phone number and encouraging readers to make a personal complaint to the organiser. The organiser received more than 200 calls, most of which were abusive (Australian Press Council 2007a). By analysing this article through focusing on the words and images used, it is clear that the newspaper saw the event as controversial and worth highlighting. It was probably assumed that the controversy would incite a reaction and sell newspapers. In fact, the online version of the article had fifty-one comments from readers, most of which were scathing of Critical Mass. It is clear that this newspaper has a particular frame for analysing protest events as divisive, which takes us back to one of the initial points made in this chapter, about Australian news reporting focusing only on 'drama, pathos, tragedy and combat' (Windschuttle 1984, pp. 311–12).

The second story published in the *West Australian* newspaper was only 131 words long, and on the surface is a routine reporting of a policy announcement. The rest of the article included comments that the Premier was optimistic the world would find solutions to global warming and that Western Australia would play a central role. The article was accompanied by an illustration of a salt-affected dam in Western Australia, with a caption that also said Premier Carpenter believed climate change would be good for Western Australia (Taylor

2006). Two days later, in response to the Premier's complaint that he had not said global warming was good for Western Australia and that the article's headline had been purposefully misleading, the *West Australian* reported that Carpenter had performed 'a back-flip' in an article headed 'Premier goes cold on global warming bonus' (see Australian Press Council 2007b). The frame and discursive device being used here is less clear-cut than the protest example, yet what it reveals to us is that there is now a dominant discourse about global warming—which is that it exists, is a bad thing and is something for which governments need to create policy to mitigate against—and governments prefer to be seen as being active in this light. Being represented as profiting from something that is damaging society is not an image governments want to cultivate.

Both of these reports led to official complaints being made about the newspapers to the Australian Press Council. The Australian Press Council is the regulatory body of the print media. It was established in 1976 with two main aims: to help preserve the traditional freedom of the press within Australia and to ensure the press acts responsibly and ethically. To carry out this role, it serves as a forum to which anyone may take a complaint concerning the press. In both cases the complaints were upheld. The Press Council found that the *West Australian* had purposefully misrepresented the Premier's response and that a casual reader scanning the headline, in conjunction with the photo, would misunderstand the policy position (Australian Press Council 2007b). In the other case the Press Council found that the article on Critical Mass did not provide balanced information, such as quotes from the government or the police who had permitted the protest, to help readers decide their own opinion. They also decided that:

> it is difficult to imagine a more grievous invasion of individuals' privacy than to print their phone number in a headline and then encourage readers to call and complain. That the newspaper subsequently published five letters to the editor, all critical of the bike protest, demonstrated that there was a non-intrusive avenue for complaint: in the newspaper's own columns. (Australian Press Council 2007a)

In effect, the Press Council is a body that facilitates self-regulation by the media, yet there is very little in the way of public accountability beyond public apologies or retraction by newspapers. Some have suggested that the Press Council's rulings are an 'extreme example' of minimal regulation in Australian media (Cunningham 2006, p. 47). The Australian Press Council responds only to complaints about newspapers, and many commentators see it as a very weak regulator of content. How else, then, is media content held to be accountable to its audience? There are examples of a minimal form of self-regulation and scrutiny of the media through watchdog functions such as the weekly *Media Watch* program on the ABC (see <www.abc.net.au/mediawatch/>) and the media section of Thursday's *Australian* newspaper. Officially, ACMA is the regulator for free-to-air commercial radio and television, pay TV, digital broadcasting content and Internet content in Australia. This government body commenced operation in July 2005, having subsumed the functions of the Australian Broadcasting Authority (ABA) and the Australian Communications Authority (ACA). ACMA's jurisdiction is defined by the *Broadcasting Services Act* (1992) (BSA), and it oversees the complaints system outlined in the BSA.

For example, the types of issue that individuals have complained about to ACMA include: inappropriate classification of television programs, vilification of particular races or ethnic and religious backgrounds, misrepresentation of the views of individuals or groups, inaccuracy of news and current affairs reporting, and excessive depictions of violence. Most investigations examine whether a broadcaster has breached the broadcasting industry Code of Practice, but the penalties the ACMA can administer are limited because codes of practice are not actually broadcasting law. Therefore, the television station usually receives a letter notifying it of the breach of the code of practice and/or a fine. An upheld complaint may also be publicised both on the ACMA's website and through the issuing of a press release.

In interview research with news producers, very few thought that bias and inaccuracy existed as serious problems in news and current affairs but they did acknowledge that sensationalising of stories does occur. They believed that journalists tend to behave ethically because of a 'fundamental truth-seeking mission of journalism in society' (ABA 2001, p. 185). Thus, bias is eliminated either by editors or ultimately by an audience that is intolerant of opinion being presented as factual observation. However, some media choose to be upfront in their delivery of opinionated journalism and news and current affairs reporting. This includes talkback radio and Internet-provided media commentary, both of which will be explored in the following section.

Interactive media

To this point we have talked about the delivery of information through media sources, both in terms of media production and how the audiences utilise the media. We have not yet canvassed the possibilities that audiences have to interact with and be directly represented by the media in Australia. There are several ways in which the audience can interact instantly with news media: we can send 'letters to the editor' to be printed in newspapers, we can phone radio stations and be put live to air on talkback, we can also SMS a television news program to 'vote' on a current news issue, or we can blog our own material and opinions on the Internet.

Talkback radio

Monthly radio ratings data are collected by the market research company AC Nielsen. Table 7.3 shows the top three radio stations in the capital cities averaged over 2007. Radio stations are usually divided into the format they mainly include every day; that is, they are primarily either a music station, a talk and news station or a sports station. Only music (M) and talk/news (TN) stations are included in the lists of the most popular radio stations.

Table 7.3 demonstrates that music radio stations are very popular stations in nearly all major Australian cities. The exceptions are Melbourne and Sydney, where talk and news radio stations are two of the top three listened to stations. Only one capital city does not include a news and talk station in its top three—Brisbane. AC Nielsen also lists radio data by time of day and age group, and demonstrates that the audience for talk and news stations increases in the older age groups. For example, in Adelaide the main talk and news station (5AA) rates only 1.4 per cent of 18- to 24-year-olds and 6.2 per cent of 25- to 39-year-olds, then leaps to 36.4 per cent of those aged 55 and over. But this doesn't tell us the content of talkback. Is it different from other media sources? Talkback radio was first used on Melbourne's 3AW in 1967. Generally talkback exists on radio stations classified as news/talk, and these stations range from public broadcasting, on ABC and SBS radio stations, to wealthy commercial stations. The content of talkback is classified as news and current affairs similarly to other media. However, it has been shown that while the issues covered may be the same, it is the amount of time given to them or the emphases made that are quite different on the commercial talkback segments (Ward 2002b, p. 29). The other factor that differentiates most talkback segments from ordinary news radio is that they are hosted by well-known and affable, even celebrity, presenters rather than by serious journalists. This point is best illustrated with reference to the notorious 'cash for comment' case.

In July 2000, the ABC *Media Watch* program revealed a scandal about John Laws, a popular talkback radio host on commercial radio station 2UE. This case, and the subsequent inquiry conducted by the then Australian Broadcasting Authority (ABA, now ACMA), became known as 'cash for comment'. *Media Watch* revealed that John Laws had made a financial arrangement, worth $1.2 million, with the Australian Bankers' Association, ensuring that Laws would no longer criticise banks on air; instead he would make favourable comments about the banking industry. The ABA also found that Laws had similar deals with other corporations, including Optus, Foxtel, NRMA, Qantas, RAMS Home Loans, Star City Casino and industry organisations such as the Registered Clubs of New South Wales and the Australian Trucking Association. The inquiry also examined the financial arrangements of Alan Jones, another 2UE talkback host, those of an Adelaide talkback host, Jeremy Cordeaux, and Howard Sattler from 6PR in Perth (Flew 2000, p. 10).

John Laws claimed that he was primarily an entertainer, not a journalist, and therefore had not breached the Commercial Radio Code of Practice, which maintains that advertisements should not be presented as though they are news (Flew 2000, pp. 11–12). The ABA found that John Laws and Alan Jones, in failing to disclose their financial agreements, has breached the code in numerous ways. The ABA also imposed new conditions on 2UE, in that it was now required to disclose all interests and clearly differentiate advertising from ordinary news and talk. Subsequent to the investigation of other radio stations, the Broadcasting

TABLE 7.3 Major radio stations in Australian capital cities

City	First	Second	Third
Adelaide	5AA (17.5 %)–T/N	MIX (15.6 %)–M	SAFM (12.1 %)–M
Brisbane	NOVA (15.4 %)–M	MMM (11.3 %)–M	97.3 (10.8 %)–M
Melbourne	3AW (15.5 %)–T/N	FOX (11.1 %)–M	ABC774 (11.1 %)–T/N
Perth	MIX (16.2 %)–M	96FM (11.7 %)–M	ABC720 (11.2 %)–T/N
Sydney	2GB (12.7 %)–T/N	2DAY (10.1 %)–M	ABC702 (9.3 %)–T/N

Source: adapted from AC Nielsen 2007.

Service Act's standards were changed so that the new rule applied to all commercial radio stations (Gordon-Smith 2002, p. 279).

This case relates to the earlier analysis of regulation of broadcasting in Australia; it also pertains to a broader issue of the power of the media to set agendas that are often less than clear-cut for the audience; that is, do all media commentators have an ethical obligation to not mislead the audience and, furthermore, a responsibility to not sensationalise stories?

Talkback radio clearly does have the power to set agendas and foster political debate. Prime Minister John Howard often used talkback to launch political issues, and even election campaigns, in the public consciousness. Ian Ward (2002b, p. 25) itemised John Howard's use of radio interviews in comparison to television interviews, doorstops and press conferences, and he overwhelmingly favoured radio over other ways of interacting with media audiences. For example, in 2001, an election year, John Howard gave 134 radio interviews, compared to forty-six television interviews, ninety-two doorstops and forty-five press conferences (see also Turner et al. 2006). He probably utilised radio most because he was able to maintain more control over the interview process than if he was being interviewed by potentially less sympathetic journalists on television. It also displayed a canny understanding of his targeted audience; it is older age groups who listen to radio (as noted above), and this is the demographic grouping most likely to vote for the Coalition.

Politicians from all political persuasions see talkback radio as a useful way to have their own political viewpoint heard, particularly as talkback radio shows by well-known hosts, such as Leon Byner, Alan Jones and Neil Mitchell, have popular listener support. However, it is not just the news/talk radio stations that attract politicians trying to increase their appeal with older sections of the population. During the 2007 election campaign, Opposition Leader Kevin Rudd also utilised radio and television to increase his presence among younger voters by appearing on the media they use—for example, he did an interview on popular FM music station 2DAY FM with Kyle Sandilands, and notoriously agreed to appear on Rove's television show on Channel Ten, which was seen by 1.4 million people. Some question this use of media as being merely part of the spin and 'celebrity-ising' of contemporary Australian politics (Megalogenis 2007).

Some politicians also see talkback as a forum for democratic debate, which listeners interact with because they do not have access to public, political discussion elsewhere. Listeners can make the most of the opportunity either to promote their own views or to ask questions of politicians on air (Young 2007, p. 245). But who rings up talkback radio to have their say? New research in Australia found that not all talkback shows and hosts should be considered the same and that they attract different audiences with different backgrounds and a range of viewpoints; that is, callers do not necessarily present a partisan viewpoint but are calling in order to provide information from their own everyday experiences to contribute to an important public conversation. Turner et al. (2006) also found that the behaviour and appeal of the host, their relationship with the callers, the selection of topics and the specific reasons why listeners call in vary between shows. For example, they suggest that there was a big difference between John Laws' 2UE show on the basis of his celebrity presence and Neil Mitchell's 3AW show: Mitchell's show foregrounds news and current affairs to show he is more of a 'hard-nosed journalist' (Turner et al. 2006, p. 116).

Australian politics and the Internet

Many believe that the Internet has dramatically changed the way we 'interface' with media, and that it can actually reinvigorate democracy and increase citizen access to the process of governance (see Chen et al. 2007, p. 161). Trevor Barr lists four main uses for media/telecommunications: modes of communication, domestic media, information/data and transactions (2000, p. 31). The Internet has facilitated new media methods in all of these fields. Examples of how we now use the Internet within these four uses of media include: attending online meetings and the everyday use of email, accessing online newspapers, accessing online database searching (for example, looking for newspaper articles), and utilising home-based banking and Internet shopping (think of the rise of Amazon and eBay). Beyond these information and consumer-oriented uses of the Internet, it has also affected the way we both access information about and participate in politics in Australia.

The claims made for the Internet—that democracy is enhanced by increased freedom of expression in information provision and participation—were also made when radio was introduced (Meikle 2002, p. 2). However, Graham Meikle (2002) believes that the Internet has provided a new tool for those who intend to create social and political change, but that this tool works together with existing media. For example, political activists use and create Internet-based alternatives to news and political commentary sources, such as Indymedia, but they also need to promote their issues by receiving coverage in more widely accessed media, such as television and metropolitan newspapers.

The Internet has also provided broader opportunities for rapid, and sometimes controversial, political commentary that might not receive coverage by major media, such as newspapers and television. In Australia, this can include blogs run by individuals (for example see the progressive Lavartus Prodeo <http://larvatusprodeo.net/> and the more liberal <http://andrewnorton.info/blog/>) or opinion and essay publishing sites (see Online Opinion <www.onlineopinion.com.au/>), and alternative media sites (see Crikey <www.crikey.com.au/> and New Matilda <www.newmatilda.com/>).

Areas for using the Internet to increase the level of interaction between government and society include online voting and online election campaigning. Online voting in elections is not yet widespread in Australia, but the 2007 federal election was the first time that vision-impaired Australians were able to vote electronically, using a pre-poll vote in designated locations within twenty-nine electorates. This approach to voting has also been used in the ACT (since 2001) and in the Victorian election of 2006 (Macey 2007). Online election campaigning has also been a more recent phenomenon in Australia, as detailed in the snapshot at the beginning of this chapter.

Recent research has been undertaken on how governments, politicians and political parties are using the Internet as part of their political communication agendas. It has been suggested that Australia lags behind other advanced democracies in governmental use of the Internet and that the influence of new public management ideas (discussed in Chapter 13) has led to the use of new technology in only basic service delivery activities or limited experiments with e-democracy (Chen et al. 2007, p. 165). For example, most federal and State government departments now provide information online, and many citizen–state transactions, such as lodging annual tax returns or downloading Centrelink claim forms, can be done online. Yet while the Internet offers new avenues for increasing participation by citizens in policy processes and decision-making, this has largely been ignored by the federal government and implemented in a top-down way by several State governments (Chen et al. 2007, pp. 167–8). In Chapter 8 we will discuss how individuals increasingly use email and the Internet to engage in politics and contact politicians. However, the converse is not really true as most Australian parliamentarians have been reluctant to use innovative communication mechanisms, such as online consultation, with their constituents. Instead most politicians' websites focus on the broadcasting of information and provide very little capacity for people to engage with them beyond sending an email that may not be answered (Chen 2007, pp. 169–73).

This chapter has shown that the media ought not be analysed as a homogenous entity, as different people utilise different forms of media and for different outcomes. The ongoing power of the media clearly resides in their ability to satisfy the needs of these different groups in society while remaining the ever-present window through which we all understand and construct the political world.

Summary

- The general public receive information about Australian politics primarily through the media, and particularly through television.
- News-makers believe that newspapers and public broadcasting are the most important sources of news.
- Australian media retain power because of their ability to set political agendas, their concentrated ownership and their capacity to construct political discourse.
- More interactive forms of media production, such as talkback radio and the Internet, are increasingly being used by politicians to distribute information to targeted audiences.

Further reading

Cunningham, Stuart and Turner, Graeme (eds) 2006, *The Media and Communications in Australia*, 2nd edn, Allen & Unwin, Sydney.

Errington, Wayne and Miragliotta, Narelle 2007, *Media and Politics: An Introduction*, Oxford University Press, Melbourne.

Louw, Eric 2005, *The Media and Political Process*, Sage, London.

Young, Sally (ed.) 2007, *Government Communication in Australia*, Cambridge University Press, Melbourne.

Useful websites

- ABC Online at <www.abc.net.au>. This is a good site for the latest news from ABC radio and television programs, and it also includes in-depth coverage of Australian political issues, particularly election campaigns (e.g. see <www.abc.net.au/elections/federal/2007/>).

- Australian Communications and Media Authority at <www.acma.gov.au> and Australian Press Council at <www.presscouncil.org.au/>. These sites provide information and research on the regulation of the media in Australia, including recent investigations into breaches of the BSA.
- Crikey at <www.crikey.com.au>. Crikey provides an irreverent look at Australian politics, but also breaks some major political stories before the traditional print and broadcast media.

CHAPTER 8
INDIVIDUAL ENGAGEMENT

This chapter will look at individual citizens as engaged political actors. It introduces the broad field of political behaviour as an important area of analysis within contemporary Australian politics. The political socialisation of individuals is highlighted, followed by detail on current debates about citizens' trust in government, attitudes towards public policy issues and changing levels of engagement and participation in politics. Individuals are not merely voters but also active citizens with opinions and actions that shape politics. Emphasis is placed on the increasing importance of public opinion and new avenues for political participation in shaping Australian society.

The topics covered in this chapter include:

- an overview of Australian approaches to understanding political behaviour and political culture
- an explanation of the way young people are socialised into our political culture
- individual attitudes towards and trust in politics and an explanation of why public opinion matters
- individual participation in political and community affairs, and explorations of generational change in participation.

SNAPSHOT Young people—are they politically active or apathetic?

Meet Eugene. He is 20 and just left his personal training business to take up a sales role with a mining company. He'll vote Liberal in his first federal election. 'I know that Howard has done a good job with the economy. I'd be happy to vote for him,' he says. But like most, politics is not something that he talks about with his mates—much less with the girls in his social group. 'Look, I read the paper every day. I'd like to think I stay aware. But politics . . . it's more entertaining listening to what they come up with, with their stupid excuses or their weaselly tactics. They never give a direct reply, do they?'

'. . . It doesn't really bother me who's running the country. I just can't be bothered with it,' Louise says. So why did she bother enrolling? 'Because you can get fined if you don't.' Louise doesn't read newspapers, either. So where does she get her political news? 'I hear it from *The Chaser*. Or maybe on the web . . . but I'm not really that interested.' (Linnell 2007)

Many would despair at these newspaper quotes collected from two young people just before voting in the November 2007 federal election. But they also force us to reflect on what politics means to contemporary young Australians.

There are ongoing debates about the political engagement of young people. Where people sit on the divide between seeing young people as apathetic *or* engaged and active often depends on how analysts understand and interpret political arenas and processes; that is, whether they mainly emphasise young people's engagement with formal political institutions such as elections and parties, or broaden this to look at how young people engage with political issues and processes and new forms of participation. Most media reporting on young people and politics, exemplified by the rest of the newspaper article quoted from above, maintains what has been labelled as 'the myth of political apathy' (Vromen 2004; see also Crawford 2006, pp. 222–30).

Nevertheless most contemporary political science explorations of young people's political engagement now investigate and interpret a more complex picture and identify that young people are engaged by political issues—from work and industrial relations to the environment to education and so on—and have continued faith in some political processes. For example, the Youth Electoral Study found that, while 81 per cent believed that it was important to vote, most young people did not really trust politicians (Print et al. 2004, pp. 16, 21). Subsequently it was argued that a charge of apathy is incorrect and that a diagnosis of 'disillusionment' with politicians, parties and the electoral system is more appropriate (Edwards 2007, p. 37). We can see this disillusionment in what Eugene says above when he talks about his lack of trust in the relationship between what politicians say and what they actually do.

It has also been suggested that the existing understanding of young people's engagement with politics gives little recognition of the broader political context for young people's engagement. This could include their experiences of family socialisation in becoming engaged (or otherwise) with politics (see Edwards et al. 2006) or the adult-focused, top-down nature of governmental structures:

> If we are interested in enhancing young people's engagement, we need to pay attention to where *they* want to have a say and find ways to hear this.

> Insisting that engagement can only be heard through conventional, adult-centric forums misses an opportunity to create links between everyday and formal political spheres. (Harris et al. 2007, p. 24)

Does the current evidence mean that young people are generally not interested in participating in politics and decision-making? The answer is no, but that to fully see and understand young people's existing participation we need to look at new spaces and new ways of 'doing' politics that do not focus on traditional political institutions such as parties and other membership-based organisations. For example, Philippa Collin (2007), building on the work of theorist Henrik Bang, points out the emergence of 'project identities' that young people use to participate in politics: these are, first, the 'everyday maker', who is involved in an ad hoc way in campaigns and issues of immediate and often local importance. One place to recognise as a new political space for and by 'everyday makers' is the social networking sites and political blogs found on the Internet. The second new participatory identity is the 'expert citizen', who is drawn into more formal consultation processes created by government and community organisations for youth participation.

These new understandings also tell us that young people do not all conceptualise politics in the same way. Previous research tended to homogenise 'generations' and portrayed all young Australians as thinking about, acting in and responding to politics in the same way. Recent analysis instead identified that there are four different types of active participant: the activist, the party player, the communitarian and the individualist (Vromen 2003). If we focused only on traditional membership-driven political institutions, we would not have the chance to understand that these new, individualised forms of political engagement have grown in appeal to some young people. Nor would we see the reinvigoration of traditions of collective action, often through new social movement organisations, that appeal to other young people.

Political behaviour

This chapter covers the broad area within political science called political behaviour. Political behaviour is concerned with the way 'people react to, and make, political decisions' (McAllister 1997, p. 241). The focus of study in political behaviour is therefore on individuals, and questions like these feature in this approach:

- Why do people vote the way they do?
- Are men more likely than women to attend a community meeting?
- How does TV affect what people understand about politics?
- What is current public opinion on Australia's climate change policy?
- What are the leadership qualities that Australians admire most?

If you are interested in the answers to these questions then you are already interested in political behaviour. The emergence of political behaviour research was a reaction against the dominant focus on formal political institutions and constitutions and the neglect of individual engagement and informal political processes. Political behaviour covers five main areas: electoral behaviour (already covered in Chapter 5), political socialisation, public opinion, political participation and political leadership (Kavanagh 1983). It tends to focus on quantitatively describing and explaining the role of individuals within politics.

Political socialisation of young people

In most explanations of individual political behaviour, emphasis has been on the resources that citizens possess, or on an individual's socioeconomic status; that is, an individual's educational level, occupation and income are seen to determine voting behaviour, participation and attitudes. We saw this in Chapter 6 when we looked at the influence of class and socioeconomic status on voting patterns for the major political parties. On the other hand, social learning theories of political behaviour emphasise the political socialisation citizens go through as a member of society, and that the beliefs and feelings they accumulate in childhood will determine political behaviour. Early socialisation studies argued that this pre-adult socialisation had important consequences for adult political values. It was believed that support for the political system learnt through childhood would sustain support for the status quo through times of social and political crisis.

Reflecting on political socialisation as a process we all go through, we can see how knowledge and attitudes towards and about politics are not just there when we are born; they are learnt and shaped by agents in society, including:

- family
- educational institutions, such as school and university
- the media
- workplaces
- peer groups, such as friends
- political and community groups, church groups, and the like.

Socialisation proceeds in ways that are both direct and indirect—all of the agents listed above do not undertake the socialising of citizens into the political system as their exclusive activity. Take, for example, a university. By reading this book for a course on Australian politics you are continuing your political socialisation through the formal practice of teaching and learning about the way politics occurs in Australia—this is relatively direct. However, you will not put away this book having been socialised into thinking about politics in a particular, concrete way. We can have no idea about the conceptual frameworks you bring with you that will assist you in understanding the way politics works. You exercise a degree of autonomy in what you absorb and the way you integrate it with information you have already received and stored. While the processes of political socialisation are universally experienced, there will always be a great deal of variation in its meaning for each person, and the variation will be constructed by personal and social factors that are specific to the location of each individual member within society.

Differentiation between political socialisation and political learning or knowledge can also be made. Political socialisation goes well beyond factual learning about political institutions and processes. Socialisation is the more important aspect of the process and has the most lasting influence. It is value laden in that it structures how you interpret information about politics and how you approach the political world. Even if you forget the nuts and bolts—the information, theory, analysis and so on presented in this book—political socialisation theories tell us that you will have continued to develop your unique approach to understanding and conceptualising politics.

Early Australian political socialisation research found that a range of agents of socialisation play a role in shaping the political outlooks of young people (Connell 1971). Agent-based socialisation has a layered occurrence and, except for the very early years of childhood when family is probably dominant, there is not a single dominating agent. Agents often act together in ways not readily discernible; that is, school, the family and the media all act in different ways to create conceptual frameworks of understandings of the political world (also see Reynolds 1991, pp. 9–32). For example, it was found that some of the nuts and bolts about politics are learnt at school, such as voting processes through the holding of elections for school captain. The family is both a source of information about and for developing psychological connections with politics. This was seen through family discussions of elections and party allegiances. For example, in Australia the way parents vote continues to be the most significant factor in influencing how their children vote. It is more significant than other social factors such as class, religion and ethnicity (Marks 1993, p. 136; see also Edwards et al. 2006).

The media are clearly an important information source about current issues. However, what young people take away from news is a very limited sense of the political world.

> What is considered to be 'news' and worth broadcasting, is a highly selected sample of what is going on in the political world at any time. The Prime Minister making a public statement is news, the Prime Minister engaged in administrative tasks is not. As a result of such selectivity in their main source of information, the children develop an extensive acquaintance with the phenomenal surface of politics well before they have made much acquaintance with its workings. It is noticeable that even in middle adolescence few have any accurate grasp of the real balance of political and social forces. The political world the children see in the media is a surface, a glittering mosaic of discrete images. (Connell 1971, p. 121)

These early findings about the process of socialisation among children and young people still resonate today. The media are often portrayed, as in the quote above, as making a limited contribution to an understanding of institutions and political process. One quantitative study argued that young people are more likely to be able to identify leaders and election policies than to identify the roles of different levels of government in Australia's federal structure because of the way the media, especially television, represent politics (Vromen 1995, pp. 82–3).

However, other studies have attempted to look beyond factual learning about political institutions to look qualitatively at how the media assist in the constructions of emotional responses to Australian politics. Ian Ward found that the way politics is presented on the nightly news leads young people to have 'oppositional' readings of politics and news; that is, the readings are labelled as oppositional because news-makers do not *intend* that teenagers see politics the way they do, which is as perpetual and pointless conflict, politicians as often untruthful, and government and politics belonging to the rich, the powerful and, particularly, older people (Ward 1992, p. 226). The level of suspicion, cynicism and lack of youth identification that the media are charged with creating is borne out repeatedly in both quantitative and qualitative studies of young people, politics and the media (see also Beresford & Phillips 1997; Evans & Sternberg 1999, pp. 104–8; Huntley 2006).

The way individuals are socialised into Australia's political culture is an important foundation for their attitudes towards ongoing political involvement. However, research on the role of the media in political socialisation leads us to believe that most people accept a specific and unidimensional image of politics. Thus, Australians will view politics more favourably only if alternative agents of socialisation such as family, friends, school and local community organisations are able to provide a persuasive alternative representation of politics.

Criticisms of the political socialisation approach state that too much emphasis has been put on the assumption that orientations towards the political system learnt in childhood are sustained throughout an individual's lifetime (Smith 2001b, pp. 126–9). Instead, we should recognise that childhood political socialisation is an important factor in adult orientations towards politics, but that socialisation is a continuous process shaped by the events, people and organisational forms that individuals come into contact with as adults. This approach would lead us to accept that young cynicism about institutionalised politics and political parties may change as individuals have more interaction with government institutions and vote at elections. The following section will look at how Australians think and feel about politics and how this in turn influences political outcomes.

Individual engagement and Australian political culture

Analysis of the distinctiveness of Australia's political culture is useful as it helps us to understand the ways people act politically. It has been argued that the 'political rules, processes and institutions of a country only make sense in the context of the political beliefs, attitudes and values of its citizens' (Smith 2001b, p. 1); that is, we ought to look at the way people think and feel about politics to understand both entrenched power relationships and how people change and influence political institutions.

The idea that people have specific feelings or orientations towards politics and the political system was developed by Gabriel Almond and Sidney Verba in *The Civic Culture* (1965). They found that individuals have three types of orientation towards politics:

- cognitive—the 'nuts and bolts' knowledge and understanding people have of politics
- affective—the way people feel about the political system, especially political leaders
- evaluative—when individuals make judgements about what ought to happen in the political world.

For example, an individual citizen may know how federal elections are used to elect the government and know that we do not vote directly for the Prime Minister (a cognitive orientation); this individual may also strongly identify with one political party for which they regularly vote (an affective orientation); and thus they make judgements about which party best represents them by examining their policy positions on such issues as health, education and taxation (an evaluative orientation). Therefore, there is an interdependence in these three types of orientation towards the nature of the political system in Australia. How you feel about a political party and how you evaluate its policy platform is based on what you know and understand about that party and the electoral system more broadly. It is this interdependence between the cognitive, affective and evaluative that structures the relationship of individuals to Australia's political culture.

We can also distinguish between micro-level political culture orientations, such as those held towards day-to-day political events like policy announcements, and macro-level political culture orientations. 'Macro-level orientations' are strongly held views that are static and define collective identity among a group of people. These can include people's religious or national identity and their broad ideological beliefs. Rodney Smith suggests that there are four elements to Australia's political culture at this macro level that unite the nation: belief in democracy, an identification with a political party, a sense of an Australian national identity, and belief in equality and a 'fair go' (2001b, p. 6). Party identification was explained in Chapter 5. We will now discuss these other facets of

Australia's political culture in the following sections on national identity and egalitarianism, and trust and democratic beliefs.

National identity and egalitarianism

A sense of a shared national identity is an idea or dominant discourse that can promote political unity among a nation's citizens. Through times of war or economic depression or major social change this shared sense of national identity is often invoked. However, we cannot simply pinpoint the beliefs underlying national identity, and it is difficult to satisfactorily answer the question: what does it mean to be Australian? Survey research has found that 'feeling Australian' was judged by most people (64 per cent saying it was very important) as fundamental to 'being truly Australian', followed by being able to speak English (62 per cent), respecting Australia's political institutions and laws (61 per cent), then having Australian citizenship (56 per cent) (Bean 2004, pp. 43–4). Similar research found that when citizens are asked about a sense of national pride in Australia they are most likely to agree with achievement in sport (92 per cent), scientific and technological achievements (91 per cent) and the armed forces (84 per cent) (Goot & Watson 2005, p. 190).

Catriona Elder (2007, pp. 6–12) points out that 'being Australian' is often best understood in terms of how individuals define what is not Australian or what is even un-Australian. She uses examples of how Australians often define themselves as different from Americans or the English, from our South Pacific neighbours or even from groups internal to the nation. She argues:

> the key group against whom ideas of Australian-ness have been made comprises the Indigenous people of Australia. However, being Australian is also defined in relation to newly arrived migrant groups, people with different regional affiliations (mainlanders versus Tasmanians, easterners versus those from the west) and the ubiquitous rural and urban divide. (Elder 2007, p. 11)

We can see here that ideas of place, space and shared feelings are very important to defining a shared sense of national identity in Australia, as are people's views on immigration and multiculturalism and their attitudes towards Indigenous Australians. These social attitudes are where views become divided among Australian citizens and politicians alike (see Wilson & Breusch 2004, p. 179; and

Goot & Rowse 2007). For example, Goot and Watson (2005) found that while people's views about levels of immigration to Australia and to multiculturalism policies were shaped by how much formal education they had received (with the more highly educated being more open to both policy types), they also suggest that overall opposition to immigration has not increased in recent years and that there are now more positive attitudes towards immigrants' contribution to the economy.

While 'feeling Australian' is important for many, acting Australian often revolves around class-derived notions of a 'fair go', mateship and egalitarianism (see Elder 2007, p. 41). The role of government in the idea of a 'fair go' is to provide appropriate welfare, services and infrastructure for all Australians so they have an equal opportunity to achieve in society and the workplace. Some have questioned whether neo-liberal economic reforms (see Chapter 13) specific to many advanced democracies in the last twenty years or so have eroded Australians' support for state intervention to provide a fair go for all (see Pusey & Turnbull 2005). Survey research has found that Australians still believe in the welfare state and provision of financial support, such as sole parent benefits, and that Australians generally are more generous in their attitudes towards the poor in society than in a comparative democracy like the US (Wilson & Meagher 2007). However, Wilson and Meagher (2007, pp. 280–1) point out that public opinion on state support is now more divided between ideas of the deserving and undeserving recipients of support. The undeserving of support, and by extension a 'fair go', include newly arrived immigrants, young people and the unemployed.

All of this recent research emphasises that while Australians like to construct unity through a sense of national identity underpinned by equality and a fair go for all, the reality of both people's opinions and the ensuing relationships with public policy outcomes are much more divided and complex. The complexity continues when we look in the next section at how Australians think and feel about the government and politicians who are responsible for policy formation and delivery.

Trust and democratic beliefs

The levels of trust and active engagement that individuals have with the political system, with governments in particular, and with democracy more broadly are often seen as indicators of social capital.

'Social capital' refers to the processes between people that establish networks, norms and social trust. Social capital is seen as being generated in communities, and it has been argued that 'social capital should be the pre-eminent and most valued form of capital as it provides the basis on which we can build a truly civil society' (Cox 1995, p. 17); that is, the connections people have with one another in communities subsequently determines the level of engagement people have with the political world.

Robert Putnam, the American academic who popularised the notion of social capital, differentiates between political participation and the generating of social capital. He defines political participation narrowly as 'relations with political institutions', and sees social capital through civic engagement as a more appropriate description for acts undertaken by individuals connected to one another through a shared sense of community (1995, pp. 665–7). Debates have emerged from the fear that Australian society has lost trust in government and other essential institutions because it has lost both the development of social capital and a sense of community (see Bean 2005; Bean & Denemark 2007; Davis 2001, pp. 220–4; Hogan & Owen 2000). For example, claims have been made about the cynicism and distrust Australians now hold for political institutions and politicians: 'A certain level of mistrust of politicians is a long-standing and healthy feature of Australian life but we have seen how healthy scepticism has changed into deep distrust, cynicism and even anger' (Young 2000, p. 181).

But is this accurate? Are we really in a period of crisis with overt cynicism and a lack of trust in political institutions and politicians? In responding to these questions there are a range of possible answers. First, we could attempt to measure cynicism by looking at political engagement. 'Political engagement' refers to such factors as how interested people are in politics, whether they talk about politics with friends and family and whether they follow politics in the news. These are all cognitive orientations towards the political world, and all of these factors are primarily measured through the use of quantitative survey-based research. If cynicism has increased we would expect Australians to be less engaged with the political world. Murray Goot has collated a series of research studies to show there is very little quantitative evidence that political engagement has declined. For example, the number of people who answer that their level of interest is 'not much' or 'none at all' has not increased in the last twenty years but has remained constant at under 25 per cent of the adult population. Furthermore, a majority, at least 60 per cent, state that they have followed recent election campaigns through newspapers and television, either often or sometimes (Goot 2002, pp. 14–19).

Second, in looking for a rising level of distrust we could examine how Australians feel about politicians and political institutions; that is, their affective and evaluative orientations toward politics. Goot reports that the general public's trust in politicians has decreased since the mid-1970s, but he argues that this is comparable to a lack of trust in other institutionalised actors, such as bank managers, lawyers and journalists (2002, p. 21). Others have found that people are increasingly suspicious of politicians: for example more than 40 per cent of Australians agreed that 'federal politicians don't know what ordinary people think' and a further 49 per cent of Australians agree with the statement that 'most politicians are in politics for personal gain'. A key problem seems to lie with people's dissatisfaction with Australian political parties (Bean & Denemark 2007, pp. 66–9) as highlighted in Chapter 6. Another interpretation is that individuals feel differently about government in a period that has seen large-scale economic change and a diminishing role for government as a provider of public services. David Burchell suggests we should not see disillusionment with government either as a rejection of politics or as the 'embrace of anti-politics'. Instead it could mean that people are just as passionate about politics but have become disillusioned with particular practices within it, be it a perception of a lack of choice between parties, a dislike for discord and party battles or a disappointment in the rate of political change fostered by governments (2002, pp. 64–8).

Polling public opinion

Public opinion is sought all the time, especially in the midst of an election campaign. Commercial pollsters and political scientists are interested to know what the general public thinks about party leaders and about which political issues are 'hot'. For example, during the federal election in 2001 public opinion was sought several times and there was a media focus on immigration, refugees and the 'war on terror'; in the 2004 federal election interest rates was seen as a 'hot' issue (see Denemark et al. 2007); and in 2007 it was climate change and the WorkChoices policy. Yet these issues of the day are not necessarily the issues that people say motivate them to engage with politics and/or to vote a particular way. The relationship between policy-making and public opinion is also not straightforward. Governments are not obliged to act in particular ways because of opinion polls undertaken by commercial pollsters. Nor can we always understand what people think and feel about an issue on the basis of a single poll. An individual's thoughts and feelings may be more complex than a quick snapshot is able to relay, or the poll may even measure an opinion that is fickle and not very important to people. When particular policy-making issues are not a feature of people's everyday lives it is difficult to ascertain the depth of their opinion. It is also impossible to tell whether people will change their actions because of the opinion they express through a poll. This means that the relationship between participation, including voting, and opinion is not straightforward.

Ian Cook (2004, pp. 187–93) lists four reasons that we can use to understand how opinion polls, and hence public opinion, enhance democratic practice in Australia:

1 Democracy is about citizens having a role in policy-making and about representatives responding to the people's will. Thus polls help policy-makers develop policies that reflect the views and values of citizens.
2 Opinion polling delivers popular will to political executives and to those in political parties. For example, political leaders can use polls to test the reception of new policy positions and to make sure that opinion is gathered from a broad range of people.
3 Opinion polls diminish the likelihood that just one section of society dominates policy-making. For example, without access to polls and popular opinion politicians may rely too much on their own judgements or on the views of those close to them. Without the use of opinion polls to gauge public opinion the only other views taken into consideration will be those of individuals and pressure groups with enough power and persuasion to contact politicians directly.
4 Opinion polling means that citizens do not have to wait until an election occurs to speak but can have ongoing input into decision-making, and policymakers are provided with ongoing access to the opinion, or the will, of the people.

However, Cook (2004) also provides two important reasons why opinion polls can also be seen as damaging to Australian democracy:

1 Polling confuses popularity with leadership; that is, opinion polls are often limited to simply indicating how popular a leader or a political party is. Few people are likely to have a deep understanding (thus their cognitive orientation) about what a government is doing and so are likely to reply in a partisan way, reflecting their affective orientation towards a leader or a party. The most popular option is not always the best policy for Australians in general as it may disadvantage some people more than others. Leaders need to collect all the information available to attempt to make decisions that are in the public interest.
2 Polls produce poll following. This often means that political leaders focus too much on media-driven fortnightly polls and what will keep them popular. This can also lead to short-term rather than long-term policy agendas for policy delivery.

Despite this mixed opinion on the value of opinion polls to democracy, they are now ubiquitous in Australian politics. Thus it is an important skill for a political analyst to be able to assess opinion polls published in newspapers. The 'Interpreting opinion polls' box provides some handy hints on how to read between the lines when wanting to understand measures of public opinion.

Interpreting opinion polls

How many people were asked for their opinion?
With a randomly selected sample, of 1000–1500 people drawn from the Australian adult population, accurate predictions about that population can be made. However, it has to be a random sample or a stratified random sample. This means that everyone has an equal chance of being included. Simply asking questions of people in the street—a convenience sample—will not give you an accurate picture of opinions of anyone else beyond the handful of people talked to in the street.

Has the newspaper reported the sampling error?
It ought to. Generally with polls undertaken with 1000–1500 Australians the sampling error is plus or minus 2 per cent. This means that if the report

states that the ALP has 48 per cent of the total two-party preferred vote and the Coalition has 52 per cent, it could in reality vary between ALP 46–50 per cent and Coalition 48–52 per cent. This variation could be between a 'safe win' or a 'too close to call' election result (based on proportions of the vote gained).

How was the information collected?
Sometimes newspapers or websites will issue 'reports' of polls done on a 'phone-in' basis. Clearly these polls represent nothing more than the people who felt strongly enough to phone in or send an email, and they are not an accurate way of measuring what the Australian population feels about an issue. Even when polls claim that they are representative, they might not be. Check to see whether the response rate is mentioned. This is the measure of how many people responded to the questionnaire and how many people refused to answer. People are more likely to answer questions over the telephone than if they are sent a questionnaire to their home. However, individuals are increasingly feeling overloaded by telephone market researchers and telemarketers, making the job of polling companies more difficult.

Has the newspaper report listed the actual questions asked and in the order they were asked?
The actual questions asked are crucial in the accurate measurement of public opinion. Watch for emotive or leading language in questions (for example, using the term 'refugees', 'boat people', 'illegals', or 'asylum seekers' may lead to different levels of support for immigration policies), question order (that is, it could make a difference whether individuals are asked about their opinion on a policy position before questions on who they intend to vote for), and including some issues and omitting others in a list, which may distort the reality of people's opinions.

Political participation

The character of democracy is based on the assumption that citizens actively participate in politics and are entitled to shape political outcomes. Some may see the act of voting as the pinnacle of political participation while others call for increased levels of participation and engagement in community affairs and political decision-making. Through exploring the types of participatory acts available to the general population we will show that participation in Australia's political culture extends far beyond attitude formation and voting in elections.

Accompanying the arguments that Australians are cynical and distrustful of politicians are suggestions that we are not interested in participating in public affairs (see Civics Expert Group 1993; Chia & Patmore 2004). However, a close investigation of the range of ways in which political engagement can be seen, as shown in this chapter's snapshot, suggests that Australians are far from politically apathetic and use a variety of ways to express opinions and demonstrate support. Choices about how to participate politically in Australia reflect different strategic choices that take into account such factors as available time, available resources, political climate and ideological position of individuals. In understanding the range of participatory acts used by Australian citizens we have divided them into:

- individual action
- collective action.

Examples of different participatory acts are detailed below with recent examples, followed by information on patterns of participation in Australian society. This evidence demonstrates that participation in Australia is changing. In recent decades there has been a decline in membership in many traditional collective action-oriented organisations, such as political parties and trade unions. Simultaneously there has been an increase in involvement with local community, environmental and human rights-type organisations that reveals a shift in approach to long-term allegiances and membership. Furthermore, the vast majority of the population engage in political acts individually: ranging from donating money, volunteering time to boycotting and buycotting consumer items over a political issue. Many individuals also now use Internet-based mechanisms to engage in politics and express a point of view.

Individual action

Individual actions include petition signing, letter writing to MPs and newspapers, boycotts and buycotts of products, donating time and money to charity and service-oriented work and becoming involved in government consultation processes.

Signing petitions

Sometimes when individuals are seeking to demonstrate the level of support for an issue they will organise a petition. This could be with either a geographic community (such as in a suburb) or a community on the basis of a shared identity (such as the local gay and lesbian community), or a group with shared values (such as those opposed to banning of 4WD vehicle use in national parks). Petitions are usually directed at decision-makers and until recently have been presented to sympathetic parliamentarians to be read into Hansard. It is possible to go to the Parliament of Australia website and run a search in the House of Representatives' or Senates' Hansards to find the range of petitions that have been tabled in parliament. More than a million Australians signed more than 900 petitions to parliament between 2004 and 2007, including a 15,000-person petition asking for a Commonwealth dental scheme to be established. In early 2008 the new federal government appointed a ten-person House of Representatives committee to review petitions and propose government action to address the issues they raise (Franklin 2008).

Collecting signatures for a petition is also a first step in increasing awareness about a political issue. By asking people to be active through signing a petition you will also be informing people about the substance of your claims. Ian McAllister found that 49 per cent of the population had collected signatures for a petition (1997, p. 247). Most Australians (83 per cent) claim to have signed a petition at some point, and only 4 per cent say they have never done it and would never do it (Wilson et al. 2005). It is easy to start a petition, and even easier to participate through signing one.

Increasingly people can also participate in online petitions. A new Internet-based pressure group, GetUp, has organised a number of petitions on such diverse policy issues as increasing funding for the ABC, on ending the Health Minister's veto of RU486, and announcing an exit strategy from the war in Iraq. One campaign that lobbied the government to end the offshore processing of refugee claims by children being held in detention attracted 100,000 signatories (Vromen 2008).

Petitions can vary in their level of success. Although it is difficult to demonstrate that a petition has dramatically changed political history, it is easy to see how a well-supported petition could place an issue on the political agenda. It is important to regard petitions as a means for individuals to express their political opinions collectively to formal decision-makers.

Writing letters, making phone calls and sending emails

Another way of attempting to get a public hearing for a particular concern or viewpoint is to write letters. If you write a letter to your local MP about an issue of concern they are generally obliged to respond to you in their role as your representative. Writing a letter, making a phone call or sending an email is clearly more individualised and more time-consuming than signing a petition. Some organisations, such as GetUp mentioned above and human rights pressure groups such as Amnesty International, provide the substance of letters to their subscribers or members and suggest they write to or email their local member of parliament or the minister responsible for policy-making on that particular issue. Other people initiate contact with their local representatives over more immediate concerns, such as planning and development decisions decided on by local governments. About a third of Australians have contacted a politician or public servant to express a viewpoint, and another 45 per cent suggest that they have not done so but may do so in the future if the right issue arose. A smaller group of people, about 14 per cent of Australians, have also written letters to the editors of newspapers or rung talkback radio to express a political viewpoint (Wilson et al. 2005).

Boycotts and buycotts

A 'boycott' is when a choice is made to not purchase a product or a service because of a political concern or issue. A 'buycott' has a similar principle, but it is when a particular product is chosen as a purchase because it is seen as representing a political viewpoint. For example, Fair Trade coffee and chocolate are advocated in buycott campaigns as providing more direct income to producers. Boycotts can be international, such as a group of nations imposing a trade ban on a nation because of human rights concerns, or they can be localised. Individuals mainly get involved with boycotts and buycotts at the local level and, like petitions and letters, they aim to increase general awareness about political issues. They are different in that they have a more direct economic impact and affect businesses more than governments.

In recent years, one very successful Australia-based boycott campaign was the boycotting of French products during the 1995–96 French government tests of nuclear weapons in the Pacific. Initially the boycott began with small hotels, cafés and restaurants refusing to sell French products, such as wines and cheeses. This led to Internet sites publishing comprehensive lists of French products and French-owned companies. There was much anti-French sentiment around Australia, and French restaurants went into decline. It was estimated that the sale of French wine fell by 40 per cent during the tests (see Thornton et al. 1997, pp. 160–1).

Boycotts and buycotts are a very contemporary form of political action, and subsequently not much evidence on Australian individuals' involvements in them has been collected. From what we do know there is clearly a growing propensity by citizens to express themselves politically this way. More than 54 per cent of Australians have engaged in a boycott or buycott, and another 28 per cent say that they would contemplate doing so in the future (Wilson et al. 2005).

One area where there has clearly been a more individually self-conscious approach to political motivations behind the purchases that people make is reflected in increasing concern for the environment in general and climate change in particular. For example a study among those who live in New South Wales found that in the previous twelve months 50 per cent had bought more environmentally friendly household products, 48 per cent avoided using plastic bags to carry shopping and 40 per cent had avoided products with excessive packaging. Even higher numbers of people have reduced water (75 per cent) and energy (73 per cent) consumption in that same period (EPA 2006, p. 5).

Volunteering time and donating money

Volunteering is widely spread among Australians: both men and women volunteer, as do people of all incomes and all ages, as well as both people who are in paid work and those who are not. People tend to volunteer for philosophical or ideological reasons because they believe it benefits the wider community (Pusey 2000, pp. 21–2). Recent research found that 41 per cent of Australians had volunteered their time in the year previously; 132 hours a year per volunteer being average (ACOSS 2005, p. vii).

Donating money is seen as another way for people to show their political commitment to a cause or an organisation. In 2004, 87 per cent of adult Australians made donations worth $5.7 billion to community organisations. A further $2 billion was provided by individuals through 'charity gambling', including fund-raising, raffles, event support and lotteries. While for many individuals charitable donations are tax deductible, not all donations are. People also choose to donate money to a broad range of organisational types and causes. Table 8.1 shows how the time and money of Australians are distributed among community organisations. It reveals that it is not the same organisations that attract people's money and time. Religious organisations gain the largest proportion of donations, but welfare services (which would include such charities as Meals on Wheels and Mission Australia) and local sport and recreation organisations attract the largest proportion of volunteer time (ACOSS 2005, pp. vii–ix).

TABLE 8.1 Individual engagement: 2004 donations and volunteering

Community sector organisation types	Percentage of all individual donations	Percentage of volunteering time
Welfare	13	28
Health (inc. medical research)	14	10
Religious	36	15
International aid	12	1
Education	7	12
Environment	5	3
Sport and recreation	4	20
Arts and culture	2	3
Others	7	8

Source: adapted from ACOSS (2005, p. 22).

Major events can also promote donations of money. One of the most significant examples of Australians donating money en masse was after the tsunami in South-East Asia on Boxing Day 2004. About $300 million was given in donations, by individuals, to international aid and development organisations (ACOSS 2005, p. viii).

Collective action

'Collective action' is activity undertaken with others, in a formal or informal group structure, to achieve a shared goal or interest, often for the creation of social and political change. Existing research has found that in general Australians are joiners (Passey & Lyons 2005, p. 78), in that they either become members or are involved in group activities for the common good and/or a shared interest. Through a focus on collective action we differentiate our approach from those who interpret society as only the sum of all individuals and the realisation of their (self) interests. Instead our view posits the importance of collective action to understanding political processes in Australia. Collective action can happen in institutionalised forms, such as through political parties, or in ad hoc ways driven by particular political issues. Collective action can be localised, such as through a community group forming to contest the transformation of parkland into a residential area. Collective action can also be global, for example when individuals simultaneously access a particular website to create a crash in the system; this sort of action has been used by internationally linked protestors on sites of multinational corporations.

Two broad forms of collective action are examined here:

- ongoing group formations of some kind
- ad hoc protest actions.

Groups

Political scientists often examine membership and involvement in community groups as a form of political participation. Wilson et al. (2005) found that in the previous two years 44 per cent of the population had worked with others on a shared community concern. However, this construction of group activity as only problem- or 'concern'-related seems quite narrow (see Smith 2001b, p. 214). It is often difficult to distinguish between involvement in different forms of community groups. For example, is being involved in a local sporting group that has a politically espoused position on the public use of open space and parkland an example of political participation? And when is a group classified as local or community-oriented? For example, a person could be a member of the local Amnesty group or the local Reconciliation group, but these concerns about human rights are much broader than a geographically contained community.

Another way of measuring group involvement is to look more specifically at types of groups and ask individuals about their level of involvement. In the late 1990s the social capital debate, mentioned earlier in this chapter, also highlighted the decline in group, or associational, involvements across liberal democratic nations (see Putnam 2000). The essence of the argument is that community cohesion has decreased due to people being less involved and not connected to one another through collectively oriented groups.

Two membership-based groups could be used to support this type of argument in Australia: both party membership and trade union membership have been in decline since the 1980s. For example, only a very small proportion of Australians are party members. Recent research found that 3 per cent of people are party members and an additional 1 per cent consider themselves active members (Wilson et al. 2005). We have little qualitative information on why party membership is so low and on how people feel about parties. Yet these low membership figures, coupled with attitudinal research that finds people have a low level of trust in parties and politicians, will be part of the explanation (see Bean & Denemark 2007).

Membership of trade unions also decreased dramatically in the same period. Density (the proportion of all workers who are union members) fell from just over half (51 per cent) in the early 1980s to the 2006 rate of less than a quarter (22.4 per cent) (Barnes 2007). Traditional areas of union strength in Australia, such as manufacturing, have contracted, and union membership remains low in the growth areas of the economy such as hospitality and retail, among younger workers and for part-time and casual workers. The reasons for union decline are partly to do with a change in Australian industry and patterns of work, as well as the lack of appeal of collective action and representation through unions for some Australians. However, it is also worth pointing to the particularly hostile political environment for trade unions during the period of the Coalition federal government (1996–2007). Many legislative measures, especially the *Workplace Relations Act* in 1996 and WorkChoices in 2006, were introduced to curtail union representation and influence within workplaces.

When social movement and community-based organisations are examined it is difficult to maintain the decline in social cohesion argument due to a decrease in associational involvement. It can be seen that while there has been a decrease in membership in parties, unions and some forms of community group, such as Rotary Clubs and other service clubs and religious organisations (see Keen 1999; Lyons 2001), the same claim cannot be made for organisations more readily associated with social movement activity, such as environmental organisations, reconciliation groups, human rights groups and women's groups. The actual activities of and values associated with social movements will be examined in Chapter 10, yet what is demonstrated here is that organisations that do not necessarily intend to influence electoral politics are often more attractive to individuals interested in political and social change (Papadakis 2001, pp. 47–50). Table 8.2 presents data on the sorts of groups Australians are members of.

TABLE 8.2 Australian membership of community groups

Community group type	Members (%)
Consumer organisations (e.g. NRMA or Choice)	54
Sporting or recreation group (inc. service clubs)	45
Financial cooperatives (inc. credit unions)	29
Religious group	24
Local community group	20
Professional society	15
Group for people with special needs	14
Environmental group or aid organisation	10
Art, music or educational group	10
Self-help health group	8
Conservation group (e.g. Landcare)	7
Rights promotion group (e.g. women, refugees)	6
Lobbying group	4

Source: adapted from Passey & Lyons (2005, p. 68).

This table shows that Australians join a range of groups and that the most popular are those that are the least recognised as overtly political actors. However, all of these groups have the potential to act on behalf of their members in trying to create policy or political change, and most do at some point. Further, the vast majority (86 per cent) of the population are a member of at least one of these community groups, with 70 per cent being a member of two or more groups (Passey & Lyons 2005, p. 66). One limitation of this data is that it focuses only on continuous membership, not a broader notion of occasional involvement with groups or organisations that some argue would be more inclusive of the ad hoc, issue-inspired political participation of women and young people (see Vromen 2003). There is no large-scale research on the reasons why some Australians find community groups based on values and identity more appealing than the more traditional political actors of parties and trade unions. Some have argued that this is due to a shift in values from material and economic concerns toward post-materialism, which emphasises social issues and quality of life (Inglehart 1990; Papadakis 2001, p. 41; Western & Tranter 2005). Nevertheless, Passey and Lyons (2005) found a direct relationship between community group involvement and individual political participation, in that members are more likely to have also acted politically in the individual activities we described above. This suggests that not only are Australians joiners but also that their collective involvements enhance their capacity to express their individual points of view.

Protest

The final point in measuring collective action is to look beyond membership of, and participation in, organisations and groups to ad hoc political events. Most Australians would associate the idea of protest politics with the more visual moments of large-scale rallies, demonstrations and blockades. Involvement in these particular political actions are expressions of collective action and collective concern over particular issues. Wilson et al. found (2005) that in the two years previously 12 per cent of Australians had taken part in a protest, march or demonstration. Yet while Australians are joiners of community groups and above the average comparatively, they are below the average in propensity to attend a demonstration. Tiffen and Gittins (2004, p. 248) found that Australians are below the average for this form of political participation and that citizens of other countries such as France and Italy are twice as likely to have attended a protest.

Despite this, in recent years protest events have occurred that attracted very large turnouts. For example, it was estimated that there were a million participants Australia-wide in the 2003 protest events against Australia's involvement in the war in Iraq, thus making it the biggest set of marches Australia had ever seen (Maddison & Scalmer 2006, pp. 1–3). Another issue that attracted very large groups of people was the marches for reconciliation held in Sydney, Brisbane, Adelaide and Hobart in May 2000. An estimated 300,000 to 500,000 people marched over the Harbour Bridge in Sydney, leading to claims that it was one of the best-attended marches ever in the city, rivalled only by the anti-Vietnam War marches in the early 1970s. Similar claims were made about the 300,000 who turned out in Melbourne, and the 40,000 in Perth, on 3 December 2000 (Burgmann 2003, p. 95).

Rallies and demonstrations are not only used to persuade the government to change a policy position, such as with the reconciliation and peace marches; they can also be used to demonstrate mass support over an issue that is primarily under the jurisdiction of the private sector. This is increasingly the case with global justice activism, which targets corporations such as multinational clothing manufacturers, banks and multinational mining companies. A large-scale rally and march, attended by an estimated 80,000 people, was held in Sydney in late 1999 to protest against the decision by News Limited to axe the South Sydney team from the National Rugby League competition. An interesting protest was organised by Clubs NSW in 2003 when about 15,000 people rallied to complain about changes to the regulation of poker machines and taxation by the New South Wales government. While it is difficult to collect information on the demographics of people who attend particular protest rallies and marches, we could presume from these diverse examples that a range of people in the community, with a range of values and issues, use these political actions as a symbol of collective action.

In conclusion, this chapter has shown that Australian political behaviour has complex dimensions that demonstrate both a decrease in trust and involvement in traditional political institutions but an increase in individual and group-based forms of participation centred around new ideas and new values. Future analyses of political behaviour will need to focus on the qualitative affective and evaluative orientations that we have towards our political culture to present a deeper understanding of the relationship Australians have with the political world.

Summary

- Political socialisation is an important process that all individuals go through. However, the lasting importance of childhood or adult socialisation varies among individuals, as does the importance of a variety of agents in the socialisation process, such as school, media, family, religion and community groups.
- Australians have cognitive, affective and evaluative perceptions of the political world. Our understanding of public opinion need not be limited to one-off media polls but can also include both historical and deeper perspectives on individual attitudes towards politics and leaders.
- Participation by individuals can take place as individual activity and as group-based, collective activity. Both types of participation are equally important democratic avenues for the involvement of individuals in politics and society, and demonstrate a range of modes of involvement. The evidence presented here challenges the broadly held view that political participation is in decline.

Further reading

Davis, Glyn and Weller, Patrick (eds) 2001, *Are You Being Served? States, Citizens and Governance*, Allen & Unwin, Sydney.

Denemark, David, Meagher, Gabrielle, Wilson, Shaun, Western, Mark and Phillips, Timothy 2007, *Australian Social Attitudes 2: Citizenship, Work and Aspirations*, UNSW Press, Sydney.

Smith, Rodney 2001b, *Australian Political Culture*, Pearson Education, Sydney.

Wilson, Shaun, Meagher, Gabrielle, Gibson, Rachel, Denemark, David, and Western, Mark 2005, *Australian Social Attitudes*, UNSW Press, Sydney.

Useful websites

- Active Stuff for Social Change at <www.active.org.au>. This site covers most cities in Australia and contains bulletin boards and email lists of current political events, such as talks, marches and group meetings. It also has links to indymedia sites.
- Newspoll Market Research at <www.newspoll.com.au>. This site of the pre-eminent political pollster gives details on different polls and has a search engine for locating polls from the past ten years.
- Australian Social Science Data Archives at <http://assda.anu.edu.au/>. This site provides access to a range of Australian databases of quantitative survey material, including on political behaviour.

CHAPTER 9
PRESSURE GROUPS

In Chapter 8 we defined 'collective action' as activity undertaken with others in a formal or informal group structure to achieve a shared goal or interest, often for the creation of social and political change. In that chapter we concentrated on the involvement of individuals in collective processes through groups or ad hoc political events. In this chapter we will examine collective action from the point of view of what groups and organisations do and the relationship between collective action and formal political institutions. This chapter concentrates on pressure groups that adopt particular strategies to have their messages heard by government. It uses a five-point typology to explain the strategic repertoire of these organisations that encompasses a continuum from the 'insider', government-focused strategy of lobbying to the 'outsider', public opinion-focused strategy of protest. Examples of pressure groups that use these strategies, and issues on which action is formulated, are highlighted throughout the chapter.

The topics covered in this chapter include:

- an explanation of how pressure groups and collective action are integral to the Australian political process
- an analysis of approaches in Australian political science on the involvements of pressure groups in politics
- an overview of existing government approaches to pressure group activity
- details on five strategies used by pressure groups—a continuum of lobbying, advocacy and service provision, strategic research, community organising, to protest.

SNAPSHOT To lobby or not to lobby—is that the right question?

TONY JONES (*Lateline*): Brian Burke, the Premier who virtually invented WA Inc. in the 1980s but ended up in prison as a result, appears to have been resurrected. With the departure of Premier Geoff Gallop, Mr Burke is emerging as a significant player in the West—even, some say, a political kingmaker. Gallop's ban on ministerial contact with Mr Burke has now been lifted by the new Premier, Alan Carpenter, paving the way for vital direct government contact. It's a remarkable reversal of fortune for Mr Burke. He was jailed in 1994 for seven months for rorting his travel expenses and then again in 1997 for six months before the second

> conviction was quashed. Before his fall from grace, some considered Burke a potential Prime Minister. Now his day job is as a political lobbyist, but there's constant speculation about the extent of his behind-the-scenes influence in Labor politics. (ABC 2006)

Brian Burke is a lobbyist. This means that he is hired by business organisations to meet with and try to influence public policy decision-makers. Some of his clients have included developers Australand, Canal Rocks and Urban Pacific, litigation sponsor IMF, mining companies Precious Metals Australia, Fortesque Metals Group and Kimberley Diamond Company (Cohen 2007). It was the work Burke did for Canal Rocks in respect to the Smiths Beach development at Yallingup that led to an investigation into his undue influence over public service officers involved in the development proposal (see Corruption and Crime Commission 2008).

The Western Australian government's Corruption and Crime Commission (CCC) has extensive powers. Established in 2004, it can tap and record phone conversations, use assumed identities, search property and compel witnesses to give evidence (Cohen 2007). It was set up to fight organised crime and monitor the public sector, and it investigates all State government departments and local government authorities (see <www.ccc.wa.gov.au/>). Public hearings were held into the Smiths Beach development in October–December 2006 and in February 2007. During this time Brian Burke's relationship with senior public servants and politicians received widespread media attention (CCC 2008). In evidence to the CCC it was heard that in the ten months to October 2006 Burke made nearly 13,000 phone calls: an average of forty-three every day. As a result of the CCC's work and the recording of Burke's phone calls, four Labor ministers were stood down (Cohen 2007). In November 2006 Burke was forced to resign from the Labor Party, and the Premier of Western Australia, Alan Carpenter, reinstated the ban on members of parliament having contact with Burke.

However, clearly Brian Burke's continued lobbying influence and access to powerful political actors did not end there. In early 2008 the Director General of the Health Department was forced to resign after having been found to be in email contact with Brian Burke, despite claiming otherwise (CCC 2008); and Kevin Rudd was repeatedly questioned, in early 2007 soon after he was elected Leader of the Opposition, about his contact with Brian Burke and a fund-raiser dinner (ABC 2007a). (For more on the Burke scandal, see Warhurst 2007, pp. 50–64.)

What does this case tell us about Australian political processes, the role of powerful lobbyists and of pressure groups more generally? Carmen Lawrence, a recently retired member of federal parliament and a former Premier of Western Australia, has been a vocal commentator on lobbying. She argues for increased scrutiny and regulation at the federal level, similar to what happened in Canada. She suggests:

> some lobbyists are clearly motivated by their own or their shareholders' interests; others by a desire to achieve particular outcomes which they believe will be of benefit to the society or some more narrowly defined sectional interest. Most people would regard such contact as a legitimate and basic right in any democracy, since politicians need to be aware of the needs and wants of various sectors of the community and to be exposed to a range of policy ideas. But it is disturbing that some are more equal than others in this process of persuasion and, worse, that a system of private lobbying, especially when it is linked to substantial campaign donations, may increase the likelihood of frank corruption. (Lawrence 2007, p. 2)

But is all pressure group activity the same? And, as acknowledged above, how do pressure groups also become an important source of information and public opinion for governments that assist them in making appropriate policy decisions?

Political actors and political communities

This section of the book emphasises the role of political actors in the Australian political process as well as questioning an understanding of Australian politics that concentrates solely on the jurisdiction of governments and formal institutions. What this means is that we need to understand Australian politics and the distribution of, and contestations over, power in a three-dimensional sense. The 'political' is not only what is done by governments, as pointed out in

Chapter 1; it is also about the way power is distributed, negotiated and contested in all parts of our lives. Some groups in society are part of that process of creating, maintaining and challenging power and work with, against or even beyond the state. Here we will discuss the importance of these forms of collective action with which individuals choose to engage.

That said, it should also be pointed out that we are not arguing that all groups and all individuals, in a one-dimensional pluralistic sense, have equivalent power to create social, political and economic change. Instead, we are suggesting that the actions of different groups, as well as the state, should be examined to obtain a multifaceted understanding of the landscape of Australian politics. This approach to understanding politics is seen as one that overcomes the state–society dualism that 'has bedevilled the discipline of political science' (Newman & Tanguay 2002, p. 388). This means that the state and broader society are often studied as topics that exist in isolation from one another, rather than starting from a position, as we do here, that sees state and society (also known as community) as interdependent.

To commence this analysis it is important to understand the make-up of the community sector or, as some analysts refer to it, the third sector, after those of government and business. Mark Lyons (2001, p. 5) defines this sector in terms of the voluntariness of individual involvement, the non-profit activity of organisations and the democratic accountability and control of these organisations. The level of commitment to these facets may vary among different organisational types as the Australian community sector is incredibly diverse. Lyons estimates that there are 700,000 community sector organisations and groups in Australia, but only 34,000 are employing organisations. Different types of non-profit community sector organisations have different capacities to generate funds. The three main sources are from charging fees for service or membership, fund-raising or government grants. Table 9.1 gives an overview of the different types of community sector organisation, and compares these organisational categories by annual income, number of paid staff and the proportion of funding that comes from government.

Table 9.1 shows that, income and staff wise, the community sector is dominated by organisations that provide community, health and education services. These organisations also derive nearly 50 per cent of their income from government funding, in that government either contracts these community organisations to provide essential health and community services that it cannot

TABLE 9.1 Understanding the Australian community sector

Type	Income ($ million)	From government (%)	Paid staff
Community services	3870	50	132,250
Health	4391	45	111,480
Education	6982	48	143,830
Other human services	376	44	12,400
Religion	1001	0	17,000
Arts and culture	466	38	6680
Sport and recreation	6491	2	98,340
Interest groups	3251	14	46,980
Economic cooperation	31,561	1	54,390
Philanthropic	80	4	434

Note:

Community services includes children's and youth services, disability services and overseas aid organisations.

Education includes private schools and private universities, university unions, P&Cs.

Other human services includes housing, employment and training organisations, legal services and community transport.

Interest groups includes professional associations, unions, employer and business associations, groups representing economic identities: motorists, pensioners etc., political parties, policy advocacy groups, environment groups and social movement organisations.

Economic cooperation includes friendly societies, credit unions, cooperatives, bodies corporate, some insurance companies that provide services rather than interest representation. Income included interest and insurance pay-outs.

Philanthropic organisations are trusts and foundations that redistribute funding.

Source: adapted from data in Lyons (2001).

provide or subsidises existing health and education services (this is further discussed in Chapter 13). Sport and recreation is another important category in that it employs many staff and as a subsector has a very high income generation, but nearly all of its funding comes from the fees charged for service as barely any is sourced from government or fund-raising. Religious (100 per cent) and community service organisations (27 per cent; that is, mostly overseas aid organisations) are the only types that raise a large proportion of their funds from fund-raising; otherwise fund-raising is not a major source of income. This is also why the philanthropic intermediary organisations are quite small as Australia does not have an extensive tradition of philanthropy as do other countries like the US and Canada (see ACOSS 2005).

The other important category in Table 9.1 is the list of organisations under 'Interest groups'. Organisations included here, such as unions and parties, are well-recognised political actors and are influential in the political process. However, there are fewer of these organisations than the other community sector types. This chapter details organised political actors that are influential in contemporary Australian politics. It is our argument that all of these service-providing (and otherwise) community sector organisations have the potential to be or are very much involved in acting on behalf of their service users and members to influence government. Therefore we will not limit our discussion only to the organisations that Lyons has labelled as interest groups.

In political science several descriptive terms are used to label political actors and groups who are outside government but try to have influence, including interest groups, pressure groups, lobby groups, non-government or community-based organisations, issue movements and social movements.

Understanding pressure groups

We have decided to use the term 'pressure group' in this book as it best describes any group of citizens who act collectively to persuade, or put pressure on, those in positions of political power to change policies or develop new policies (Cook 2004, p. 138). All of the terms in the definition box are used to refer to groups who seek to persuade governments either to incorporate particular viewpoints or to change policy direction. Yet the specific term used often reflects particular understandings of the way the state works and the perceived importance and power of collective action within the political process. Political scientists often talk about interest groups, but we have purposefully chosen not to use this term as it implies that, following the public choice approach, interests can be rationally aggregated into a form of action directed at the state, to which the state duly responds (see Marsh 1995, p. 80). Instead we suggest that political pressure and persuasion happen in myriad ways that do not always reflect people's self-interest and are not always rational.

As with any categorisation, the lines of distinction between different types of collective action is often unclear. There is not always a clear empirical difference, for example, between the practice of pressure groups and social movements; that is, many small but formalised organisations see themselves as part of broader social movements for the creation of social and political change, but will also operate within government-led policy-making initiatives and be seen as pressure groups (see Richardson 2000; Newman & Tanguay 2002, p. 399). A potential resolution to this categorical tension will be discussed in the later section 'Strategic repertoires of Australian pressure groups' but first we need to explore further how political scientists discuss the involvement of pressure groups in Australian politics.

Authors who write about interest groups tend to focus on powerful groups involved in influencing the political process. They describe groups that promote or protect a particular interest or issue and try to make government change or reinforce an existing policy position. It is, however, recognised that all interest groups are not created equal and that there are 'insider' and 'outsider' groups (see Matthews 1997, pp. 270–1). The insider/outsider distinction was developed more than twenty-five years ago by Wyn Grant to differentiate between alternative strategic approaches used by organisations (Grant 2004, p. 408). Insider groups often have an economic focus, have financial backing and have direct access to government. They are also often seen as groups who are protecting their own interests in their relationship with government.

Recognition of the insider status of a particular group is usually dependent upon the period being examined and on the government in power. For example, trade unions are categorised as outsider groups when there is a Coalition federal government in office because they do not have direct access and political influence. Trade unions were classified as insider groups when the ALP was in power federally from 1983 to 1996, and this was attributed to the corporatist-style Accord Agreement between the government and unions. However, the influence of unions on even the ALP is argued to be diluted now (see Griffin et al. 2004). When a Liberal–National federal government is discussed it is often suggested that such groups as the National Farmers Federation, which has links with the

National Party, and the Business Council of Australia have prioritised insider status.

Outsider interest groups usually have limited resources and limited access to government. They are often labelled as groups that promote (rather than protect) interests or values. Examples often used are small organisations such as the feminist Women's Electoral Lobby, the Gay and Lesbian Rights Lobby, anti-abortion Right to Life groups and so on. Groups of this type are interested in promoting a particular view of social life and are not motivated primarily by economic interests. They are, however, also interested in governments instituting legislative change that conforms with their views (see Beresford 2000, pp. 118–26).

There are limitations in using only these associated binary categories—insider/outsider, promoter/protector—to explain how groups are involved in political processes. It is rare to find a group that always fits neatly into one or the other category and, as we have seen, this can change over time. These categorisations reflect distinctive understandings of power relationships in two main ways: first, they prioritise the collective action undertaken by the groups, which is directly aimed at the state, and the groups are subsequently seen and categorised in this light, and second, the categorisations tend to prioritise the economic foundations of these groups at the expense of any ability they may have to engage in social or political persuasion, aside from their economic influence.

Ian Marsh (1995) has made an important contribution to the analysis of the roles of organisations in shaping Australian politics, in that he differentiates between interest groups and issue movements and sees both as reflective of a period in Australian politics in which Australians are no longer being represented by, or even reliant on their allegiance to, the two major party groupings (Marsh 1995, pp. 47–81). Thus, he believes that Australians now turn toward (what we call) pressure groups and social movements to better represent their interests and political views within the political system.

Marsh makes two primary distinctions between pressure groups and social movements: first, that pressure groups lobby or attempt to reform the state in the guise of creating further equality, whereas movements are more interested in challenging the whole scale values of the state, and second, he refers to the material/post-material classification of American political scientist Ronald Inglehart, which suggests that new social movements are an expression of post-materialist values based on such factors as participation, lifestyle and nature

(Marsh 1995, p. 47). Australian pressure groups are grouped into four main categories on the basis of whom they represent in negotiations they have with governments:

- **producer groups:** organisations that represent individuals involved in the production of goods and services, such as trade unions and employer groups
- **welfare state client groups:** organisations that represent individuals receiving benefits from the state, for example, health education, housing and income support
- **welfare state producer groups:** organisations that provide services to clients whose funding is partially or wholly provided by government, for example health and education providers and welfare agencies
- **professional groups:** organisations that seek to manage the complex growth of regulation of professional occupations and represent members.

Table 9.2 provides examples of some of the organisations in Australia that fit these four pressure group categories. The table also includes the website addresses for all to enable you to compare and contrast the purposes of the organisations. While these four broad categories are useful in distinguishing between the different purposes of different organisations, especially in terms of whom they represent, very little is learnt about what they actually do and on what kind of ideological premise they base their action. To best understand the role of pressure groups in the Australian political system we need also to look at the different strategies they utilise.

To this point in the chapter we have explained what pressure groups are and whom they represent. We have until now neglected the role of government in both granting access and inviting pressure groups into the political process. There are two ways we can understand the active role of government in fostering relationships with pressure groups: first through recently established formal consultation processes, and second through the debate over how much regulation needs to exist over the relationship between those who seek to persuade and those who make decisions.

Consultation is about government listening to views and taking them into account when making public policy decisions. Pressure groups are increasingly involved in consultation processes with government over policy decision-making. Consultation assumes that there needs to be some kind of exchange between the

TABLE 9.2 Examples of Australian pressure groups

Producer groups	Welfare state: Client	Welfare state: Producer	Professional groups
Business Council of Australia <www.bca.com.au>	Australian Council of Social Services <www.acoss.org.au>	Smith Family <www.smithfamily.com.au>	Australian Medical Association <www.ama.com.au>
Australian Council of Trade Unions <www.actu.asn.au>	Australian Consumers Association <www.choice.com.au>	Australian Red Cross <www.redcross.org.au>	Real Estate Institute <www.reiaustralia.com.au>
National Farmers Federation <www.nff.org.au>	Mental Health Council of Australia <www.mhca.com.au>	Independent Schools' Council of Australia <www.isca.edu.au>	Royal Australian College of General Practitioners <www.racgp.org.au>
Australian Chamber of Commerce and Industry <www.acci.asn.au>	Returned & Services League of Australia <www.rsl.org.au>	National Disability Services <www.nds.org.au>	Law Council of Australia <www.lawcouncil.asn.au>

government and the public, but that government is obliged to make the final, binding decision. Government does not give power to others in the consultation process, but there is a degree of reciprocity because government acknowledges that those being consulted have some influence and can change the direction of policy (see Edwards 2001). Consultation is carried out in the following five main ways:

- meeting key community contacts
- conducting surveys of public opinion
- arranging pressure group meetings
- organising public meetings
- releasing discussion papers and inviting public comment (see Bishop & Davis 2001).

Consultation is different from the pressure group strategic repertoires (discussed below) because consultation and its political agenda is at the discretion of governments (either federal, State or local), and usually takes the form of an invitation to participate in the decision-making process. Some State and local governments have been the leaders in using consultation processes with a commitment to new governance processes and devolved decision-making (Head 2007, p. 449). Recent initiatives by the federal government, such as Community Cabinets, suggest a new agenda for consultation and participation at the federal level.

> Community Cabinet meetings are part of the Prime Minister's commitment to ensure consultation with the Australian people on the things that concern them, whether they are national or local matters. These meetings give people in the community an opportunity to meet Cabinet members in person and ask questions directly about issues important to them. Community Cabinet meetings will be held at various venues across Australia and will generally be held on Sundays.
>
> *Source*: Department of the Prime Minister and Cabinet <www.pmc.gov.au/community_cabinet/index.cfm>.

Despite these new participation and consultation agendas, few analysts see that they herald a new era of governance whereby decisions are made by deliberation and consensus among equal players. There are still major differences in power and responsibility between government on the one hand and community and business representatives on the other. Instead, as Head (2007, p. 452) points out, pressure group conflicts remain central to decision-making, and existing consultation processes have not demonstrated an open commitment by governments to 'power-sharing' as they retain control through regulation, funding and service contracts.

The second role of government, after providing arenas for consultation, is as a regulator of the access and power that pressure groups have. There is continuous debate in Australia about the lack of transparency and decisive regulation of how pressure groups and business and community sector organisations generally gain access to and influence political decision-makers (see Fitzgerald 2007; Lawrence 2007; Warhurst 2007). Australia has very little regulation, and there are a variety of means through which pressure group representatives can gain access to and influence politicians and public servants. Recently the Australian Parliamentary Research Group (2007, p. 58) released a manifesto that called for a series of measures to increase transparency and accountability in Australian political processes, and one focus was on the lack of regulation of some lobbying and advocacy activities. The group suggested that every minister and government agency establish a publicly accessible website that lists every instance of lobbying activity. Lobbyists would need to be registered and release information about their organisation, including their organisation, staff, clients and contact details. A new register of lobbyists to be kept by the government agency, Prime Minister and Cabinet was announced in January 2008, but this new directive made no commitment to registering individual instances of lobbying activity and making this information publicly available (see <http://democratic.audit.anu.edu.au/misc/ruddmincodeconduct.pdf>). No matter what, as John Warhurst (2007, p. 77) points out, a new regulatory system of pressure group activity will be expensive and complex. It will put extra pressure not just on governments but also on both well-resourced and less well-resourced pressure groups and the community sector more generally. Yet many think these costs are worthwhile as 'regulating lobbyists would send important messages to the general population about open government' (Warhurst 2007, p. 79)—an important gesture in an age when, as we saw in Chapter 8, citizens are increasingly cynical about government and politicians.

Strategic repertoires of Australian pressure groups

In this book we have chosen to emphasise how different pressure groups use different strategies and approaches to promote their message within Australian political processes. Recent work in this field argues that an examination of strategies used and existing resources held by pressure groups is able to present a more sophisticated understanding of both insider- and outsider-oriented pressure groups and their status within Australian politics (McKinney & Halpin 2007).

Choices over which strategy pressure groups use are affected by:

- the resources available to them, such as incoming funds, paid staff and volunteers
- their total funding, from such sources as government, corporations, philanthropy or membership

- any particular political issues; that is, some issues will dictate what is the best strategy to use to communicate a group's point of view
- the economic and political climate, such as a judgement on which strategy will be received best by the intended recipient, and whether the prevailing economic and political climate will be amenable to that strategy
- the philosophy or ideological foundations of the group.

Pressure groups can be seen to adopt one, or different combinations of, the five strategic approaches described in the box 'Strategies used by Australian pressure groups'. This list of five strategies has been constructed as a continuum from the strategy that is most explicitly directed at government (lobbying) to the strategy that is often least likely to be explicitly directed at government (protest). We could also label this as a continuum from reformist strategies to strategies that start to challenge the state and may be more akin to social movement action. This list of strategies contextualises Wyn Grant's (2000) insider/outsider formulation in that insider strategies are lobbying and advocacy and service provision, and outsider strategies are community organising and protest. Strategic research can be utilised as either an insider or outsider strategy.

Each of these strategies will be examined in detail below.

Strategies used by Australian pressure groups

Lobbying includes direct approaches made to government representatives with the intent of persuading them to accept a group's perspective. It is done through such means as organised meetings, attending political functions, political donations, petitions, letter-writing, providing submissions to government inquiries and responding to policy proposals.

Advocacy and service provision strategies are used when pressure groups speak *on behalf of* those less collectively organised to speak up to the state themselves. For example, service-delivering community organisations and charities often advocate for policy reforms to reduce and prevent poverty and inequality, and thus speak on behalf of the poor and the homeless.

Strategic research is the production of systematically collected evidence and research. It will be undertaken to enable pressure groups to be in an authoritative position, and to persuade government and the general public of their claims.

Community organising is when pressure groups facilitate political change by working with other groups in society. It is different from advocacy in that groups work together in the creation of change within communities and less emphasis is put on making claims on the state. This strategy prioritises networking, distribution of information to the general public and resource-sharing between groups.

Protest is the use of such tactics as demonstrations, rallies, sit-ins, crashing websites and civil disobedience to protest symbolically against, and disrupt, the actions of others, including the state.

Lobbying

Lobbying is the main strategy focused on in existing considerations of pressure group activity. This strategy is targeted directly at government and is most invested in persuading government to act in the interests of a particular group or political issue. The tactics available within the strategic repertoire of lobbying include having formal or informal meetings with decision-makers, being invited to participate in official advisory committees and paying to attend functions that guarantee access to a minister or other influential parliamentarian. These approaches demonstrate the importance of guaranteed access to powerful political actors in generating successful lobbying activities.

Lobbying by pressure groups falls into two approaches: those for whom lobbying is their main activity, and those who choose to combine lobbying with other strategies. There was an increase in the first approach in the 1990s, particularly through the growth of organisations that are contracted by other pressure groups to do lobbying on their behalf. In one estimate there are now more than a thousand lobbyists based in Canberra alone and more than $1 billion is spent on lobbying federal and State governments annually (Fitzgerald 2007). The major political parties and many producer groups realised that they can 'buy in' the skills they need for a particular issue or campaign, rather than totally construct campaigns in-house. Lobbying organisations are traditionally associated with US-style politics but play an increasingly important role in Australia as they intersect with the established industries of public relations, advertising and 'spin doctors' discussed in Chapter 7.

Many large law and accounting firms have specialised government relations or public affairs departments that engage in lobbying activity. Specialist lobbying organisations often have established communication links with a particular political party and are hired by organisations that want to convey a particular political message to that party. Other lobbying organisations attempt to be bipartisan and will often have individuals on staff who have previously worked for both of the major parties as, for example, policy advisers. Former politicians of all persuasions are also often found working in lobbying organisations (see Warhurst 2007, pp. 10–13).

Specialist lobbying services are filling a gap as there is a perception that outsiders have very little understanding of the way political processes within government actually work. This belief is reflected in the quote below from a Canberra-based lobbyist, who worked previously both as a political adviser for the ALP and as a journalist:

> The old mates' club died out years ago. The key skill is knowing how the system works; where the pressure points are, how the bureaucracy interacts with government, how Senate committees work, how ministers reach decisions. It is not something you can read in a book. (Schmidt 2001, p. 58)

Lobbying tactics used by business associations illustrate the organisations that represent Ian Marsh's producer group category and, to a lesser extent, the professional pressure group category. Marsh points out that producer groups are different from the other groupings due to their scale, wealth and reach and because they generate political influence due to their economic significance (2000, p. 181). We also saw the power of individual lobbyists in the snapshot. Currently about 600 individual lobbyists have official parliamentary passes, administered by the Department of Parliamentary Services, to enable their access to federal parliamentarians. However, this list is not yet publicly accessible unlike more transparent lobbyist lists in Canada and the US (Fitzgerald 2007, p. 3).

Business groups form representative associations that act on their behalf in processes of lobbying and consultation to enable them to shape policy processes and/or to exercise veto power (see Head 2007, p. 448). One example is in the Business Council of Australia text box.

Business Council of Australia

The Business Council of Australia (BCA) was formed in 1983 as a forum for Australia's business leaders to contribute to public policy debates through lobbying and strategic research (see <www.bca.com.au/>). Some of the issues it lists on its website as needing public policy reform include: fiscal discipline in the federal government budget, overhaul of federal–State relations, tax reform, efficient infrastructure development and streamlining of business regulation. The BCA is an association of chief executive officers (CEOs) from a hundred of the largest Australian corporations. This includes Australian listed companies, such as Lend Lease, Wesfarmers, Visy, Macquarie Bank and Qantas, and multinational subsidiaries like Shell Australia and Rio Tinto, and one statutory authority (Australia Post). It is 'now widely acknowledged as the nation's premier big business lobby group' (Shields 2005, p. 300).

Paul Broad (2001) undertook survey research with twenty-five major Australian business associations to assess whether their relationship with government had changed. He found that fifteen of the organisations estimated that 70 per cent or more of their time was taken up by public policy-related activities. High-profile organisations and mining organisations estimated that they spent nearly all of their time on this type of work. Organisations that were less government focused tended to spend more time providing services and training for their membership, including educating them about workplace health, safety and environmental issues. Most organisations had increased the amount of lobbying they did of individual senators and independents. Broad attributes much of this shift to two factors: first, most peak national business associations now see that it is their primary role to be involved in public policy issues and, second, with frequent changes in government at national and State levels there is often a re-negotiation of the relationship and the 'regulatory burden' on business (2001).

Business- and industry-oriented pressure groups occupy a privileged position of access and power that is shared by very few other types of pressure group. This does not mean that business and government always have a harmonious relationship. The relationship often shifts over time, and can be dependent on such factors as the political party in power, the state of the economy, the climate of opinion toward business and the ability of shared business interests to act together (Ravenhill 1997).

Lobbying is also successfully used as a strategy by pressure groups that have less resources and are less powerful than business-led pressure groups. Some pressure groups use lobbying together with other reformist strategies, such as service provision and advocacy. Presenting petitions to parliaments and providing submissions to government inquiries are two tactics used to lobby and persuade government when direct access to parliamentary members is not guaranteed. It is clear that for some of these representatives, primarily community-based service-providing groups, the only opportunity they have to be involved in government-led decision-making is by attempting to persuade members of parliament in forums such as these (for more on parliamentary committees see Chapter 4). Direct access is rare for groups that do not have established networks and ample resources; however, some pressure groups, in recognition of their representative function, will be invited to join advisory committees.

The important focus of analysis here is that transparent processes are established for organisations without direct access to government, but the same impetus for transparency is not levelled at exclusive meetings of government actors with other lobbyists; that is, organisations without direct access may be able to influence the policy process, but the parameters of influence are established through formal, government-led consultation initiatives.

Advocacy and service provision

Advocacy is about acting on behalf of disadvantaged social groups who are not collectively organised, and as a pressure group strategy it is also about being critical and challenging access to and the distribution of power. 'At its core advocacy is about the ways we seek to influence the distribution of political, social and economic goods. It's about how we get access to power, opportunity, benefits' (Hogan 1996, p. 158). Consequently pressure groups use advocacy tactics to argue publicly for or to criticise new policy-making directions and the distribution of government resources. It was established at the beginning of this section that different strategies come to the fore at different times, often depending on the surrounding political and economic climate. Ken Moffatt and his co-writers suggest:

> While advocacy is acknowledged as an essential element of community practice, funding bodies do not fully endorse this activity. In a climate of political conservatism, advocacy on behalf of marginalised groups is interpreted as 'special interest group' activities. (Moffatt et al. 1999, p. 315)

The implication is that these 'special interest' groups are not able to represent marginalised sections of society properly to policy-makers (Sawer 2002). Carol Johnson (2000) argues that this shift is one that privileges an idea of mainstream Australia while constructing groups that advocate for particular interests as divisive; that is, social conservatives believe groups in Australian society that arguably have less access to power and resources, such as indigenous Australians, people with disabilities, people from non-English-speaking backgrounds, the homeless, the poor, young people and so on, do not need advocacy organisations to speak on their behalf.

Recent research based on an email survey of Australian non-government organisations found that advocacy-oriented organisations (58 per cent) acknowledged that their key messages were often critical of the federal government. However, a majority also believed that they were at least moderately successful in having their message heard by government (Maddison et al. 2004, p. 31). Where they were divided was around the *types* of organisation that believed their advocacy work was less likely to be listened to by government. Organisations concerned with women's issues were most likely to say that they were not at all successful in being heard, and both women's issues and human rights organisations thought that they had become less successful in having their message heard since the mid-1990s. The barriers to organisations having their messages heard were most likely to be that the federal government was not interested, that the media was not interested and that they did not have the analytical resources available to do this work. The extent of government funding did not seem to have a clear relationship to whether or not organisations were able to comment on government policy. However, up to a quarter of organisations acknowledged that their funding agreement restricted their capacity to comment on government policy (Maddison et al. 2004, pp. 32–7). Recent federal government policy has moved away from this approach, and in early January 2008 Deputy Prime Minister Julia Gillard announced that contracts would be renegotiated to remove clauses that prevent non-government organisations (NGOs) and other community groups from criticising the government (ABC 2008).

The other dimension to advocacy and service provision is the changing role of the community sector as it increasingly delivers services that were once the sole preserve of the public sector (see also Chapter 13). Mark Considine (2003, p. 63) sees this shift as 'the most radical change to state–society relations since the advent of the modern welfare state'. He argues that this increased focus on a service provision role for many community organisations has started to erode the distinctiveness of the sector. This is because there is less focus on the particular needs of community-based service users and time for associated advocacy work, with increased emphasis on fulfilling the administrative burden imposed by the government agency purchasing service provision (Considine 2003, p. 75).

Despite this sometimes hostile political context, advocacy-oriented pressure groups continue to play an important role in Australian politics. One important group is the Australian Council of Social Service (ACOSS), the peak council for community welfare organisations. Its website states that the aims of ACOSS are:

> to reduce poverty and inequality by developing and promoting socially, economically and environmentally responsible public policy and action by government, community and business while supporting non-government organisations which provide assistance to vulnerable Australians. (<www.acoss.org.au/About.aspx?displayID=1>)

ACOSS has always had a limited resource base as the people it represents, the unemployed and those in poverty, do not have the resources to fund advocacy. As a result successive federal governments have provided funding for undertaking advocacy work to ACOSS and many other peak representative organisations. It has long been considered that it is important for government to enable disadvantaged groups to participate in the formulation and implementation of policy. ACOSS itself has argued for continued funding to peak organisations because they provide a crucial role in promoting participation in liberal democracies by:

- representing the interests of disadvantaged groups, who might otherwise be without a direct voice
- promoting the free flow of a range of ideas and viewpoints
- encouraging a more competitive environment for the development of policy and program options (ACOSS parliamentary submission cited in May 1996, p. 255).

The argument being presented here is that the inclusion of such groups as ACOSS in the policy-making processes enhances the democratic nature of those processes. However, groups, such as ACOSS, have had to adapt their role as policy advocates. In the past the role of organisations of this type was primarily to appeal on behalf of disadvantaged people, on the basis of social or moral values. Now these organisations are expected to be able to present persuasive arguments based on research and rationality (May 1996, p. 250). This is particularly seen with the government-led shift away from the large-scale funding of various representative organisations that commenced in the 1970s, and toward the establishment of government-fostered consultative mechanisms. One clear example of this is the federal defunding of the Australian Youth Policy and Action Coalition in the late 1990s and its replacement with the National Youth Roundtable: fifty Australian young people were selected annually to participate in a dialogue with the government; they then returned to their communities and consulted young people to develop a comprehensive picture of their views and attitudes. The Roundtable did not claim to be representative or to foster participation, as its focus is on the processes of consultation. It was disbanded in early 2008.

Seeing service provision alone as a strategy used by groups in collective action is sometimes contentious. This is because many would not see that providing a service influences political processes. However, there are some obvious examples of service provision reflecting broader concerns in advocating political and social change. For example, groups reflecting a feminist ideological position can be found running refuges for women and families who need to be supported to get away from violent situations. Another important example is community legal centres, which are independent organisations that provide legal advice and advocacy for a wide range of individuals and groups in the broader community. The services are particularly targeted at people on low incomes or those who are otherwise disadvantaged in their access to justice, such as indigenous Australians. As well as providing direct legal advice and assistance, legal centres carry out a range of related activities aimed at addressing systemic problems. These activities include law reform, test case litigation, referrals and community legal education, such as books, pamphlets, classes, videos, radio programs, training kits and so on.

Strategic research

Strategic research is concerned with mapping alternative approaches and specifies potential differences, intentions, effects and costs of various policy programs. It is often undertaken by pressure groups generally, and think tanks in particular, to persuade others of specific viewpoints. Strategic research can be used as either an insider or an outsider strategy as it can be used simultaneously to influence the opinion of both government and general public opinion.

Research is undertaken by a range of people acting within a number of institutions. Most people think of universities as the primary place where research is undertaken; however, there are many locations for producing research that can potentially influence policy-making, the media and public opinion. Examples of these locations are:

- universities (by individual academics)
- university research centres (for example, Social Policy Research Centre)
- government research centres (for example, Australian Institute of Family Studies)
- parliamentary committees and commissions of inquiry
- pressure groups (for example, the Smith Family and trade unions)
- think tanks (for example, Centre for Independent Studies, Australian Strategic Policy Institute)
- consultants (for example, Access Economics).

Three main types of research are carried out by social scientists working in these locations:

- basic or curiosity-driven research, which expands our understanding of social and political processes
- applied research, which makes us capable of influencing the social and political processes by answering questions on policy problems
- strategic research, which is concerned with mapping alternative approaches and specifies the potential differences, intentions, effects and costs of various policy programs (Keen 1993).

It is the third type, strategic research, that we examine as part of the strategic repertoire of Australian pressure groups.

Strategic research is often undertaken by pressure groups to persuade others of specific viewpoints or directions for policy-making. Strategic research differs from applied research in that it explores the impact of different policy-making approaches. It is more concerned with the long-term goals of policy-making than thinking about broad policy 'problems' as applied research does. Strategic research differs from basic research in that it is less abstract and less theoretical. While basic research often aims to uncover 'truth' about the social and political world, strategic research seeks to find the solution to fundamental problems and to advance new policy programs.

Pressure groups that use strategic research as a strategy come from a variety of ideological backgrounds. Arguably there has been an increase in the number of specialised think tanks in Australia in recent years. Think tanks are independent, non-government organisations that focus mainly on conducting strategic research with the intention of influencing public opinion and policy outcomes (Stone 1991, p. 200). Ian Marsh highlights the emergence since 1975 of conservative think tanks, which promote the values of classical economic and political liberalism (1995, p. 78). Two mentioned organisations, the Centre for Independent Studies (CIS) and the Institute of Public Affairs (IPA), are funded by publication subscriptions, membership and private donations. They both publish journals and have paid research staff, and these staff regularly write opinion pieces in major newspapers. Marsh argues that these conservative think tanks have been influential in publishing strategic research, especially through formulating 'agendas concerned with economic liberalisation, privatisation, deregulation, labour market reform and contraction of government' (1995, p. 79).

Progressive groups also utilise strategic research, yet have not been as prolific as such organisations as CIS and IPA. For example, in the past, unions often produced in-house strategic research. This is now done less often as unions experienced a rapid decrease in their membership and have limited money to spend on functions that do not directly service their members. When pressure groups, including unions, can no longer afford paid staff to undertake strategic research they will often commission university researchers to do the research for them, because universities have both the resources and academic legitimacy to collect persuasive evidence. One example is the research report *Australia at Work* (see van Wanrooy et al. 2007), which was co-funded by the Australian Research Council and Unions NSW, and undertaken by the University of Sydney-based Workplace Research Centre. It used survey data to investigate Australians' experiences of industrial relations reform and WorkChoices in particular. The publication of the research helped supplement the advocacy, community organising and educating strategies undertaken by Australian unions as part of their Your Rights at Work Campaign. However, as often happens to strategic research that intends to influence policy outcomes, the report also became quite controversial and was extensively criticised by Liberal Party politicians, other pressure groups and some in the media (for example see ABC 2007b). This demonstrates that fundamental to what think tanks do, and to strategic research itself, is the contribution to public discourse, and inevitably these discourses and ideas are contested by those who do not agree with research findings and recommendations.

Community organising

Community organising is a political process pressure groups use to work together and obtain social justice for disadvantaged citizens through collective action. It is underpinned by a belief in participatory democracy. Community organising came to prominence in many developed countries in the late 1960s and early 1970s, at the same time as other new movements that aimed to create social and political change. Many initial community projects were funded by the federal Whitlam government, through the Australian Assistance Plan, so communities could take the responsibility for creating change at the grassroots level. New organisations, called regional councils, were set up to facilitate these processes. Community organising projects still exist in disadvantaged geographic communities, for example projects among the Aboriginal population in Redfern in Sydney and Fitzroy in Melbourne. In recent years these grassroots projects have seen a resurgence and are often funded by local councils to give local communities a say in development processes and other localised decisions.

Furthermore, pressure groups often use this strategy to prioritise the importance of instilling values and changing public opinion through the provision of information on issues and political ideas. This is particularly the case when pressure groups believe there is no point trying to reform and lobby the government. In their community education role, pressure groups may hold public meetings, debates and teach-ins, and they may also publish leaflets. Some groups will use community organising as an offshoot of their lobbying and advocacy work, while others will reject lobbying activity as cooperation with the state and will tend to prioritise protest actions. Ken Kollman (1998) refers to this kind of educative, public opinion-focused strategy, which is less obviously aimed at the state, as 'outside lobbying'. He suggests that it is important because it 'simultaneously communicates [signals] to policy-makers the salience of policy issues among constituents and increases the salience of issues among constituents [expands the conflict]' (Kollman 1998, p. 58).

Pressure groups use community organising strategies to bring together diverse members of a community, whether that community is based on a shared geographical space, such as a suburb, or on a shared identity, such as ethnicity. For example, ethnicity-based organisations will often practise community organising when they are trying to create a network of people with shared interests and identity. Networking and community organising tactics are also used in bringing together diverse groups for a common cause. For example, the anti-war in Iraq protests that culminated across the world in February 2003 relied on email and the Internet to bring together a diverse range of environmental pressure groups, unions, church and religious groups, political parties, human rights and peace pressure groups and individual activists to organise local events.

The importance of grassroots community organising has recently been emphasised as a successful strategy that was used by unions in attempting to change the culture of union political practice and persuade the public about industrial relations. This campaign started in 1999 when the Australian Council of Trade Unions (ACTU) released a report, called Unions@Work, that signalled a major policy shift and was the first big overview of union activity in about ten years. The report argued that unions needed to move towards more grassroots organising strategies. It emphasised using new technology and suggested using email and websites extensively to promote campaigns. It also suggested that unions needed to build alliances with community organisations to influence public debate, particularly when the political environment internationally had been hostile to collective action undertaken by unions. This new direction culminated in the Your Rights at Work campaign, which influenced the outcome of the 2007 federal election. This campaign was based on organising local community-oriented Your Rights at Work groups that campaigned in workplaces and throughout the election campaign against WorkChoices. The campaign's primary focus was on changing public opinion about workers' rights and about unions as well as potentially changing people's vote.

What becomes apparent is that groups will often use strategies, such as community organising, that have an internal or general public focus when they want to build membership, strengthen coalitions and networks, or change ideas and cultures of practice.

Protest

Of the five strategies that have been examined here, protest receives the most media attention; that is, when we think of citizens interacting with government we will rarely be provided with visual images of strategic research or lobbying by pressure groups. We are more likely to think of direct action events, such as Earth Hour in 2007, when households and workplaces around Australia turned off their lights to conserve energy and acknowledge global warming, or the *Sea Shepherd* chasing Japanese whaling ships in early 2007 and 2008, or the Clubs NSW mobilisation against increases in poker machine taxes in 2003. All of these protest events received extensive media coverage and little condemnation, instead being portrayed as a normal expression of public opinion (see Grant 2004). This demonstrates that protest events for some pressure groups, have become a normal part of their strategic repertoire and are used to influence both governments and public opinion.

Protest comes in a variety of forms, such as rallies, marches, strikes, sit-ins, blockades, stunts and collective acts of civil disobedience. It will also just as often be called non-violent 'direct action'. Protest can be used by groups to commemorate or mark an event; for example, the annual International Women's Day marches usually held on the first Saturday in March around Australia and the rest of the world. Protest can also be used by groups to publicise a political issue and bring together a large group of people; for example, the large rallies organised in support of East Timorese independence in 1999. Some pressure groups will use protest in combination with other activities, such as lobbying or advocacy, and they will be using it for two reasons: to bring together a group of people who share a viewpoint, and to grab government and media attention. Other organisations will use protest activities as their primary strategy to challenge society as they do not see that directly lobbying government will bring about social and political change. These groups are usually part of social movements and will be discussed in more detail in the following chapter.

Here we shall look at contrasting examples of various types of protest by looking at three different environment pressure groups that use this strategy. Note that all of these groups have a broader strategic repertoire than protest, which includes strategic research and occasionally using lobbying and advocacy.

Stunts by paid activists

Greenpeace is one of the world's most widely recognised environmental protest organisations. Its Australian branch opened in the mid-1980s. It regularly utilises stunts by its paid activists to highlight the environmental issues on which it is campaigning. On its website it suggests that its use of non-violent direct action (NVDA) becomes necessary when 'lobbying or negotiations with decision-makers fails. Greenpeace uses NVDA as a means of peaceful protest to expose global environmental problems and force solutions that ensure a green and peaceful future' (see <www.greenpeace.org/australia/about/work/methods/non-violent>). For example, it has raised banners in unusual places, such as on Flinders Street Station, Melbourne, to protest against genetically engineered foods in 2008; on the Sydney Opera House in 1986 protesting against French nuclear testing; and on a container ship due to be loaded with nuclear waste in October 2000, when four activists also chained themselves to the container. Recently it has also been involved in anti-whaling campaigns. Greenpeace receives a high level of media attention for these stunts. Another of its other high-profile campaigns has been on reducing climate change, but this was not seen benevolently. In August 2002 three Greenpeace climbers scaled the flagpole at Parliament House in Canberra and protested to the government by unfurling a banner reading 'Ratify Kyoto Now'. Seven Greenpeace activists were arrested and charged with Commonwealth trespass.

Civil disobedience and blockading forests

The Wilderness Society (TWS) was established in Australia in 1976 to protect wilderness in Tasmania and to save the Franklin River from being dammed. TWS continues to have a major focus on forest protection, and is the only environmental pressure group with forest campaigns in most states: New South Wales, Victoria, Tasmania, Queensland and Western Australia. TWS has organised a number of non-violent civil disobedience campaigns that have involved activists 'sitting-in' for weeks or months at a time. Examples of long-term blockades include the Tasmanian Franklin dam blockade in 1982, protests against wood-chipping in the forests of south-eastern New South Wales in 1989 and the Jabiluka anti-uranium mine protest in the Northern Territory in 1998 (Williams 1998).

The blockading of the Franklin River dam site in 1982 was an important event for Australian environmental activists as it represented a coming of age for the environmental movement. It mobilised large numbers of activists and supporters around the issues, developing skills and resources, and it helped environmentalism become an influential force in Australian political life. However, few forestry companies look favourably on blockading of their day-to-day business. In 2004 Gunns, a Tasmania-based woodchip company, launched a court case to sue twenty environmental activists and organisations, including TWS and Greens Senator Bob Brown, for damage to its company and disruption of its operations. At the time of writing the case is proceeding, with fewer defendants and a narrower claim, through the Australian legal system (see <www.gunns20.org>).

Rallies and marches

Rallies and marches are often used to create awareness of an issue and can also, potentially, lead to a new group solidarity on that issue. Large turnouts at rallies and marches are also symbolically important because they are often used as evidence of the support base an organisation, or a political issue, has in the broader community. Friends of the Earth (FoE) has a long history of working on anti-military issues nationally, including protesting against arms fairs and US military bases during the 1980s and campaigning against uranium mining and nuclear testing and dumping in the 1980s and 1990s. FoE also regularly uses community organising and educating tactics to create broad levels of support among the general community, not just among political activists. For example, in 2000–02, FoE was extensively involved with other community and environmental organisations in protesting against the building of a new nuclear reactor at the Lucas Heights site in Sydney where there is an existing reactor. Local community groups in the Sutherland Shire of Sydney were very successful at bringing together large groups of people when they organised rallies and marches on this issue.

This chapter has demonstrated that pressure groups seeking to influence and change Australian politics adopt a range of strategies that depend on both their power in society and the resources available to them. The following chapter will look at how social movements attempt to change social and political values and the nature of Australian society itself.

Summary

- It is important to examine the interaction between pressure groups and government so as to best understand the Australian political process. Pressure groups are important within this process because they promote vibrant democratic practice and a broad range of viewpoints.
- Previous understandings of pressure groups are limited because they do not fully examine the process and strategies that groups utilise.
- Examining the strategies pressure groups use helps us to understand their different agendas and the different levels of access they have to power and decision-making.

Further reading

Davis, Glyn and Weller, Patrick (eds) 2001, *Are You Being Served? States, Citizens and Governance,* Allen & Unwin, Sydney.

Marsh, Ian 1995, *Beyond the Two Party System: Political Representation, Economic Competitiveness and Australian Politics,* Cambridge University Press, Melbourne.

Sawer, Marian and Zappala, Gianni (eds) 2001, *Speaking for the People: Representation in Australian Politics,* Melbourne University Press, Melbourne.

Warhurst, John 2007, *Behind Closed Doors: Politics, Scandals and the Lobbying Industry,* UNSW Press, Sydney.

Useful websites

- Australian Medical Association at <www.ama.com.au>. The AMA website provides access to speeches, media releases, policy positions and discussion papers dealing with medical, political, medico-legal and public health issues relevant to the doctors for whom the association lobbies.
- Australian Council of Social Service at <www.acoss.org.au>. The ACOSS website includes a 'News and media' section that highlights the current advocacy campaigns the organisation is involved in. It also includes a section that provides access to its research publications.
- Australian Council of Trade Unions at <www.actu.asn.au>. The peak trade union website lists the current campaigns in which Australian unions, and unions internationally, are engaged. It also provides access to educational resources for workers and policy-oriented submissions made to government inquiries.
- National Farmers Federation at <www.nff.org.au>. The federation website details the major policy positions taken up by the organisation in its lobbying and advocacy work on behalf of Australian farmers.

CHAPTER 10
SOCIAL MOVEMENTS

This chapter moves beyond an examination of the participation of individuals and the strategies used by pressure groups to highlight examples of the practices of participatory democracy and collective action through movements for change in Australia. Major established movements such as the labour, women's, environment, indigenous, gay and lesbian, global justice and peace movements will be discussed here. We will also examine the conservative, neoliberal movements that formed to respond to and reject the forms of participatory democracy advocated by progressive movements for change. Social movements share four dimensions: an active network of individuals groups and organisations; a sense of shared identity; a conflict with powerful political actors; and the use of protest and direct action strategic repertoires.

The topics covered in this chapter include:

- an explanation of how processes of social change and collective action underpin understandings of social movements
- an overview of the various ways to theorise social movements—an analytical schema is proposed to assist in understanding Australian social movements
- an analysis of recent Australian social movement activity, including counter-movement activities
- the possibilities for future social movement action.

SNAPSHOT Protesting for peace: the 2003 anti-war movement

The peace marches that took place around the world on the weekend of 15 February 2003 were a powerful social movement action that attracted hundreds of thousands of people in cities everywhere. It was estimated that there were a million participants Australia-wide, making it the biggest set of marches Australia had ever seen. The aim of the protest event was simple: to demonstrate the strength of public opinion against Australia entering in the invasion of Iraq with other 'coalition of the willing' nations and therefore to try to persuade the Australian government to withdraw its active support.

The organisers and speakers at Australian rallies demonstrated the breadth of this new anti-war network. The rallies included representatives from several different movements and pressure groups including: trade unions, political parties such as the Australian Greens, the Australian Democrats and the Australian Labor Party, socialist organisations, Muslim community associations, Christian church representatives and the National Union of Students.

On Monday 17 February every major newspaper in Australia featured the march on its front pages. During the week that followed the marches were portrayed as a peace movement action, but many people who attended were labelled, by the media, as not being the predictable participants in such protests events:

> Glenyce Pitt and Shirley Childs had never taken to the streets for a cause before the weekend peace rallies. Both were long-time Liberal voters, but they did not support John Howard's resolve for war with Iraq. 'I just think there are other ways people can achieve peace,' said Ms Pitt, 66, who described herself as 'pretty much a dyed-in-the-wool Liberal voter' and who marched in the Adelaide protest. (Karvelas & McGarry 2003)

The marches were controversial for the federal government as they were directly in conflict with the government's position on both its alliance with the United States and its intention to send troops to fight in the war. The Prime Minister, John Howard, criticised the protestors, arguing that they were merely sympathisers of Saddam Hussein, President of Iraq:

> I mean, we are all accountable for the actions we take and people who demonstrate and who give comfort to Saddam Hussein must understand that and must realise that it's a factor in making it much more difficult to get united world opinion on this issue.

Federal Opposition Leader Simon Crean responded, arguing that Mr Howard had insulted 'ordinary' Australians: 'The Prime Minister's comments today are a disgrace. The Prime Minister is questioning the loyalty of more than half a million mums and dads who marched for peace around Australia last weekend' (both quoted in Martin 2003, p. 5).

From these quotations we can see how this particular moment of protest had competing constructions in Australia political discourse. It was simultaneously a people's movement of 'ordinary' Australians and an event that brought together a cross-section of movement participants whom the Prime Minister criticised for being misguided. Protest events, and the subsequent media and political response, are an important part of social movement analysis in helping us to understand the role of movements in creating social and political change. It also shows how appeals to people's value positions and public opinion generally are an important dimension of social movement action and subsequent success.

But why is this one symbolic weekend important to understanding Australian politics? It is worthwhile for us to understand the role social movements play because action undertaken by social movements is an indicator that social change is underway in broader society. For example, the wave of feminist activism in Australia in the early 1970s demonstrated that society's attitudes towards and treatment of women was changing. Now, many people are surprised at the issues that women protested about because we take these rights for granted. For example, women were involved in everything from chaining themselves in pubs that had separate areas for men and women to making demands that men and women should be paid the same amount for the same work and that women should be able to work in the public service after they were married, to family and relationship concerns making access to contraception, abortion, childcare and no-fault divorce easier.

Beyond these examples of the way society has changed several questions remain to be answered: is social movement activism relevant to democracy today? Why should we even look at action that happens outside or beyond the state? What is the relationship between social movements, social change and democracy?

Processes of social change

To understand social movements and their relationship with political processes we need to posit some definitional boundaries. In the introduction to this book we argued that the study of politics is the study of interactions of unequal power between individuals and (formal and informal) institutions, groups and organisations within a community. This chapter explores how change happens in these unequal power relationships at the societal, or social, level. Social movements often emerge during times of political and social upheaval. For example, the Australian labour movement emerged in the late nineteenth century during a period when Australia was renegotiating its political and social structures. The emergence of the environment, women's, indigenous and gay and lesbian movements is regularly identified with the late 1960s and early 1970s, a time when rapid social and political change was happening in many developed, liberal democratic countries. Hence analysis of the processes of social change is important to an evaluation of recent social movement action in Australia.

'Social change' is when the values, norms, practices and belief systems of a society change. These changes in values are mainly instigated by social movements and usually have an effect on institutional structures, such as government and policy processes.

Movements can be instrumental in opposing political change. They also suggest alternative and innovative ways of ordering and changing both society and political institutions. Movements, like pressure groups, can also work together with governments to shape new policy programs. The activities of social movements are interwoven with a shift in social attitudes on such issues as the limitations on the economic uses of the environment, institutionalising equality between men and women, creating equal rights and opportunities for indigenous Australians, and the acceptance of gays and lesbians. For example, the environment movement has had an important historical role in both changing social values and increasing understanding of the effect human behaviour has on the natural environment. For example, an issue that commenced as a theoretical proposition is now recognised to be one of the most important environmental issues of our times: global warming and climate change. There is extensive international debate over the requirements for the developing and developed world's adaptation to the threat of climate change. Environment movement organisations continue to campaign internationally to set policy-oriented reduction targets for greenhouse gas emissions as well as trying to change values and practices within society to make them more energy efficient.

Processes influenced by participatory democracy were fundamental to the emergence of New Left social movement groups based around environmental and women's issues in the early 1970s in Australia (Catt 1999, pp. 43–5). Not all groups associated with social movements espouse participatory democracy in all of their decision-making processes; some allow representatives to be chosen for some decision-making roles. Nevertheless there is a tendency within most progressive Australian movements to argue that all of their participants ought to have the opportunity to participate in deliberation and decision-making.

There has been extensive debate about the level of importance that ought to be attached to social movements in understanding political processes. We take the position that social movements have been active participants in the creation of social and political change in Australia and are therefore worth examining in addition to pressure groups that principally seek to influence the behaviour of governments by using lobbying and advocacy strategies. Those who study social movements tend to focus on individuals, organisations and events and the interdependence between them (della Porta & Diani 2006, p. 2). This chapter introduces existing theoretical positions on social movements that shape Australian analyses. This will be followed by a discussion of new forces and focuses shaping social movement action in Australia to identify the challenge that social movements present.

Conceptualising movements for change

Social movements come into being and to a large extent exist apart from formal political institutions, such as parliament and political parties. Yet similarly to pressure groups social movements use the strategies of protest and community organising. The social movement repertoire, however, focuses on mostly non-violent direct action through marches, vigils, public meetings, demonstrations, statements to the media and civil disobedience to achieve social and political change (Tilly 2004, p. 3). Social movements are often depicted as lacking an overarching institutional structure and existing as coalitions of groups, organisations and individuals. For example, we might talk about 'the environment movement' and the participants could include individual recyclers, pressure groups like the Australian Conservation Foundation, localised Landcare groups and the Australian Greens Party. There is no central coordinating body or 'head office' for the Australian environment movement. Social movements aim to create social change through challenging fundamental social values. This means they are concerned equally with changing the consciousness of participants as with influencing government policy (in the manner of the pressure groups discussed in Chapter 9). For example, it is equally important to the existence of the environment movement that participants share an environmental consciousness and a commitment to green-based values and practices as it is that government institutes pro-environmental policies.

There are four major ideas in understanding social movements that we discuss here:

- political opportunity structures
- cycles or waves of protest
- post-material value structures and identities and
- the importance of discursive structures.

First, the state and institutionalised power structures are crucial to any understanding of Australian social movement activity because they provide the 'political opportunity structure'. Political opportunities are possibilities for movement intervention, and they include a level of disruption or degree of openness within the state from which movements can gain leverage (see della Porta & Diani 2006, p. 16). For example, the environment movement surfaced in Australia over the Franklin Dam debate mentioned in Chapter 9 during a period of political disruption between the jurisdiction of the State of Tasmania and the conservative federal government in the late 1970s and early 1980s. After the Australian Labor Party (ALP) was elected in 1983 the movement was successful in stopping the dam. This happened only because of the existence of political opportunities, and the movement was able to take advantage of and gain publicity for, interest in and commitment to its cause.

Second, through placing emphasis on periods and the historical context of social movement action (see Tilly 2004, p. 3) the concept of 'cycles of protest' (Tarrow 1994, p. 153) has been developed. This idea suggests social movements do not arise individually but are part of a general period of social unrest, and are facilitated by changes in the political opportunity structure. As part of this cyclical idea, movement activity is believed to start as informal networking, then collective action such as protest occurs, then social movement organisations are established, then eventually there is a decline in protest activity and organisations consolidate to form long-term agendas (Nash 2000, p. 122). For example, in a study of the New South Wales Gay and Lesbian Rights Lobby, Flynn (2000) focuses on a historical reading of events from the Lobby's activist past, and notes the interaction and influence the group has had in creating government policy change on such issues as decriminalisation of homosexuality, age of consent and new legislation on recognition of same-sex relationships.

Third, post-materialism as a sociopsychological understanding of people's political motivations was developed by an American political scientist, Ronald Inglehart (1977). Post-materialism has been an important dimension in political science's explanation of social and political change in general. Post-materialists have interpreted social movements through looking for broad shifts in social and political values. Emphasis is placed on the alternative character and a specific historical, generational origin of new values. Thus, post-materialists tend to highlight societal shifts toward valuing non-material goods, such as the natural environment, public interest and debate, freedom of speech and a more humane society. Inglehart believes post-materialist goals have been represented by the political and social movements that emerged in the 1960s and 1970s, which attempted to create major change in liberal–democratic societies. Discussions and negotiations over identity are also an important element of social movement emphases on value orientations. Ian Parsons (1999) suggests that notions of identity are articulated by movements in terms of pride in that identity, and he comments on women's, gay and lesbian, indigenous and disabled groups acting within Australian society: 'The growth of [these] movements has been geared towards the development of a proud identity among groups that had experienced discrimination and oppression at the hands of the established power structures' (1999, p. 14). Therefore action is underpinned by group assertion of the value of who the activists are, their uniqueness in terms of developing and sharing a particular identity. For many groups the development of a shared—or, rather, a collective—identity has been a priority of movement mobilisation (Melucci 1996, pp. 68–86).

Fourth is the emerging importance in social movement studies of the roles of ideas and/or dominant discourses that shape and constrain cultural opportunities for social movements to develop and become influential (della Porta & Diani 2006, p. 18).

This next section introduces four indicators of social movement action. This is a synthesis of the theoretical positions on social movements discussed so far. Some authors, when writing about Australian politics, barely differentiate between pressure groups, political parties and social movements in the creation of political and social change (see Beresford 2000; Singleton et al. 2006, pp. 407–30). We clearly think the differentiation is an important one in understanding political processes. Mario Diani (1992) developed four indicators of social movement dynamics, and we will apply them here to understand recent Australian social movement activity. The indicators are:

- **Networks:** social movements are not organisations but are dense, informal, interactive networks of individuals, groups and/or organisations.
- **Values:** to be considered a social movement, this interactive network needs to have a shared set of values and solidarity, and create a sense of belonging and collective identity.
- **Conflict:** social movements either promote or oppose social change and are engaged in political or cultural conflicts. They create 'oppositional relationships between actors who seek control of the same stake—be it political, economic or cultural power' (della Porta & Diani 2006, p. 21).
- **Protest:** social movements use protest and direct action events that largely occur outside the main institutional arenas.

The difference between social movements and political parties and/or pressure groups is not based primarily on differences in organisational characteristics or on varying patterns of participation. This is because social movements are not actual organisations but are seen principally as networks of interactions, which may include formal organisations such as pressure groups and other community-sector organisations. But a single organisation ought not to be studied and subsequently labelled as the social movement; it is the existence of a network that indicates the existence of a movement for change. The differentiation between social movements and other political organisations is also important when it comes to the role of conflict as constituting social movement action. Della Porta and Diani (2006, p. 23) point out that there are other broad coalitions, based on such issues as human rights or social exclusion, that have shared values but do not engage in conflict with the state or other political actors. They suggest these are better characterised as 'consensus movements'.

Social movements are also more than a single protest event. Social movement analysts interpret protest events as part of the broad cycle of movement activity, even though protests may be the most visible part of what social movements do. Analysts identify the presence of a vision of the world and of a collective identity that assists protest participants to place their action in a wider perspective. Hence, single contentious episodes, or protests, need to be understood as part of a longer-lasting action or campaign. A one-off community-based protest over the development of a local park, for example, ought not be considered as social movement activity unless it is seen to develop the participants' sense of collective identity; that is, if the event happens in isolation from the other indicators that Diani (1992) highlights, then we cannot label a protest alone as an indicator of movement activity. However, it is rare that protests happen unconnected from pressure group activity and networks, or are not based on conflict with or disruption of the state. What tends to happen is that a protest is not properly interpreted by the social movement scholars, who would 'reveal' the extent of the network, conflict and shared values the protest encapsulates.

For example, Critical Mass (discussed in Chapter 7) is a monthly meeting of bicycle riders that happens in cities all around the world. The groups ride en masse through the streets with a different destination at each meeting. Their international website states: 'Critical Mass is not an organisation, it's an unorganised coincidence. It's a movement . . . of bicycles, in the streets.' They also say there is no 'official line' on what Critical Mass represents or what its aims are. However, a social movements analyst would investigate this phenomenon and ask such questions as: what is the protest about? Why do these people come together to protest each month? How is the Critical Mass network sustained? Does the disruption that occurs when the bikes take over the streets from the usual cars make this a movement event? What shared values do the participants have? Green values? And so on. In this way analysts could identify the protest event as well as the existence of networks, shared values, and the level of conflict with or disruption of authority and those in power.

To this point in the chapter we have examined new theoretical viewpoints on social movements and, following this, adopted Mario Diani's synthesis to arrive at four indicators of social movement action. The following sections will study these indicators within the Australian context.

Movements in Australia

The late 1960s and early 1970s were an important period of social, political and economic change in Australia and in other liberal–democratic nations such as the United States, United Kingdom, France and Canada. Anti-Vietnam War protests led to widespread challenge of traditional forms of authority and emphasised participatory politics. In Australia this was coupled with the election of the ALP

Whitlam government in 1972, which led to various claims for new priorities within formal political institutions; for example, women's greater equality in society, Aboriginal land rights, encouragement of multiculturalism as a national goal, and the protection of the natural environment were all prioritised. Many of these claims were not made by traditional political actors such as parties, unions or established community groups but by emerging social movements. At that time there seemed to be a rejection of the 'old-style' movements represented by the Australian labour movement, because they clashed with new politics based on identity and/or anti-materialism. Here we will briefly discuss the important role the labour movement played, and reject the suggestion that unions are no longer relevant as movements for change in Australia as this is a one-dimensional argument used to distinguish clearly between 'old' and 'new' movements (see Nash 2000, p. 103). However, we acknowledge that the role of unions has changed, and varies depending on governments and periods of economic and social change.

Ian Marsh argues that nine major social movements have emerged in Australia since the 1960s: women's, peace, environment, consumers, gay and lesbian rights, animal liberation, ethnic, Aboriginal rights and the 'new right' (1995, p. 71). To this we also add the recent global justice movement and re-emergence of a peace movement around the war in Iraq as well as considering the Australian labour movement as a movement in its own right. For the ease of analysis, we see animal rights as part of a broad environmental justice movement, and have chosen to label ethnicity-based groups and consumer groups as pressure groups that engage with the state, mainly using lobbying strategies and rarely, if ever, using protest actions (akin to the 'consensus movements' mentioned above). We are thus left with seven progressive movements of interest to our analysis seen in Table 10.1 and the eighth 'counter' movement presented by neo-liberal and conservative groups.

Table 10.1 takes the seven progressive social movements and compares them along the four criteria for recognising the existence of social movements. The 'networks' column lists the types of formal and informal group that form the movement's network as well as mentioning whether the movement has an affiliation with any particular political party or institutionalised actor. These networks are usually implicit, and are generally not formalised by any codification or formal agreement. For example, while the Australian Greens Party is generally accepted as playing a role in the environmental movement, there is no formalised connection between it and other environment-based groups. On the other hand,

TABLE 10.1 Contemporary progressive Australian social movements

	Networks	Shared values	Conflict	Major protest events
Labour	Australian Labor Party, existing union networks, formal peak bodies (e.g. ACTU), some cross-movement work with environmental, anti-global and grassroots groups	Labourism	With Coalition federal government over industrial law reform	Your Rights at Work Campaign, 2005–07; Maritime Unions of Australia dispute, 1998
Global justice	Strong links with environmental and grassroots-oriented community groups, anti-war movement, some left-oriented unions	Anti-capitalism and anti-corporate globalisation	With multinational corporations and international groups: World Trade Organisation and World Economic Forum	Against World Economic Forum in Melbourne, 2001; against APEC, Sydney, 2007
Anti-war	Human rights and community groups, global justice movement, most unions, church groups, Muslim community groups	Peace	With federal government over Australian commitment to military intervention in Iraq and in war on terrorism	Major international anti-war protests, February 2003
Environment	Australian Green Party, green groups: both those working at grassroots and those working on governmental reform	Green consciousness	With multinational corporations; lesser extent with all government over green and justice issues	Anti-nuclear reactor, 2001, Jabiluka anti-uranium mine, 1998
Women	Feminists working in bureaucracy, service providers and informal groups	Feminism	With federal Coalition government over retreat from policies on gender equity, childcare, maternity leave etc.	Annual International Women's Day (March) and Reclaim the Night (October) marches
Gay and lesbian	Community-oriented service providers, law reform groups and informal groups	Sexuality rights and identity	With governments over law reform	Annual Mardi Gras parade in Sydney (February)
Aboriginal	Community-oriented service providers, Land Councils, ATSIC	Indigenous rights and identity	With legal system over land rights, reparations for stolen generation	Major marches in support of reconciliation, 2000

many of the unions that make up the Australian labour movement do have formal links with the Australian Labor Party.

The 'Shared values' column refers to the collective identity that the movement uses to mobilise participants; that is, it is implied that the groups and individuals who participate in movement activity share a broad set of values. These are a generalised set of values and will differ in their detail among groups and individuals. These values are rarely written down as a formalised treatise. For example, there is no single text that instructs people on how to act or think as a feminist, a 'greenie' or a global justice activist. Even further, many social movements encompass diverse views and engage constantly in debates about appropriate value systems and strategies.

The 'Conflict' column broadly outlines what institutional forms the movement has defined itself as being in opposition to. This includes attempts to reform those particular institutions or attempts to initiate law or policy-making reform in favour of the aims of the movement.

The 'Protest' column refers to specific activity that has been undertaken by the movement. The protests mentioned reflect the period considered in Table 10.1 and the specific activity undertaken by these social movements. The main movement in Table 10.1 that can be considered as 'new' within this period is the global justice movement. It is the only movement to have engaged in protests that have helped to launch the movement into the public consciousness for the first time during this period. The peace movement is a re-emergent movement that both mobilised traditional anti-war activists and created new coalitions and new protest events. All of the other movements are well established and seldom use protest or other forms of direct action as their primary form of mobilising support or generating attention.

New movements? Institutionalised movements?

The period being examined here, from the mid-1990s onwards, was particularly hostile, or even impervious, to progressive movements' calls for social change. This is not to say that progressive movements have been unsuccessful in making claims or that their activity has not been important; rather, that a conservative economic and political climate necessarily affects the type of action undertaken or initiated and the possibilities for creating social change. Therefore there is a change in the political opportunity structure that constrains and enables movement action. This can also affect whether social movements choose to concentrate on creating change in government policy or focus more on attracting new participants and organisation at the grassroots level. If a government has demonstrated that it is particularly disinterested in responding to claims made by social movements, the movements may also focus on a different concentration of power, in both a formal and an informal sense, including other levels of government, corporations and international organisations.

Much of what social movements have done in recent years has been to generate publicity for their cause and to obtain media attention. This action has been directed at challenging dominant discourses in society and attempting to reframe debates and values in the favour of the movement's goals. Yet striving for media attention may end up detracting from the seriousness of the issues the movements are attempting to place on the public agenda. This presents movements with the following dilemma:

- only those actions that attain media coverage become widely publicised
- media coverage tends to increase with the novelty, disruption and violence of collective acts
- media coverage is unlikely to reconstruct the precise interactions between political actors, especially if they involve disruption or violence between demonstrators and police (Scalmer 2002, p. 41).

Courting media attention is clearly relevant to our understanding of the anti-war in Iraq protests on the weekend of 15–16 February 2003 discussed in the snapshot. However, this dilemma is most likely to be seen in reporting on protest events organised by participants in the global justice movement. Here media reports have concentrated on the violent interaction between the police and the participants, and accusations of violence were made against both groups (see Iveson & Scalmer 2000). The media coverage of both movements concentrated on the visual aspects of the individuals involved, such as labelling them as 'rent-a-crowd' activists as opposed to 'ordinary Australians', who are less likely to be motivated to protest (Karvelas & McGarry 2003).

Some have suggested that protest activity is now widely accepted as a normal part of a vibrant democracy within which the state and movements have clearly negotiated and demarcated roles. The usual intention of social movements is to disrupt the action of their opponents, but now protests and mobilisation, through marches and rallies, are becoming part of the conventional repertoire of participation and democratic practice. We saw this in Chapter 9 when we were looking at the range of strategies available to pressure groups to call upon the state to institute reform. We can also see this through the recognition that much protest activity is sanctioned by, and organised with, the police. For example, the annual Sydney Gay and Lesbian Mardi Gras marches, the Australia-wide indigenous Reconciliation marches and the annual International Women's Day marches all have police cooperation, and the police have redirected traffic to make sure the marches and rallies run smoothly. Furthermore, most pressure groups in Australia will, at some stage, hold a protest event to publicise their cause. Groups recognise that a protest event is useful both to mobilise their participants and to grab the attention of the media and/or decision-makers. Most are able to organise events like rallies and marches that are legal, thus not prohibiting participation by those who fear arrest or police harassment. Research has shown that more than 60 per cent of the Australian population are willing to participate in a 'lawful' demonstration (Papadakis 2001, p. 46).

However, not all movements are routinely organised and/or institutionalised in the same way or even to the same degree. When we look again at Table 10.1 we can see that the movements that seem to have routine protest events—women, gay and lesbian, indigenous—are those that have also relied on lobbying activities, such as contacting politicians, reforming the law and appearing in government inquiries. Success in legislative change and law reform may suggest that individuals, organisations and groups that share a value system are homogenous in terms of their strategic action and protest activity. This is clearly not an accurate picture of Australian social movements today as there are always radical actors within movements who would reject lobbying and negotiation with governments. There are also mobilisations of new groups whose actions are less media-driven and less state-directed, and therefore may be less noticeable. This rarely means that movements no longer exist. Instead, it may mean that movement formations are prioritising collective identity processes. This idea also relates to the cyclical pattern of protest adopted by movements for change and the proposition that movements still survive, even when less visible, by adopting 'abeyance structures', which focus on internal activities undertaken by a small committed group of activists (Sawyers & Meyer 1999, pp. 187–8). For example, Anita Harris has argued that there exists a new and younger group of active feminists who are taking the Australian women's movement into new terrain. She talks chiefly about the discursive production of feminism when she suggests 'it is critical to look in places often disregarded as sites for feminist work', such as zines, web pages, creative writing and performance (Harris 2001). Harris is arguing that to understand the women's movement and feminist action we need to look for 'dispersed activism' rather than a single leader or movement, and we need to look especially at the Internet, popular culture and the media and feminist production therein.

In this examination of the factors that have shaped Australian social movements we can also examine recent instances of cross-movement activity to identify important and successful movement mobilisation. Some actions have relied on cross-movement support, which has seen new alliances formed between labour, environmental and global justice groups that have, through their organisational forms, promoted particular issues or protests. These include supporting refugees and asylum seekers in 2001 and 2002, anti-war in Iraq protests in 2002–03 and support for East Timor's independence in 1999.

All these protests, which create cross-movement support and participation, may be indicators of the emergence of new value frameworks based on the concepts of 'community unionism' and/or 'environmental justice'. As the terms indicate, coalitions are being formed between unions and environmental groups, between community service groups and environmental groups, between identity movements, such as indigenous movements, and environmental groups. This is not always a new phenomenon, as the Green Bans that occurred in the early 1970s were an example of a union, the Builders' Labourers Federation (BLF), acting on claims presented by the new social movements of that era. However, it has also been argued that the Green Bans were not really coalitions between movements but an example of a radical union acting upon the arguments and *values* presented by new social movements, including the environmental and women's movements (see Burgmann & Burgmann 1998).

Through the development of 'environmental justice' or 'community unionism', social movements broaden their value base to appeal to a new constituency and to offer more complex analyses of social and political change. For example, in the ACTU (1999) document written to address falling union membership, Unions@Work, mention was made of the need to develop the social movement approach to broaden unions' appeal and reach. It argued that unions ought to build alliances with community organisations and new social movements and to further develop transnational links between unions. New coalitions help unions to compete in public debate, particularly during periods where there is a hostile federal government. A recent example of a union and community organisation coalition was a 2003–04 alliance between the New South Wales Teachers' Federation and parents and citizens groups that led to the formation of a new network, the Public Education Alliance. The campaign involved public forums, an advertising campaign and lobbying of the Premier and the education minister. The campaign's success included teacher professional development and reduction in class sizes (Tattersall 2005, p. 103).

The environmental justice approach has been adopted by groups that are not governed by traditional environmental concerns, such as forests, climate change and mining, but are instead locating the equity and distributive issues of poverty, development and aid within an environmental framework of analysis. The environmental justice approach has also been an important point from which to link with the anti-capitalist/anti-corporate value position of the global justice movement by prioritising social justice and equality. Coalitions between environment groups and community organisations have not been straightforward due to the clash between ecosystem or nature-centred approaches of the environment movement with the human-centred values of community development (Hillman 2002, p. 349). Despite this apparent clash in values, new environmental justice campaigns have emerged at several levels including at the international level, where there is emphasis on the disproportionate share of climate change that developing countries experience while developed countries make the biggest contribution to greenhouse gases. At the national level, campaigns about the degradation of natural rivers and increase of salinity have pointed out the interference and resultant damage from land clearing, pollution and large dams. At the local level there have been campaigns against increased urban development and corporate polluters that use an environmental justice framework (Hillman 2002, pp. 351–2).

Global justice movements in Australia and abroad

The global justice movement is the newest Australian social movement. One of the main protests led by the global justice movement that Australia has seen was in Melbourne at the blockade of the World Economic Forum (WEF) meeting on 11 September 2000 (known as S11). About 10,000 people were present on the day, and much of the commercial media reporting focused on the visual spectacle of the expected violence between police and protest participants. Two main international targets of this movement have been the WEF and the World Trade Organisation (WTO). The WEF consists of multinational corporation representatives who discuss issues of economics and trade. It is different from the WTO, which is made up of representatives of governments who negotiate binding agreements on trade.

The S11 2000 protests in Australia revealed the potential for cross-movement alliances in supporting the broad agenda against corporate globalisation. A range of groups including environmental groups, community-based Marxist and libertarian groups and unions came together to protest in Melbourne. A similar coalition of groups had been mobilised for the anti-MAI (Multilateral Agreement on Investment) campaign in 1999. Networks were also important in terms of the international links with those who had been active in the protests against the WTO meeting in Seattle, US, in November 1999 and the template these earlier protests provided (see Bramble & Minns 2002).

The networks of the global justice movement are transnational in nature, and this emphasis has been reinforced through the World Social Forums held annually since 2001, mainly in Brazil, at the same time as the WEF meets in January in Switzerland. Related examples include the first European Social Forum, held in Florence in November 2002, and the first Asian Social Forum, held in January 2003. The first United States Social Forum was held in 2007. Australia has had small Social Forum events in Sydney, Melbourne and Brisbane. These international social forums, and associated protests such as in Genoa, Italy, in 2001, have involved hundreds of thousands of people meeting to deliberate about and protest against inequality and corporate globalisation. These events are all underpinned by a general belief that through social and economic justice 'another world is possible'. There is a broad opposition to neo-liberal economics. For example, an activist attending the World Social Forum is quoted as saying: 'Global justice is not anti-globalisation, because we support the type of globalisation present at the World Social Forum: people to people globalisation' (Becker 2007, p. 206).

In addition to new transnational movement networks between the developed and developing world, and a new site of conflict with international corporate power, the global justice movement has also deployed new strategies of creative resistance and protest such as 'culture jamming'. This strategy uses parody of corporate advertising and creative distortion of well-known imagery to make a political statement. It can also include graffiti, public performance art, hactivism of Internet sites and flash mobs. For example, in Australia, S11's culture jamming included the anonymous groups that hacked into Nike's website and redirected 900,000 hits to the S11 website over a nineteen-hour period, and the use of John Farnham's song 'You're the Voice' as the movement anthem, which led to threat of legal action by Farnham unless they desisted (Iveson & Scalmer 2000, p. 6).

A more recent, yet smaller protest event of about 5000 protestors in Australia associated with the values of the global justice movement was against the Asia Pacific Economic Cooperation (APEC) meeting held in Sydney in September 2007 (Kirby 2007). The meeting was attended by national leaders such as President Bush of the US and President Putin of Russia, and hosted for the first time by the Australian Prime Minister. However, the effect of using the policing of protests to intimidate people ought also to be taken into consideration. For example, among the charges made against police subsequent to this protest event were that up to 200 officers had removed their identity badges and that eighteen arrests were made. Before the protests even occurred, there was much discussion of the use of a police-owned water cannon and a 'blacklist' of people who would not be allowed to attend (see Berkovic & Box 2007). The small mobilisation and large police presence possibly indicates the long-term difficulty of generating support for global justice ideas and the movement generally in Australia. Confrontation and violent clashes between demonstrators and police have also been noted as part of the cycle of protest as a movement evolves and initially relies on tactics of civil disobedience (della Porta & Diani 2006, pp. 190–1; see also Burgmann 2003, pp. 312–17).

One of the highlights of the movement against the APEC meeting was, in what could be construed as a culture-jamming moment, the intervention made by the political satire television show *The Chaser*. Members of the *Chaser* team were charged by police with breaching security at APEC after they used a hire car with a Canadian flag and mock security passes to join the official APEC motorcade. When they were stopped one of the members of the team stepped out of the car dressed as Osama bin Laden. The story was covered by international media, and attracted more than two million viewers when shown on the comedy team's television show the following week. This points out that protests now occur in a variety of symbolic and culture-oriented ways in contemporary social movement politics.

This overview of progressive Australian social movements demonstrates that broad networks are being mobilised by a variety of value positions that conflict with recent directions taken by the state. Evidence about social movement action provides an example of Lukes' three dimensions of power in that there is:

- a concentration on explicit conflict between the state and movements
- an exposure of the informal processes used by both political and corporate actors to retain power
- a broad critique of the neo-liberal values that various movements actively oppose.

However, part of seeing power in three dimensions is to recognise that new groups are forming, and established groups are being strengthened, which run campaigns counter to progressive movements for social change.

Australian counter-movements

Counter-movements arise in reaction to the successes obtained by progressive social movements, and the two types of movement develop in symbiotic dependence during the course of mobilisation. In general, the relationship between movements and counter-movements is something that has been defined as loosely coupled conflict in which the two sides rarely come together face to face (della Porta & Diani 1999, pp. 212–13).

The values of counter-movement groups contradict those of progressive social movements. Australian counter-movements cannot be considered social movements in the sense that we have been discussing in this chapter because they are not underpinned by beliefs in participatory democracy, nor do they contribute to progressive social change. However, this does not mean that they do not influence public opinion and broader social and political values. Most social movement scholars tend to examine progressive movements for change, whereas conservative movements are under-researched. We argue that we should also recognise counter-movements as examples of collective action that have been described as 'anti-political movements, interested in the management of popular acquiescence and consent, and uninterested in the development of local democracy and governmental accountability' (Roche 2000, pp. 231–2). Recent examples in Australia include what Ian Marsh labels 'neo-liberal' movements (1995), and active participants in these networks are mainly think tanks such as the Institute of Public Affairs and the Centre for Independent Studies. Other examples are movements that have centralised around conservative political parties such as One Nation and the Shooters Party. The growth of the Internet has provided many counter-movement organisations with space to develop a network and consolidate value systems. Some sites, such as the innocuously named Australian News Commentary, explain that they are set up specifically to counter what they perceive as left-wing bias in mainstream media political analysis (see <www.australian-news.com.au/about.htm>).

Table 10.2 lists the progressive movements we have examined and examples of groups that act as counter-movements to them.

In a recent event in Australian history we can see the 'loosely coupled conflict' between counter-movement and progressive movement groups. The precipitative event was what was labelled the 'Cronulla riots' of December 2005. This large-scale mobilisation was provoked by counter-movement organisations, then followed by a series of mobilisations and events by groups formed around anti-racism sentiments. The riots began as a dispute over the use of the beach between local, mostly male residents of Anglo-Celtic heritage from the Sutherland Shire

TABLE 10.2 Active counter-movements in Australia

Progressive movement	Counter-movements
Women's movement	Pro-life and anti-abortion groups, anti-Family Court men's groups
Gay and lesbian movement	Conservative religious and church-based groups, e.g. Festival of Light
Environmental movement	Mining and forestry-funded groups or corporations, e.g. Gunns
Peace movement	Pro-guns and pro-military groups, e.g. Sporting Shooters of Australia
Indigenous and ethnicity movement	Anti-immigration groups, pro-nationalism groups, e.g. Australian League of Rights, Australia First
Labour and global justice movement	Conservative think tanks and pro-market liberalism groups, e.g. H.R. Nicholls Society, Centre for Independent Studies, Institute of Public Affairs

and Cronulla and youths of Middle Eastern descent. It spiralled into several days of violent clashes characterised by assaults, expressions of white pride and racism. Many participants from both sides were arrested, and some were charged with violent behaviour and assault-related crimes. It was subsequently revealed that this event was not a random outbreak of violence but had been advertised, promoted and partly organised by the Patriotic Youth League. A counter-movement network partner, the Australia First Party, distributed anti-immigration leaflets around Cronulla and had been urging people to rally at Cronulla Beach on the Internet (see Hannan & Baker 2005). Other known conservatives were also implicated in inciting violence, such as talkback radio personality Alan Jones, who ACMA found had broadcasted material that was 'likely to encourage violence or brutality' (ACMA 2007a).

Few political or media commentators saw this event as a confrontation on the basis of race, instead portraying it as an unfortunate example of violence fuelled by alcohol, and believed that the guilty would be dealt with by the police. For example, in his Australia Day speech a month or so later the Prime Minister suggested that Australian values would prevail:

> Racial intolerance is incompatible with the kind of society we are and want to be. Within limits, all Australians have the right to express their culture and beliefs and to participate freely in our national life. And all Australians have a civic responsibility to support the basic structures and values of Australian society which guarantee us our freedom and equality. The criminal behaviour of last December should be met with the full force of the law. And I do not believe it calls for either national self-flagellation or moral panic. (Howard 2006a)

Others, especially academic commentators writing in online media, saw the event as chiefly an indicator of an underlying Australian racism against people from Asia and the Middle East (for example Kell 2005; Hage 2006) and a reaction against policies of multiculturalism in Australia. Subsequently, several events were organised by anti-racist activists under the rallying call of 'those 5000 people who rioted at Cronulla do not speak for us' (Burchell 2006, p. 6). Other more general responses included the frequent use of imagery depicting the Australian flag, which revealed a community gathering strength and expressing solidarity and unity (Cubby 2006, p. 85). Here we can see the discursive battle over who could speak about 'being Australian' between the progressive groups and the counter-movement.

Counter-movements are also supported by particular dispositions within intellectual thought. Conservative values and books are an important foundation to the success of a counter-movement. The promulgation of values to support campaigns can be seen particularly in movements counter to progressive social movements based on identities, such as the women's, gay and lesbian and indigenous movements. The progressive movements aim both to promote new value systems and to create change in society; the counter-movements mobilise specifically to oppose a shift in values and understanding. As highlighted in Chapter 9, Carol Johnson observed that conservative groups classify and denigrate people who promote new identities as 'special interests' who do not act or speak for 'ordinary Australians' (2000, p. 65). Similarly, Marian Sawer argues:

> The Prime Minister himself has told us that elites engaging in 'black-armband history' are displaying contempt for the national pride felt by ordinary Australians and that feminists promoting equal opportunity are showing contempt for the values of ordinary women. (2003b)

The 'history wars' of late 2002 and early 2003 are an example of a counter-movement campaign that challenged progressive values based on identity. Conservative political historians and journalists challenged broadly accepted facets of Australian indigenous history since white settlement. This debate arose subsequent to the publication of *The Fabrication of Aboriginal History* by Keith Windschuttle (2002). The book aims to redress the understanding of the frontier killings by white settlers of indigenous inhabitants of Tasmania in the early nineteenth century. Windschuttle uses historical sources of evidence to substantiate his argument that historical scholars have been incorrect in their estimates of the numbers of indigenous Australians killed in Tasmania. Windschuttle questions the extent of the violence against the Aboriginal inhabitants and argues that it was not genocide, but a 'settlement remarkably free of death by violence, disease being the great killer' (*Australian* 2002).

Robert Manne argues that 'Windschuttle's revisionism is by no means limited to corpse minimisation. Equally important is his attempt to discredit the common moral understanding of what he calls the "orthodox school" of historians' (2002); that is, this was the public airing of a vociferous debate about the numbers of Aboriginal people killed in Tasmania, with progressive historians on one side and conservative historians on the other (see Reynolds 2001). These opponents are unlikely to agree on their estimates of the numbers killed, as they are persuaded by different sources of evidence. What is important to understand about this public debate is how counter-movement campaigns use their own values to discredit the arguments of those they disagree with. Ostensibly the argument is about which form of historical evidence has more credibility, but it is really a debate on who is entitled to present the truth of the matter.

This makes it important to analyse the underlying power relationships and value systems in historical and political writing. Furthermore, we can choose to accept that, no matter who we believe, 'the death of an individual, Aboriginal or settler, by violence or disease, had moral ramifications, and that the destruction of Tasmanian Aboriginal society was a tragedy with moral implications for Australia today' (*Australian* 2002, p. 10).

Little is known about the full extent of the influence or effectiveness of counter-movement organisations in Australia. Hopefully future research will examine the existing relationships between conservative political actors and counter-movement groups. Undoubtedly counter-movements have played a role internationally with Christian fundamentalist and extremist nationalist groups often mimicking the tactics and strategies used by their counterpart progressive movements. These groups are also linked with the subsequent rise of radical conservative governments and political parties in various parts of the world (see, for example, Betz & Immerfall 1998).

Social movement society?

In the international social movements literature it has been suggested we now have a 'social movement society'. Three main factors establish the idea of a movement society:

- protest has moved from being a periodic feature of democratic politics to a permanent aspect of modern life
- protest is used with greater frequency, by more diverse groups of people, and is used to represent a wider range of demands than ever before
- the professionalisation and institutionalisation of protest may be changing social movements into a process that occurs within the arena of conventional politics (Meyer & Tarrow 1998, p. 4).

We have highlighted the increasing use of creative protest as a political strategy by individuals and groups in communicating political messages. In this chapter we also explored the question of institutionalisation of movement action, and found that it was true for *some* sections of *some* movements. However, future research on Australian movements will need to highlight the diversity in action taken within movements and to explore the value and identity structures that movements create and sustain.

Social movements in Australia are expressions of the need to create political and social change. We have seen that social movements have both challenged and changed existing political institutions. However, this change is not universally welcomed as we have also seen how a conservative political climate can foster counter-movements that respond to progressive movements. Australia's political future will continue to be shaped by power contestations between these different forces for change.

Summary

- Social movements have played an important role in the Australian political landscape in terms of the practice of participatory democracy and their influence on processes of social and political change.
- Interpretations and analyses of Australian social movement activity highlight the four indicators of networking, conflict with authority, protest and shared values.
- Social movements have had an ambivalent influence on, and relationship with, the state. This can be understood through an examination of the interplay between media exposure, political opportunities, political and protest cycles and less visible identity-building work.
- Recent social movement activity is usefully analysed through an examination of cross-movement actions such as focusing on anti-war coalitions, environmental justice or social movement unionism.
- The only movement that is 'new' in Australia is the global justice movement. Other movements have a more institutionalised focus.

Further reading

Attwood, Bain 2003, *Rights for Aborigines*, Allen & Unwin, Sydney.

Burgmann, Verity 2003, *Power, Profit and Protest*, Allen & Unwin, Sydney.

Doyle, Timothy 2001, *Green Power: The Environment Movement in Australia,* UNSW Press, Sydney.
Scalmer, Sean 2002, *Dissent Events,* UNSW Press, Sydney.
Scalmer, Sean and Maddison, Sarah 2006, *Activist Wisdom: Practical Knowledge and Creative Tension in Social Movements,* UNSW Press, Sydney.
Willett, Graham 2000, *Living Out Loud,* Allen & Unwin, Sydney.

Useful websites

- New Mardi Gras at <www.mardigras.org.au>. This site is the information point for the organisation of the annual Gay and Lesbian Mardi Gras parade in Sydney.
- Reconciliation Australia at <www.reconciliation.org.au/i-cms.isp>. Reconciliation Australia is an independent, not-for-profit organisation established in 2000 as the peak national organisation building and promoting reconciliation between Indigenous and non-Indigenous Australians.
- Tim Longhurst at <www.timlonghurst.com/tag/culture-jamming/>. This blog discusses culture-jamming practices and other forms of Internet activism in Australia.

PART III
POLICY PROCESSES

CHAPTER 11
FEDERALISM

FEDERALISM IN ACTION

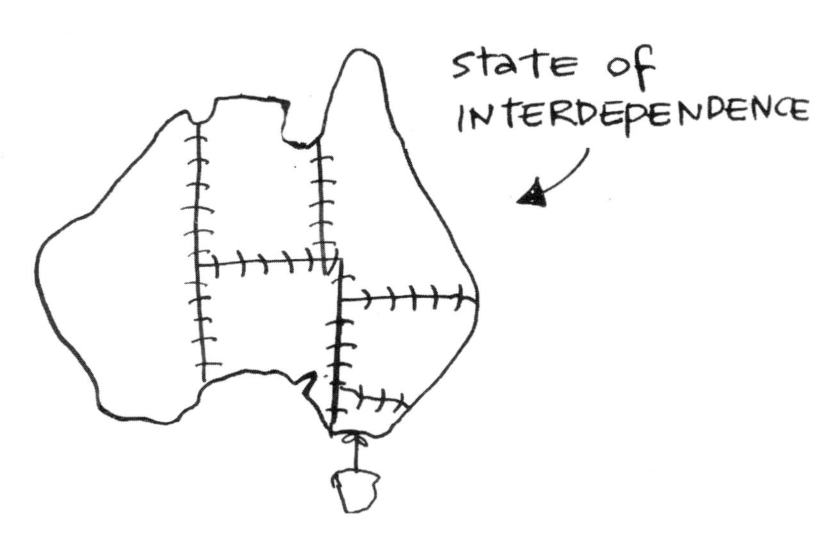

In the third part of this book we examine some of the ways policy decisions are made, implemented and challenged in Australian politics. This requires an understanding of institutional components of the system, as well as looking more broadly at elements of how policy is developed and delivered. We also consider the specific question of Australian policy towards our relationships with other countries.

This chapter looks in detail at the federal system of government in Australia. We explain how Australian federalism differs from other types of federalism by looking at three key institutional features. We then investigate continuing disputes within Australian federalism over sharing and coordination of powers, and look at different ways of analysing this contestation. A complete assessment of Australian federalism requires recognising and examining more than formal institutions; it requires analysing the processes at work in the dynamics of our federal system.

Topics covered in this chapter include:

- the role of the national level of government, and interactions between it and the States
- how Australian federalism is different from other federal systems
- four approaches to analysing and understanding Commonwealth–State relations
- the importance of examining process in understanding how federalism works.

SNAPSHOT Can federal–State cooperation save the Murray–Darling?

The Murray–Darling Basin is probably the most important water catchment area in the country. But a combination of overuse and drought has left it parched and degraded, and new initiatives are needed to save this essential natural resource.

The basin extends from Queensland to South Australia and covers extensive territory in New South Wales and Victoria. It generates 40 per cent of the national income from agriculture and grazing. It contains more than twenty rivers and groundwater storage. (See a map of the basin at <www.environment.gov.au/water/mdb/index.html>.)

Over the last century the massive water resources of the Murray–Darling have been managed through cooperative arrangements between the States. This began with the establishment in 1915 of the River Murray Waters Agreement between New South Wales, Victoria and South Australia, overseen by the River Murray Commission created two years later. By the 1980s concerns about environmental degradation, including salinity, were growing. In response, in 1987 the Murray–Darling Basin Agreement was created to oversee water management and distribution, overseen by the Murray–Darling Basin Commission. Those involved in the management of the basin now include New South Wales, Victoria, South Australia, Queensland, the Australian Capital Territory and the Commonwealth (MDBC 2006a; MDBC 2006b).

By the end of the twentieth century extraction levels from the system had reached 80 per cent of the average annual flow. This meant that in drought years the amount of water being extracted from the river system was greater than the flow of water (Lowe 2004, p. 251). In 2002 States agreed to reduce their levels of extraction, and in 2003 they began to consider enclosing irrigation pipes to reduce evaporation and consequent salinity. In 2003 the Council of Australian Governments allocated $500 million in compensation to farmers losing irrigation entitlements (Lowe 2004, pp. 251–2).

These measures were insufficient to improve the health of the Murray–Darling. Early in the new millennium, record low inflows were being reported. The system was so dry that the federal government and State premiers proposed urgent modifications to water-sharing and implemented contingency plans for 'at-risk' towns (Howard 2007a). On 25 January 2007 the Prime Minister announced a new initiative, the National Plan for Water Security (Howard 2007b), a $10.05 billion fund to fix irrigation channels, improve irrigation methods on farms to reduce wastage, and tackle overallocation of water (Howard 2007c, 2007d).

Crucially, the plan relied on the States' referral of some of their decision-making powers to the Commonwealth, under section 51 (xxxvii) of the Constitution, so that the federal government could oversee a range of policy issues relevant to the task of managing the Murray–Darling Basin. The plan allowed for consultation with the States and Territories, but coordination and final decision-making would rest with the federal government.

In justifying his plan, the Prime Minister argued that an overallocation of water resources had occurred 'under the surveillance of the States' (Howard 2007e). He said:

> States issue water licences, States control property rights. The Commonwealth has very little direct constitutional power in relation to these things and we have all rather hoped that the pretty unwieldy, ad hoc arrangements concerning the Murray–Darling Basin might work, but plainly they don't . . . when you look at the map, those rivers run across the borders, the Great Artesian Basin lies underneath the borders. Those lines on the map mean nothing, and we have to think as Australians, and not as Queenslanders or New South Welshmen, or Victorians. (Howard 2007e)

In another interview he said:

> We are offering to take over a huge problem generated entirely by the States, that's the problem of overallocation within the Murray–Darling Basin. We didn't create it. The Commonwealth doesn't make water allocations. We're not responsible for the overallocations, but we are prepared to fix that problem . . . it's an offer that I very earnestly encourage the States to accept, [it] does involve a referral of power to the Commonwealth, it won't work otherwise and it can't go ahead otherwise. (Howard 2007f)

Initially, the then Prime Minister sought to reach agreement with State and Territory governments on his proposal (Howard 2007d). However, consensus was impossible to achieve. Although New South Wales, Queensland and South Australia reached agreement with the Commonwealth in February 2007 (Howard 2007b) after making amendments to the plan, Victoria remained opposed. Negotiations with Victorian Premier Steve Bracks broke down in July, with the Premier citing the rights of Victorian irrigators and a suspicion that the federal government would use the plan to privatise water supplies as reasons for the disagreement (Kenny & Henderson 2007; ABC News 2007b).

This led the federal government to claim it had the constitutional jurisdiction, under several heads of power including the corporations power and the external affairs power, to legislate to achieve a national water plan without the cooperation of the States (Howard 2007g). In August 2007 the federal government passed the *Water Act 2007* (Cwlth). This legislation established a new Murray–Darling Basin Authority with the task of developing a sustainable management plan in relation to water allocation and use from the river system. It gave effect to the National Plan for Water Security announced in January.

Why did the federal government initially appeal for the support and cooperation of the States in trying to achieve this plan? Why did most of the States agree to the plan but one remain opposed? How was the federal government able to legislate to implement the plan, despite the opposition of Victoria? What happens when federal and State governments disagree over policy? Are some issues genuinely 'national' in character? If they are, how can they best be tackled in a federal system?

A distinctively Australian federalism

The colonies that became States at Federation had possessed their own governments before 1901. The system of government they developed was based on the Westminster system inherited from the United Kingdom. The Westminster system of government led to the adoption of important features of our parliamentary system, including an executive drawn from the legislature, a Prime Minister decided by the party retaining the majority of seats in the lower house of parliament and unwritten conventions, which determine many of the procedures and practices by which the nation is governed. But in order for the colonies to preserve their powers, this form of government was integrated in the Australian system of government with federalism.

A federal system is one with a division of governmental power between central and regional political entities.

This resulted in three distinctive institutional features of federalism in Australia:

1 a division of government between national and State/Territory levels
2 the Senate
3 the institutionalisation of a 'hybrid' form of federalism.

We will discuss each of these features in turn.

The Commonwealth

The national level of government established by the Australian Constitution is known as the federal, or Commonwealth, government. Helen Irving's account of the writing of the Constitution tells how the drafters tried to delineate which powers and matters belonged to the national government and which would be retained by the States. They believed that things like defence were matters that 'made the colonies a nation'. This moved them beyond being a collaborative group of independent political entities that simply shared a common history, heritage and outlook (1997, p. 79) and moved them towards thinking of themselves as united as a single nation with a unified and coherent outlook on some national matters.

When the Constitution was drafted for Federation the States attempted to rein in the power of the national government by nominating its powers in section 51 of the Constitution. This was intended to mean that the policy areas within which Commonwealth can legislate are specified in this section of the Constitution. They include trade, telegraph services, defence, lighthouses, quarantine, census statistics, currency, immigration, marriage and divorce, pensions and railways. Because referenda have not usually been successful, the text of section 51 has changed very little since Federation. However, the interpretation of section 51 has changed considerably. For example, one clause that has allowed the Commonwealth to legislate in areas not previously considered to be its domain is the 'external affairs' power (section 51 (xxix)), which grants the Commonwealth power to enact laws with respect to 'external affairs'. This includes the ratification of international treaties, either directly with other countries or in the form of multilateral treaties. Thousands of treaties have been signed on issues as diverse as human rights, labour relations and environmental policy (Charlesworth et al. 2006, pp. 26–7). The impact of the interpretation of the external affairs power will be discussed below in the legal approach to examining Commonwealth–State relations.

'Bilateral treaties' are agreements between Australia and one other country. 'Multilateral treaties' are agreements signed by three or more countries. Examples of multilateral treaties that Australia has ratified are United Nations human rights treaties, including the International Covenant on Civil and Political Rights.

Some of the powers granted to the Commonwealth in the Constitution are 'exclusive', which means that the power to deal with them is exclusively held by the Commonwealth and the States have no direct say. An example of an exclusive power is defence. In many policy areas the Commonwealth and the States share responsibilities; these are called 'concurrent' powers. This can result from the Commonwealth's constitutional ability to give 'tied grants'—grants to the States to which conditions are attached (section 96). The Commonwealth's tied grants allow it to influence policy areas not specified in section 51. The Constitution also states that where there is an inconsistency between a federal and a State law, the federal law will prevail (section 109). This means that if there is a direct dispute and disagreement over a matter covered by both a national and a State law, the national law will be the one that is considered enforceable and the State law will be inoperable. All this means that despite the fact that the text of the Constitution has changed very little in the more than a century since Federation, the powers of the Commonwealth have expanded considerably through other means.

This expansion does have a limit, however. The Constitution protects Australian federalism at its most fundamental level. In an interpretation outlined in the High Court in *Melbourne Corporation v The Commonwealth* (1947) 74 CLR 31 and reaffirmed in *Austin v Commonwealth* (2003) 215 CLR 185, the federal government is not permitted to discriminate between States or to legislate to threaten their very existence. This is called the 'state immunity' principle.

The Senate

A second institutional feature of federalism in Australia is the Senate—the upper house of the federal parliament. The Senate was discussed in Chapter 4, so here we will only summarise two relevant points:

1. The Senate was designed to provide equal representation for the States in the national parliament, although in practice senators often act in the interests of their party rather than their State.
2. The Senate possesses almost identical powers to the House of Representatives, under section 53 of the Constitution, except in relation to money bills. This means that all legislation must pass through both the House of Representatives and the Senate, and the Senate can amend or block legislation if it chooses.

A 'hybrid' form of federalism

The federal aspects of the Australian parliamentary system were integrated *with* the Westminster system of responsible government. The two systems were combined into one resulting in a 'hybrid' form of federalism (Emy 1978, p. 181; Saunders 1990; Galligan 1995, p. 38; Parkin & Summers 2002, p. 5). This has been called a 'Washminster' mutation (Thompson 1980); the name derives from the federalist components' origins in the US (hence the first part of the name 'Washminster', which derives from Washington DC) and the Westminster components' origins in the United Kingdom.

It has been argued that these two systems not only were different in their institutional construction but also were designed for different purposes.

- Federalism was designed to divide government and to achieve equal representation for, and participation in decision-making by, the States. This was achieved by establishing State governments with residual powers, providing for equal representation for the States in the federal Senate, and granting the Senate coequal powers with the House of Representatives. These federal elements of our parliamentary system were written into the Constitution.
- The Westminster system was designed to provide a clear chain of accountability between the people, the parliament and the executive so as to ensure legitimacy and accountability of government. To make this possible it is important that government is formed by winning a majority of seats in the lower house (Painter 1997a, pp. 195–6). This ensures that the executive is accountable to the legislature, and the legislature is in turn accountable to the people. Many of the Westminster features of the parliamentary system are not written down in the Constitution.

The existence of this hybrid therefore creates particular tensions in Australian politics, which are commonly expressed in two ways. The first is as a dispute over the question of who has a 'mandate' from the people after an election. Governments that hold the majority in the lower house usually claim a mandate to implement the policies they championed during an election race. Yet the Senate can also claim its own mandate, and if the government does not have a majority there the Senate can argue that it was elected to amend legislation proposed by government and, if necessary, to block legislation altogether. Discussion in

Chapter 4 about the role of the Senate as a house of review, and its role as a representative body, augments this claim for a separate mandate. The second way that the tensions between these two systems of governing can be expressed is through the distinction between written and unwritten rules of parliament. The written elements tend to relate to the federalist elements of the Constitution. The unwritten elements tend to outline the Westminster elements of the constitutional framework. But because the Westminster elements are not written down, there is considerable dispute over their enforceability. These tensions manifested themselves clearly in the 1975 constitutional crisis.

The 1975 constitutional crisis

On 11 November 1975 the Labor federal government led by Gough Whitlam was dismissed from office by the Governor-General, Sir John Kerr.

Whitlam had been elected in 1972 after twenty-three years of conservative Liberal–Country Party government. His government was interventionist and increased public spending on education, medical services, housing, transport and regional development. It also championed reforms to the public sector to enhance efficiency.

But the government did not hold a majority in the Senate and was forced to a double dissolution election in 1974 in which it was returned to government but with a decreased lower house majority. After the 1974 election the Senate was deadlocked with twenty-nine senators from the Labor Party, twenty-nine from the Opposition and two independents. By 1975, following the resignation of one Labor senator and the death of another, the Labor Party only held twenty-seven Senate seats.

Until 1975 it had been an unwritten convention that outgoing senators be replaced by a member of the same political party. But in a flouting of the unwritten convention both the Senate vacancies, one from New South Wales and one from Queensland, were filled with appointees who were hostile to Labor. In October 1975 the Senate refused to pass the government's budget, which effectively prevented the government from functioning.

The government held a majority in the lower house and claimed that the Senate had no right to block supply because to do so would override the principles of responsible Westminster government. The Senate argued that it had the power to refuse the budget. A stalemate was reached. On 11 November 1975 the Governor-General dismissed the Whitlam government and appointed the Leader of the Opposition, Malcolm Fraser, as caretaker Prime Minister until an election could be held. An election was held on 13 December 1975 in which the Coalition led by Malcolm Fraser won a majority in both houses of the federal parliament.

This event demonstrated a clear conflict between the federal elements of the Constitution, which were written down in the form of the powers of the Senate, and the Westminster elements of the system of government that were not written down.

Sources: Beresford 2000, pp. 51, 175; Hawker 1975, p. 16; Parkin & Summers 2002, pp. 15–17; Whitlam 1977, p. 222.

We have clarified that federalism in Australia is a hybrid system that produces particular tensions within the parliamentary arena. Outside the parliamentary area, tensions between levels of government over powers, areas of policy responsibility and mechanisms for cooperation and collaboration over policy are also common. Tensions in Australian federalism reflect changing priorities, expectations and outcomes of government over time. It is therefore important to analyse the dynamics of Australian federalism outside the parliamentary arena to understand its role in policy outcomes. There are several ways of doing this, and below we consider four different approaches to examining Australian federalism.

Examining Commonwealth–State tensions

There are different ways of conceptualising federalism. James Gillespie defines federalism as 'a system of government in which authority is constitutionally divided between central and regional governments' (1994, p. 60). Brian Galligan has argued that the 'essence of federalism is the division of political power and government institutions between two levels of government, both of which are sovereign in limited fields and neither of which is subject to the other in certain core areas' (1989, p. 3). As these examples show, definitions of federalism share a conceptual and institutional delineation between centres and regions, but some also try to include a recognition that each entity must be entitled to claim some degree of autonomy from the other and the need for some mechanism to share and collaborate over cross-jurisdictional powers.

> The extent of sharing of, or cooperation or collaboration over, areas of jurisdiction is reflected in attributes used to describe different types of federalism. 'Cooperative federalism' is used to describe a federalism within which different levels of government seek to achieve agreement on mutually determined courses of action and cooperate to try to achieve them. 'Coordinate federalism' is used to describe a federalism within which different levels of government tend to leave each other to their own affairs and conceive of themselves as having discrete realms of operation and jurisdiction (Singleton et al. 2006, p. 77).

The division and delineation of jurisdictional autonomy, overlap and interdependencies between the central and regional entities are subject to considerable variation between countries. In Canada, for example, demands for regional autonomy have historically been strong, which has resulted in greater devolution of powers to the regions than is the case elsewhere (Holmes & Sharman 1977, p. 10). A new analysis of federalism in Asia argues that while federalism is relevant, it requires distinctive styles and hybrids in the region that differ from Western federalism (He 2007, pp. 10–18). Sometimes the subcentral entities within a federal system may reflect ethnic or religious diversities, sometimes the differences between regional entities are based on economic strength and resource bases, and sometimes the boundaries of the regions are determined historically. Indeed, Thompson has argued that federalism is a system of government usually resorted to by societies so divided that federalism represents the only way they can achieve unity (1994, p. 21).

The interactions between and within arenas of government in federalism are complex and difficult to disaggregate. In an effort to clarify these complex relationships, many studies focus on formal institutional mechanisms for the sharing of and collaboration over powers between the central and regional governments. Other approaches focus more on relationships and processes of cooperation and collaboration between governments, or on people's sense of identity. These approaches produce four different ways of analysing the fortunes of Australian federalism:

1 a legal approach, which focuses on the interpretation of the Commonwealth's constitutional powers by the High Court

2 an economic approach, which focuses on mechanisms of revenue collection and distribution
3 a governmental approach, which examines cooperation and coordination between levels of government. This has also been called a state-assertiveness approach (Gillespie 1994, pp. 67–9) or a political approach (Galligan 1989, pp. 3–4)
4 a cultural approach, which recognises people's identification with their region.

The legal approach

The legal approach to interpreting federalism focuses on analysing important High Court decisions as they have influenced the balance of forces within Australian federalism. The High Court has the authority to determine a Commonwealth or State law as invalid if it exceeds the constitutional prerogative of its tier of government. As noted above, it also has the power to decide whether a Commonwealth law and a State law are inconsistent with each other, in which case, under section 109 of the Constitution, the State law is considered inoperable.

Immediately after Federation, the High Court tended to interpret the Constitution in such a way as to preserve the ex-colonies' desire to protect their powers as much as possible from Commonwealth interference. This meant that the High Court supported the view that the Commonwealth and States had separate spheres of jurisdiction and that the States should be 'shielded' against Commonwealth intervention. Thus, the view was held that the Constitution established an 'implied immunities' doctrine, in which both levels of government would be immune from each other's laws, and a 'reserved powers' doctrine, in which the Commonwealth's ability to interfere in matters that were reserved to the States was limited (Selway & Williams 2005, pp. 478–9; Blackshield & Williams 2006, pp. 297, 303).

This attitude, however, was not to last long. In 1920 these ideas were overturned in the celebrated *Engineers* case (*Amalgamated Society of Engineers v Adelaide Steamship Co. Ltd* (1920) 28 CLR 129) in which it was found that States could be subject to federal industrial arbitration. This meant that an area previously under State jurisdiction was opened up to Commonwealth intervention. Despite the Court's claim that the decision was based in a literal reading of the Constitution, the decision greatly expanded the scope of Commonwealth intervention in State affairs (Galligan 1995, pp. 34, 173–4).

More than twenty years later the High Court again expanded the Commonwealth's powers. Until the *First Uniform Tax* case (*South Australia v The Commonwealth* (1942) 55 CLR 373), the States had levied income-based taxes. In 1942 the Commonwealth imposed uniform income-based taxation rates, and the High Court upheld its right to do so. Although the States were legally entitled to continue to levy their own income taxes, the Commonwealth promised to withhold federal grants to States that continued to levy their own income tax by the amount raised by the State government (Holmes & Sharman 1977, pp. 136–41). This eliminated any incentive for the States to continue to levy their own income taxes.

Several decades later *Koowarta v Bjelke-Petersen* (1982) 153 CLR 168 upheld the Commonwealth's power to sign international multilateral human rights treaties and to enact domestic legislation to implement them. The *Koowarta* case concerned a complaint by an Aboriginal man in Queensland that a State-based law discriminating against Aboriginal people with regard to land title contravened the Commonwealth *Racial Discrimination Act 1975*. The Commonwealth was allowed to implement this legislation under the external affairs power (section 51 (xxix) of the Constitution).

Later in *Tasmanian Dams* (*Commonwealth v Tasmania* (1983) 156 CLR 1) it was held that any matter of genuine international concern that was the subject of an international treaty fell within the ambit of the external affairs power (Galligan 1995, pp. 177–8). The *Tasmanian Dams* case concerned the protection of a World Heritage value wilderness area in Tasmania and a proposal to build a hydro-electric dam that would have flooded the area. The outcomes in these cases gave the federal government new scope to legislate in areas previously under the jurisdiction of the States, such as human rights and environmental protection.

A further example is the Toonen case, in which a gay man in Tasmania lodged a complaint with the United Nations Human Rights Committee on 25 December 1991, that Tasmanian State laws criminalising gay sex were discriminatory, they violated his right to equality and they constituted an arbitrary interference in his right to privacy. The complaint was lodged after an unsuccessful decade-long campaign to repeal the laws. The lodging of the complaint was possible because the federal government had ratified the International Covenant on Civil and Political Rights (ICCPR) and its First Optional Protocol allowing complaints of violations of this treaty to be lodged directly with the United Nations (Gelber 1999).

In 1994 the United Nations Human Rights Committee upheld the Toonen complaint and asked the Australian government to take measures to remedy the problem. But the Tasmanian government refused to change its laws. Instead the federal government passed the *Human Rights (Sexual Conduct) Act 1994*, which enshrined protection from arbitrary interference in private consensual sexual activity between adults, a right codified in the International Convention (Gelber 1999, pp. 330–4). The federal government's legislation contravened Tasmania's anti-gay laws, which meant that under section 109 the Tasmanian laws could have been declared inoperable. The High Court agreed to hear a case that would have done exactly that, but it was never heard because on 1 May 1997 the Tasmanian parliament repealed its law.

In *Teoh* (*Minister of State for Immigration and Ethnic Affairs v Ah Hin Teoh* (1995) 183 CLR 273), the impact of treaty ratification under the external affairs power was taken even further, and the High Court found that ratification of an international treaty gave rise to a 'legitimate expectation' that it would be upheld in domestic policy if there was some ambiguity in the domestic legislation concerned. This appeared to undermine the long-held principle that treaty ratification does not automatically incorporate its terms into domestic law and that the passage of domestic legislation is needed (Patapan 2000, p. 61). The Labor federal government at the time immediately challenged the finding and introduced legislation (Administrative Decision (Effect of International Instruments) Bill 1995) into parliament to have it overturned. This legislation lapsed when an election was called (Patapan 2000, p. 62). Similar bills then appeared in federal parliament again in 1997 and in 1999, which sought to entrench the idea that international instruments do not automatically give rise to legitimate expectations in domestic policy. However, it appears that the general principle anchored in the rule of law, that ambiguities in domestic legislation may be clarified by resorting to international legal principles and standards, is still being upheld in the High Court, for example in the *Lam* case (*Re Minister for Immigration and Multicultural Affairs; Ex parte Lam* (2003) 195 ALR 502) (see Lacey 2001, 2004).

Finally, in 2006 one of the most important judgments for Australian federalism was handed down in the High Court. In the *WorkChoices* decision (*New South Wales v Commonwealth of Australia; Western Australia v Commonwealth of Australia* (2006) 231 ALR 1), the High Court upheld the federal government's industrial relations regime as a valid exercise of the Commonwealth's constitutional corporations power (section 51 (xx)). The decision allows the Commonwealth to use the corporations power to regulate any activities of a corporation, including the internal workplace relations of a corporation and any matter associated with it. As a result, the federal government has the power to regulate a vast range of areas. There are few areas of Australian contemporary life that do not involve corporations, and in the context of the privatisation, corporatisation and outsourcing of services previously owned and run by governments over the last few decades the implications of this decision are far-reaching. The decision is also likely to influence the way different levels of government negotiate, given that the Commonwealth has a trump card: it can threaten to take over an area if the States do not perform adequately (Kildea & Gelber 2007). Even though the Rudd Labor government promised to repeal WorkChoices as soon as possible in its first term, the implications of the High Court judgment for the extent of Commonwealth jurisdiction will persist. For example, the legislation passed to enable the federal government to manage the Murray–Darling Basin (discussed in the snapshot at the beginning of this chapter) relied for its constitutionality in part on the corporations power as outlined in the *WorkChoices* case.

This section demonstrates that a legal approach to examining Australian federalism tends to lead to the conclusion that the Commonwealth is expanding its powers and encroaching on State areas of policy responsibility. This could mean that the States' policy role is decreasing, or even that the States are ceasing to operate in the ways intended at Federation (Craven 1992, p. 55). However, this interpretation relies on evidence derived from one source, and the picture it portrays might not be wholly accurate. This is because federalism is not a 'zero-sum game', meaning that as one tier of government gains the other necessarily and proportionately loses (Sharman 1989, p. 99; Gillespie 1994, p. 64). Federalism is a dynamic system of overlapping and shared policy responsibilities. A more accurate view may be gauged by investigating evidence drawn from other approaches.

The economic approach

A second approach to examining Australian federalism focuses on the financial relationship between the Commonwealth and the States, and in particular on the financial dominance of the Commonwealth government. For chronological accounts of changes in federal financial relations see Summers (2002, pp. 94–101), Gillespie (1994, pp. 76–87) or Singleton et al. (2006, pp. 109–16). Here, we will summarise the primary mechanisms and institutions of financial federalism.

Federation created a national government, which was empowered to effect internally free trade by removing domestic customs and tariffs and by imposing uniform national customs and excise on imports. Tariffs and other taxes had previously been collected and spent by the colonies themselves. Federation meant that the States were both relinquishing their income from intercolonial tariffs and granting the Commonwealth the power to collect national tariff, customs and excise duties. This meant that disputes arose at the time of drafting the Constitution over how the monies collected by the Commonwealth would be distributed. An agreement was reached that the Constitution would contain provisions for the allocation of funds to the States for the first ten years after Federation (sections 81–105). In the long term, however, it would be left up to parliament to decide on the future allocation of funds (Galligan 1995, pp. 217–23).

The Commonwealth therefore was granted exclusive control over customs and excise, but all other taxes were available to both levels of government (Summers 2002, p. 93). Although this arrangement sounds equitable, it had the immediate effect of ensuring Commonwealth financial dominance. At Federation, customs tariffs amounted to 75 per cent of overall tax revenue (Galligan 1995, p. 219). This meant that the federal government earned more money than it spent. The States had responsibility for carrying out policy in a range of areas including education, health and housing, yet their revenue base was too small to fund these programs themselves.

> The situation where the Commonwealth earns more revenue than it spends, and the States earn less revenue than they need to cover their expenditures, is called 'vertical fiscal imbalance'.

This immediate financial benefit on the part of the national government was enhanced by later developments, and the Commonwealth continued to hold the upper hand in revenue collection and distribution. The three main mechanisms that produce Commonwealth–State financial tensions are:

1 the Commonwealth Grants Commission
2 the Commonwealth's use of 'tied grants' under section 96 of the Constitution
3 taxation.

1 Commonwealth Grants Commission

The Commonwealth Grants Commission was established in 1933 to assess claims made by States for special assistance. In the early 1980s the commission changed from making extra payments to States on the basis of need to calculating general revenue assistance on the basis of a formula of per capita relativities. The commission works according to the principle of horizontal fiscal equalisation. This means that grants are allocated differentially to States in an attempt to ensure that each State can deliver services to its residents at a comparable standard to other States (Galligan 1995, p. 234; Gillespie 1994, p. 75). The commission's principle of fiscal equalisation states that:

> State governments should receive funding from the pool of goods and services, tax revenue and health care grants such that, if each made the same effort to raise revenue from its own sources and operated at the same level of efficiency, each would have the capacity to provide services at the same standard. (CGC 2004, p. 4)

The methods used to calculate relativities are reviewed every five years (CGC 2004, p. 1).

> The attempt to equalise the States' capacity to provide comparable levels of services is called 'horizontal fiscal equalisation'.

The distribution of general revenue assistance this way is highly controversial. If Commonwealth funds were distributed on a per person basis, the larger and more populous States would receive a bigger slice of the revenue pie than they currently receive. For example, in 1994–95 if funds had been distributed on a per person basis, New South Wales, Victoria and the ACT would have received $1.5 billion more (Painter 1997a, p. 203). Those States with healthy earning capacities and larger populations in effect subsidise the economically weaker States. Funds are redistributed away from the wealthier States such as New South Wales and Victoria. The larger States have therefore historically seen horizontal fiscal equalisation as unfair (Summers 2002, p. 105; Painter 1997a, p. 203).

2 Tied grants

The Commonwealth is entitled under section 96 of the Constitution to make individual payments to States 'on such terms and conditions as the Parliament thinks fit'. These payments are also known as section 96 grants, tied grants, specific purpose grants (Galligan 1995, p. 228) or specific purpose payments (Painter 1997a, p. 201). Tied grants allow the Commonwealth to specify how the money will be spent by the recipient State. This provision was designed to allow the federal government to make one-off payments to poorer, less populous and disadvantaged States (Galligan 1995, p. 221) and to direct funds to specific programs that need funding (Painter 1997a, p. 201).

Over the longer term these grants have proved particularly controversial because they allow the Commonwealth to direct State spending. Although some tied grants were made as early as 1910–11 (Summers 2002, p. 94), their use increased significantly from the 1970s. As a proportion of total grants to States by the Commonwealth, tied grants comprised 30 per cent in 1972–73, then reached a peak of 49 per cent in 1975–76 under the Whitlam Labor government, returned to 26 per cent in 1982–83, and rose again to 35 per cent in 1992–93 and 42 per cent in 2000–01 (Summers 2002, pp. 97–100; Painter 1997a, p. 201).

Some analysts have argued that States have retained wide jurisdiction in spending, even where tied grants are involved, often because the conditions attached to the grants are very general or because the conditions reflect negotiations completed before the funds were granted. Nevertheless, it appears that during the eleven years of Coalition government from 1996 to 2007 there were instances of highly interventionist funding arrangements, including the imposition of conditions relating to matters outside the core reason for the funding (Parkin & Anderson 2007, pp. 304, 306). This, combined with a willingness on the part of the Commonwealth to bypass the States entirely to implement elements of its policy agenda and to force the States to comply with federally determined policy initiatives via joint funding arrangements (Solomon 2007, p. 39), bolsters the claim that financial arrangements continue to operate as a source of Commonwealth influence over ostensibly State policy areas.

3 Taxation

There are several areas in which the States' taxation powers have been curtailed. It has already been noted that from the 1940s the federal government established a practical monopoly over the collection of income taxes, which became an increasing proportion of overall revenue after World War II (Summers 2002, pp. 94–6). This was partly driven by expanded expectations of national government following the two world wars and the 1929 Depression.

Also, in the 1990s the High Court found many State licensing fees to constitute 'customs and excise' (under section 90 of the Constitution). This prohibited the States from levying them, although subsequent to this decision the federal government effectively arranged to collect these revenues on behalf of the States (Parkin & Anderson 2007, p. 297).

The single most important change in taxation since the imposition of uniform income tax was the introduction of the GST in 2000. Since that time GST revenues have been channelled directly to the States, which has meant a large amount of money has been allocated to State government coffers with no federal strings attached and with no need for the States to request the funding from the Commonwealth. The GST revenue replaced previous unconditional general revenue grants, but was offset in part by a corresponding abolition of many State-based taxes (such as financial institutions duties and stamp duties) (Parkin & Anderson 2007, pp. 297–9). Although Parkin and Anderson argue that overall the financial position of the States was strengthened by this change, Solomon argues to the contrary that their increase in resources gave the States 'no greater freedom' because the federal government demanded compliance with other financial policies in return (Solomon 2007, p. 37).

These accounts tell a story of the Commonwealth's continued ability to manipulate financial relations in such a way as to influence policy in States' jurisdictions. The logical conclusion to be drawn from this is that the Commonwealth financially dominates the federal system and that this dominance is at the expense of the States.

However, this approach may not provide the complete picture. For example, the States probably prefer not to raise their own income taxes because they avoid the political costs and dissatisfaction associated with doing so, they can shift the blame for poor performance to the federal government, and when the expenditure occurs at the level of policy and service delivery the States still exert a great deal of control over how and where the money is spent (Painter 1997a, pp. 201–2). Furthermore, the States' retention of GST revenues gives them a robust financial grounding that they take into future negotiations. And since policy in most areas is still carried out by and within the States (even if it is federally funded), the States can exert influence over policy implementation. The economic approach, then, leaves us with unclear conclusions as to the relationship between the Commonwealth and the States. With this in mind, it is important to consider the third approach to assessing Commonwealth–State relations: the governmental approach.

The governmental approach

The governmental approach analyses relations between the Commonwealth and States from the perspective of intergovernmental relations; that is, cooperation, interchange and collaboration between different levels of government over policy-making.

There are a very large number of intergovernmental committees, meetings, agencies and agreements in Australia, and it is not possible to detail them all. For example, Sharman details the 'proliferation' of intergovernmental organisations in conjunction with the increasing complexity of governmental tasks after 1951 (1989, pp. 107–9). Nevertheless, examinations of intergovernmental relations have been conducted, including those by Painter (1987; 1998) and Carroll and Painter (1995). In assessing intergovernmental relations here, we will focus on two key examples: the Council of Australian Governments (COAG) and national competition reforms.

A key institution of intergovernmental cooperation is COAG, which was established in 1992 to provide a forum for regular meetings of the Prime Minister, premiers, chief ministers and the president of the Australian Local Government Association. This body replaced earlier intergovernmental meetings of heads of government, particularly the Special Premiers' Conferences, which had begun in 1990 and were perceived to have been dominated by the Commonwealth (Edwards & Henderson 1995, pp. 22–3). Early studies indicated that COAG operated as a 'genuinely federal' institution because it provided a forum for genuine cooperation and coordination between governments. In policy areas where the Commonwealth required joint action with the States, or where the States needed a process to coordinate their actions and/or lacked powers, COAG facilitated genuine bargaining and give-and-take (Carroll & Painter 1995, p. 10).

Examples of the kind of agreement reached in COAG include the National Action Plan for Salinity and Water Quality 2000, a $1.4 billion, seven-year agreement between the federal, State and Territory governments to support practical measures in rural and regional areas to rehabilitate waterways, improve native vegetation, improve engineering works or change land and water use (NAPSWQ 2007). In 2004 an agreement on research involving human embryos and prohibition of human cloning was reached. The agreement banned human cloning and established a national regulatory regime to oversee the use of assisted reproductive technology (COAG 2004).

During the later Howard government years, however, COAG was criticised as being a forum in which the federal government sought ratification by the States of its own policy agenda. Solomon cites in evidence the implementation of the National Competition Policy (Solomon 2007, p. 42) as do Singleton et al. (2006, pp. 117–18), who cite the Commonwealth's success in securing agreement from the States to fund debt reduction, the States' acquiescence to Medicare and housing agreements despite disagreements over funding levels, and the States' compliance with the abolition of certain taxes in return for GST revenue. Even where genuine negotiation and collaboration have occurred, it has been argued that they led to the eventual ceding of State powers to the Commonwealth (Parkin & Anderson 2007, p. 303). The successful negotiations in 2007 between the Commonwealth and New South Wales, Queensland, South Australia and the ACT, discussed in the snapshot, are a clear example of the federal government negotiating in such a way as to secure agreement from the States, even though they were effectively ceding some of their powers to the Commonwealth.

In addition, Parkin and Anderson argue that the Howard government engaged in extensive 'regulatory' federalism, in which formal regulatory structures such as intergovernmental forums were used to impose regimes and incentive structures to ensure the States' compliance with central policy demands. Examples of this are the federal government requiring States to use a Commonwealth-approved, standardised student report card in return for school funding, and making university funding contingent on universities offering individual contracts to staff (Williams 2008, pp. 19–20).

A particularly clear example is the National Competition Policy (NCP) Agreement, which commenced in 1995 under the Keating Labor government but was to be largely implemented by the later Howard Coalition government (Parkin & Anderson 2007, pp. 301–2).

National competition policy

In the 1980s Australia began to restructure its economy to establish a more competitive market environment, including by floating the dollar and deregulating financial markets. By the 1990s COAG was considering how to achieve greater competitiveness in government enterprises. In October 1992 an Independent Committee of Inquiry into a National Competition Policy was established, chaired by Professor Fred Hilmer. The final report of that committee has become known as the 'Hilmer Report', and it formed the basis for competition policy in Australia.

Source: <www.ncc.gov.au/articleZone.asp?articleZoneID=16#Article-87>. The Hilmer Report is available at <www.ncc.gov.au/publication.asp?publicationID=219&activityID=39>.

The NCP had a wide-ranging reform agenda, which included privatisation, corporatisation and regulatory change. As a direct result of this agreement the States and Territories undertook large-scale reforms and in return received significant Commonwealth funding. This means that the States were persuaded to implement the federal government's reform agenda through the payment of incentives. Non-compliance led to financial penalties (Parkin & Anderson 2007, p. 301; Solomon 2007, p. 42). For example in 2006 funding worth $3.97 million to Western Australia was removed due to its failure to implement reforms to water planning (Howard 2006b). Parkin and Anderson argue that the NCP process 'reduced the scope for discretionary action by the States'. Even if the States disagreed with the measures being requested of them, the financial penalties for not doing so were so significant that compliance was ultimately secured. The result was that 'national-level policy and program priorities' were interposed into areas under State constitutional jurisdiction (Parkin & Anderson 2007, pp. 302–3; Hollander 2006).

In the past a governmental approach to examining Commonwealth–State relations has tended to produce more positive assessments of the fortunes of the States in Australian federalism than the results provided by a legal or an economic approach (Parkin & Anderson 2007, p. 304, and see for example Gillespie 1994, p. 68; Sharman 1989, p. 100). This is primarily because the governmental approach takes a less formalistic approach to calculating the balance of forces, and it is able to discern complex interrelationships between players which are not visible in the first two approaches. This approach is better able to take two-dimensional or three-dimensional aspects of the exercise or assertion of power into account than the first two discussed here. The governmental approach benefits from being able to recognise the continuous participation and contestation of the States and Territories in policy decision-making and delivery, and from identifying and allowing the examination of complex mechanisms for intergovernmental cooperation and collaboration. This means that these approaches have tended to draw optimistic conclusions about the fortunes of Australian federalism.

More recent analyses, however, have tended to draw a more pessimistic view of intergovernmental relations from the point of view of federalism, and have provided evidence of an increasingly assertive Commonwealth government in intergovernmental relations. It may be the case that the years of Coalition government represented a genuine change in the tone and nature of intergovernmental relations.

The election of the Rudd Labor government in late 2007 may change this outlook. The first meeting of COAG following the election discussed a 'new framework for cooperative Commonwealth–State relations' and sought to tackle significant issues in health, education, climate change, infrastructure and housing (Rudd 2007a)—all policy areas in which both the Commonwealth and the States play significant roles. The media consistently reported the federal government's stated desire to reduce blame shifting, achieve greater cooperation and simplify Commonwealth–State relations (for example Uren 2008; Steketee 2008; Kelly 2007). The new government has set targets, including reducing the number of people waiting for elective surgery by 25,000, guaranteeing access to early childhood education for four-year-olds, reducing by 50 per cent in five years the number of people turned away from homeless shelters, and eliminating the twenty-year difference in life expectancy between indigenous and non-indigenous Australians within a generation. It will establish working groups and implementation plans (Steketee 2008).

A New South Wales government inquiry into options for a new national industrial relations system concluded with a report in late 2007 which outlined new mechanisms for a sharing and interchange of powers between the States and the Commonwealth. This system would permit either a referral of powers or simultaneous, identical State and Commonwealth legislation, thus requiring high levels of cooperation between the different levels of government (Williams 2007b; Marris 2008a, 2008b).

It remains to be seen whether the changes to federalism that will be ushered in by the Rudd government will mark a return of intergovernmental relations to an era of genuine cooperation and bargaining.

Cultural federalism

Despite differences of opinion over the relative influence and power of federal, State and Territory governments, it remains the case in Australia that culturally people still perceive differences between the regions in which they live. People in their everyday lives identify as a Queenslander, a Western Australian and so on. This brings a new but often overlooked dimension into the frame: that of cultural federalism.

It can be argued that Australians have become enculturated as federal people, although few people are consciously aware this. Cultural federalism is for the most part subtly pervasive and widespread. Examples include interstate sports competitions, such as the State of Origin Rugby League games, which allow residents of New South Wales and Queensland to invent and engage themselves in ultimately harmless territorial wars over a piece of turf only about a hundred metres long. Alternatively, surveys since the 1960s indicate that both State and nation are important components of Australians' construction of their own identity, although nation is often ranked ahead of State (Smith 2001b, p. 281). When asked how they identify, most people will respond both with a national and a State or Territory nomenclature. Rodney Smith argues that fully rounded State identities as such are elusive, in the sense that it is difficult to argue how a Western Australian identity differs from, say, a Queensland one. However, an allegiance to State or Territory remains an important component of a cultural construction of Australianness (2001b, pp. 291–3). For example, Queenslander homes are said to be an 'icon' that gives residents a sense of 'cultural identity' (Martin 2007). Western Australians' geographical isolation is said to give them a sense of parochialism, separateness and cultural isolation (Gallop 2000). It is popularly believed that certain identifiable qualities can be attributed to the residents of different regions in Australia, regardless of the machinations of governmental power.

In addition to identifying with one's State or Territory, Smith argues that Australians are culturally both aware and supportive of federalism itself (2001b, p. 305). This means that federalism has entwined itself in our daily lives in virtually incalculable ways. When viewed from a cultural perspective, Australian federalism can be seen as both constructing, and a construction of, federally (and other) divided identities. This implies that federalism is vital and organic, capable of acting and interacting with actors, and of reinforcing itself and being reinforced in cultural ways. It may well be that extra-institutional approaches to analysing federalism, such as a cultural approach, will play an increasingly important role in analysing Australian federalism in the future.

Understanding Australian federalism

Most analyses of Australian federalism recognise the increasingly influential role of the Commonwealth in day-to-day Commonwealth–State relations and in policy areas. Constitutionally, the Commonwealth has successfully expanded the interpretation and reach of its powers in ways unforeseen at Federation. Financially, it is evident that the Commonwealth dominates decisions on expenditure and has continued to do so since the introduction of the GST in 2000. In intergovernmental forums and arrangements, it is easier to see the continuing and vital role that the States and Territories play as important actors in federal relations. Nevertheless, even here the Commonwealth has displayed a tendency since the mid-1990s to try to achieve its own policy agenda via incentives and penalties.

Does this imply that federalism itself is at risk from developments in contemporary Australian politics, because the Commonwealth is influencing States' affairs in increasingly widespread ways? Or does it imply that the nature of federalism is changing but that Australia will remain a viable federation for the foreseeable future? It is still true that the States and Territories carry the weight of responsibility for implementation of policy change. Additionally it is extremely unlikely that the Commonwealth would completely take over large areas of State responsibility, such as hospitals or secondary schools, despite its probable constitutional ability (since the *WorkChoices* decision) to do so. Such a move would require the devotion of considerable Commonwealth resources to running departments and offices remote from the coalface of policy implementation. This would be expensive and would not automatically result in better outcomes for the end-users (patients or students) than the current system. The possibility of duplication of services would render such a move vulnerable to charges of wastefulness and inefficiency.

When viewed from the perspective of multidimensional understandings of power, Australian federalism remains a site of considerable contestation. It is still true that the States and Territories—as well as the Commonwealth—are important actors within that site. Federalism is as much about institutional frameworks and arrangements, such as the Constitution or financial agreements, as it is about processes of coordination, bargaining and negotiation between different levels of government, processes that undergo continuous change. Federalism is changing, but this need not mean that federalism itself is at risk.

As we move through the twenty-first century, the system of government within which participants operate must try to keep pace with technological, cultural, social and economic change. Analyses of federalism that are flexible enough to recognise these changes are more likely to produce results that reflect the complexities of contemporary Australian political practice and policy-making processes. We argue, then, that understanding Australian federalism requires being responsive to changes and taking into account the roles of a variety of actors and participants. This produces a complex picture of the fortunes of Australian federalism.

Summary

- The Australian governing framework combines a Westminster and a federal model into one hybrid system of government. The Westminster elements tend to rely on unwritten rules of conduct, and the federal elements tend to be more explicit in the Constitution.
- There are tensions between the Westminster and federal systems, which express themselves in arguments over whether the House of Representatives or the Senate has a 'mandate' to carry out policy and whether the written or unwritten rules should be more important in a dispute.
- Examining federalism from a legal or economic approach produces results that imply the Commonwealth is increasingly dominating in policy areas that are ostensibly the responsibility of the States.
- Examining federalism from a governmental approach reveals more complex processes involved in contemporary federal dynamics.
- Regardless of the influence and power of the Commonwealth vis-à-vis the States and Territories, culturally people in their everyday lives display a resilient identification with their region as well as their nation.

Further reading

Galligan, Brian 1995, *A Federal Republic: Australia's Constitutional System of Government*, Cambridge University Press, Melbourne.

Painter, Martin 1998, *Collaborative Federalism: Economic Reform in Australia in the 1990s*, Cambridge University Press, Melbourne.

Smith, Rodney 2001, *Australian Political Culture*, Pearson Education, Sydney.

Useful websites

- Federal government entry point: <www.australia.gov.au>. From this site you can access every State and Territory's home page and get information about the State and Territory governments.
- COAG: <www.coag.gov.au>. From this entry point you can read communiqués about COAG meetings and access intergovernmental agreements.

CHAPTER 12
POLICY ANALYSIS

Although policy-making is often portrayed as the decisions made by a government as to whether it should do A or B, it is in fact a continually contested, inherently 'messy' activity involving a diverse range of actors and interests that need to be reconciled. In the first part of this chapter we look at what is 'public policy' and explore the different approaches and concepts political scientists use to make sense of the policy process. We develop a framework for analysing policy issues that recognises and accommodates the complexity of policy-making. In the second part of the chapter we apply these concepts and techniques to three different areas of policy in Australia: the economy, health and industrial relations.

The topics covered in this chapter include:

- defining public policy and exploring who is involved in the policy process
- developing a framework for the critical analysis of policy-making, drawing on the work of scholars within the 'structured interaction' perspective
- examining how the preferences and actions of political actors in the policy process are shaped through ideas, institutions and interactions
- case studies of three contemporary policy issues: developing a national curriculum for schools, private health insurance and the management of interest rates.

SNAPSHOT Australia's policy climate change—ratifying the Kyoto Protocol

The international scientific community has overwhelmingly acknowledged climate change and increasing greenhouse gas emissions as the cause of significant and possibly irreversible damage to the earth's atmosphere (Intergovernmental Panel on Climate Change 2001; Bureau of Meteorology 2004). Frequent droughts, extreme weather and increased temperatures are all consequences of this human-induced pollution.

The Kyoto Protocol is an international agreement between states to reduce greenhouse gas emissions. It is linked to the United Nations Framework Convention on Climate Change (UNFCCC), but stands on its own as a 'firm and binding commitment' legally requiring states that have signed and ratified the protocol to comply with individual targets set for the reduction of emissions (UNFCCC 2008). Under the principle of 'common but differentiated responsibilities', the protocol places a heavier burden on developed states, taking into account the historically greater emissions of these states and the fact that they can pay the cost of cutting emissions with greater ease. In 2007, 176 countries had ratified the protocol.

Australia signed the Kyoto Protocol in 1998, but did not ratify it. Ratification is a further step to signing an international treaty, involving an expression from the executive government of a state that it intends to be bound by the treaty's provisions. The government's position, as articulated by Prime Minister Howard in Question Time, was:

> It is not in Australia's interests to ratify the Kyoto Protocol . . . because the arrangements currently exclude—and are likely under present settings to continue to exclude—both developing countries and the United States. For us to ratify the protocol would cost us jobs and damage our industry. (House of Representatives Hansard, 5 June 2002, p. 3163)

In 2004 the Senate Environment, Communications, Information Technology and the Arts Committee (Senate Environment Committee) conducted an inquiry into whether Australia should ratify the protocol. After considering submissions from businesses and environmental groups and evidence from climate change experts and public servants, the committee's report recommended against ratification (Senate Environment Committee 2004). However, a dissenting report was issued by the Labor Party, the Australian Democrats and the Greens. All these political parties explicitly supported ratification.

Ratification was also advocated by numerous environmental groups, including the Climate Change Action Network, Friends of the Earth and Greenpeace, which campaigned to change the government's stance on the issue. For example, to coincide with the start of the 2007 APEC meeting in Sydney, Greenpeace activists painted the message 'Australia pushing export coal' on the side of a coal ship docked at Newcastle to draw attention to the inconsistencies between coal exports and the spirit of the Kyoto Protocol (Greenpeace 2007). Although they acknowledged the limitations of the protocol, these groups argued that in refusing to ratify it Australia was acting out of step with the international community and needed to be seen as a good global environmental citizen, serious about tackling greenhouse gas emissions (Senate Environment Committee 2004, pp. 9–10).

The business community's opinion on the Australian government's position was mixed. Some business associations (for example, the Australian Wind Energy Association and Environment Business Australia) saw the importance of ratifying the protocol as promoting certainty, so companies could invest and take advantage of the opportunities created for renewable energy products. Others in the businesses community (Woodside Energy, the Australian Chamber of Commerce and Industry and the Plastics and Chemicals Industries Association) were opposed to ratification, concerned about the economic impact of legally binding emissions targets (Senate Environment Committee 2004, pp. 10–12, 19–20).

The Kyoto Protocol polarised the major parties during the 2007 federal election campaign. A report released by the UN Framework Convention on Climate Change in the week before the election reported that greenhouse gas emissions from industrialised countries were approaching an all-time high. Despite a poll conducted in October 2007 by the *Age* that revealed 88 per cent of respondents supported ratification, Prime Minister Howard maintained his position: 'My view is that there's a serious challenge . . . My view is also that the world is not coming to an end tomorrow and that like all of these things we have to get a commonsense, balanced approach' (AAP 2007). Conversely, ratifying the Kyoto Protocol was one of Labor's major election campaign promises.

Although many groups had lobbied unsuccessfully to alter the Howard government's position on Kyoto, the change of government after the 2007 federal election also brought a swift change in policy. Within hours of being sworn in as Prime Minister, Kevin Rudd acted to ratify the protocol as the first official act of his government. Rudd argued that 'Australia's official declaration today that we will become a member of the Kyoto Protocol is a significant step forward in our country's efforts to fight climate change domestically and with the international community' and pledged a series of commitments, including reviewed emissions and renewable energy targets and a national emissions trading scheme (Rudd 2007c).

An international alliance of business and energy industry leaders, representing more than 150 companies including Westpac, Coca-Cola, Virgin and Nike, welcomed the ratification and called for future climate change policy to be guided 'primarily by science', with the establishment of legally binding emission targets, so that companies could invest with certainty in researching and developing low-carbon technology. Australia's energy industry was also reported to have united in support of Rudd's commitment to ratify Kyoto (Murphy 2007).

However, the ratification was also seen by many with a degree of scepticism, representing little more than a symbolic (albeit important) step. It was argued that the government had lagged in setting the policy direction on climate change and that strategic economic decisions had already been taken by companies (Hewett 2007). Greenpeace and the Climate Change Action Network also warned that much of the difficult policy work was still to come. They argued that the Australian government had taken little action so far in reducing emissions and now needed to work hard on making the switch from coal to renewable energy (Franklin & Ryan 2007).

Australia's changing position on the ratification of the Kyoto Protocol illustrates the complex policy issues underlying what might on the surface seem a relatively straightforward act of executive government. It also raises broader questions about the nature of the policy process in Australia. Despite the dramatic step of ratifying the Kyoto Protocol, did a change in government really affect a policy change? Is the government the only actor involved in shaping climate change policy? Was it responding to policy change or leading it? This snapshot also reveals that the Kyoto Protocol was not simply about protecting the environment. What other issues were involved?

What is public policy?

Public policy can be defined as what governments do (or choose not to do) in order to achieve a certain aim or purpose. This definition is both clarifying and confusing. It clarifies that public policy is about governments' decisions in a range of policy areas and that it involves action and inaction. At the same time, it is confusing because it talks only about government and not about the multitude of other political actors who contribute to the development of public policy and policy delivery.

Some definitions of public policy do include both the formal institutions of government and informal actors, networks and stakeholders. Others acknowledge the power of ideas (the third dimension of power) in driving policy development.

For example, we can view policy as the 'instrument of governance' that results from the 'competition between ideas, interests and ideologies that impels our political system' (Althaus, Bridgman & Davis 2007, p. 5). This recognises that public policy results from complex interactions (such as those we have described throughout this book) and that it is not a linear and uncontested process originating in the executive, passing through the legislature and being implemented by the public service. However, there are different ways of viewing the interaction between official policy-makers within the system of government and other players in the policy arena.

Considine critiques what he calls the 'standard view' of policy, which emphasises the use of governmental authority to commit resources to achieve a desired outcome (1994, p. 3). This approach, he argues, is too instrumental because it emphasises the formal, governmental institutions involved in policy formation and delivery and discounts the complex interactions in the development and consequences of policy-making. Instead he advocates a view of policy that focuses on process, not just outcomes. He defines policy as the 'continuing work done by groups of policy actors who use available public institutions to articulate and express the things they value' (1994, p. 4). Both the contestation within policy-making acknowledged above and this view of policy as a process fit well with the overall approach of this book—an approach to understanding contemporary Australian politics that looks beyond formal institutions and seeks to take the roles of a broad range of political actors and networks into account.

In focusing on the processes of policy-making, as well as the arenas within which it occurs, we are investigating the many ways in which policy is influenced and shaped in often invisible ways. Ultimately, we are examining a particular context for the exercise of multi-dimensional power. Thus, we can develop a definition of public policy (see box), which is derived from the works cited.

> 'Public policy' is decided in a process of continuous contestation. It is the formation, articulation and implementation of political actors' goals via public institutional arrangements.

Policy analysis

In this section, we expand on the fundamental principles of public policy developed above to create a framework by which we can analyse the policy issues presented later in the chapter. Policy-making takes place in arenas characterised by authority and conflict but which also present opportunities for cooperation and collective action. In the field of political science, the question of how best to analyse policy is just as contested as the policy processes it seeks to explain. Although there is no agreed method of policy analysis, since the mid-twentieth century a number of distinct approaches have emerged, roughly grouped in two camps. The first camp consists of those who see policy-making as a rational and ordered process, which can be analysed according to scientific principles (Althaus, Bridgman & Davis 2007; Fenna 2004). The second camp sees policy-making not as an irrational and chaotic process but as one characterised by continuous and symbiotic patterns of interaction between political actors (Colebatch 2002; Considine 1994; Stone 2002). Given our approach to power as a relational concept with multiple dimensions (see Chapter 1), we are most persuaded by the second method, which forms the basis of our analytical framework. In establishing this framework and analysing the debates in public policy analysis, we look at three aspects of policy-making:

- The **processes** involved in the creation of public policy. Are they linear and rational, or dynamic and contested?
- The range of **actors** involved in making public policy. Is public policy made by governments? Do non-government organisations have a role?
- The **interactions** between political actors. How do actors interact with one another? What shapes their preferences and strategies? What role do ideas play?

Policy processes: rational or interactional?

A common way in which social scientists try to make sense of the complex interactions that take place in the development of public policy is to simplify the process into a number of discrete stages, called the 'policy cycle' (examples include Howlett & Ramesh 2003; Althaus, Bridgman & Davis 2007; Hogwood & Gun 1984). The underlying logic of this approach is based on applied problem-solving: although it is a theoretical construct, each of the stages in the policy cycle is intended to correspond with one of the steps you might take if you could solve a real-world problem in a rational and systematic way.

The policy cycle model proceeds according to a number of discrete stages. Problems are recognised and come to the attention of the government, which formulates a number of policy options before choosing its preferred course of action (or inaction). The government and the public service consequently implement this policy choice, the results of which are monitored and evaluated by various policy actors before being fed back into the cycle.

The policy cycle framework is useful in that it allows the analyst to disaggregate a complex process into a simple sequence of stages that can be investigated and compared individually. It can be applied to different levels of policy-making (from local government to international organisations) and can take account of a range of different policy actors, although it does heavily emphasise the government as the key decision-maker (Howlett & Ramesh 2003, pp. 14–15).

However, the framework does suffer from a number of difficulties. Scott (2006, p. 573) argues that instead of conceptualising policy-making as a linear cycle, it is more appropriate to view policy-making as an ongoing, evolutionary process with constant feedback between the stages. We cannot assume political actors will actively seek policy solutions to recognised problems; they may just react to circumstances according to their own interests and pre-defined values. The model fails to explain how or why the policy process moves from stage to stage without stopping at a particular point (Howlett & Ramesh 2003, p. 14), and it assumes that policy has both a starting point and an end point that are discernable. Finally, the policy cycle framework does not tell us much about how and why actors participate in making policy and how different perspectives and values are reconciled and resolved, nor does it talk about contestation over resources, power and ideas or discourses.

The simplicity of the policy cycle framework is a fundamental weakness. As it is based on the logic of rational, systematic and linear decision-making, the model has been criticised on the basic ground that it does not reflect reality (Everett 2003; C. Howard 2005). As Stone (2002, p. 7) observes, the policy cycle is 'a production model, where policy is created in a fairly ordered sequence of stages, almost as if on an assembly line', thus reflecting a desire to imbue a scientific, analytical rationality upon the formation of policy and to move it away from the irrationality of politics. However, we argue that policy and politics are inherently intertwined, as at the heart of public policies lie values (Smith et al. 2006, p. 132). Policy actors do not recognise problems and seek solutions, rather '[t]he world of policy is populated by a range of players with distinct concerns, and that policy-making is the intersection of these diverse agendas, not a collective attempt to accomplish some known goal' (Colebatch 2006, p. 1).

Nonetheless, while the policy cycle is an unsatisfactory tool with which to analyse policy formation, it should not be disregarded. The model has a symbolic importance, and in part reflects the policy cycle thinking that has become entrenched in the Australian public sector, particularly in the formation and evaluation of economic policy (Mascarenhas 1996, pp. 218–27; Palmer 2006). As we will see in the case study on interest rate policy, the scientific rationality with which monetary policy is created and evaluated is closely linked to the neoclassical ideology of the free market, and highlights the important (and inseparable) relationship between policy analysis and politics. As Stone (2002, p. 8) suggests, 'analysis is itself a creature of politics; it is strategically crafted argument, designed to create ambiguities and paradoxes and to resolve them in a particular direction'. In this way the policy cycle could be viewed as a normative model, if not entirely accurate as a description of how the world works then a prescription for how policy-making ought to occur.

We argue that it is more fruitful to analyse the policy-making process through the lens of what Hal Colebatch terms 'structured interaction'. Fundamentally different to the policy cycle framework:

> The structured interaction perspective does not assume a single decision-maker, addressing a clear policy problem: it focuses on the range of participants in the game, the diversity of their understandings of the situation and the problem, the ways in which they interact with one another, and the outcomes of this interaction. It does not assume that this pattern of activity is a collective effort to achieve known and shared goals. (Colebatch 1998, pp. 102–3)

The structured interaction framework does not disregard the importance of government and the hierarchy of authority in approving and implementing policy decisions in public service departments, but acknowledges that the policy process has two dimensions: the vertical and the horizontal. The vertical dimension is concerned with rule, or the downward transmission of authorised policy decisions to subordinate officials to implement and evaluate (Colebatch 2002, p. 23). However, the vertical dimension is complemented by a horizontal dimension that focuses on the relationship among policy participants in the various organisations outside the line of authority; how linkages between policy actors are formed and sustained, the frameworks that participants use to understand policy and the institutional context within which action is undertaken (Colebatch

2002, pp. 23–4). The use of a structured interaction approach will become clearer throughout the chapter as it is discussed in the context of participants and interactions, and then applied to three case studies.

Participants in the policy process

As we have argued, public policy involves a set of choices and competing values and interests. Many theories of public policy place great emphasis on government as the key actor involved in determining public policy, or the politicians and bureaucrats who head the institutions and departments that approve policy decisions (Considine 1994, pp. 5–6). A good example is Thomas Dye's definition of public policy as 'anything a government chooses to do or not to do' (Dye 1972, p. 2). However, in the structured interaction perspective, it is not assumed that government is the only actor and makes the critical policy decisions—the question of who is involved in the policy process is much more important. Who participates in the issue will help to shape what that issue is (Colebatch 2002, p. 36). As policy-making is not only about hierarchy and rule, but also negotiation and consensus:

> It is more fruitful to suspend judgement about who (if anyone) is 'making policy', and concentrate on identifying the people who are participating in the policy process, how they got there and what they do, and then determine whether we would want to identify any of them as 'policy-makers'. (Colebatch 2002, p. 25)

Who participates in the policy process (who we term 'political actors') varies across different policy issues, and includes government, business and community actors—both individuals and groups. Broadly defined, political actors include 'any individual or group able to take action on a public problem or issue' (Considine 1994, p. 6). One of the most important things to note about participants in the policy process is that they are not necessarily those with 'policy' in their title; rather, these actors are diverse and have varying motivations (Colebatch 2006, pp. 1–2).

As we saw in the snapshot, the government is without doubt a key actor in the policy process. Nonetheless, we can't assume that 'the government' is a single, coherent entity. Even within the broad label of 'the government' there are numerous political actors at work, often with differing perspectives and preferences: for example, the Prime Minister, Cabinet, ministerial staff (see Anderson 2006), ministerial advisers and department officials. If we extend our conception of government to include the broader parliamentary arena, political parties, individual parliamentarians and committees (Holland 2006) come into play. The judiciary can also be regarded as a policy actor (see the discussion of judicial activism in Chapter 3). In addition, there is a universe of quasi-independent government bodies undertaking policy work, such as the Reserve Bank, which operate within a prescribed statutory framework and with defined policy responsibilities but with a greater degree of autonomy than government departments (Argy 2000, p. 99).

But as noted, the government is not the only actor in policy processes. Although government ministers may make official pronouncements on policy that legitimate the process, like announcing the ratification of an international commitment, 'they do so after a wide range of other groups have had their say . . . In practice the circle of policy makers is always much wider than a roll-call of elected and appointed officials' (Considine 1994, p. 6). The activities, strategies and impacts of several of these political actors have been examined throughout this book: the media, business, individuals, pressure groups and social movements (see Part II—Political actors).

Participants in the policy process—whether they are government, community or business—often join together as 'policy collectives' to find mutual support, share knowledge and address policy problems of common concern. Policy collectives are also referred to as 'policy communities' or 'policy networks'. Two common examples are organisations set up to facilitate cooperation between government departments, and government sanctioned bodies established to facilitate and institutionalise consultation with non-government actors. The latter group is often referred to as 'peak bodies', and includes organisations such as the Australian Council of Trade Unions and the National Council for Women. Not all the relevant or interested policy actors are included in these collectives, and which groups are favoured in government consultations is prone to changing political climates (Hancock 2006, pp. 60–1), giving rise to two dichotomous groups of policy actors: 'insiders' and 'outsiders'. This may create concern that it is policy elites who determine policy and not the people (Smith et al. 2006, p. 133). However, in recent years there has been a trend to greater participation and consultation in policy-making, both between government agencies and between government, business and the community sectors (Colebatch 2006, pp. 5–6). For more on insider/outsider groups and consultation processes, refer back to Chapter 9 'Pressure groups'.

Policy interactions

So far we have established that public policy is decided in a process of constant contestation, and it is shaped by the interactions of numerous policy actors—government, community and business. The next question we need to ask is how policy actors interact, and what shapes these interactions?

Political scientists have developed numerous theories by which they analyse the interactions that take place during the policy process. Many of these are applications of broader theories designed to explain political interactions in all facets of society, which have simply been adopted to the public policy context. Examples include Marxism, rational choice theory, pluralism and institutionalism. We will not discuss the specifics of each theory here; an introduction to these and other approaches can be found in Howlett and Ramesh (2003, pp. 20–49), Fenna (2004) or Laffin (1997, pp. 52–7). The central questions addressed by all these theories are which actors are most influential in the policy process? What shapes their strategies? What degree of agency do they have in making policy? Some theories emphasise the importance of individuals and groups as the drivers of policy. Others focus on the importance of institutions in shaping the choices available to policy actors (Scott 2006, p. 574).

Although complex, policy-making is not chaotic. The term 'structured interaction' implies that the interaction between policy actors takes place according to a set of rules. In analysing the context of policy-making, it is important to recognise that policy actors invariably operate within a set of institutions and structures, whether they are defined as formal rules, organisations and processes or as informal practices and norms (Considine 2005, pp. 1–7). These structures not only shape who participates in the policy process, but how they participate—their strategic behaviour (see the discussion of these strategies in Chapter 9). Some of the structures that shape policy interactions include:

- notions of legitimacy, authority and expertise
- policy arena—particularly the institutions of government
- previous behaviours and decisions
- the dominant policy discourse.

In the contested world of policy-making, Colebatch (2002, pp. 26, 28–30; 2006b, p. 41) argues that participants seek to create stability in their interactions. Some policy actors (both inside and outside of government) are recognised as legitimate and become institutionalised in the policy process because they carry authority, or are regarded as experts. Authority holders are those with a legal right to use public or state power, for example ministers and civil servants (Considine 2005, p. 30). An example of an expert body that we have already encountered in this book is the Australian Law Reform Commission. Established by the Whitlam government in 1975 to conduct inquiries and provide expert policy advice, it has been institutionalised as an authoritative and legitimate actor in the policy process. However, both authority and expertise are essentially social constructs that frame the world in particular ways and give certain actors standing to participate in the policy process.

This standing is also dependent upon the arena in which the policy contest takes place. For the general public, the most visible arena is the institutions of government. This is a vast arena, ranging from local councils to the federal Cabinet, the public service and statutory authorities. However, it is only one of many sites for the resolution of competing ideas. Other arenas include policy communities or networks, the media and professions or workplaces. As we will see in the next chapter, there is also scope for contestation and policy formulation to take place at the point where policy is implemented or delivered.

Political actors' preferences, choices and actions are further shaped by the opportunities that are available to them and the decisions that have been made before them. Policy is often a product of practice: of 'what can be done conveniently and systematically, what works, what is consistent with the expectations that others have of us . . . Scope for choice is limited by the action already in place and the commitments which it embodies' (Colebatch 2002, pp. 15, 17). Considine (2005, pp. 2–3) argues that what may be announced as a 'new policy' is rarely written on a sheet of blank paper. Instead, the new policy is 'pencilled in the margins and spaces of other, previously negotiated commitments'. The importance of existing policy arrangements is illustrated in two of the case studies to be discussed, education and health policy.

Finally, actors are both enabled and constrained by how policy issues are socially constructed and framed. Policy issues are not naturally occurring, but are 'framed' by the participants in a policy debate (Colebatch 2002, pp. 46–7). Some political actors may complain that their policy ideas are not being taken seriously. In this way, Luke's third dimension of power—what is considered to be socially acceptable and in the 'mainstream'—serves to restrict the activities and opinions of these policy outsiders. In this context, power is therefore understood as the 'capacity to act within and on behalf of this established framework of signs and values' (Considine 2005, p. 55).

Political scientists conceptualise this framework of mainstream ideas as the prevailing 'policy discourse'. According to Considine (2005, pp. 55, 74), a discourse is a 'larger narrative used to control what is said and what is understood about what is said' and can be used by political actors to downplay unwanted issues and promote favoured accounts of 'current predicaments', 'emerging crises' and 'unique opportunities for reform'. We looked at the importance of discourse in setting the policy agendas of the major Australian political parties in Chapter 6, and the influence of ideology and prevailing ideas will be further illustrated in the three policy case studies presented below.

Contemporary policy issues

In this section we apply the theories of policy formulation discussed previously to an analysis of three key policy areas in Australian politics: education, health and the economy. Rather than painting a broad, historical picture of policy development in these areas (see Parkin et al. 2006 for this approach), we present case studies of individual policy issues designed to highlight the complexity and contested nature of different aspects of the policy-making process. First, a case study on the development of a national education curriculum illustrates the challenges raised by policy-making in a federal system in which the interests of different levels of government must be accommodated. The second case study on private health insurance demonstrates the impact of competing party ideologies and how these ideas are further constrained by a prevailing free-market ideology. Finally, a brief examination of interest rate policy continues our assessment of the influence of the market economy, in particular the extent to which governments are losing their capacity to develop monetary policy and the democratic consequences this may produce.

Case study 1: Establishing a national education curriculum

Kevin Rudd thinks that schoolchildren should learn about great Australian poets such as Henry Lawson and Banjo Paterson. John Howard prefers Shakespeare to *Big Brother*. Federal Treasurer Wayne Swan points to post-war migration and financial deregulation as important historic events, while Deputy Opposition Leader and former Education Minister Julie Bishop argues that students 'should not be forced to interpret Shakespeare from a feminist or Marxist perspective' (Fraser 2007; Maiden 2007; Ferrari 2006). The personal differences of opinion among these politicians illustrate just how contentious a policy area education can be. What subjects and topics should be taught in schools? How should they be taught and who should teach them?

What follows is a brief account of the policy processes behind the continuing development of a national curriculum for Australian schools. A national curriculum encompasses the basic idea that no matter which State children attend school in or what type of school they are enrolled in (Catholic, public or independent), the subjects and topics taught will either be the same or be underpinned by common elements. Curricula in Australian schools are currently determined and implemented at the State and Territory level, which has resulted in each State or Territory developing its own distinctive syllabi and programs for educational assessment. A report undertaken by the Australian Council for Educational Research found that more than twenty-seven different mathematics courses, twenty history courses and eighteen English courses are taught in schools throughout Australia (Bishop 2007).

Developing a common curriculum is not a 'new' policy issue—it has featured prominently in the media as a key public debate in recent years (see in particular the opinion pieces of former Liberal staffer Kevin Donnelly published in the *Australian* and online at <www.onlineopinion.com.au/author.asp?id=95>). Previous unsuccessful attempts were made under the Keating and Howard governments to establish a national curriculum. In 1993 the Keating government tried to withhold more than $2 billion in education grants to the States when they refused to cooperate on the issue of a national school curriculum (Topsfield 2007). In 2006 John Howard convened an Australian history summit and appointed a panel of 'experts', including controversial historian Geoffrey Blainey and political commentator Gerard Henderson, to write a common history curriculum for Australian schools. The composition of the panel was criticised by New South Wales Education Minister John Della Bosca as ideologically unbalanced (Macdonald 2007) and the document it produced, *The Guide to the Teaching of Australian History*, was quickly forgotten after the Howard government's electoral defeat in 2007. The failure of these policy initiatives is a pertinent example of the fact that policy-making cannot simply be conceived as a government (or governments) deciding to pursue a particular agenda, then implementing its will through the machinery of the public service. Rather, public policy involves complex negotiations between numerous political actors, structured by the institutional and social settings in which these interactions take place.

The dynamic of Australian federalism is perhaps the key element structuring the development of a national curriculum policy. Although the national curriculum has bipartisan support from the Labor Party and the Liberal–National Coalition at the federal level, attempts to reach agreement with and between the States have been difficult. While this may be attributable to disputes over policy content, it may also be a matter of process. The Rudd government has criticised the approach of the previous government as too 'top-down' in trying to dictate rather than facilitate policy development: 'you can either have Mr Howard's approach, which is to try and force parts of that new national curriculum on the states and territories, and meet great resistance, or you can work with the states and territories around one table to develop collaboratively' (Kevin Rudd, quoted in Peake 2007).

In another attempt to achieve consensus, Prime Minister Kevin Rudd announced in January 2008 the appointment of a specialist panel to design and implement a national curriculum for all Australian school students from kindergarten to year 12 (ALP 2008). The National Curriculum Board will have until 2011 to consult and negotiate with the States and Territories to set a national curriculum in four key subject areas: English, history, maths and science. The board will consist of twelve members, comprising representatives from every State and Territory as well as the Catholic and independent school sectors. The composition of the board places the State and Territory governments as primary actors in the political process, alongside the federal government.

Although the Labor Party's approach to policy negotiation has been described by former Education Minister Julie Bishop as 'astounding political naivety on the part of federal Labor to think the state governments are all of a sudden going to roll over and adopt a national curriculum of their own free will' (Peake 2007), at the COAG meeting of premiers and chief ministers in December 2007 all States and Territories agreed to implement a national curriculum (Karvelas 2007). This show of cooperation may have been facilitated by fortuitous circumstances. In 2007, the year before the establishment of the board, the States had begun to cooperate independently of the federal government in developing nationally consistent curricula through such mechanisms as the Council of the Australian Federation (ALP 2008; Grattan & Tomazin 2008).

There is also probably little coincidence in the fact that this cooperation comes at a time when Labor governments are in power not only in the federal arena but also in all Australian States and Territories. However, the power of State/federal conflicts should not be underestimated, and this division has the potential to cut through party loyalty. For example, in 2006 the federal Liberal government threatened to withhold $1 billion in Commonwealth funding to Western Australia unless the State abandoned its outcomes-based education curriculum. Despite belonging to the same political party, this action was not met with favour by the Western Australia Liberal Opposition. Liberal education spokesperson Peter Collier expressed his party's views:

> I do not support the use of federal funding as a bargaining tool to influence educational policy . . . The role of the State in education and other service industries would become redundant . . . This is a federal minister with nothing better to do with her time than interfere with the responsibilities of the States. (Strutt 2006)

As Kevin Rudd has acknowledged, achieving cooperation between the States is an 'arduous task' requiring 'charm and diplomacy', given that the development of education policy in this area involves numerous competing interests:

> You know, one of my experiences as a bureaucrat in years past is . . . that this is a pathway sewn with good intentions and non-achievement. I actually know how tough this is. Six State, two Territory curriculum bodies and then if you go out beyond that to the Catholic and independent sectors—I think one of the advices I had was that we've got 34 separate organisations contributing to the development of curricula across the country at the moment. (ALP 2008)

Although the National Curriculum Board accommodates State and Territory input into the policy process and comprises the 'best and brightest educationalists' (King 2007), its composition excludes the direct participation of some pressure groups. While these groups may have a specific interest in the development of a national curriculum and are also formed of education experts and practitioners, their participation strategies are limited by their status as 'outsiders'. For example, teachers' unions have not been given representation on the board—an omission that has been heavily criticised by these bodies, for example, the Australian Education Union and the Teachers Union (Rudra 2008a).

Nonetheless, the federal government has promised that the curriculum's development will take place on a 'consultative basis' (ALP 2008). Education Minister Julia Gillard explained that 'the National Curriculum Board of experts will be required to publicly release exposure drafts of its work for consultation with parents and teachers to ensure their work is concise, practical and understandable' (King 2007). The idea of a national curriculum is widely supported by professional associations, for example, the Secondary Schools Principals Association and the Australian Science Teachers Association. However, the thoroughness and inclusiveness of the consultation process with groups, associations, interested individuals and unions remains to be determined as the process progresses. It is important to appreciate that 'teachers' are not a homogenous group, nor do they necessarily hold common interests in education. For example, teachers are represented by multiple unions at both federal and State levels, as well as in non-government schools and by numerous professional associations for different specialisations within the teaching profession (*Aussie Educator* 2008). Interestingly, there has been no mention of involving or consulting schoolchildren in this process.

In addition to identifying the complex universe of political actors involved in the process of policy development, the structured interaction perspective enables the policy analyst to gain insight into the various competing issues and values underlying the national curriculum debate. The ALP put forward several arguments for a national curriculum:

- assisting the 80,000 children who are disadvantaged in transferring from interstate schools each year
- making sure that schools in all States and Territories meet international standards and addressing significant differences in achievement between the States and Territories through the implementation of a 'highly rigorous curriculum'
- raising school retention levels, as a long-term contribution to economic capacity (ALP 2008; ALP 2007e).

These justifications indicate that the Rudd government views the development of a national curriculum as the appropriate policy measure to address standards of education and increase economic performance. A similar view has been advocated by the Business Council of Australia in its support for the common curriculum (Ranck 2007). However, political actors have different perceptions of the underlying causes and issues involved in the policy debate. The Australian Democrats claim that the national curriculum debate is simply a smokescreen to hide what they see as the inequitable funding of education between public and private schools (Topsfield 2007). A chronic shortage of teachers and federal investment in education could also be regarded as fundamental underlying issues (Caldwell 2007).

Another dimension to the debate is ideological: the perception that those developing school curricula are doing so in a way that is incompatible with how we view (or ought to view) the world. This dimension is most strikingly illustrated in the comments of Julie Bishop, who argued at a History Teachers Association of Australia conference:

> We need to take school curricula out of the hands of the ideologues in the State and territory education bureaucracies and give it to a national board of studies, comprising the sensible centre of educators . . . Some of the themes emerging in school curriculum are straight from Chairman Mao. We are talking serious ideology here. (Quoted in Ferrari 2006)

State governments promptly rejected this argument, suggesting that the federal government was 'politicising education and the curriculum in a way that is concerning' and that 'the idea that the federal government is an ideology-free zone is laughable' (NSW Minister for Education Carmel Tebbutt, quoted in Patty 2006). Political commentator Clive Hamilton even described the federal government as pursuing an 'ideological jihad against schools' (Patty 2006).

As much as governments would like to project the neutrality and objectivity of policy-making to the public and the media, it is impossible to remove politics and ideology from policy-making; a critical perspective on policy analysis reveals that it is very much part of policy development. Rather, the key is to acknowledge and recognise the extent to which it shapes the preferences and actions of political actors in the policy process.

Case study 2: Private health insurance

The provision of healthcare in Australia is undertaken by a two-tiered system. The national public health insurance system, Medicare, insures all Australians to receive care and treatment in public hospitals without additional costs. Almost two-thirds of Australian hospital beds are in public hospitals (AIHW 2004, p. 9). The remaining third are supplied by a private healthcare system, which operates alongside publicly delivered health services. Private hospitals may operate as non-profit or for-profit organisations. Around 42 per cent of Australians currently have private health insurance (AIHW 2006).

One of the key dimensions of conflict in the area of health policy is how health services ought to be paid for (Gray 2006, p. 504). Should the government use taxation revenue to implement a collective, nationally administered payment system, or should the provision of healthcare be left to the market and services paid for by individuals from their own pockets? The rationale for government intervention is that access to health services (as a matter of life and death) should be available to everyone, regardless of their capacity to pay. In countries like Australia, where private healthcare systems duplicate public care, private health insurance provides choice, a level of care and faster access to hospital facilities above those available under the public system, to those who can afford to pay for it. For example, private patients can benefit from shorter waiting periods for elective surgery. However, there is no convincing evidence that as a corollary, waiting times in public hospitals are also reduced (OECD 2004, p. 3; Dawkins et al. 2004).

Since the 1990s a number of policy changes have been made to health insurance aimed at increasing the proportion of Australians with private cover (Hall & Savage 2005; Butler 2002). The 1996 budget reduced expenditure on public health benefits (for example, restricting the availability of the Health Care Card and raising the cost of medications and home care), and increased expenditure to 'underpin' the private sector (Gray 2006, p. 509). This included a $2 million publicity campaign promoting private health insurance and the introduction of the Private Health Insurance Incentives Scheme. Under this scheme, low- and middle-income individuals and families electing to take out private health insurance were offered subsidies, while those on middle to high incomes choosing not to obtain private cover were required to pay a Medicare levy of 1 per cent of their taxable income.

However, these measures did not achieve their intended effect, as by June 1998 only 30.6 per cent of the population was privately insured. Subsidies for private health insurance were expanded after the 1998 election, and in January 1999 a 30 per cent across-the-board rebate on private health insurance premiums for new and existing policies was introduced. According to the government, the rebate was intended to 'restore the balance in our health care system. A balanced system will ease the burden on Medicare and the public health system and give more Australians greater choice and access to private hospitals' (Commonwealth Department of Health and Ageing 2008). As Gray (2006, p. 510) argues, this measure failed to increase the percentage of the population subscribing to private health insurance to any significant extent (less than 1 per cent in the first nine months of the scheme's operation) and predominantly benefited middle to high income earners who already held private health insurance, 'reducing their contribution to total health financing'.

A year later (July 2000), the government introduced yet another initiative, Lifetime Health Cover, which further encouraged citizens to take up private health insurance by allowing private health insurance providers to charge differential premiums depending on age. Again the initiative was supported by an $8.7 million media campaign urging people to 'run for cover'. By September 2000, 45.8 per cent of the population was covered by private health insurance (Gray 2006, p. 511).

Looking at this policy from an authoritative choice perspective emphasises the rational decisions made by leaders in positions of authority and their subsequent implementation. Private health insurance subsidies are the direct result of a decision made by the Howard government to 'restore the balance in our health care system', as the best available policy option to counter the effects of falling subscriptions to private health insurance. However, the provision of health insurance in Australia is also an excellent illustration of a policy process that is constantly contested, evolving and far from linear. Australia is unique in that it is the only state to have historically introduced universal public health insurance programs before subsequently abolishing them with a change in government. A public national health insurance scheme was introduced by the Whitlam government in 1975, abolished by the Fraser government, then reintroduced by the Hawke government as Medicare in 1984 (Kay 2007, p. 578; Gray 2006, p. 498). From an authoritative choice perspective, this seems to be evidence of a government 'changing its mind'. However, to explain why this occurs we need to look at the ideological positions of the major political parties, the range of policy actors and their status as participants when different governments come to power.

Two political actors that supported the public subsidisation of private health insurance were the Australian Medical Association (AMA) and the Australian Health Insurance Association (AHIA). Both these actors enjoyed privileged positions in the policy process and good access to government ministers. As an expert professional association, a key health service provider and a pressure group, the AMA has historically occupied a prominent place in health policy development, whereas private health providers such as the AHIA achieved influence as a sympathetic interest to the government's neo-liberal policy agenda (Gray 2006, pp. 594–5). The interests of the AHIA in securing profits through the greater adoption of private health insurance policies are quite apparent, although this justification for supporting the government's policy was never used. Instead the AHIA argued that those opposed to the rebate were, 'in effect, running an ideological campaign which is aimed, in the last resort, at putting more money into the pockets of people working in the public sector' (ABC 2004).

A coalition of groups called the 'National Medicare Alliance' mobilised during the debate in opposition to the policies of the Howard government. This coalition included such groups as the Health Issues Centre, the Public Health Association of Australia, ACOSS, the Doctors Reform Society, Australian Consumers' Association and the Australian Nursing Federation. However, Gray argues that these groups had little influence on the policy debate as, in comparison to the health insurance lobby and the AMA, they were relatively underresourced and hence 'unable to get their views onto the political agenda or to attract significant media attention' (2006, pp. 518–19).

Like the policy debate over the introduction of a national curriculum, there is an underlying ideological dimension. Although the proposals and the nature of their implementation may have been motivated by a belief that an increase in private health insurance would lead to a corresponding decrease on the pressures on the public health system, the economics of this assumption can be questioned (Fiebig et al. 2006, p. 1; Dawkins et al. 2004). As Australian Consumers' Association spokesperson Nicola Ballenden argued: 'I guess it depends on your perspective—whether you think $2.2 billion is really a reasonable amount of money to spend on a 1 per cent increase in private health insurance, when we don't know whether it will take any pressure at all off the public system' (ABC 2004).

The Dean of Medicine at the University of Sydney, Stephen Leeder, suggested that 'it must remain, I think, an open question as to whether the real goal was to take pressure off the public system, or whether it was to put energy into the private system' (ABC 2004). Indeed, health policy in Australia has been characterised by the historical persistence of diverging policy positions driven by ideological differences between the two major parties. The Liberal–National coalition favours a private health insurance scheme, whereas the ALP supports a national publicly administered system (Gray 2006, p. 498).

After the Howard government came to power in 1996, Health Minister Dr Brendan Nelson explained his government's position:

> The previous government's policy position was mostly to say that private health insurance and the private health sector was supplementary to Medicare. Labor thought it had a role but in their view a relatively minor role compared with Medicare—and a role which would phase out over time. This government, however, holds a view that we need a robust and healthy private health financing sector . . . the government's message is loud and clear: that the private sector is a vital component of the long-term viability of Medicare and the public hospital system. (Nelson 1997, p. 54)

Each political party carries its own 'policy paradigm', or a set of assumptions about social, political and economic institutions that shape the way in which policies are framed and how they can be reformed (Kay 2007, p. 583). Nelson's statement clearly indicates the Howard government's commitment to private markets and explains the privileged position that such groups as the AHIA were able to occupy.

Underlying structures in Australian society beyond these party positions also constrain the policy choices available to actors. For example, despite the historical divergence of the policy positions of the major parties on private health insurance, the status of Medicare is such that it cannot be completely dismantled. In this sense, 'public opinion' can of itself be an important political actor. The Australian Survey of Social Attitudes found that nearly 70 per cent of Australians were willing to pay more taxes to increase spending on health and Medicare, 'reflecting the service's wide use and popularity' (Wilson et al. 2005, p. 111). Although it has been downgraded, elements of the Medicare system have survived the Coalition government. Attempts in 2003 to extend private health cover to out-of-hospital expenses was met with criticism by a Senate Select Committee of Inquiry and failed to pass the Senate (see Gray 2004, pp. 44–7). Viewed as politically unpopular, the proposal to extend private health insurance was dumped before the 2004 federal election. As John Howard has reflected on his personal and his party's position:

> It is true that in my past . . . I was a critic of Medicare and I formed the view ten and a half to eleven years ago that the Australian people had said to me, 'Well, John, we note what you say, but we want you to know what we believe. And we believe that Medicare fundamentally is a good system.' (Quoted in Kay 2007, p. 580)

At the same time, the Labor Party has moved to support a two-tier system and the public subsidisation of private health insurance. The Rudd government has given no indication that it will act to dismantle the private health cover scheme. Rather, the Parliamentary Secretary for Health, Jan McLucas, has stated that Labor is:

> committed to maintaining all of the rebates as they currently exist, maintaining lifetime health cover and the Medicare levy surcharge . . . We will have a viable and effective private health insurance system in Australia that will ensure that Australians can access quality private health insurance. (*Australian* 2008)

Consequently, as Gray (2006, p. 499) argues, the policy gap between the two major parties appears to have narrowed, and they now support a large role for the private sector in complementing the operation of Medicare, or what Kay (2007, p. 581) describes as a 'universalism plus choice' policy synthesis.

Case study 3: Interest rates—the trend to policy privatisation

The previous two cases studies highlighted the complexity of interactions between the numerous actors and the diverse interests involved in the development of policy. However, in both cases these actors were centred on, and operated within, the institutions of government. Interest rate policy presents a fascinating contrast as a public policy that is determined, implemented and essentially exists within the institutions of the neoclassical market economy. It is an area of policy-making that we argue is increasingly being removed from the institutions and control of the state to the private market and raises difficult questions of policy accountability that cannot be solved through electoral means.

The management of interest rates is always a fiery political issue. Governments like to take credit when interest rates are low, but often distance themselves from responsibility when rates are high. For example, the Howard government promoted its ability to manage interest rates extensively throughout the 2004 federal election campaign (see the 2004 federal election snapshot on the *Powerscape* website: <www.allenandunwin.com/powerscape>). Treasurer Peter Costello praised Australia's stable rates, warning that 'we can't afford to have inexperienced management, people blundering with economic policy' (Costello 2004). However, exactly who determines interest rate policy is often a source of confusion.

The Reserve Bank of Australia (RBA) is the body responsible for setting interest rates. The manipulation of short-term interest rates is the main way in which the government implements its economic (monetary) policy strategy, and has a strong economic and employment impact by affecting the cost of credit (for example, home loans), exchange rates, property and asset prices and the future prospect of inflation. Before the 1980s interest rates were determined 'at the political level' and the RBA was 'just another agent of government' similar to the Treasury and other government departments, and its role was to 'implement government policies' (Argy 2000, p. 110). During the process of financial deregulation in the early 1980s many of the financial controls originally set by the government were removed, and the RBA was no longer required to act as a regulatory agent of the federal government.

Today the Reserve Bank is largely independent of government in the design and operation of monetary policy and setting interest rates. According to the bank's website, 'the Reserve Bank Board makes decisions about the interest rates independently of the political process—that is, it does not accept instruction from the government of the day on interest rates' (RBA 2008). As we explained earlier in this chapter, it is an example of a quasi-independent government body operating within a prescribed statutory framework but with a significant degree of autonomy. The RBA's activities are subject to the provisions of the *Reserve Bank Act 1959* (Cwlth) and the *Statement on the Conduct of Monetary Policy* (2007), an agreement formed between the government and the RBA. The statement:

- sets the objectives of monetary policy as maintaining currency stability, full employment and the economic prosperity and welfare of the people of Australia
- recognises the RBA's independence from government in the conduct of monetary policy, subject to communication between the bank and the government
- sets a target for inflation at 2–3 per cent over the course of an economic cycle, according to which the RBA sets short-term interest rates.

There are several reasons why the Reserve Bank, and in turn the development of interest rate policy, are becoming more independent of government. The first, as we have mentioned, is the changing economic landscape following financial deregulation of the 1980s. At the same time as financial markets have been regulated, other instruments of government intervention in the economy (fiscal policy, wages policy, fixed exchange rates) have also been scaled back. This, and the Reserve Bank's own strong performance in achieving inflationary targets, have incrementally increased its role.

The second reason is the nature of economic policy-making as a specialist or expert activity and the perceptions of expertise and authority associated with it. Unlike other policy areas, such as health and education, where proximity to government confers authority and legitimacy, in many areas of economic policy governments are viewed with scepticism. The issues involved in monetary policy are very complex and require more technical expertise than Cabinets can obtain, and financial markets need to be assured that control of monetary policy is in 'professional hands', safe from the short-term electoral interests of politicians (Argy 2000, pp. 111–12). The perceived credibility of the bank is necessary in order to preserve the confidence of markets, which creates positive effects on inflation and future interest rate expectations.

Therefore, the formation of official monetary policy is largely a closed shop, dictated by economic orthodoxy and expert opinion. However, it is important to note that the RBA is not the only player in setting interest rates. Although it is the only body that can set short-term interest rates, the sheer volume of money that private financial markets deal with means that they have a significant influence on the level of long-term interest rates, exchange rates and asset prices. Furthermore, commercial entities directly influence the decisions of the Reserve Bank's board, given that their actions are structured by the demands and expectations of markets and business, for example, financial institutions.

With the increasing independence of the Reserve Bank comes the problem of accountability. If elected governments no longer control monetary policy, can voters still hold governments to account when interest rates get too high? Who can be held accountable in the government's place? As Argy (2000, p. 111) notes, 'no central bank can ever be fully accountable, given the complexity and range of factors impacting on economic outcomes at any one time, which makes it difficult to apportion blame or credit'. Although the Reserve Bank is notionally held accountable to the government by the requirements that it issue six-monthly reports on its activities and appear before a parliamentary committee to answer questions, this was not always the case. Previously banking regulation in Australia occurred behind closed doors, as the effect of public statements by the RBA ran the risk of negatively influencing the bank's objectives and the conduct of monetary policy (Argy 2000, pp. 111–12). Finally, one of the most difficult problems faced by the RBA is evaluating the outcome of its interest rate policies, given that there is still disagreement among economists about the effectiveness of inflationary targets in promoting economic growth and employment (see Argy 2000, p. 112).

As we have seen, the 'official' conduct of monetary policy is shaped by the economic orthodoxy that control of interest rates is a scientific, technical and professional matter, which should not be in the hands of politicians who succumb to short-term interests dictated by the electoral cycle. Independent control of monetary policy bestows 'credibility' upon the policy process. This approach to the management of monetary policy is captured by Argy (2000, p. 121) in the concept of 'policy privatisation':

> In the last two and a half decades economic policy has tended to become more responsive to private markets and more distant from consensual politics. This 'privatisation' process has partly manifested itself in a transfer of control over some policy variables from governments to private markets . . . the policy responsibilities of [quasi-independent government bodies] have been gradually amended to make them more compatible with private market values while their role as a vehicle for resolving social conflict has diminished.

However, despite their scientific guise, monetary policy decisions (like all policy decisions) are not value neutral and have important consequences for the welfare of Australians. What we are potentially seeing is the creation of a democratic deficit—as external constraints and pressures mount and legislating in a global environment becomes an increasingly complex activity, the trend inevitably becomes for governments to delegate policy responsibilities to non-elected, 'non-majoritarian' institutions (Thatcher & Stone-Sweet 2002). However, this process of 'policy privatisation is threatening to further weaken support for our political institutions by rendering the political system less responsive to the preferences and expectations of the community, albeit unrealistic and incompatible at times' (Argy 2000, p. 123). Once public policy-making is decoupled from parliamentary institutions without opportunity for popular participation, this lack of accountability may fuel popular discontent with government and disaffection with the policy process (see Papadopoulos 2003).

Although the three case studies have examined very different policy areas, in each instance policy-making is not simply a matter of 'what governments choose to do' after undertaking a rational cost–benefit analysis of each policy problem. As the case study on private health insurance showed, such a straightforward analysis is not possible in reality. Governments are shaped by their ideologies, their actions constrained by social expectations and by the policy decisions of previous and present political actors. The process behind the development of the national curriculum showed that these actors have their own agendas and distinct policy preferences, and therefore any policy resolution or outcome requires extensive negotiation and consultation. Finally, using the example of interest rates, we sought to question the assumption that governments can actually exercise control over the policy process, particularly in an increasingly liberal economic environment, and highlight some of the difficulties of policy evaluation and accountability that the practice of delegating the responsibility of policy formulation raises.

Summary

- Policy-making is a process of continuous contestation and involves the participation of numerous political actors.
- Although the government is a key actor and its institutions (parliament, Cabinet and the public service) form the central arena in which policy is developed and implemented, many political actors participate in the policy process, including groups from the business and community sectors and the media.
- The actions, decisions and preferences of policy-makers are shaped in a complex and symbiotic process of interaction. These interactions are constrained by overarching structures, or rules of the game, including the notions of legitimacy, authority and expertise, previous policy decisions, governmental institutions and dominant ideologies and discourses.

Further reading

Colebatch, Hal 2002, *Policy*, 2nd edn, Open University Press, Buckingham.

Colebatch, Hal (ed.) 2006, *Beyond the Policy Cycle: The Policy Process in Australia*, Allen & Unwin, Sydney.

Considine, Mark 2005, *Making Public Policy: Institutions, Actors, Strategies*, Polity Press, Cambridge.

Johnson, Carol 2007, *Governing Change: From Keating to Howard*, rev. edn, API Network, Curtin University of Technology, Perth, WA.

CHAPTER 13
POLICY DELIVERY

In this chapter, we explore the role of key institutions in policy delivery: the public sector and the public service, and business and the community sectors. We will look at the contemporary role of the public sector and the public service in the context of political and economic changes since the 1970s and 1980s. We will investigate the influence of these changes on political actors and policy delivery in the contemporary Australian state, particularly on perceptions of accountability. We will argue that the contemporary framework for policy delivery encourages the participation of a wide range of political actors but that the forms of action they may take are often constrained.

The topics covered in this chapter include:

- defining the public sector and the public service
- explaining changes in conceptions of the appropriate role of the public sector in the contemporary Australian state
- examining how these developments have affected the operation of the public service and other actors in policy delivery
- investigating challenges of accountability and efficiency in contemporary policy delivery
- understanding the limits on the modes of participation by an ever-increasing range of actors.

SNAPSHOT From insiders to outsiders: 'mainstreaming' women's policy

The women's movement in Australia in the 1970s advocated the integration of women's policy issues into the governmental agenda, to address such issues as violence against women, equal pay, maternity leave, childcare and the right to work. In order to help achieve this the distinctive idea of the 'femocrat' arose: 'senior public servants committed to feminism and employed to develop, execute and oversee women's policy programs within the state bureaucracy' (van Acker 1999, p. 119). The strong presence of femocrats in Australia has been described as 'distinctive' (Eisenstein 1996, p. xiii) in comparison with other countries in which the women's movement was also prominent, such as the United States. The strategy was not without its critics. Conservatives criticised it for using the government to threaten the nuclear family; progressives criticised femocrats' reliance on a bureaucracy that was contrary to women's interests, claimed that they did not represent women, and argued that they excluded non-white, indigenous, working-class and immigrant voices (Eisenstein 1996, p. xv).

Nevertheless the influence of femocrat ideas contributed directly to the development of policy machinery designed to promote women's interests at the highest levels of government. In 1973 the federal Labor government of Gough Whitlam created a position of Prime Ministerial Adviser on Women's Affairs, and in 1974 a small section in the Department of Prime Minister and Cabinet was created to support that role (Eisenstein 1996, p. 18; Sawer 1990, p. 10). By 1976 the Women's Affairs Branch (later the Office of Women's Affairs, then the Office for the Status of Women) became 'the nucleus of a network of women's policy units' in the Commonwealth public service (Sawer 1990, pp. 33, 42). At a State level, women's advisers and units were created in premiers' departments in the mid-1970s in Victoria, South Australia and Tasmania, and in the 1980s in the Northern Territory, Western Australia and the Australian Capital Territory. But the existence of these units was never secure. For example in 1982 the Tasmanian Liberal government of Robin Gray abolished the position of women's advisor, although it was reinstated in 1989 after a Labor government was elected (Sawer 1990, p. 140). For more detail on the women's movement in Australia, see Chapter 10.

More recently, however, women's policy advice mechanisms have been more comprehensively downgraded at both Commonwealth and State or Territory level. Federally, the Office for the Status of Women suffered significant cuts to its budget and staff after the Howard Liberal government was elected in 1996 and women's policy advice units elsewhere in the bureaucracy were 'silenced or stifled' (Summers 2003, pp. 128, 130). Then in 2004 the OSW was moved away from the Department of Prime Minister and Cabinet, renamed the Office for Women and located in the Department of Family and Community Services. This was criticised as a loss of 'its unique focus on women's needs and issues' and the 'dumping of women from the political agenda' in favour of seeing women only in terms of their family roles (Summers 2004, p. 13). In New South Wales the Department for Women was abolished by the Labor government in the April 2004 mini-budget, to be replaced with an Office in the Premier's Department. Despite being described by the government as an 'elevation', this change was accompanied by significant staff reductions and the halving of its budget (Maddison 2004, p. 595; Maddison & Partridge 2007, p. 44).

Some of these changes were justified in terms of a shift to 'gender mainstreaming', a strategy of promoting gender equality within and across mainstream departments and programs rather than in separate, discrete women's units (<www.un.org/womenwatch/osagi/gendermainstreaming.htm>). Yet gender mainstreaming has been criticised as vulnerable to misuse by legitimising the dismantling of specialist expertise and advocacy on behalf of women (Sawer 2006, pp. 125–6; Bacchi et al. 2005, p. 46). In support of this, it has been argued that the institutional changes discussed here were accompanied by a change in rhetoric from both Labor and Liberal politicians, who shifted away from recognising a need to guarantee women's equality and 'expunged' women from their political agenda (Summers 2003, p. 123).

This brief history demonstrates that political actors, in this case feminists, can agitate and argue successfully in favour of significant changes to the infrastructure that develops and delivers policy for their community base. But at the same time, any changes or improvements achieved are still vulnerable to pressures from alternative, or competing, political actors. In what ways did the public sector and the public service respond to feminists' demands? Why did changes occur to policy delivery for women? What were the factors influencing those changes?

The public sector and the public service

The public sector is the name given to all the people who work in any capacity for a government, at federal, State, Territory or local government level. It is also called the government or governmental sector, and it is contrasted with the business and community sectors. It includes nurses in public hospitals, postal workers, police officers, council building inspectors and garbage collectors, teachers in public schools, academics and administrators in public universities, roads and transport authorities, and so on. The public sector has been categorised as 'the staff employed by the state to carry out the instructions of the elected government, and to administer or manage its institutions' (Hughes 1998, p. 363). This means that decisions about what is to be carried out by the public sector are made by elected representatives—by governments. Also, such decisions are binding on all members of a society. One cannot opt out of governmental decisions—their effect is compulsory and universal (Hughes 1998, p. 335), like paying income tax or abiding by the road rules. This definition of the public sector is very broad.

It also means the public sector is made up of more than the public service. The public service refers to government departments and is one component of the public sector. The 'public service' is the title given to those workers employed within federal, State and Territory government departments under terms determined by specific legislation. These Acts began to be enacted in the colonies in the late nineteenth century, and have continued to be amended as requirements have changed in the more than a century that has passed since then (Nethercote 1996, p. 224). For example, the federal public service is made up of those people employed under the *Public Service Act 1999* (Cwlth). Federally it is called the Australian Public Service (APS), and it consists of all those departments and agencies whose staff are employed under the Act. Each department is administered by a minister with responsibility for that portfolio. The Acts governing the public service in each State and Territory vary in terms of the titles used (for example in New South Wales it is the *Public Sector Employment and Management Act 2002* and in Western Australia the *Public Sector Management Act 1994*). They have also changed relatively recently, and most States and Territories have new Acts that have been implemented since the 1990s. We will discuss the reasons for this later when we discuss changes in contemporary policy delivery.

The Acts set out the terms and conditions under which the public service operates. Public servants have traditionally had their own distinct conditions of employment in Australia, which have been different from those afforded employees in business or community organisations. Public servants have in the past tended to have strong levels of employee protection, such as protection against arbitrary dismissal, and training, staff development and career path opportunities (Nethercote 1996, p. 224).

The legislation regulating the public service also grants heads of public service departments certain powers on behalf of the minister administering the department. The role of each department is to advise the minister on policy, to deliver the policy to the public and to monitor its implementation.

The public service is wide-ranging in its responsibilities and capabilities, which may include such diverse tasks as sending peace-keeping forces to East

Timor, monitoring quality in university education, issuing passports or improving the health of indigenous people. For example in 2008, sixteen Commonwealth portfolios existed with responsibilities including:

- agriculture, fisheries and forestry
- broadband, communications and the digital economy
- defence
- families, housing, community services and indigenous affairs
- health and ageing
- immigration and citizenship
- resources, energy and tourism.

There are also many statutory agencies and authorities, including the Australian Competition and Consumer Commission, formed in 1995 to administer the *Trade Practices Act 1974* and other Acts, the Civil Aviation Safety Authority (CASA), which was established in 1995 under section 8 of the *Civil Aviation Act 1988*, and the National Library of Australia (NLA), which is an agency within the Department of the Environment, Water, Heritage and the Arts and whose role is defined by the *National Library of Australia Act 1960*.

Statutory agencies and authorities are created by a specific piece of legislation and primarily have responsibility for delivering services or regulating government activities, sometimes within or in conjunction with a government department. They are an important part of the public sector framework because they are created by government statute and are ultimately under the direction and control of a minister. However, on a day-to-day basis they operate by and large independently of government and may even be critical of government policies. This criticism can be seen by government as a healthy aspect of its governance, but sometimes it can undermine the relationship between the government that creates the agency and the agency itself. Ultimately, the government has statutory control over the functions and role of agencies and authorities but not their day-to-day operations.

Aboriginal and Torres Strait Islander Commission

ATSIC was established in 1990 under the *Aboriginal and Torres Strait Islander Commission Act 1989* and tasked with strengthening the economic, social, cultural and heritage development of indigenous people. Its board was elected by indigenous people.

Yet criticism of the organisation was widespread (Robbins 2007, p. 323), and its relations with the Coalition government of 1996–2007 were strained (Sanders 2005). Criticisms raised included the government seeking to hold ATSIC responsible for the failure to improve indigenous health and education (Robbins 2007, p. 323) and alleging financial mismanagement (Sanders 2005, pp. 162–3). The chair of ATSIC, Geoff Clark, lost public confidence due to reporting of a pub brawl in which he had been involved, and allegations of rape made against him (Sanders 2005, p. 159; Robbins 2007, p. 322).

At the same time the government was pursuing broader policies of rejecting self-determination, 'mainstreaming' indigenous affairs and adopting 'practical reconciliation', which meant focusing on delivering concrete outcomes in health, education and standards of living and rejecting 'symbolic' measures, such as an apology for past practices, including the removal of children from their families referred to as the 'Stolen Generations' (Robbins 2007, pp. 315–16).

In 2004 the federal government devolved a number of programs away from ATSIC and to other Commonwealth departments and agencies, and in March 2005 the government abolished ATSIC altogether (Robbins 2007, p. 322).

There are different ways in which the government can effect its policy decisions, and these alternatives place a different emphasis on the role of the public sector on the one hand, and business or community sectors on the other, in policy delivery. The public sector has an important, but not the sole, role in policy delivery, as can be seen from the list below. Policy delivery can be undertaken in the following ways:

1 Government can provide the service itself. An example is when the government provides primary school education, which is publicly funded.
2 Government can produce goods or services for commercial sale to earn revenue. An example is Sydney Water Corporation, which is a statutory corporation owned by the New South Wales government.
3 Government can subsidise other organisations to provide goods or services. An example is when the government subsidises a private bus company to

provide bus services in an area not covered by a public transport network. In this example, government funding is being provided to business to provide a service that government is unable to provide itself, but which it has a responsibility to deliver.

4 Government can regulate activities undertaken by business, that is, privately owned service providers. An example is the sale of prescription medicines manufactured by pharmaceutical companies and sold for profit. The sale of such medicines is regulated by public authorities including the Therapeutic Goods Administration, whose tasks are to safeguard public health and safety and to decide which medicines are permitted on the Australian market (adapted from Hughes 1998, pp. 336–7).

In the first of these options the government is undertaking the activity, or providing the service, itself. In these cases the public sector plays the primary role in policy delivery, and business or the community sector plays only a tangential role in providing support or related services or goods, such as providing raw materials or equipment. In the second option government-owned services are being delivered in a business-like mode. In the third and fourth options business plays a central and obvious role in policy delivery. Importantly, the mix of these modes of operating has shifted over time, in conjunction with changes in conceptions of the purpose and role of the public sector overall. We will turn now to a discussion of these changes to explain how and why the roles of business and the community sector in policy delivery have increased substantially in recent years.

Change in the public sector

Significant changes have been wrought in the last two decades to the ways policy decisions are implemented. Here we want to outline the traditional view of how the public sector operates, and outline reasons for changes in conceptions of the public sector and the public service over time. This will provide a framework within which it is possible to examine the influence of these changes on policy delivery.

The 'statist' view of the public sector

As we argued in Chapter 2, one of the historical features of a liberal democratic state is an antipathy towards government, an inherent hostility to and antagonism towards the potential for government to become too powerful and to interfere too much in citizens' lives. Despite this, the state has played an active role throughout Australia's post-Federation history in national development.

More generally during the twentieth century, the ideal of limited government began to be overtaken by new demands for government intervention in liberal democratic societies. Especially after the Great Depression of the 1930s and World War II, the idea that government had a responsibility to take care of all people, instead of simply letting them fend for themselves, gained currency. People looked to governments to solve complex social, economic and political problems like unemployment, poverty and disease or, more recently, such issues as environmental sustainability and the protection of human rights. These demands meant that governments expanded considerably, both in size and scope. Governments began to take on roles not previously envisaged for them, and the size of the public sector grew. It has been reported that by 1980 in Australia, about a quarter of gross domestic product (GDP) was the result of government expenditure and about a fifth of total employment was government-based (Schwartz 2003, pp. 45–6).

In the area of welfare governments responded to public pressures to safeguard people's interests, including by expanding pension programs and unemployment benefits and providing health, education and transport services. The state began to take on responsibility for providing an adequate standard of living for all members of society. This aspect of expanded government intervention became known as the 'welfare state' or 'welfare statism' (Jamrozik 2001, p. 1; Hughes 1998, p. 340). Jens Alber has described the welfare state as 'a polity in which state responsibilities extend beyond the mere maintenance of internal order and external security to a public responsibility for the well-being of citizens' (cited in Jamrozik 2001, p. 2). It has been argued that the form in which the welfare state developed in Australia was qualitatively different from other, especially European, countries because it relied heavily on establishing minimum living wages rather than an emphasis on residual welfare payments (Bell 2000, pp. 194–5; Castles 1985). Residual welfare is designed to help those who fall between the cracks or are unable to fend for themselves. Others who are capable of ensuring an adequate standard of living for themselves are not assisted by the state at all. By contrast, establishing minimum living wages for all sought to ensure that all people were provided, by the state, with an adequate minimum standard of living.

This expanded understanding of the role of the government in delivering policy to solve complex social problems is called 'statism' because it is reliant upon the state—and not the free market—for solutions. In the statist model the government is responsible for providing jobs, ensuring adequate standards of living, protecting the environment or delivering adequate health and education services. The state is seen as the primary means by which this may be achieved. In this model, not only is the state capable of intervening to provide services and goods demanded by its people, but also it is imperative that the state does so in order to respond to incidences of failure—incidences where the market is incapable of providing sufficiently for all community members.

An increasing role for the market

However, in the mid-1970s, criticisms arose regarding both the size and the role of government in developing and delivering policy capable of solving complex economic, social and political problems. The perception that it was the role of government to provide services and to ensure a certain standard of living for all came into question. Instead, a greater role for business in providing services, and in engaging in economic enterprise that would deliver higher standards of living via the market, was embraced.

Over time a market-oriented approach to policy delivery became dominant, an approach where the market—and not government—is represented as the best and most appropriate means by which enhanced standards of living can be achieved. Government is still regarded as having a role to play, but its role is limited in important ways. This contrasts dramatically with the statist approach, in which government is required to intervene because the market is incapable of providing adequately for all. The market-oriented approach has also been called an approach based on 'economic rationalism', 'economic liberalism' and 'neo-liberalism', as we explained in Chapter 2.

Both major political parties in Australia embraced this change (Marsh 2002, p. 23). Importantly, although this change has been primarily spoken of in economic terms, Marsh also argues that it has affected sociopolitical strategy (and therefore policy delivery) much more broadly than in purely economic terms (2002, p. 19). A wide variety of policy areas and approaches was affected by this shift, not just economic policy.

The areas in which this shift from government responsibility for policy delivery and implementation to a market approach took place were as diverse as the public sector itself. They include trade, education, immigration, welfare, transport, environmental services, utilities, urban development, farming and agriculture, tourism and health, among others. The idea that the market would deliver services in every policy area more efficiently and effectively than government could or should came to dominate.

Effects of change

This change in an understanding of the appropriate role of the state led to significant structural and organisational changes within the public sector. The changes are too numerous to cover them all in detail, but some of the most important and visible changes include:

- changes in permanent staff numbers and budget allocations for the public service
- commercialisation and privatisation of policy delivery
- outsourcing of policy delivery
- contract-based oversight of policy delivery
- a results-focused (or output-based) approach to policy management.

The first and most visible change was a significant reduction in the size and budget of the public service. The rationale for this reduction was that it was necessary to ensure overall economic sustainability. It was argued that the old-style government provision of a range of goods and services substituted for more effective provision by business, cost too much money, produced uncompetitive and inefficient monopolies, and was ineffective in achieving policy goals (Johnson 2000, pp. 25–6; Beresford 2000, p. 59). In 1987 Labor released an economic statement in which the then Treasurer (and later Prime Minister) Paul Keating championed the theory that reducing public sector costs would free capital to be used more effectively and efficiently elsewhere (Kelly 1992, p. 329). Inefficiencies in government provision of goods and services were considered to be a reflection of broader inefficiencies in what came to be regarded as a highly regulated and subsidised economy. For example, the 1988–89 Annual Report of the Industries Assistance Commission (IAC) argued in favour of deregulation of the economy to remove 'inefficiencies', stating that economic gains of $16 billion per year, or 5 per cent of GDP, could be achieved (IAC 1989, p. 19). The IAC was recast in 1989 as the Industry Commission, and was a precursor to the Productivity Commission created in 1998 (<www.pc.gov.au>). The changing names reflected the changing parameters within which the commissions conducted their work.

From the 1980s to the turn of the twenty-first century, staffing and budget levels in the public sector and the public service were significantly reduced. Bell stated that more than 300,000 jobs were lost in State and Commonwealth government employment (2000, p. 197), and Davis demonstrated that federal public employment budgets were reduced by 17 per cent in the decade between 1985 and 1995 (1997, p. 211).

Precise calculations of staff numbers are difficult to pin down, but the figures shown in Table 13.1 report the number of staff employed under the Public Service Act. They have been derived from Australian Public Service Commission reports.

A clear indication of a reduction in the size of the public service exists from 1988 levels to 2000. However, from this point on an increase in staffing is seen. The increase in the first four years of the century was explained in the 2003 *State of the Service* report as resulting from the introduction of new or expanded policy responsibilities in security and border protection, as well as increased workload (APSC 2003, p. 1). Approximately a quarter of the strong growth in 2006 was reported as being due to changes to Medicare arrangements, which brought 5000 employees under the coverage of the Public Service Act. Changes to some other agencies had the same effect, but some new infrastructure was also created (APSC 2006, p. 12). In addition, as discussed in Chapter 4, there has been a substantial increase in the use of ministerial advisers who, while not strictly a part of the public service, are on the government payroll and are supplementing if not replacing the traditional role of the public service in providing advice to ministers.

These increases in the size of the public service since 2000 appear to belie the dominance of neo-liberal orthodoxy in governmental arrangements with its consequent presumption of a reduction in staffing levels. Nevertheless, they are only one aspect of the overall picture presented here. Viewed in the context of other changes to the public sector and public service, the overall picture of an increasing role for the market and outsourcing of policy delivery to business and the community sector remains viable.

A second effect of a changed understanding of the role of the state has been the commercialisation and privatisation of many government services. Some

TABLE 13.1 Staff employed in the public service

Date	No. of staff	Date	No. of staff
1988	169,398	1998	121,262
1989	165,218	1999	113,268
1990	161,383	2000	110,954
1991	164,085	2001	118,644
1992	164,478	2002	123,494
1993	161,426	2003	131,711
1994	149,859	2004	131,522
1995	144,839	2005	133,596
1996	135,074	2006	146,434
1997	126,284	2007	155,482

Sources: for figures from 1988 to 1997: APS Statistics (December 1997) <www.apsc.gov.au/publications98/statsdec97.pdf>; for figures from 1998 to 2002: *State of the Service* reports 1998, p. 10; 1999, p. 8; 2000, p. 54; 2001, p. 31; 2002, p. 5; 2003, p. 5; 2004, p. 7; 2005, p. 9; 2006, p. 12; 2007, p. 11, available at <www.apsc.gov.au/apsprofile>.

government services are now run as competitive businesses, having been retitled government business enterprises (GBEs) (Schwartz 2003, p. 55; Davis 1997, p. 214). Other government assets, such as the Commonwealth Bank and Qantas, have been sold. Commercialisation and privatisation aim to increase efficiency and promote competition between government providers of goods and services and their business and community counterparts. The National Competition Policy adopted by the Commonwealth and the States in 1994, and discussed in Chapter 11, promotes open competition between the public sector and others in the marketplace. Policy and services previously delivered exclusively by government have been put out to tender, and government monopolies in many policy areas have been abolished (Davis 1997, pp. 214–15). However, privatisation remains a controversial issue.

Privatising New South Wales' electricity supply

In December 2007 New South Wales Premier Morris Iemma announced a plan to privatise the State's electricity infrastructure by granting long-term leases to business to run generators while retaining State ownership of the generators. Retail operations were also to be sold.

In support of its plan, the New South Wales government claimed that consumers in Victoria were paying less for their energy supplies following privatisation of that State's electricity supplies, and that the New South Wales government needed the $15 billion it would save from privatising electricity to spend on other services, including nurses, teachers and police (Costa 2008). But Unions NSW claimed that 86 per cent of the New South Wales population opposed the privatisation because they believed it would lead to increased prices, the loss of jobs and foreign ownership of assets (Norrington 2008).

A third, and related, effect of the changed view of the role of the state has been the outsourcing of some policy delivery from the public sector to the business and community sectors. This manifests in many forms, including privately constructed and operated roads with tolls to allow the private construction firm to recoup its construction and maintenance costs, private hospitals, the use of tax incentives to encourage higher income earners to take out private health insurance, and private universities. An example of the involvement of community institutions in policy delivery is outlined in the box 'Services to the unemployed'.

Services to the unemployed

Services to assist the unemployed in seeking work were provided from 1946 to 1998 primarily by the federal government, in the form of the Commonwealth Employment Service (CES). Some state government services and private job placement agencies existed during this time as well. But in 1996 the federal government flagged significant changes to the ways employment services were delivered, with the aims of increasing the quality of services provided, reducing government expenditure and assisting people to obtain jobs. In May 1998 the CES was abolished, employment services were contracted out and funding for employment services was halved.

Centrelink and Job Network (a network of providers who successfully tender to provide services to the unemployed) were created to assist with job hunting, administering job seekers' obligations in return for financial assistance, and to provide job matching and training (Webster 1999, pp. 34–5, 37).

By March 2000, 92 per cent of Job Network services were provided by business and community sector organisations (Eardley et al. 2001, p. 9).

One particular controversy has been the effect of awarding contracts to church-based organisations. In being awarded the contracts, the organisations agreed to comply with legislative requirements, including anti-discrimination laws. However, religious organisations are exempt from many anti-discrimination provisions, and complaints were made that people seeking work at these organisations were being discriminated against in their employment prospects on the grounds of their religion. In response, the Human Rights and Equal Opportunity Commission attempted to draft guidelines according to which both the principle of religious freedom and the principle of non-discrimination in employment could be reconciled, but the guidelines produced even more heated debate. On the one hand, church-based organisations argued that they had the right to establish religious institutions and to express their religion in their activities. On the other hand, prospective employees felt they had a right not to be discriminated against on the ground of their religious belief (Patapan 2001, pp. 13–14). The issue remains a highly contentious one.

This example indirectly highlights a fourth effect of the newly dominant understanding of the appropriate role of the state; that is, the emergence and increasing incidence of contractual relationships between the government, which is overseeing and regulating service provision, and the business or community organisation that delivers it. Agreements between the government and service providers are governed by contracts, which tend to include performance indicators and targets for bonuses (Davis 1997, p. 215). The details of these contracts might not be fully available for public scrutiny. For example, critics of a privatised women's prison in Victoria in the late 1990s (which was later returned to government operation) found it impossible to gain access to the terms of the contract under which the prison was operated (George 2003, p. 26; see also George & Lazarus 1994). Another effect of the influence of complex contractual relationships is an increasing difficulty in clearly delineating organisations as purely 'public' or 'private' (Patapan 2001, p. 15).

Finally, others recognise the emphasis of the new approach to policy delivery on results. Schwartz argues that when policy-making is separated from policy management and implementation, a concurrent shift takes place in how policy delivery is managed. Rather than policy being controlled in terms of inputs (such as the amount of money allocated or the number of people working on it), control begins to focus on outputs and results (such as the cost per person benefiting from the policy). This has led to the use of outcome-based performance measures to determine the effectiveness and efficiency of policy delivery (Schwartz 2003, p. 50). The achievement of output targets is rewarded, and underperformance is punished. The most common mechanisms for determining output measurements tend to be budget-related (Painter 1997b, p. 40).

Conceptualisations of change

These trends have been gathering pace since the 1980s. In the early 1990s US authors David Osborne and Ted Gaebler wrote an influential book called *Reinventing Government* (1993). In it, they criticised the failure of old-style governments, with their 'sluggish, centralized bureaucracies, their preoccupation with rules and regulation, and their hierarchical chains of command'. Policy delivery was simply not working, they said. Old-style governments were 'big, cumbersome, expensive' (1993, p. 12). Instead, they acknowledged and promoted the emergence of a new type of entrepreneurial government, one which was 'lean, decentralized, and innovative ... flexible, adaptable, and quick to learn new ways when conditions change ... [able to] use competition, customer choice and other nonbureaucratic mechanisms to get things done as creatively and effectively as possible' (1993, p. 2). They called this 'entrepreneurial government'. Entrepreneurial government was characterised by its promotion of competition instead of monopolies, measuring performance on outcomes instead of on inputs, and by being goal-driven, customer-focused and market-oriented (1993, pp. 19–20). Osborne and Gaebler wrote in laudatory terms about the new entrepreneurial model.

They summarised the change as one of government taking on the role of 'steering rather than rowing' (1993, p. 25); that is to say, it became the role of government to oversee policy directions but not to undertake the day-to-day tasks of policy implementation and evaluation. The government is still steering, or overseeing, policy delivery in crucial ways (Hughes 1998, p. 337). But the government steers the boat while others—business and community organisations—do the actual rowing. This is a useful analogy for understanding the new mode of governing.

Others have called the contemporary model for government a 'purchaser–provider distinction' (O'Brien & O'Donnell 2002a, p. 61) or a 'policy-provider split' (Schwartz 2003, p. 50). The new model has also been characterised as 'managerialism', 'New Public Management' and 'post-bureaucratic government'. It has been viewed as a move from the state's role as an administrator to a manager of market-oriented processes which mirror business practice. Moreover, this transformation has been legitimised by the use of a language of consumer choice and efficiency in policy delivery (O'Brien & O'Donnell 2002b, pp. 1, 4–5). Finally, the new *modus operandi* for the state has been described as governance, as opposed to government. Rhodes traces the genealogy of the use of the term 'governance', seeing it as signifying the shifts described here in how society is governed (1997, pp. 46–52).

Concerns and criticisms

A range of concerns and criticisms has arisen from these extensive changes, and these discussions have been canvassed in many critical publications in the area of public sector management and public policy (see Boston (ed.) 1995; Rhodes 1994; Weller & Davis 1996; Considine & Painter 1997).

One major concern has been a criticism of reduced policy coherence. 'Policy coherence' is the ability to direct and achieve coordinated, logical and consistent policies and policy outcomes, and to control government machinery and mechanisms for attaining them. Recently there has emerged a questioning of the government's ability to direct policy outcomes in an increasingly complex and multilayered environment. This problem is magnified in a context in which policy delivery is overseen in contractual relationships, which produces fragmentation and loss of expertise (Di Francesco 2001, pp. 104–7). One way in which this idea has been expressed is the 'hollowing out' thesis: the argument that the state is becoming hollowed out, smaller and fragmented because its core capacities are being increasingly assumed by non-government entities (Rhodes 1997, pp. 53–5). This process has been described as the state 'retaining its form but losing any real influence' (Davis 1997, p. 209).

Moreover, some commentators have argued that the performance of the managerialist state has been relatively poor, especially when weighed against the considerable costs in terms of the time and resources spent on reorganisation, the turbulence of rapid change and loss of staff. Operational efficiency has tended to be emphasised over effective and high-quality policy delivery (Considine & Painter 1997, pp. 88–9).

Privatisation of 000 services in Victoria dropped

In 1994 the Victorian government contracted out the management of 000 ambulance service call centres to a US-based technology company called Intergraph.

In 1997 the Victorian Auditor-General found that there had been serious mismanagement of the tender process. In 2000 a Metropolitan Ambulance Service Royal Commission was initiated to investigate a range of criticisms about the call centres, including poor call-response times and allegations of impropriety in the awarding of contracts. During the inquiry the Royal Commissioner expressed disappointment with government attempts to curtail the commission's terms of reference (Birnbauer 2002; Gough 2001). In November 2001 the commission announced its findings, including that Intergraph had falsely reported its call response times, staff had insufficient medical knowledge, and government monitoring of their contract was insufficient (Abbott 2001).

In 2002 the Victorian government recommenced operation of the ambulance call centres.

There is evidence that when some services were initially contracted out to business, the cost to government was reduced because the service provider had underestimated the real costs involved in providing the service. As these anomalies have been corrected over time, however, the cost savings to government are harder to identify, and the effectiveness of service delivery has been undermined in some instances. Areas where this has occurred include school cleaning services, water filtration in South Australia, job placement for the unemployed and the outsourcing of information technology services (Quiggan 2002, pp. 89, 95–101). It appears that overall the extent of the changes has been considerable, but the benefits are not always obvious or have not necessarily been worth the cost.

The public service and accountability

The 'traditional' view of the public service

The traditional view of the public service is one of a non-political, impartial and semi-independent administrative bureaucracy designed to be an instrument of government, and made up of permanently employed public servants. The traditional bureaucrat was 'rule-bound' and operated in a hierarchical environment in which long-practised methods were little questioned (Yeatman 1997, p. 18). Promotion was based on seniority (length of service), not on merit.

This ideal of a non-political bureaucracy is based in the theory of bureaucratic organisation derived from Max Weber (1864–1920), a German sociologist who developed a highly influential theory of modern bureaucracy based on the technically efficient and impartial application of rules. Weber argued that a 'pure' modern democracy is free of status privileges, and instead is organised by a bureaucracy that is guided by impersonal criteria for making decisions. The rules according to which decisions are made can be learnt and applied impartially. Abiding by these rules ensures a levelling of economic and social differences and the creation of a modern mass democracy (Gerth & Mills 1948, pp. 187, 196–224; Weber 1969, p. 340 cited in Gelber 2003, p. 25). Bureaucracy is 'rational' and impartial in the sense that the rules are carried out in the same way for all people, via mechanisms capable of neither favour nor discrimination.

This model of bureaucracy epitomised the public service as it developed in liberal democracies like Australia. Public servants carried out functions authorised by law, within a hierarchy of authority headed by the minister overseeing the department's functions. Public servants gained specialised knowledge of the rules by which they, and policies, operated and had job security, which allowed them to perform their roles according to impartial rules.

In Australia, this bureaucratic model was merged with the Westminster system of responsible government to ensure accountability. As described in Chapter 4, a system of responsible government means that the government, or executive, is held accountable to the legislature, or parliament, through parliamentary procedures such as questions posed to ministers. The legislature is then held accountable to the people through mechanisms such as elections. This ensures a 'chain of accountability' from the government through the parliament to the people and ensures legitimacy by allowing the people to check the activities of their elected representatives. The executive branch of government is in practice made up of the Cabinet and the Prime Minister, who direct the work of the government and who are supported in that role by departments of the public service for which they are responsible.

It is also a feature of the Westminster system that the public service is part of the chain of accountability within responsible government. The public service's role is to advise the minister on policy and to manage and oversee the implementation of government policy. Because ministers are responsible to parliament for the activities of their departments, the activities of the public service can in turn also be scrutinised as part of the democratic process. This is a feature unique to the public service. Traditionally, accountability mechanisms in the public service have included financial accountability (the responsibility to disclose fair and accurate records of the expenditure of public funds), as well as broader accountability, including accurately reporting a department's activities to the minister responsible and engaging and consulting with stakeholders (Corbett 1996, pp. 196–200).

These features of the public service help to explain why public servants had a special job security and status of employment. First, there was a need to differentiate elected ministers from non-elected officials who were required to carry out parliamentary policy directions. Second, the public service was supposed to be non-political in the sense of holding allegiance to no one political party and being prepared to serve whichever party was in government.

The contemporary public service

However, the contemporary public service, like the contemporary public sector, operates in a managerialist environment. This has led to a number of important changes in how the public service operates, which have distanced it from its traditional role.

One of the most important changes has been a change in employment conditions. These changes have attempted to ensure that public sector employees have no greater rights or status than employees in commercial businesses. Job security began to be reduced by the Fraser Coalition government as early as the 1970s, but more substantial employment reforms were undertaken by the Hawke Labor government in the 1980s. This included the expanded use of temporary staff and the creation of the Senior Executive Service, which reclassified a stratum of the most senior officials into a less secure form of contract-based employment (Halligan 1997, p. 52). The Commonwealth Public Service Board, which oversaw employment matters, was abolished in 1987 (Nethercote 1996, p. 224). In 1994 a federal government public inquiry was launched into the terms of the *Public Service Act 1922*, specifically examining employment conditions in the public service. The inquiry's report, entitled the McLeod Report (Public Service

Act Review Group 1994), advocated more flexible employment practices in the public service. Many of its recommendations were subsequently adopted by the next federal government after 1996 and incorporated into the *Public Service Act 1999* (see the report's recommendations at <www.apsc.gov.au/publications96/apsactreview.htm>). Since that time employment conditions in the public service have much more closely resembled those of business (O'Brien & O'Donnell 2002a, p. 74).

There has been a great deal of commentary regarding the potential within new modes of public sector management and public service operation for accountability to be undermined. The new focus for performance measurement for public sector managers is on results, instead of on 'traditional concerns' such as inputs and accountability (O'Brien & O'Donnell 2002a, p. 61, citing Gray & Jenkins 1995, p. 80). Much of the detailed internal regulation of behaviour in the old-style public service has been eradicated.

Furthermore, Painter makes an important point regarding the importation of new management practices from business (1997b, pp. 41–2). The public service has a specific role as a creation of and for government. In carrying out its role, it has traditionally emphasised ethical, political and social concerns. However, these concerns are not always or primarily present in business, where profits tend to be the bottom line. The importation of business management practices into the public service can therefore override the special role of the public service as an arm of a democratically elected government, with responsibilities that reach beyond efficiency and productivity. The core concerns of democratic and accountable governance can be pushed aside in the pursuit of budget targets and efficiency. Yeatman makes a similar point: the public service has an obligation to deliver policy fairly and equitably in accordance with community needs, and this obligation 'sits uncomfortably with' the demands of a managerialist state (1997, p. 15). There is also a related point to consider: are some activities intrinsically or inherently the kind of activity that government—and not business—ought to provide? Boston has engaged insightfully with this question ((ed.) 1995), and he argues that the contracting out of core governmental activities poses significant risks for appropriate policy delivery.

This means that in the contemporary public service and public sector a number of questions have been raised regarding how well accountability can continue to be achieved. Rod Rhodes warned in the mid-1990s of a 'potential disaster' arising from trends towards privatisation and outsourcing of functions

(1994), and recent research on the Commonwealth Job Network confirms the existence of an 'accountability deficit' (Mulgan 2006). When the government devolves responsibility for large elements of policy delivery to non-government actors, the risk of accountability mechanisms suffering is enhanced. On the other hand, government retains the overall responsibility for policy direction and regulation, which provides mechanisms for accountability to be maintained.

Policy delivery in the contemporary Australian state

Thus far we have elaborated on how the public sector and the public service operate in contemporary Australian politics, and outlined some criticisms regarding the market orientation and managerialist approach to its organisation. It is time now to consider the effect of these changes on policy delivery.

It is important to consider the extent to which the contemporary mode of operation in the public sector enhances or detracts from possibilities for interaction between it and other political actors. Policy goals are decided in a process of continuous contestation. Contestation requires the engagement of a range of actors with differing views about how best to move forward, and about which policy approach might best help solve complex problems such as unemployment, poverty, salination, indigenous health or climate change.

On the one hand, it seems clear that the direction of contemporary policy making provides enhanced institutional opportunities for actors and networks from business and the community to gain access to, and engage in very concrete ways with, policy delivery. The opening up of policy implementation in these ways provides direct mechanisms by which these actors may become involved in policy implementation and delivery. This implies that it is more possible than ever before for non-government actors to become involved in policy implementation in their areas, in ways that they see as most helpful to themselves or their community base. There is some evidence that this is taking place, as the example of employment services for people with disabilities demonstrates (see box).

People with disabilities

In 2002 the national industry association for disability services, the Australian Council for Rehabilitation of the Disabled (ACROD), surveyed community–business partnerships that were offering employment opportunities to people with disabilities. They surveyed nearly 8500 partnerships and released a report entitled 'Mutual Benefit: Community and Business Getting Together—a focus on partnerships in the disability sector'.

They found the partnerships involved a diverse range of activities, including the production of art works, commercial lighting and recycled sawdust briquettes.

One partnership in Victoria was between Minibah Services and SITA Environmental Solutions, a waste management company. Minibah arranged for people with disabilities to assist SITA in managing a transfer and recycling operation, which provided an opportunity for the employees to earn award-based wages and produced low-cost recycled goods for the marketplace (ACROD 2002).

However, there are potential problems with this opportunity expansion that need to be addressed. The first of these is that providing the institutional opportunity may be inadequate, if the infrastructural and financial support to make the participation of non-government political actors viable is not provided. ACROD, cited in the box 'People with disabilities' speaking in positive terms about community–business partnerships opening up employment opportunities for people with disabilities, has also highlighted the potential risks involved in the government's devolution of responsibilities for people with disabilities to business and community entities. There is a particular risk associated with inadequate government funding provision to the organisations empowered to carry out the required tasks (see the box 'Disability services and cost shifting').

Disability services and cost shifting

ACROD released a policy document entitled 'Disability Services: Policies for the Next Federal Government' in which it claimed that 'cost-shifting' by government may place disability services at risk. Cost shifting occurs where the government funds business or community organisations to carry out tasks it previously carried out itself. The risk occurs to disability services when the government's funding formula does not fully reflect the cost of policy delivery.

ACROD recognised in the report that the government has redefined its role as a 'purchaser' of welfare and community services rather than a

> provider of those services, while seeking to retain control over how services are delivered. This means community organisations are caught between cost pressures from inadequate funding for policy delivery on the one hand and a lack of independence in policy implementation on the other.
>
> ACROD called on the government to increase its financial commitment to the devolution of services to community organisations involved in disability services (ACROD 2001).

This example highlights one of the major difficulties associated with the contemporary devolution of policy delivery to non-government actors, which is the risk associated with inadequate funding. Given that this devolution has occurred within an environment that places greater emphasis on financial efficiency and budget-led accounting, this risk is very high.

A second potential problem in the contemporary model for policy delivery is its market orientation. Is it the case that some policy areas do not fit well with a market orientation, which rests on the assumption that a supply and demand approach can fix a vast range of economic and social problems and which prioritises cost efficiency? The kind of issue that falls into this category could include services for people with disabilities or the homeless.

It appears that the contemporary framework within which policy delivery takes place both enhances opportunities for engagement in policy delivery by new actors within policy networks and communities who are stakeholders in their policy area, and at the same time constrains their participation to activities that are consonant with a pro-market orientation. This process therefore both enables and constrains participation in policy delivery in the contemporary Australian state.

Summary

- The public service has traditionally played the role of an impartial bureaucracy, carrying out the wishes of elected government officials. This has ensured transparency and accountability.
- In the last three decades the state's role has changed to one of 'steering instead of rowing'. This has led to significant changes in the manner in which policy is delivered, and the inclusion of a range of business and community actors in policy delivery.

- Contemporary concepts of the appropriate role of the state open up new opportunities for policy actors to engage with the state in policy delivery, but at the same time they constrain their actions to those consistent with a market-oriented approach.

Further reading

Considine, Mark 1994, *Public Policy: A Critical Approach*, Macmillan Education, Melbourne.

Considine, Mark and Painter, Martin (eds) 1997, *Managerialism: The Great Debate*, Melbourne University Press, Melbourne.

Weller, Patrick and Davis, Glyn (eds) 1996, *New Ideas, Better Government*, Allen & Unwin, Sydney.

Useful websites

- Australian Public Service Commission: <www.apsc.gov.au>. This website provides information on the operation and standards of the public service.
- Centre for Research in Public Sector Management, University of Canberra: <www.blis.canberra.edu.au/crpsm>. This centre conducts research into the contemporary operation of the public sector. It holds conferences and seminars and provides access to useful publications in the area.
- The Centre for Public Policy, University of Melbourne: <www.public-policy.unimelb.edu.au>. This centre holds conferences on public sector operations and offers courses in public sector management, public policy and social policy.

CHAPTER 14
AUSTRALIA IN THE WORLD

In this, the final chapter on policy processes, we will investigate Australian foreign policy. Since Australia's international relationships both affect and are affected by domestic policy processes, it is important to study foreign policy as a component of policy more generally. Also, understanding Australia's place in the world is an essential component of understanding contemporary political practice because of the increasing interconnectedness between states in the global era and the interdependencies between domestic and international policy processes. We see this chapter therefore as an important part of understanding the range of pressures on, and interaction within, policy development in the contemporary era.

This chapter investigates Australia's orientation to the international community through its foreign policy over time. We argue that Australia's place in the world has demonstrated both continuity and change. The continuity rests in alliances with great powers, especially the United States. The change relates to how Australia projects itself on the world stage and how it perceives its role. We argue that recently Australian foreign policy has demonstrated a very high level of synergy with that of the United States, raising questions about the nature of and justifications for our most influential alliance. This has been combined with a rhetoric of 'national interest' that conceals a range of interests at work. We will investigate what these might be.

The topics covered in this chapter include:

- continuity and change in Australia's historical alliances with great powers
- investigating alternative conceptions of the 'national interest' from 1996 to 2007
- three trends in foreign policy since the 1990s: the Australia–United States alliance, Australia's role in the Asia-Pacific region, and non-compliance with international human rights norms
- how understanding foreign policy is an important component of understanding contemporary Australian politics and policy-making.

SNAPSHOT The 2004 tsunami—aid responsibilities vs 'national interests'

On 26 December 2004 an earthquake off the coast of Sumatra, Indonesia, triggered a tsunami. Waves travelling at hundreds of kilometres per hour hit Indonesia, Thailand, India, Sri Lanka, the Maldives and eventually Somalia (Shergold 2005, p. 44). Hundreds of thousands of people were killed, and half a million people were displaced. The international community responded immediately, as did Australia. As well as providing support to Australians and their families directly affected by the tsunami (Shergold 2005, pp. 44–5), humanitarian assistance in the form of aid and relief workers was immediately forthcoming from the Australian government. An initial aid package for the region was announced the day after the tsunami and Australian Defence Force (ADF) and Australian Federal Police (AFP) resources were committed to the humanitarian effort (Ravenhill 2007, p. 210). By the end of the year the government had committed $60 million in humanitarian assistance for Indonesia, the Maldives, Sri Lanka and Thailand (Ravenhill 2007, p. 210). The Australian public also responded generously, raising nearly $300 million in public donations.

Australia provided focused assistance specifically to Indonesia. Within a week of the disaster Australia had provided aircraft, helicopters, water purifiers and medical staff to Aceh. The ADF had established an emergency hospital with X-ray and resuscitation facilities (Sukma 2006, p. 223). On 31 December *HMAS Kanimbla* left to provide on the ground assistance (Shergold 2005, p. 46).

In addition, on 5 January the Prime Minister announced longer-term assistance in the form of the Australia–Indonesia Partnership for Reconstruction and Development (Shergold 2005, pp. 45, 47), a $1 billion package over five years. The package was negotiated in less than a week. It is managed by a ministerial level Joint Commission comprising the foreign ministers and economic ministers of both countries, and overseen jointly by the Australian Prime Minister and Indonesia's President. This has been described as an 'unusually high level of political involvement for a bilateral development cooperation program' (Dawson 2006, pp. 129–30).

Australia's assistance was credited, along with cooperation over the Bali bombings of October 2002, with significantly improving Australia's relationship with Indonesia in the wake of East Timor's independence. It was viewed positively as Australia reaching out to help its neighbours in a time of need (Ravenhill 2007, p. 211; Kelton 2006, p. 242; Sukma 2006, pp. 222–3).

But the $1 billion reconstruction package was not without its critics. The most strident criticism has emerged from AID/WATCH, an activist community organisation that monitors Australian overseas aid (<www.aidwatch.org.au>). In a 2006 report written by AID/WATCH, the reconstruction package was criticised on several grounds.

First, it was argued that the package was announced unilaterally by Australia at a time when international donors were meeting in Jakarta to discuss the appropriate mechanisms of response (O'Connor et al. 2006). Australia decided to go it alone, announcing a substantial aid package without consulting other nations involved in the reconstruction effort, including the US, India and Japan.

Second, the package was made available to all areas in Indonesia, not just those that had been affected by the tsunami. Three months after the tsunami, agreement was reached on the allocation of funds. A significant proportion of the funding was allocated to rehabilitation assistance in non-tsunami-affected areas of Indonesia, a total of $791 million. Of this total, $50 million was allocated to a Government Partnership Fund designed to support the exchange of capabilities between Australian and Indonesian government officials (O'Connor et al. 2006, Table 8). The linkages between government agencies enabled by the package have been described as unusual for an official development cooperation program (Dawson 2006, p. 131). Thus, the AID/WATCH report contends that the main thrust of the package was not tsunami relief but a series of other infrastructure and support programs, despite the announcement of the package as part of the Australian response to the tsunami. Some of the measures announced as part of the package, including the Government Partnership Fund, reflected projects conceived by the Australian government well before the tsunami struck (O'Connor et al. 2006).

Finally, half of the package is not a donation but rather a $500 million loan, which Indonesia is required to repay from 2015. This is a departure from the normal practice since 1997 when the Australian government stopped giving aid in the form of loans (O'Connor et al. 2006). However, the loans are highly concessional; they attract no interest, have a repayment period of forty years, and no repayment of principle is required for the first ten years (Dawson 2006, p. 138).

Australia's response to the tsunami raises a number of questions about Australia's responsibilities in the region. As a developed nation, Australia is expected to respond with assistance and aid during disastrous events, and it has done so. Yet the assistance and aid we provide does not appear to be constraint-free.

Australia appears to have been pursuing some objectives in its post-tsunami aid program that were not directly related to the tsunami itself. What are some of the national priorities Australia might be pursuing through its aid programs? Is it appropriate for Australia to pursue objectives in this way? How have Australia's actions been interpreted in the region? What are the conflicting pressures at play in determining foreign aid and foreign policy?

Continuity and change: Australia's historical alliances

Since 1901, Australia's isolated location, vast size and relatively small population have combined to produce somewhat of a split personality in international relations. On the one hand Australia has tended to rely heavily on alliances with more powerful nations that, it was hoped, would act as protector in the event of an emergency. On the other hand, Australia has at times fiercely defended its capacity for independence in policy and decision-making, in programs to secure Australia's security and in external affairs generally.

Australia's alliances with other nations have also demonstrated both continuity and change over time. Continuity derives from our historical alliances with more powerful nations, first with Britain and, since World War II, increasingly with the United States. There is also continuity in our attempts to engage economically with the Asia-Pacific region. However, within these broad brush strokes there have been changes in some more specific foreign policy concerns.

Immediately post-settlement in Australia, ties to Britain were paramount and included the inheritance of largely British legal and political systems and a national identity as British citizens living overseas. These beginnings ensured that an attachment to Britain as the primary focus of Australia's perception and projection of its identity persisted for a considerable time, at least throughout the first two-thirds of the twentieth century. During the period from Federation in 1901 until the 1970s, the dominant element of foreign policy considerations was security (Horner 1993, p. 83), conceived of as the need to defend Australian soil from invasion and Australian citizens from harm. Security was considered to be best assured by retaining links with a more powerful nation (Gelber 1993, p. 66), and that meant alliance with Britain.

In the post-World War II period, without relinquishing its relationship with Britain, Australia increased its cooperation with the United States in matters of defence and security (Horner 1993, p. 90). The 1951 ANZUS agreement between the United States, Australia and New Zealand, for example, committed its member countries to assist one another in the event of an act of war or invasion, ensuring that any risk to Australia's security could potentially involve United States support. During the Cold War, Asia was viewed as a threat.

By the 1970s, however, both the means of assuring Australian security and the issues considered essential components of foreign policy began to shift. In 1976 the government released a Defence White Paper (Department of Defence 1976) which signalled a shift in the focus of security policy towards enhancing stability and cooperation in Australia's geographical region: South-East Asia and the Pacific (Viviani 1993, pp. 45–6, 49).

A 'White Paper' is a document produced by the government that outlines its policy priorities and outlook in a specific portfolio area. It expresses the government's prevailing interpretation of the context in which policy development in that area is to take place.

This focus was reinforced in a report commissioned by the government which became known as the Dibb Report in 1986 (Dibb 1986) and in another Defence White Paper published in 1987 (Department of Defence 1987). These reports elaborated on the idea that the pursuit of stability in political relations and economic interaction with countries in the region would enhance Australian security (Gelber 1993, pp. 71–2). This is not to say that self-reliance meant Australia was turning its back on its relationship with the US. On the contrary; that alliance remained strong during this period. However, self-reliance did involve a shift in focus and an attempt to pursue regional interests in conjunction with the alliances Australia had been involved in with the United States and Britain (Gelber 1993, p. 72).

In 1987 two government departments that previously existed separately were amalgamated to create the Department of Foreign Affairs and Trade (Viviani 1993, p. 41). The creation of a single department responsible both for trade issues and foreign affairs signalled the government's commitment to achieve economic reform both domestically and internationally, via combined foreign and export policies (Viviani 1993, p. 59). In December 1989 the then Foreign Minister Gareth Evans released a statement entitled *Australia's Regional Security* in which 'cooperative security' was promoted via cooperation and consultation, and as amounting to more than military defence and inclusive of environmental, migration, economic and other concerns (Cotton & Ravenhill 1997, p. 5). This confirmed that the ambit of security policy had widened to involve more than military defence.

By the period of Labor federal government from 1983 to 1996 foreign affairs policy involved a stronger engagement with the Asia-Pacific region. This shift was led tentatively at first by Prime Minister Bob Hawke and gathered pace significantly under the leadership of Prime Minister Paul Keating. Early attempts by the Labor government were regarded by some commentators as having made 'little progress' (H. Smith, 1993, p. 19), but after Keating became Prime Minister in December 1991, he was seen as a leader who promoted a visionary approach to establishing Australia as an important power in the Asian region (Goldsworthy 2001, p. 16) on the basis of the view that Australia's future lay in enhancing relationships in the region (Murray 1997, p. 243). Keating said, 'I brought with me to the prime ministership [a] ... conviction ... that our future lay comprehensively in Asia' (2000, p. 15). This did not mean that other foreign policy objectives were erased from the government's consciousness. Indeed, the Australian government supported United States policies towards military participation in the Gulf War of 1990–91, actions that produced criticism of Australia in the Asia-Pacific region (Bell 1997, p. 211).

The Howard era: changing meanings of 'national interest'?

After the election of the Coalition government in 1996, foreign policy was reappraised. The result was in many senses a reaffirmation of longstanding alliances with more powerful nations in order to achieve security, rather than a wholesale change of direction. But there was also a discernible shift away from a commitment to some of the broader elements of security adopted since the 1970s. In the contemporary era notions of security became narrower again, conceived in predominantly defence and military terms. In this section of this chapter we will examine how this dynamic played out.

The newly installed Coalition government released its first White Paper on foreign and trade policy in 1997, entitled *In the National Interest* (DFAT 1997; see <www.defence.gov.au/ARMY/LWD1/pdfs/docs/In_the_National_Interest.pdf>). This paper recognised that Asia was a 'centre of power and influence with different cultural traditions' (cited in Milner 2001, p. 33) but also put forward a new official catchphrase for foreign policy of 'Asia first, but not Asia only' (Cotton & Ravenhill 2001, p. 3). This meant that more traditional alliances with both the US and Britain were reaffirmed (Goldsworthy 2001, p. 10).

Other changes introduced by the federal government included a move away from regionalism towards bilateralism; key bilateral relationships were regarded as those with the United States, Japan, China and Indonesia. Multilateralism was downgraded, with the government declaring it would be selectively pursued only where doing so was in accordance with a perceived national interest (Gyngell & Wesley 2007, p. 221; DFAT 1997, p. iii; Cotton & Ravenhill 2007, p. 7). Overall, the federal government stressed 'national interest' above all else. This was reinforced in a subsequent 2003 White Paper entitled *Advancing the National Interest* (DFAT 2003).

Some commentators began to argue that the government's emphasis on 'national interest' cloaked changed meanings of the term. One argument was that the Australian government was increasingly viewing foreign policy priorities and its international obligations through the lens of what it perceived to be Australian 'values'. Wesley, for example, argued that the government's approach displayed a logic that was:

> more strongly determined by domestic politics and a vision of Australian values than anything that has come before ... The new logic is one in which events in and relationships with the outside world are interpreted and responded to according to a certain conception of the values of the majority of Australian society. (2002, p. 47)

This meant that foreign policy became determined more than ever before according to the same political calculations as domestic policy (Wesley 2002, p. 54) rather than in the more traditional view of international relations and dealings between states. This view is supported by McDonald (2005, p. 153) and Ungerer (2007, p. 13) and was acknowledged by the Prime Minister himself when he referred to the 'old boundaries' such as that between 'domestic and foreign policy' being 'fuzzier now' (cited in Kelton 2006, p. 229).

A second argument, supported by Wesley (2002) and Flitton (2003), was that in making its policy decisions, the Australian government seemed convinced of the weight and importance of Australia as a player in the global arena, a sense of self-worth that was based more on hubris than an objective calculation of national power in global terms. This sense of self-belief persisted despite strong condemnation of Australia's role in several important events by other countries and by intellectuals. In this view, 'national interest' equates with the Australian government's self-perception as a country exerting power in its geographical region.

A third argument put forward by Weiss, Thurbon and Mathews is that the federal government's actions in both the international and national arenas have trampled on what is objectively in Australians' interests in many policy areas (2007, p. 2). Whether in the purchase of defence equipment, not on the basis of what served Australia's military best but what was American, or in reducing quarantine regulations to cater to the United States' commercial interests, the government's actions displayed a 'pattern of betrayal' (2007, pp. 3–4) of Australia's security and prosperity. Their analysis of an undermining of national interests by a government that used 'national interest' as its flagship statement of governance is supported by Grant's analysis of the Australia–US alliance (2004), Borgu's analysis of air combat capabilities (2004) and Hamilton's analysis of climate change policy (2001). Weiss, Thurbon and Mathews have argued that the term 'national interest' was used as a cover for calculating what was necessary to secure Howard's personal status and electoral success, and to undermine Labor's legacy (2007, pp. 234–5). The evidence in favour of this argument is strengthened by widespread acknowledgement of the increasingly important role of the Prime Minister himself in foreign policy-making (Kelton 2006, p. 229; Cotton & Ravenhill 2007, p. 6).

Critics of these interpretations put an alternative view: that since September 11 terrorism has become the central, dominant and driving theme of foreign policy developments (Ungerer (ed.) 2007), underpinned by an entirely new conception of security in the world (Hirst 2007, p. 227). They argue that this explains the trajectory of Australian foreign policy and that it 'cannot be explained by notions of "mateship" and shared values alone' (Ungerer 2007, p. 4). Perhaps it is the combination of elements that speaks forcefully to the meaning of 'national interest' in the era under study.

To what extent do these interpretations of 'national interest' from 1996 to 2007 stand up to scrutiny? Did the government display a tendency to view outside events through a domestic lens? Has Australia displayed arrogance in its dealings with its neighbours and regional events? Has it undermined national interests in the name of securing them? Has it placed the United States' interests above our own? We will try to shed light on these claims and make an assessment of Australia's place in the world by examining three sets of events in foreign policy processes since the mid-1990s. We will examine:

1 the Iraq war and the Australia–US alliance
2 Australia's role in human rights protection in the Asia-Pacific region
3 Australia's non-compliance with international human rights norms.

The Iraq war and the Australia–US alliance

The alliance between the United States and Australia has been a defining feature of Australian foreign policy since 1996. In many respects, including the waging of wars in Afghanistan and Iraq and the conclusion of a bilateral Free Trade Agreement, the role of the United States in influencing Australian policy decisions has been paramount. Here we will discuss the ways in which Australian and United States policy approaches have dovetailed during this period.

Within two days of the terrorist attacks in the United States on September 11, 2001 Prime Minister Howard formally activated ANZUS for the first time in its history (Sales 2007, p. 4; Doig et al. 2007, p. 28). The Australian government unequivocally supported the United States' decision to wage war first in 2001 in Afghanistan, underpinned by United Nations Security Resolutions and because the organiser of the terrorist attacks, Osama bin Laden, was believed to be hiding there. Then in 2003 war began in Iraq, on the ground that dictator Saddam Hussein possessed weapons of mass destruction (WMDs) and represented a threat to regional and world security. Australia deployed troops and committed resources as part of the 'Coalition of the Willing' in Iraq (Bell 2007, pp. 25–42). In May 2003, the cost estimated by Access Economics of Australia's involvement in the war on Iraq over two years was $700 million (Richardson 2003, p. 26).

In relation to the decision to wage war in Iraq, Australia unreservedly supported the United States' positions on its legality, its justification and its continuation. Hence, the decision to participate in the 2003 Iraq war was particularly revealing of the nature of the alliance. This decision was initially justified on the basis of intelligence shared between the United States, the United Kingdom and Australia (Gyngell & Wesley 2007, p. 138). The intelligence was claimed to reveal that Saddam possessed chemical and biological weapons and potentially could manufacture a nuclear weapon. But this information was publicised selectively; dissenting opinions were silenced and some information that was known to be incorrect nevertheless made its way into the public arena (Doig et al. 2007, pp. 32–4). Additionally, the information released was used to support arguments that linked Iraq and terrorism 'in the public imagination' (Doig et al. 2007, p. 29), and the nuanced and qualified way in which some of the intelligence had initially been presented within government circles was lost in the context of the release of information to the public (Gyngell & Wesley 2007, p. 138). The reason for this appears to have been to enable Australia to justify its support for a decision—to oust Saddam Hussein—which had already been made in Washington, in order to strengthen its alliance with the United States (Doig et al. 2007, pp. 26–9; McDonald 2005, pp. 154–7).

Support for the war in Iraq was not universal. Some countries, including France and Germany, strongly opposed it (Skotnicki 2003), and the United Nations Security Council did not endorse the military intervention that began there on 20 March 2003. Indeed, some have argued that the war was illegal under international law (for example Simpson 2005; see also conflicting legal opinions in *MJIL* 2003).

Despite a quick declaration of victory by the United States on 1 May 2003, the war in Iraq continues. It has become marked by insurgent tactics that are difficult to combat with traditional military tactics, and Iraqi and United States casualties have been high (Kelton 2006, pp. 238–9; Frost 2007, p. 413). As the war began to raise serious questions about the timing of troop withdrawal and the viability of a stable Iraqi government, the federal government continued to support Australia's involvement on the ground that its relationship with the United States required doing so (Frost 2007, p. 414).

A raft of related scandals has occurred since. In 2004 reports emerged of systematic abuse of Iraqi prisoners in the Abu Ghraib prison, and raised questions about the Australian government's knowledge of the abuse before it received media attention (McDonald 2005, pp. 154–5). In 2005 the Australian Wheat Board (AWB) scandal exposed payments by the then Australian export monopoly of kickbacks to the Iraqi regime between 1997 and 2003 in return for securing wheat exports for Australian farmers. The Volcker report released by the United

Nations revealed that AWB had illegally paid more than US$221 million to the Iraqi regime in contravention of the United Nations oil-for-food program, designed to provide humanitarian relief to Iraqi citizens (Kelton 2006, pp. 235–6; Botterill 2007, p. 4). Subsequently the Australian government launched the Cole inquiry, which concluded that twelve executives may have broken the law (Botterill 2007, p. 4) and that DFAT's procedures for preventing corruption had been inadequate (Frost 2007, p. 416). It also concluded that neither public servants nor the relevant ministers knew of the illegal payments, but opinion polls showed that the public did not believe the government had not known (Lenihan 2007, p. 66). Evidence suggested the government had been warned of potentially illegal payments as early as 2000 (Cotton & Ravenhill 2007, p. 19), raising questions over the adequacy of oversight by the minister and DFAT. The AWB scandal also highlights the broader foreign policy issue of placing the economic interests of domestic farmers and markets ahead of humanitarian objectives.

The detention of Australian citizen David Hicks in Guantanamo Bay prison for five years without trial provides further evidence of the nature of the US–Australia alliance. Hicks was captured in Afghanistan on 9 December 2001 after having trained with Al-Qaeda. From the beginning the Australian government's position was that since Hicks could not be charged with any offence existing under Australian law at the time of his arrest, his fate would be decided by the United States. However, it has been argued by critics that prosecution could have occurred in Australia (Hovell & Niemann 2005; Sales 2007, p. 5). Hicks was therefore left in the custody of the United States military, which transported him to Guantanamo Bay, Cuba. Citizens of other countries, including the United Kingdom, France, Russia, Spain and Sweden, were also detained at Guantanamo Bay, but their governments secured their return so that they could be tried in their own countries and in their own courts (Hovell & Niemann 2005, p. 118). The Australian government did not seek Hicks' return.

In June 2004 Hicks was charged by the United States Department of Defense with conspiracy to commit war crimes, attempted murder and aiding the enemy (Hovell & Niemann 2005, p. 117). The Military Commission was strongly criticised, including by the Law Council of Australia's independent observer who described it as 'flawed' and said a 'fair trial of David Hicks is . . . virtually impossible', and by the UK government (Hovell & Niemann 2005, p. 117; Sales 2007, p. 5; THLDT 2007). Even the United States Supreme Court declared the commission unconstitutional and illegal, but Congress then passed new legislation enabling it to operate. Hicks finally faced trial in March 2007. This time the charges were providing material support for terrorism and attempted murder (Bikundo 2007, p. 494). He pleaded guilty to the former charge and returned to Australia to serve the remaining nine months of his sentence in Adelaide's Yatala prison.

The Australian government began to respond to criticism of the delay in processing Hicks and consequent denial of due process only in early 2007 after the public outcry reached new heights (Sales 2007, p. 7; Stead 2007). At that time Prime Minister Howard simply asked the United States to speed up Hicks' trial (Bikundo 2007, p. 495). The staunch criticism of the Australian government's stance on Hicks, and the extraordinary concessions regarding legal process granted to the United States, was hardly ameliorated by this development.

A further aspect of the United States–Australia alliance during this period is the Free Trade Agreement concluded in 2004. Opinion on the benefits of the agreement to Australia are divided, with evidence that in some areas such as the beef industry the interests of United States producers have been prioritised over those of domestic farmers. For example in the area of foreign investments, United States investments in Australia worth less than $800 million are now exempt from scrutiny by the Foreign Investment Review Board, whose scrutiny is designed to ensure that the investment is productive for Australia. Before the conclusion of the FTA the figure was $50 million. In the area of quarantine the FTA has required Australia, until now free from 'mad cow' disease, to relax its quarantine standards for meat imports from BSE-infected countries (Weiss et al. 2004, 2006, 2007, pp. 66–7, 75–85). Foreign policy analysts concluded that 'most observers' felt the agreement did 'not serve the interests of key agricultural sectors' (Cotton & Ravenhill 2007, p. 4), and it is known that the United States pursues 'asymmetric reciprocity' in such agreements (Ravenhill 2007, pp. 201–2). The motivation for signing the agreement is widely believed to have been to garner political favour with the United States and cement the alliance (see also Leaver 2007).

This brief overview of Australia's role in important aspects of its alliance with the United States since 1996 does appear to support the argument that Australia has adopted stances that uncritically support the United States' policies and are designed to meet the US' needs even where these may conflict with some interpretations of what is in Australia's interests. Australia has played second fiddle to its more powerful ally. Significant decisions, including our involvement in the Iraq war, the use of intelligence in policy-making, the treatment of Australian citizens and the making of a long-term binding agreement on trade, demonstrate complete accord with—perhaps even deference to—the United States. Many observers have noted that the extent and depth of this alignment were explained by the government as arising from shared 'values' (Cotton & Ravenhill 2007, pp. 4, 8). This means that even if we were to interpret these events as having been driven by a new terrorism-dominated security agenda, they still serve as a reminder of how closely Australia's interests had been considered to ally with those of the United States during this period.

Australia's role in the Asia-Pacific region

There has been considerable debate over Australia's role in the Asia-Pacific region since the late 1990s, especially in regard to the protection of human rights. Australia has been described as pursuing a 'new interventionism' in the Pacific (Cotton & Ravenhill 2007, p. 4). On the other hand, Australia is often asked to intervene to assist other states. What has Australia's role in the region been? First, we will consider regional issues, then we will consider specific events in relation to Australia's relationship with other countries.

Relations with the region

During the 1997–99 Asian financial crisis economies and currencies crumbled, and as a result many countries in the region, including Thailand, Indonesia and South Korea, were granted financial assistance by the International Monetary Fund (IMF), assistance to which Australia made a significant contribution (Goldsworthy 2001, p. 18). Despite some positive recognition of Australia's contribution to the rescue packages (Milner 2001, p. 40), Australia was also criticised by countries in the region for a perceived indifference to their financial hardship, a paternalistic attitude in trying to instruct Asian states in how to fix their economies and a sense of haughtiness in congratulating itself on avoiding the worst of the economic downturn (Cotton & Ravenhill 2001, pp. 5–6).

One of the longer-term outcomes of the financial crisis was the preference for, and conclusion of, a variety of bilateral agreements, including trade agreements with Singapore in 2003 and Thailand in 2005 (Cotton & Ravenhill 2007, p. 9), a security declaration with Japan in 2007 (Bisley 2008) and continuing negotiations with China (Frost 2007, p. 405). Bilateral agreements on counter-terrorism were also secured with Malaysia, Thailand, the Philippines, Indonesia, Brunei, East Timor, Cambodia, Papua New Guinea, India, Pakistan and Fiji (Cotton & Ravenhill 2007, p. 12).

The period of the Howard government also saw the emergence, then consolidation, of the 'Howard doctrine': the idea that Australia was prepared to act regionally in the same manner as the United States acts globally; that is, to intervene (militarily if necessary) in other countries' affairs in the interests of security. This idea emerged from a 1999 article in the *Bulletin* magazine in which the Prime Minister portrayed Australia as playing the role of a deputy sheriff to the United States in the region (Milner 2000, p. 180). Howard repudiated the statement in the short term. Then United States President George W. Bush, during a visit to Australia in October 2003, responded to media questions about Australia's role in the region with the comment that Australia was not just a 'deputy sheriff [but] ... a sheriff' (Kelly 2003).

In 2004 the Australian government refused to sign ASEAN's Treaty of Amity and Cooperation, which commits states to non-interference in each other's internal affairs. Grounds for the refusal included that it would undermine Australia's capacity to launch pre-emptive strikes in the region (McDonald 2005, p. 163). After criticism from the region, and in the context of a desire to participate in the East Asian meetings, the government eventually agreed to sign the treaty, but with the reservation that doing so did not limit its other commitments with non-ASEAN states and on security matters (Cotton & Ravenhill 2007, p. 11).

East Timor

Australia played an important role in the lead-up to and after the 1999 referendum on independence, which secured autonomy for East Timor and ended Indonesia's occupation of the territory. Although Australia was in part responding to the human rights demands of the international community and sectors of the Australian public, these events also raised an intense debate over the appropriateness of our role.

Until the late 1990s Australian foreign policy towards East Timor had been dominated by bipartisan support for maintaining a close and constructive relationship with the Indonesian government (Burchill 2000, pp. 169–72), which had annexed the East Timorese territory in 1975–76. This emphasis on maintaining fruitful relations with Indonesia meant that successive governments had supported Indonesia's occupation of East Timor. As an indication of this, former Prime Minister Whitlam stated in 1976 that 'despite Indonesia's invasion of Timor, the relationship between Australia and Indonesia must be preserved' (Viviani 1999, p. 85 citing a speech in Townsville, 2 May 1976). This official attitude persisted even after the 1991 Dili massacre on 12 November 1991, in which Indonesian troops opened fire on thousands of East Timorese youths at Dili's Santa Cruz Cemetery who were involved in a memorial procession that had developed into a protest march. The number of dead was estimated at more than a hundred (Hodge 1994, p. 197).

Nineteen ninety-eight saw the demise of the controversial Soeharto regime in Indonesia, which had claimed government in a bloody coup in 1965 in which at least 500,000 civilians were killed (Cotton 2000, pp. 7, 11). The newly installed Indonesian government, led by President Habibie, began to discuss East Timor's future autonomy (Kingsbury 2000, p. 26). The Australian Labor Party, after losing government federally, officially adopted a pro-independence policy, and Minister for Foreign Affairs Alexander Downer began to promote the involvement of the East Timorese people in developing a solution to the intransigent question of the territory's independence (Cotton 2001, pp. 214–17).

In 1999 the debate moved to a new level as reports emerged of violent activities in East Timor by militias in favour of retaining East Timorese integration with Indonesia. There was some evidence that these militias were taking direction from the Indonesian military (Burchill 2000, p. 169). When the UN announced that a referendum on independence would be held, the question emerged of whether a UN-led peace-keeping force ought to be sent into the territory before or after the referendum. The Australian government supported the idea of sending in a peace-keeping force after the referendum, but others, including Portugal, argued that peace-keeping was required earlier (Cotton 2000, p. 15).

In order for logistical arrangements to be made so that the referendum could be conducted, the UN established the UN Mission in East Timor (UNAMET) in June 1999 (Martin 2001, pp. 37ff), to which Australia contributed substantially in terms of finances, logistical support and staff.

The referendum produced a 78.5 per cent majority in favour of independence (Burchill 2000, p. 169). After the result was announced on 4 September 1999, the UN compound came under siege as escalated violence broke out across East Timor, including wholesale destruction, killings and forcible movement of East Timorese people to West Timor. Within days Australia had committed itself to participate in a UN-led peace enforcement mission with support from other nations in the region and the US. On 15 September the UN created the peace enforcement force INTERFET (Martin 2001, pp. 94, 103, 114), which eventually deployed 9000 troops from eighteen countries and in which Australia played a leading role (Cotton 2001, pp. 221–4).

Australia has continued to provide support to East Timor since that time in various forms, such as a $32 million police assistance program to help develop local police capacities (O'Keefe 2007, p. 142). However, instability persists.

Many people credited the post-referendum intervention with saving lives. However, some countries in the region, including Indonesia, Malaysia, Thailand and Korea, criticised what they perceived as Australian heavy-handedness, arrogance and preparedness to act to protect what it perceived as its own interests in the region (Milner 2000, p. 179), including Australia's stake in the oil and gas reserves of the Timor Sea under the 1989 Timor Gap Treaty (King 2002, p. 82). New crises continue to arise, such as an attempted coup in February 2008, which means Australia is likely to continue its involvement in East Timor for the foreseeable future.

Solomon Islands

A further indication that Australia has been more interventionist in the region than it had previously been, and that the East Timor experience has provided a 'model for intervention' in unstable and fragmented states in the region, is the Solomon Islands (O'Keefe 2007, p. 131).

After years of unrest, by 2003 violence had become severe in the Solomons. Following the release of a report by the Australian Strategic Policy Institute (ASPI) recommending large-scale intervention, which contributed 'significantly' to the Australian government's understanding of the situation (Morgan & McLeod 2006, p. 418), the Solomon Islands Prime Minister requested intervention, the Solomon Islands parliament passed enabling legislation, and the Australian government intervened (O'Keefe 2007, pp. 133–4). The Regional Assistance Mission to Solomon Islands (RAMSI) deployed more than two thousand troops, federal police and protective services and was supported by other governments in the region. Within a year the mission was scaled down to only a hundred troops. However, while the lawlessness was relatively successfully tackled in the short term, the underlying problems that had induced the violence, including socioeconomic factors, were not addressed. RAMSI was criticised for inadequately seeking to deal with these underlying causes. In 2006 riots again broke out, and additional military and police were deployed (O'Keefe 2007, pp. 133–5; Morgan & McLeod 2006, pp. 412, 414, 419–20).

The Australian government acknowledged that the Solomon Islands intervention represented a new approach to the South Pacific. The government even claimed that the world expected Australia to play such a role in the region (AFP 2003). Although the Solomon Islands intervention was undertaken in response to a request for assistance, the deployment of Australian troops and police to strife-torn neighbouring countries raises broader questions about Australia's perception of its own role in the region. It demonstrates a greater preparedness on Australia's part to act, even militarily if necessary, to be seen to play a leading role in the region and to be interventionist in regional crises.

Papua New Guinea

Papua New Guinea (PNG) has appeared to suffer from similar problems of social disorder and poverty. Australia has a long history of providing aid to the country, but in 2003 problems of lawlessness were also widespread and in 2004 the Australian government increased cooperation to try to strengthen local governance. The Enhanced Cooperation Program included an $800 million support package tied to the deployment of police and civil servants to train locals and thus increase domestic capabilities, enabled by domestic legislation. But the intervention produced criticisms of conditional engagement. In particular, the immunity of Australian police from local prosecution for any alleged offences was regarded suspiciously. In 2005 the PNG Supreme Court found this immunity to be unconstitutional, leading to the departure of Australian police. The impasse was not able to be resolved—PNG wanted assistance to be unconditional, and the Australian government wanted immunity for its police on the ground (O'Keefe 2007, pp. 136–8; Hirst 2007, pp. 245–9). The PNG experience provides further evidence of a 'gradual yet dramatic increase' in Australia's preparedness to intervene in the region, justified by perceptions of state failure and augmented by security concerns that link weak states with the potential for terrorism (O'Keefe 2007, pp. 141–7).

On the whole, the picture of Australia's role in the Asia-Pacific region is one of greater preparedness to intervene. This is notable for the fact that, although the interventions themselves may have been requested by regional states, Australia has also demonstrated an insensitivity to perceptions of heavy-handedness.

Non-compliance with international human rights norms

We noted earlier that the Australian government after 1996 announced its intention to move away from multilateralism in the pursuit of national interests. A clear example of multilateralism is Australia's engagement with the United Nations human rights treaty system. We will discuss this engagement here with a view to discerning the ways in which, and extent to which, Australia's current engagement appears conditional or selective.

We have already discussed how the Australian government is able, under the constitutional external affairs power, to ratify multilateral human rights treaties and then to enact domestic legislation to implement the terms of those treaties (see Chapter 11). One such example is the International Convention on the Elimination of All Forms of Racial Discrimination (ICERD), ratified in 1975, and the subsequent *Racial Discrimination Act 1975* (Cwlth), which implements its terms. Another consequence of ratifying such treaties is that the Australian government is required to lodge regular reports and attend meetings with the United Nations committees overseeing signatory nations' compliance with the treaties. In the case of the ICERD, the relevant committee is the Committee on the Elimination of Racial Discrimination (CERD), to which Australia is required to report every two years (CERD 2000a).

In August 1998 Australia became subject to the CERD's 'early warning procedures'—the first Western government to do so—and was asked to provide information to the committee regarding amendments to the *Native Title Act 1993*. After considering Australia's report, in 1999 the CERD concluded that the amendments were racially discriminatory and amounted to a contravention of Australia's obligations under the racial discrimination convention (Evatt 2001, p. 4). In particular, the CERD was concerned about the extinguishment of native title rights and the lack of participation in the formulation of the legislative amendments by indigenous peoples (Gelber 2001, p. 2). The Australian government reacted angrily to these criticisms, with the Attorney-General producing a press release claiming that 'the Committee's comments are an insult to Australia'. The Attorney-General also called the committee's findings 'unbalanced' and claimed the committee misunderstood and misrepresented Australia (Williams 1999).

The CERD continued to criticise Australia's native title regime after the passage of the *Native Title Amendment Act 1998*, as well as other policies including mandatory sentencing in Western Australia and the Northern Territory, the lack of an entrenched protection against racial discrimination, the government's unwillingness to apologise to or consider compensation for the Stolen Generations, over-representation of indigenous people in jail, low standards of living in indigenous communities, the winding back of funding and powers of the Human Rights and Equal Opportunity Commission (CERD 2000b), and the Australian government's position regarding its responsibilities towards international bodies and treaties (CERD 2000c). It also criticised the mandatory detention of asylum seekers (Kinley & Martin 2002, pp. 469–70).

In response to this raft of criticisms the Australian government announced a 'whole-of-government' review of the operation of the treaties committee system as it affects Australia (Downer 2000a). On 29 August 2000 the Minister for Foreign Affairs, the Attorney-General and the Minister for Immigration and Multicultural Affairs made a joint announcement regarding the outcomes of this review (Downer 2000b). The review's outcomes included a recommendation that the government take 'strong measures' to 'improve the effectiveness of the United Nations human rights treaty bodies'. The review criticised the treaty committee system for paying insufficient attention to the decisions of democratically elected governments and implied that they work beyond the scope of their 'mandates' and that they were not focused on their 'primary objectives' (Downer 2000b). In the media, the government expressed the view that the CERD should focus its efforts on those countries where egregious breaches of human rights occur, rather than on the Australian issues they had commented on, which were matters for 'domestic political debate' (Downer 2000c).

The review announced that Australia would henceforth adopt a more 'strategic' approach to interaction with the treaty committee system, a 'selective' approach to reporting to committees where 'appropriate', would grant permission to members of the Committee on Human Rights to visit Australia only where there is a 'compelling reason' to do so, and would refuse to sign the Optional Protocol to the Convention on the Elimination of All Forms of Discrimination Against Women. This prevented complaints being lodged of violations of the treaties' terms directly with the United Nations.

Reaction to the government's refusal to sign the Optional Protocol included a group of seven international law experts who wrote to the government describing its decision as 'perverse' and 'ironic' given that Australians had worked for more than twenty years in the international arena to draft the protocol (Charlesworth et al. 2000, p. 67). A chorus of women's organisations and individuals joined in the criticism (O'Loughlin 2000; Nicholson 2000; Gilchrist 2000; Halliday 2000, p. 12). The government defended its position by saying again that the United Nations should focus its attention on countries with egregious violations of human rights (Garran 2000). On issues of racial discrimination, the Howard federal government continued to display an attitude of hostility towards international criticism of Australia's record on human rights issues (Kent 2007, pp. 247–8).

In 2004 the Australian government considered the question of whether to ratify the Optional Protocol on the Convention Against Torture, which would, among other things, allow regular visits by international bodies to detention centres in Australia. A report prepared by the parliamentary Joint Standing Committee on Treaties recommended against ratification of this protocol, arguing that since Australia complies substantively with the Convention Against Torture and because the Australian government was concerned that the United Nations was not focusing on the 'most pressing of human rights violations' there was no need to ratify the protocol (JSCT 2004, pp. v–vi). This stance was entirely consistent with the Australian government's position on international monitoring of domestic human rights concerns, which was increasingly isolationist and defensive. The government's rejection of international norms has been described as a 'constant theme' in human rights oversight of Australia's performance (Kent 2007, p. 243).

Another indication of the juxtaposition of national interests against multilateral concerns emerged in the Australian government's arguments regarding the 1997 Kyoto Protocol on Climate Change (see snapshot in Chapter 12). In signing this protocol the Australian government defied world opinion and scientific demands to reduce greenhouse gas emissions, and instead obtained concessions that included an increase of 8 per cent in domestic greenhouse gas emissions from 1990 levels on the grounds of economic need. It has been argued that this represented a rejection of Australia's previously recognised obligations to the most vulnerable people of the world (McDonald 2003; Krishnapillai 2002).

Asylum seekers

Finally, it can be argued that Australia's treatment of asylum seekers arriving onshore has been a powerful illustration of the previous government's approach to its international human rights obligations. On 26 August 2001, in what is now known as the *Tampa* incident, the Australian government requested a Norwegian freighter called the *Tampa* to rescue more than 400 asylum seekers whose boat was sinking in international waters. After doing so, the captain of the *Tampa* proceeded towards Australian waters and Christmas Island, then in Australia's migration zone. But the Australian government denied him permission to enter Australian waters, and for two days the ship remained at sea. After the captain of the *Tampa* reported worsening conditions on board, he issued a mayday and headed towards Christmas Island. The Australian government continued to deny him permission to dock, and one day later Australian SAS troops boarded the ship (Gelber 2003, pp. 23, 181).

In a policy dubbed the 'Pacific Solution', the asylum seekers were then sent to Nauru and Papua New Guinea for the processing of their claims. The Australian government brokered the deals and provided financial support to make this possible, and stated that its primary concern was to prevent the asylum seekers from setting foot in Australia (Maley 2003, p. 187). Subsequently the Australian government legislated to toughen migration laws regarding asylum seekers in several ways, including by excising Christmas Island and other islands from Australia's migration zone (Gelber 2003, p. 29).

These events were regarded by many commentators as a gross breach of Australia's obligations under international law, including the United Nations Convention Relating to the Status of Refugees (Fonteyne 2002, p. 18). They were criticised by refugee advocates both within Australia and internationally as setting a new precedent for the abrogation of responsibility towards asylum seekers on the part of developed nations (Maley 2003, p. 187). Some saw the incident as amounting to Australia turning its back on the international responsibility of providing safe haven for those in need (Fonteyne 2002, p. 21).

However, the policy proved popular domestically. Within a week of the *Tampa* incident a Newspoll showed 50 per cent of people favouring the rejection of all boats carrying asylum seekers, and a further 38 per cent supporting the idea that only some boats should be allowed to enter Australia depending on the circumstances (Newspoll 2001). The *Tampa* incident was credited, along with the September 11 terrorist attacks, with forming the basis for a convincing Coalition federal election victory on 10 November of the same year, features of which were a campaign in favour of 'border control' (Maley 2003, p. 188) and the slogan 'We decide who comes to this country and the circumstances in which they come' (Ramsey 2001).

Other legislative and policy stances support the charge of insufficient compliance with human rights norms in relation to asylum seekers. These include the mandatory detention of unauthorised arrivals, first invoked by the federal Labor government in 1989 (McMaster 2001, p. 67), reduction of opportunities for judicial review of decisions by the Department of Immigration (Fonteyne 2002, p. 20), the ability to draw adverse inferences from asylum seekers' lack of identity documents (Gelber 2003, p. 29), the introduction of temporary protection visas and the forcible return of vessels to Indonesia to prevent asylum seekers reaching Australian territory (Kent 2007, p. 236). Immigration policy appeared to contravene the Convention and Protocol Relating to the Status of Refugees and the International Convention on Civil and Political Rights, both of which Australia has ratified. They breach provisions safeguarding freedom from inhuman and degrading treatment, freedom from arbitrary detention and the right to due process (Fonteyne 2002, p. 20; Kent 2007, p. 235).

Challenges to the legality of these policies in the High Court of Australia have tended to fail. In 2004 the High Court determined that if an asylum seeker whose claim had been rejected was unable to be deported, he or she could be detained indefinitely (see snapshot in Chapter 3). The same year a case arguing that the conditions of detention were so bad that detention was not legally valid also failed; it was held that a child born in Australia to non-citizen parents was not entitled to citizenship and could be deported; and the legality of detaining children was upheld (Gelber 2005, pp. 311–13, 315–16).

Australia's stance on both compliance with the United Nations human rights treaty system and international environmental standards has been widely condemned in human rights and environmental circles (see for example Kinley & Martin 2002; Evatt 2001). Australia's respect for human rights 'diminished' in the period under discussion (Kent 2007, p. 229). And despite its strengthened bilateral relations with many countries, agreements reached with other countries did not invoke human rights concerns (Kent 2007, p. 230).

The previous Australian government moved from full participation in multilateral human rights systems towards non-compliance or conditional compliance with international human rights norms. International standards were overridden or ignored, and this appears to have occurred on the basis of narrowly and domestically calculated 'national interests'.

It is too early to assess the likely foreign policy direction of the Rudd government. In its pre-election statements, the ALP promised to strengthen the alliance with the United States by making a greater commitment to security and development in the Asia-Pacific (McLelland 2007a). It also criticised the disengagement of the Howard government from the international community, including its refusal to ratify Kyoto, the Optional Protocol on the Convention on the Elimination of All Forms of Discrimination Against Women and the United Nations Protocol on Torture. It declared its opposition to Australia's involvement in the war on Iraq, promised to initiate a phased withdrawal of troops from Iraq, and pledged to focus security and foreign policy resources on the Asia-Pacific region, citing problems in East Timor, the Solomon Islands and Papua New Guinea as examples of the need for a new type of intervention (McLelland 2007b).

Since the Rudd government's election, some aspects of foreign policy have already altered: the government has restated its promise to bring Australian troops home from Iraq (Flitton 2008); in March 2008 it entered into a Papua New Guinea–Australia Forest Carbon Partnership designed to help save PNG's rainforests by enabling PNG to sell carbon credits through a global emissions trading scheme (Hammer 2008); it ratified the Kyoto Protocol; and it terminated the 'Pacific Solution' aspect of immigration policy, although indications are that other aspects of asylum seeker policy, including mandatory detention, will remain in place (Skehan 2007).

Australia internationally

In sum, these trends appear to have amounted to reconstructions of the meaning of Australia's national interests. There does appear to be considerable evidence that foreign policy has been increasingly determined by perceptions of Australian 'values' and a desire to express those values through policy decisions. There has been a growing correlation between domestic and foreign policy imperatives on security, regional relations and human rights. There is also evidence that Australia has behaved in a heavy-handed manner in the region and been somewhat indifferent to criticisms of aspects of its interventions. Finally, the evidence seems strong that 'national interests' have been heavily determined through the lens of the United States' priorities and a desire to emphasise former Prime Minister Howard's position in the alliance with our strongest ally. This last argument was bolstered further by Howard's invited speech to the American Enterprise Institute in Washington DC in March 2008, in which he criticised the Rudd government's policies on foreign and domestic issues.

To understand the events examined here thus requires an understanding of complex interplays between international and domestic concerns and pressures in policy processes. Apparent contradictions between regional and domestic perceptions of the importance of Australia's role, as well as between international and domestic expectations of compliance with human rights norms and standards, may seem difficult to understand, but they can be explained through the framework of domestic constructions of national interests. Security, the war on terrorism, a preparedness to act to solve crises within our region, and the maintenance and strengthening of alliances with our most powerful ally appeared to support 'national interests'. At the same time, multilateralism, international human rights concerns such as those to do with asylum seekers, and compliance with multilateral human rights treaties were perceived as antagonistic to 'national interests'.

This leads us to three questions. First, what are the implications for understanding Australian foreign policy from this analysis? Second, where is Australia heading in terms of what could be called its conception of international citizenship, its place in the world? Finally, what does this story tell us about policy-making more generally in the contemporary era?

In answer to the first question, it seems that the interplay between foreign and international concerns and domestic or national considerations is increasing and is increasingly complex. This means that understanding Australia's international engagement requires more than ever before an understanding of the frameworks and processes of Australian national politics. This is why an analysis of Australia's foreign policy has been included in this book.

Answering the second question requires considering whether Australia has evolved from being a paragon of international citizenship, assisting in the creation and maintenance of a comprehensive multilateral regime respected by a majority of Western nations and capable of supporting and enhancing human rights among the world's people, to a pest bent upon securing its own narrowly defined interests at the expense of more universal concerns.

At the end of World War II Australia participated actively and enthusiastically in developing the international multilateral human rights framework that it has recently eschewed. The Minister for External Affairs in the post-war government, H. V. Evatt, played a major role in the drafting of the Universal Declaration of Human Rights and the Charter of the United Nations. It has been argued that, at that time, Australia expressed a commitment to principles of collective social justice and multilateralism through this engagement in setting up the most multilateral human rights regime of the twentieth century (Kent 2001, pp. 258–9). However, despite the positive influence of Evatt's contribution at the time, other studies have been more critical of Australia's participation even at this early stage in the multilateral system. Charlesworth, for example, argues that Australia displayed a 'reluctance' towards ceding sovereignty over human rights issues to international bodies from a very early stage. She notes that in 1942 Evatt himself called Australia's record 'acutely disappointing' in this regard, and he bemoaned the States' determination to preserve their residual powers against international interventions (1993, p. 219). In the Australian parliament, he was accused of ignoring Australia's national interests (Buckley et al. 1994, p. 304).

Over subsequent decades the principles of multilateralism and universal human rights standards continued to conflict, as governments of different hues struggled to reconcile them. And indeed such reconciliation is not always easy or straightforward. But from the examples we have discussed in this chapter, in the first years of the twenty-first century principles of multilateralism and universal human rights standards found it particularly difficult to find purchase in the political landscape.

Finally, this picture of contemporary Australian foreign policy demonstrates the many, and potentially countervailing, pressures on government in policy-making. Policy at all levels is influenced by overt and covert practices of power, as different groups attempt to influence government decision-making. It is also influenced in less visible ways, such as the imposition of perceptions of Australian 'values' on decisions about Australia's place in the world. In this context, it is important to remember that pressures can continue to affect policy processes. Just as policy directions and emphases have changed in the recent past, so may they change again in the near future.

Summary

- Until the 1970s Australian security was achieved via a reliance first on Britain, then the United States, and was conceived primarily in terms of military defence.
- By the 1970s this perception was changing, and Australia began to engage more strongly with the Asia-Pacific region and to include broader issues, such as diplomacy, human rights and environmental concerns, in its conceptions of foreign policy.

- From 1996 to 2007 the Australian government reconstructed foreign policy priorities on the basis of changed and contested meanings of 'national interest'.
- This has produced complex interactions. Understanding foreign and international policy considerations therefore requires understanding the national framework of Australian political processes.

Further reading

Burke, Anthony and McDonald, Matt (eds) 2007, *Critical Security in the Asia-Pacific*, Manchester University Press, Manchester.

Cotton, James and Ravenhill, John (eds) 2001, *The National Interest in a Global Era: Australia in World Affairs 1996–2000*, Oxford University Press, Melbourne.

——(eds) 2007, *Trading on Alliance Security: Australia in World Affairs 2001–2005*, Oxford University Press, Melbourne.

Firth, Stewart 1999, *Australia in International Politics: An Introduction to Australian Foreign Policy*, Allen & Unwin, Sydney.

Useful websites

- Lowy Institute for International Policy: <www.lowyinstitute.org>. This institute is an international policy think tank that engages in debate on key issues of Australian foreign policy.
- Australian Strategic Policy Institute: <www.aspi.org.au>. This is an independent policy institute that seeks to inform the public about foreign policy.
- The Strategic and Defence Studies Centre is located at the Australian National University: <http://rspas.anu.edu.au/sdsc/index.php>. Its members engage in scholarly research with a view to influencing policy debates.

BIBLIOGRAPHY

AAP 2005, 'WA: I'm not finished with electoral reform: Gallop', AAP, 23 May.

——2007, 'World won't end tomorrow due to climate change, says Howard', *AAP Newswire,* 18 November, <www.news.com.au/story/0,23599,22778836–1702,00.html> [31 March 2008].

AAP and Munro, Ian 2007, 'Hicks deserves fair go if he is genuinely sorry, say MPs', *Sydney Morning Herald,* 29 December, p. 6.

Aarons, Mark 2008, 'Labor's ties that grind', *Sydney Morning Herald Online,* 1 March, <www.smh.com.au/articles/2008/02/29/1204226991323.html> [31 March 2008].

ABA, see Australian Broadcasting Authority.

Abbott, Royal 2001, 'Ambulance report says company acted illegally', Australian Associated Press, 29 November, <www.aap.com.au> [March 2004].

ABC 2004, 'Call for health insurance rebate funds to go to hospitals', *7.30 Report* February 2004, <www.abc.net.au/7.30/stories/s103128.htm> [31 March 2008].

——2006a, 'The right stuff', *Four Corners,* 17 July, <www.abc.net.au/4corners/content/2006/s1688866.htm> [March 2008].

——2006b, 'Fall and rise of Brian Burke', *Lateline,* ABC Online, 8 February, <www.abc.net.au/lateline/content/2006/s1565572.htm> [31 March 2008].

——2007a, 'Rudd under fire over Burke meetings', *7.30 Report,* 1 March, <www.abc.net.au/7.30/content/2007/s1860887.htm> [31 March 2008].

——2007b, 'Hockey defends criticism of WorkChoices study', *7.30 Report,* 2 October, <www.abc.net.au/7.30/content/2007/s2049308.htm> [March 2008].

——2008, 'Government remove criticism ban from NGOs', *ABC Online,* 9 January, <www.abc.net.au/news/stories/2008/01/09/2135037.htm> [March 2008].

ABC News 2007a, 'Mixed response for PM's reconciliation plan', 12 October, Document, <www.abc.net.au/news/stories/2007/10/12/2057390.htm> [May 2008].

——2007b, 'Murray stoush set to go to High Court', *ABC News,* 25 July, Document, <www.abc.net.au/news/stories/2007/07/25/1987632.htm> [May 2008].

AC Nielsen 2007, 'Radio Ratings Archive', *Nielsen Media Research*, <www.nielsenmedia.com.au/MRI_pages.asp?MRIID=11> [1 April 2008].

ACT Bill of Rights Consultative Committee (ACTBoRCC) 2003, *Towards an ACT Human Rights Act: Report*, May, <www.jcs.act.gov.au/prd/rights/reports.html> [31 October 2007].

Age 2007, 'Shoddy justice for Hicks', 29 December, p. 18.

Agence France Press (AFP) 2003, 'World expects us to take lead in Pacific—Australia', 14 October.

Albanese, Anthony 2007, Member of the House of Representatives, interview conducted by Anika Gauja, 18 July.

Allison, Lyn 2007, Member of the Senate, interview conducted by Anika Gauja, 14 August.

Almond, Gabriel and Verba, Sidney 1965, *The Civic Culture*, Little Brown, Boston.

Althaus, Catherine, Bridgman, Peter and Davis, Glyn 2007, *The Australian Policy Handbook*, 4th edn, Allen & Unwin, Sydney.

Amnesty International 2005, 'The impact of indefinite detention: The case to change Australia's mandatory detention regime', <www.amnesty.org/en/library/info/ASA12/001/2005> [20 February 2008].

Anderson, Geoff 2006, 'Ministerial staff: New players in the policy game' in *Beyond the Policy Cycle: The Policy Process in Australia*, ed. Hal Colebatch, Allen & Unwin, Sydney.

Arblaster, Anthony 1994, *Democracy*, 2nd edn, Open University Press, Buckingham.

Argy, Fred 2000, 'Arm's length policy-making: The privatisation of economic policy' in *Institutions on the Edge? Capacity for Governance*, eds Michael Keating, John Wanna and Patrick Weller, Allen & Unwin, Sydney.

Attwood, Bain 1999, *The Struggle for Aboriginal Rights: A Documentary History*, Allen & Unwin, Sydney.

——2003, *Rights for Aborigines*, Allen & Unwin, Sydney.

Attwood, Bain and Markus, Andrew 1998, 'Representation matters: The 1967 referendum' in *Citizenship and Indigenous Australians*, eds Nicholas Peterson and Will Sanders, Cambridge University Press, Melbourne, pp. 118–40.

——2007, *The 1967 Referendum*, 2nd edn, Aboriginal Studies Press, Canberra.

Aussie Educator 2008, 'Associations and unions', <www.teachers.ash.org.au/aussieed/education_unions.htm> [31 March 2008].

Australian 2002, 'Tragedy and truth in history debate', 28 December, p. 10.

——2008, 'ALP backs private health insurance', 20 February, <www.theaustralian.news.com.au/story/0,25197,23247246–12377,00.html> [31 March 2008].

Australian Broadcasting Authority (ABA) 2001, *Sources of News and Current Affairs*, ABA, Sydney.

Australian Bureau of Agricultural and Resource Economics (ABARE) 2003,

'Agricultural biotechnology: Potential for use in developing countries', ABARE eReport 03.17, October, <www.abareconomics.com/publications_html/economy/economy _03/economy_03.html> [28 May 2008].

Australian Communications and Media Authority (ACMA) 2007, 'Digital media in Australian homes—2006', <www.acma.gov.au/webwr/_assets/main/lib100845/digital_media_in_aust_homes–2006.pdf> [31 March 2008].

——2007a, '2GB breaches code by broadcasting material that was likely to encourage violence or brutality and to vilify people on the basis of ethnicity', media release, 10 April 2007, <http://internet.aca.gov.au/WEB/STANDARD/pc=PC_310133> [18 July 2008].

Australian Constitution, <www.aph.gov.au/senate/general/constitution/>.

Australian Council for Rehabilitation (ACROD) 2001, 'Cost shifting jeopardises disability services', media release, 18 October, <www.acrod.org.au/ACRODdoc/newsoct.htm> [April 2004].

——2002, 'Launch of "Mutual Benefit: Community and Business Getting Together—a focus on partnerships in the disability sector"', media release, 1 August, <www.acrod.org.au/ACRODdoc/mrel1–08.pdf> [April 2004].

Australian Council of Social Services (ACOSS) 2005, *Giving Australia: Research on Philanthropy in Australia,* Prime Minister's Community-Business Partnerships, Canberra, <www.acoss.org.au/upload/publications/papers/301__Giving%20Australia%20Summary.pdf> [31 March 2008].

Australian Council of Trade Unions (ACTU) 1999, *Unions@Work,* <www.actu.asn.au/Archive/Papers/unionswork.aspx> [31 March 2008].

Australian Electoral Commission (AEC) 2007, 'National seat status newsfile no 131', <www.aec.gov.au/pdf/publications/newsfiles/131/no131_colour.pdf> [31 March 2008].

Australian Film Commission 2007, *Get the Picture: What People are Watching: Pay TV,* <www.afc.gov.au/gtp/pdfs/paytv.pdf> [31 March 2008].

Australian Institute of Health and Welfare (AIHW) 2004, *Australian Hospital Statistics 2002–03,* catalogue number HSE 22, Canberra, <www.aihw.gov.au/publications/index.cfm/title/10015> [31 March 2008].

——2006, *Australia's Health 2006,* AIHW, Canberra.

Australian Labor Party (ALP) 2007a, 'Federal Labor's education revolution—a school computer for every student in years 9–12', media statement, 14 November, <www.alp.org.au/ media/1107/msloo140.php> [14 January 2008].

——2007b, 'A digital education revolution', *Election 2007 Policy Document,* <www.alp.org.au/download/labors_digital_education_revolution_campaign_launch.pdf> [14 January 2008].

——2007c, 'Fresh ideas for work and family', <www.alp.org.au/media/1007/msir170.php> [31 March 2008].

——2007d, '2007 National Platform and National Constitution', <www.alp.org.au/download/2007_national_platform.pdf> [May 2008].

——2007e, 'New directions for our schools: Establishing a national curriculum to improve our children's educational outcomes', <www.alp.org.au/download/now/new_directions_national_curriculum.pdf> [31 October 2008].

——2008, 'National curriculum board announcement', press conference, Queanbeyan Public School, 31 January, <www.alp.org.au/media/0108/pcdpmpm310.php> [31 October 2008].

Australian Parliamentary Research Group 2007, 'Be honest minister! Restoring honest government in Australia', <http://arts.anu.edu.au/democraticaudit/misc/aspgbe honestminister.pdf> [18 July 2008].

Australian Press Council 2006, 'State of the news: Print media in Australia Report 2006', <www.presscouncil.org.au/snpma/ch01.html> [31 March 2008].

——2007a, 'Adjudication no. 1344', February, <www.presscouncil.org.au/pcsite/adj/1344.html> [31 March 2008].

——2007b, 'Adjudication no. 1349', March, <www.presscouncil.org.au/pcsite/adj/1349.html> [31 March 2008].

Australian Public Service Commission (APSC) 2003, *State of the Service Report 2002–2003*, APSC, Canberra.

——2006, *State of the Service Report 2005–2006*, APSC, Canberra.

Bacchi, Carol, Eveline, Joan, Binns, Jennifer, Mackenzie, Catherine and Harwood, Susan 2005, 'Gender analysis and social change: Testing the water', *Policy and Society*, vol. 24, no. 4, pp. 45–68.

Bach, Stanley 2003, *Platypus and Parliament: The Australian Senate in Theory and Practice*, Department of the Senate, Canberra.

Baldino, Daniel 2005, 'Australia and the World' in *Howard's Second and Third Governments*, eds Chris Aulich and Roger Wettenhall, UNSW Press, Sydney.

Bale, Tim and Roberts, Nigel 2002, 'Plus ça change…? Anti-party sentiment and electoral system change: A New Zealand case study', *Commonwealth and Comparative Politics*, vol. 40, pp. 1–20.

Barnes, Alison 2007, 'Australian unions in 2006', *Journal of Industrial Relations*, vol. 49, no. 3, pp. 380–93.

Barr, Trevor 2000, *newmedia.com.au: The Changing Face of Australia's Media and Communications*, Allen & Unwin, Sydney.

Bartlett, Andrew 2007, Member of the Senate, interview conducted by Anika Gauja, 8 August.

Bean, Clive 1997, 'Australian Democrats: Electoral performance and voting support' in *Keeping the Bastards Honest: The Australian Democrats' First Twenty Years*, ed. John Warhurst, Allen & Unwin, Sydney, pp. 69–86.

——2004, 'Voting and citizenship' in *The Vocal Citizen*, ed. Glenn Patmore, Arena, Melbourne, pp. 42–53.
——2005, 'Is there a crisis of trust in Australia?' in *Australian Social Attitudes: The First Report*, eds Shaun Wilson, Gabrielle Meagher, Rachel Gibson, David Denemark and Mark Western, UNSW Press, Sydney, pp. 122–40.
Bean, Clive and Denemark, David 2007, 'Citizenship, participation, trust and efficacy in Australia' in *Australian Social Attitudes 2: Citizenship, Work and Aspirations*, eds David Denemark, Gabrielle Meagher, Shaun Wilson, Mark Western and Timothy Phillips, UNSW Press, Sydney, pp. 58–80.
Bean, Clive and McAllister, Ian 2002, 'From impossibility to certainty: Explaining the Coalition's victory in 2001' in *2001: The Centenary Election*, eds John Warhurst and Marian Simms, University of Queensland Press, Brisbane, pp. 271–86.
——2005, 'Voting behaviour: Not an election of interest (rates)' in *Mortgage Nation: The 2004 Australian Election*, eds Marian Simms and John Warhurst, API Network, Perth, pp. 319–34.
Bean, Clive, McAllister, Ian, Gibson, Rachel and Gow, David 2004, *Australian Election Study 2004*, ASSDA, Australian National University, Canberra.
Bean, Clive, McAllister, Ian and Gow, David 2008, *2007 Australian Election Study*, Australian Social Science Data Archive, Australian National University, Canberra.
Becker, Marc 2007, 'World Social Forum', *Peace and Change*, vol. 32, no. 2, pp. 203–20.
Bell, Roger 1997, 'Reassessed: Australia's relationship with the United States' in *Seeking Asian Engagement: Australia in World Affairs, 1991–1995*, eds James Cotton and John Ravenhill, Oxford University Press in association with Australian Institute of International Affairs, Melbourne.
——2007, 'Extreme allies: Australia and the USA', in *Trading on Alliance Security: Australia in World Affairs 2001–2005*, eds James Cotton and John Ravenhill, Oxford University Press, Melbourne.
Bell, Stephen 1997, *Ungoverning the Economy: The Political Economy of Australian Economic Policy*, Oxford University Press, Melbourne.
——2000, 'The role of the state: Welfare state or competition state?' in *The Politics of Australian Society: Political Issues for the New Century*, eds Paul Boreham, Geoffrey Stokes and Richard Hall, Longman, Sydney, pp. 192–206.
Bennett, Scott 1999, 'The decline in support for Australian major parties and the prospect of minority government', *Research Paper No. 10*, Department of the Parliamentary Library, Canberra.
——2005, 'Compulsory voting in Australian Elections', Research Brief No. 6, Australian Parliamentary Library, <www.aph.gov.au/library/pubs/RB/2005–06/06rb06.pdf> [31 March 2008].
Bennett, Scott and Lundie, Rob 2007, 'Australian electoral systems', Research Paper No. 5, Australian Parliamentary Library, <www.aph.gov.au/library/pubs/RP/2007–08/08rp05.pdf> [31 March 2008].

Beresford, Quentin 2000, *Governments, Markets and Globalisation: Australian Public Policy in Context,* Allen & Unwin, Sydney.

Beresford, Quentin and Phillips, Harry 1997, 'Spectators in Australian politics: Young voters' interest in politics and political issues', *Youth Studies Australia,* vol. 16, no. 4, pp. 11–16.

Berkovic, Nicole and Box, Dan 2007, 'Four banned by police lose appeal—APEC 2007', *Australian,* 7 September, p. 11.

Berlin, Isaiah 1969, *Four Essays on Liberty,* Oxford University Press, Oxford.

Betz, Hans-George and Immerfall, Stefan (eds) 1998, *The New Politics of the Right: Neo-Populist Parties and Movements in Established Democracies,* Macmillan, Basingstoke.

Bikundo, Edwin 2007, 'The trial of David Hicks and the law on the use of force', *Current Issues in Criminal Justice,* vol. 18, no. 3, pp. 494–7.

Biotechnology Australia 2003, 'Farmers adopt a pragmatic approach to GM crops', media backgrounder, 18 August, <www.biotechnology.gov.au/assets/documents/bainternet/BA_Media_Farmersurvey_National20050415155924.pdf> [28 July 2008].

——2004, 'Survey finds Australian perceptions of risk changing', media backgrounder, 11 February, <www.biotechnology.gov.au/assets/documents/bainternet/BA_Media_MillwardBrown_Feb0420050331170347.pdf> [28 May 2008].

Birnbauer, William 2002, 'Bracks axed $4m enquiry despite royal commissioner's plea', *Age,* 12 November, p. 1.

Bishop, Julie 2007, 'Greater national consistency in curricula', media release, 8 May, Minister for Education, Science and Training, <www.dest.gov.au/ministers/bishop/budget07/bud18_07.htm> [31 March 2008].

Bishop, Patrick and Davis, Glyn 2001, 'Developing consent: Consultation, participation and governance' in *Are You Being Served? States Citizens and Governance,* eds Glyn Davis and Patrick Weller, Allen & Unwin, Sydney, pp. 175–95.

Bisley, Nick 2008, 'The Japan–Australia security declaration and the changing regional security setting: Wheels, webs and beyond?', *Australian Journal of International Affairs,* vol. 62, no. 1, pp. 38–52.

Blackshield, Tony and Williams, George 2006, *Australian Constitutional Law and Theory,* 4th edn, Federation Press, Sydney.

Blackstone, Sir William 2001, *Blackstone's Commentaries on the Laws of England* (first published in 1830), vol. 1, W. Morrison ed., Cavendish Publishing, London.

Bodey, Michael 2007, 'News flagship gains the most readers', *Australian,* 16 February, <www.theaustralian.news.com.au/story/0,20867,21233221-7582,00.html> [13 January 2008].

Bolt, Cathy 2004, 'Australia still ponders GM spread', *Australian Financial Review,* 15 January, p. 5.

Borgu, Aldo 2004, *A Big Deal: Australia's Future Air Combat Capability*, Australian Strategic Policy Institute, Canberra.

Boston, Jonathon 1995, 'The limits to contracting out' in *The State Under Contract*, ed. Jonathon Boston, Bridget Williams Books, Wellington.

Boston, Jonathon (ed.) 1995, *The State Under Contract*, Bridget Williams Books, Wellington.

Botterill, Linda 2007, 'Doing it for the growers in Iraq? The AWB, Oil-for-Food and the Cole Inquiry', *Australian Journal of Public Administration*, vol. 66, no. 1, pp. 4–12.

Bowler, S. and Denemark, D. 1993, 'Split ticket voting in Australia: Dealignment and inconsistent votes reconsidered', *Australian Journal of Political Science*, vol. 28, pp. 19–37.

Bracks, Steve 2003, 'Victoria's parliament transformed', media release, Office of the Premier (Victoria), 28 March.

Braithwaite, John 1989, *Crime, Shame and Reintegration*, Cambridge University Press, New York.

Bramble, Tom and Minns, John 2002, 'Activist perspectives on the Australian anti-capitalist movements', refereed paper presented at the Jubilee conference of the Australasian Political Studies Association, Canberra, October, <www.arts.anu.edu.au/sss/apsa> [May 2008].

Bramble, Tom and Kuhn, Rick 2007, 'The transformation of the Australian Labor Party', *Joint Social Sciences Public Lecture*, 8 June, Australian National University, Canberra.

Brennan, Sean, Behrendt, Larissa, Strelein, Lisa and Williams, George 2005, *Treaty*, Federation Press, Sydney.

Brett, Judith 2002, 'The Liberal Party' in *Government, Politics, Power and Policy in Australia*, 7th edn, eds John Summers, Dennis Woodward and Andrew Parkin, Longman, Sydney, pp. 169–88.

——2003, *Australian Liberals and the Moral Middle Class*, Cambridge University Press, Melbourne.

Broad, Paul 2001, 'Australian business associations: Their strategies for surviving the 1990s and beyond', *Labour and Industry*, vol. 11, no. 3, pp. 27–54.

Brown, Bob 2004, *Memo for a Saner World*, Penguin, Melbourne.

Brown, Helen 2007, 'Victoria and NSW to lift ban on GM canola', *Australian Broadcasting Corporation Transcripts*, 27 November.

Buckley, Ken, Dale, Barbara and Reynolds, Wayne 1994, *Doc Evatt: Patriot, Internationalist, Fighter and Scholar*, Longman Cheshire, Melbourne.

Burchell, David 2002, 'Perpetual disillusionment' in *The Prince's New Clothes: Why Do Australians Dislike Their Politicians?*, eds David Burchell and Andrew Leigh, UNSW Press, Sydney, pp. 62–80.

——2006, 'An email from the ether: After the Cronulla events', *Australian Universities Review*, vol. 48, no. 2, pp. 6–8.

Burchill, Scott 2000, 'East Timor, Australia and Indonesia' in *Guns and Ballot Boxes: East*

Timor's Vote for Independence, ed. Damien Kingsbury, Monash Asia Institute, Monash University, Melbourne.

Bureau of Meteorology 2004, *Submission to the Senate Environment Committee on the Kyoto Protocol Ratification Bill 2003 (No. 2)*, Submission 15, <www.aph.gov.au/senate/committee/ecita_ctte/completed_inquiries/2002-04/kyoto/submissions/sublist.htm> [31 March 2008].

Burgmann, Meredith and Burgmann, Verity 1998, *Green Bans, Red Union: Environmental Activism and the New South Wales Builders Labourers' Federation*, UNSW Press, Sydney.

Burgmann, Verity 2003, *Power, Profit and Protest*, Allen & Unwin, Sydney.

Burke, Anthony and Gelber, Katharine 2005–06, 'Can human rights save us?', *Arena Magazine*, issue 80, pp. 43–5.

Burke, Anthony and McDonald, Matt (eds) 2007, *Critical Security in the Asia-Pacific*, Manchester University Press, Manchester.

Butler, J.R.G. 2002, 'Policy change and private health insurance: Did the cheapest policy do the trick?', *Australian Health Review*, vol. 25, no. 6, pp. 33–41.

Butt, Peter, Eagleson, Robert and Lane, Patricia 2001, *Mabo, Wik and Native Title*, 4th edn, Federation Press, Sydney.

Caldwell, Brian 2007, 'Rudd has a long way to go to become the education prime minister', *Sydney Morning Herald*, 6 December, p. 15.

Canberra Times 2007, 'Humanity back on the political agenda', 27 December, p. 16.

Carroll, Peter and Painter, Martin 1995, 'The federal politics of microeconomic reform: An overview and introduction', in *Microeconomic Reform and Federalism*, eds Peter Carroll and Martin Painter, Federalism Research Centre, Australian National University, Canberra.

Carroll, Peter and Painter, Martin (eds) 1995, *Microeconomic Reform and Federalism*, Federalism Research Centre, Australian National University, Canberra.

Carson, Lyn and Gelber, Katharine 2001, *Ideas for Community Consultation: A Discussion on Principles and Procedures for Making Consultation Work*, report prepared for the NSW Department of Urban Affairs and Planning, Sydney, February.

Carswell, Andrew 2006, 'Chain gang chokes city' in *Daily Telegraph*, 25 November, <www.news.com.au/dailytelegraph/story/0,22049,20817018-5001021,00.html> [31 March 2008].

Cass, Deborah and Burrows, Sonia 2000, 'Commonwealth regulation of campaign finances—public funding, disclosure and expenditure limits', *Sydney Law Review*, vol. 22, no. 4, pp. 447–526.

Castles, Frank 1985, *The Working Class and Welfare: Reflections on the Political Development of the Welfare State in Australia and New Zealand, 1890–1980*, Allen & Unwin, Sydney.

Catt, Helena 1996, *Voting Behaviour: A Radical Critique*, Leicester University Press, London.

——1999, *Democracy in Practice*, Routledge, London.

Cave, Peter 2007, 'Government acknowledgement of Aboriginals too little, too late',

Australian Broacasting Corporation, The World Today, 12 October, <www.abc.net.au/world today/content/2007/s2057790.htm> [May 2008].

Chaples, Ernie 1997, 'The Australian voters', *Politics in Australia*, 3rd edn, ed. Rodney Smith, Allen & Unwin, Sydney, pp. 354–71.

Charlesworth, Hilary 1993, 'The Australian reluctance about rights', *Osgoode Hall Law Journal*, vol. 31, no. 1, pp. 195–232.

——2002, *Writing in Rights: Australia and the Protection of Human Rights*, UNSW Press, Sydney.

Charlesworth, Hilary, Chiam, Madelaine, Hovell, Devika and Williams, George 2006, *No Country is an Island: Australia and International Law*, UNSW Press, Sydney.

Charlesworth, Hilary, Torre, E. Dell, Kinley, David, Joseph, S., McCormack, T., Mathew, P., Rothwell, D. and Wright, S. 2000, 'Howard's human rights stance a concern', *Australian Financial Review*, 8 September, p. 67.

Chen, Peter, Gibson, Rachel, Lusoli, Wainer and Ward, Stephen 2007, 'Australian governments and online communication' in *Government Communication in Australia*, ed. Sally Young, Cambridge University Press, Melbourne, pp. 161–80.

Chia, Joy and Patmore, Glenn 2004, 'The vocal citizen' in *The Vocal Citizen*, ed. Glenn Patmore, Arena, Melbourne, pp. 1–21.

Chong, Agnes, Emerton, Patrick, Kadous, Waleed, Petitt, Annie, Sempill, Stephen, Sentas, Vicki, Stratton, Jane and Tham, Joo-Cheong 2005, *Laws for Insecurity? A Report on the Federal Government's Proposed Counter-Terrorism Measures*, 23 September, <www.amcran.org/images/stories/Laws%20for%20Insecurity%20Report.pdf> [24 October 2007].

Civics Expert Group 1993, *Whereas the People . . . Civics and Citizenship Education*, Australian Government Publishing Service, Canberra.

Cohen, David 2007, 'The strife of Brian', *Age*, 28 February, <www.theage.com.au/news/in-depth/burkes-backyard/2007/02/27/1172338625209.html> [31 March 2008].

Colebatch, Hal 1998, *Policy*, Open University Press, Buckingham.

——2002, *Policy*, 2nd edn, Open University Press, Buckingham.

——2006a, 'Mapping the work of policy' in *Beyond the Policy Cycle: The Policy Process in Australia*, ed. Hal Colebatch, Allen & Unwin, Sydney.

——2006b, 'Accounting for policy in Australia', *Public Policy*, vol. 1, no. 1, pp. 37–51.

Colebatch, Hal (ed.) 2006, *Beyond the Policy Cycle: The Policy Process in Australia*, Allen & Unwin, Sydney.

Collin, Philippa 2007, 'Policies for youth participation and the development of new political identities' in *Are We There Yet? National Youth Conference Proceedings*, ed. Ani Wierenga, Peer Reviewed Papers, Youth Affairs Council of Victoria, Melbourne, pp. 11–18. <www.yacvic.org.au/includes/pdfs_wordfiles/YACVic_Conf_Papers.pdf> [31 March 2008].

Committee on the Elimination of Racial Discrimination (CERD) 2000a, *General Guidelines Regarding the Form and Contents of Reports to be Submitted by States Parties under Article 9, Paragraph 1, of the Convention,* CERD/C/70/Rev.5, 5 December, <www.unhchr.ch/tbs/doc.nsf/0/abe104e5613b4321c12569e7004f1ffa/$FILE/G0046522.pdf> [28 May 2008].

——2000b, Summary record of the 1393rd meeting, CERD/C/SR.1393, 29 March.

——2000c, Summary record of the 1395th meeting: Australia, Tonga, Zimbabwe, CERD/C/SR.1395, 3 April.

Commonwealth Department of Health and Ageing 2008, '30 per cent rebate', <www.health.gov.au/internet/main/publishing.nsf/Content/health-privatehealth-rebate-consumers-rebate.htm> [31 March 2008].

Commonwealth Grants Commission (CGC) 2004, *Report on State Revenue Sharing Relativities 2004 Review,* CGC, Canberra, <www.cgc.gov.au/method_review2/2004_review_report/2004_review_report> [18 January 2008].

Connell, Robert W. 1971, *The Child's Construction of Politics,* Melbourne University Press, Melbourne.

Connolly, Steve 2008, 'Disaster fear in council mergers', *Sunday Mail,* 27 January, p. 11.

Considine, Mark 1994, *Public Policy: A Critical Approach,* Macmillan Education, Melbourne.

——2003, 'Governance and competition: The role of non-profit organisations in the delivery of public services', *Australian Journal of Political Science,* vol. 38, no. 1, pp. 63–78.

——2005, *Making Public Policy: Institutions, Actors, Strategies,* Polity Press, Cambridge.

Considine, Mark and Painter, Martin (eds) 1997, *Managerialism: The Great Debate,* Melbourne University Press, Melbourne.

Cook, Ian 1999, *Liberalism in Australia,* Oxford University Press, Melbourne.

——2004, *Government and Democracy in Australia,* Oxford University Press, Melbourne.

Corbett, David 1996, *Australian Public Sector Management,* 2nd edn, Allen & Unwin, Sydney.

Corruption and Crime Commission (CCC) 2008, 'Report on the investigation of alleged misconduct concerning Dr Neale Fong, Director-General of the Department of Health', <www.ccc.wa.gov.au/pdfs/report-alleged-misconduct-fong-neale.pdf> [31 March 2008].

Costa, Michael 2008, 'Vic power prices lower under private sector', media release, 15 January.

Costar, Brian and Curtin, Jennifer 2004, *Rebels with a Cause: Independents in Australian Politics,* UNSW Press, Sydney.

——2007, 'The independent challenge to big party dominance in Australia', paper presented at the First Annual International Conference on Minor Parties, Independent Politicians, Voter Associations and Political Associations in Politics, 29 November–1 December, Birmingham University, UK.

Costello, Peter 2004, 'Transcript, the Hon Peter Costello MP, Treasurer, doorstop interview 11 August 2004', Australian Government, Treasury.

Cotton, James 2000, 'East Timor and Australia—twenty-five years of the policy debate' in *East Timor and Australia*, 2nd edn, ed. James Cotton, Australian Defence Studies Centre in association with Australian Institute of International Affairs, Canberra.

——2001, 'The East Timor commitment and its consequences' in *The National Interest in a Global Era: Australian in World Affairs 1996–2000*, eds James Cotton and John Ravenhill, Oxford University Press in association with Australian Institute of International Affairs, Melbourne, pp. 213–34.

Cotton, James and Ravenhill, John 1997, 'Australia's "engagement with Asia"' in *Seeking Asian Engagement: Australia in World Affairs, 1991–1995*, eds James Cotton and John Ravenhill, Oxford University Press in association with Australian Institute of International Affairs, Melbourne.

——2001, 'Australia in world affairs 1996–2000' in *The National Interest in a Global Era: Australian in World Affairs 1996–2000*, eds James Cotton and John Ravenhill, Oxford University Press in association with Australian Institute of International Affairs, Melbourne, pp. 3–9.

——2007, 'Trading on alliance security: Foreign policy in the post–11 September era', in *Trading on Alliance Security: Australia in World Affairs 2001–2005*, eds James Cotton and John Ravenhill, Oxford University Press, Melbourne.

Cotton, James and Ravenhill, John (eds) 2001, *The National Interest in a Global Era: Australia in World Affairs 1996–2000*, Oxford University Press in association with Australian Institute of International Affairs, Melbourne.

——2007, *Trading on Alliance Security: Australia in World Affairs 2001–2005*, Oxford University Press, Melbourne.

Coultan, Mark 2007, 'YouTube revolutionaries upstage the party machine', *Sydney Morning Herald*, <www.smh.com.au/news/federalelection2007news/rudd-faces-youtube-revolution/2007/10/25/1192941243230.html> [31 March 2008].

Council of Australian Governments (COAG) 2004, *Research Involving Human Embryos and Prohibition of Human Cloning Agreement*, <www.coag.gov.au/ig_agreements/human_cloning.htm> [21 January 2008].

Cox, Eva 1995, *A Truly Civil Society*, ABC Books, Sydney.

Craig, Geoffrey 2003, *The Media, Politics and Public Life*, Allen & Unwin, Sydney.

Craven, Gregory (ed.) 1992, *Australian Federalism: Towards the Second Century*, Melbourne University Press, Melbourne.

Crawford, Kate 2006, *Adult Themes: Rewriting the Rules of Adulthood*, Pan Macmillan, Sydney.

Crosby, Lynton 2000, 'The Liberal Party' in *Howard's Agenda*, eds Marian Simms and John Warhurst, University of Queensland Press, Brisbane, pp. 64–70.

Cubby, Ben 2006, 'The Australian way', *Griffith Review*, no. 13, pp. 77–106.

Cunningham, Stuart 2006, 'Policy' in *The Media and Communications in Australia*, 2nd edn, eds Stuart Cunningham and Graeme Turner, Allen & Unwin, Sydney, pp. 43–63.

Cunningham, Stuart and Turner, Graeme (eds) 2006, *The Media and Communications in Australia*, 2nd edn, Allen & Unwin, Sydney.

Dahl, Robert A. 1964, *Modern Political Analysis*, 3rd edn, Prentice-Hall, Englewood Cliffs, NJ.

Dalton, Russell and Wattenberg, Martin 2000, 'Partisan change and the democratic process' in *Parties without Partisans: Political Change in Advanced Industrial Democracies*, eds Russell Dalton and Martin Wattenberg, Oxford University Press, Oxford.

Dalton, Russell and Weldon, Steve 2005, 'Public images of political parties: A necessary evil?', *Party Politics*, vol. 28, no. 5, pp. 931–51.

Daskal, Jennifer 2007, 'This was a trial? Gitmo Justice I', *International Herald Tribune*, 2 April, pp. 1, 6.

Davies, Amanda and Tonts, Matthew 2007, 'Changing electoral structures and regional representation in Western Australia: From countrymindedness to one vote one value', *Space and Polity*, vol. 11, no. 3, pp. 209–25.

Davis, Glyn 1997, 'Toward a hollow state? Managerialism and its critics' in *Managerialism: The Great Debate*, eds Mark Considine and Martin Painter, Melbourne University Press, Melbourne, pp. 208–23.

——2001, 'Government by discussion' in *The Enabling State: People before Bureaucracy*, eds Peter Botsman and Mark Latham, Pluto Press, Sydney, pp. 219–31.

Davis, Glyn and Weller, Patrick (eds) 2001, *Are You Being Served? States, Citizens and Governance*, Allen & Unwin, Sydney.

Davis, Rex and Stimson, Robert 1998, 'Disillusionment and disenchantment at the fringe: Explaining the geography of the One Nation Party vote at the Queensland Election', *People and Place*, vol. 6, no. 3, <http://elecpress.monash.edu.au/pnp/free/pnpv6n3/davistim.htm> [May 2008].

Dawkins, Peter, Webster, Elizabeth, Hopkins, Sandra and Yong, Yongsay 2004, *Recent Private Health Insurance Policies in Australia: Health Resource Utilization, Distributive Implications and Policy Options*, Melbourne Institute Report No. 3, <http://melbourneinstitute.com/publications/reports/phi2004.pdf> [31 March 2008].

Dawson, Scott 2006, 'The Australia–Indonesia partnership for reconstruction and development' in *Different Societies, Shared Futures: Australia, Indonesia and the Region*, ed. John Monfries, Research School of Pacific and Asian Studies, Australian National University, Canberra.

Debelle, Penelope and Schmidtke, Malcolm 2004, 'A party from nowhere', *Age*, 4 October, <www.theage.com.au/articles/2004/10/03/1096741899963.html?from=storylhs> [31 March 2008].

della Porta, Donatella and Diani, Mario 1999, *Social Movements: An Introduction*, Blackwell, Oxford.

——2006, *Social Movements: An Introduction*, 2nd edn, Blackwell, Oxford.

Denemark, David, Meagher, Gabrielle, Wilson, Shaun, Western, Mark and Phillips, Timothy 2007, *Australian Social Attitudes 2: Citizenship, Work and Aspirations*, UNSW Press, Sydney.

Denemark, David, Ward, Ian and Bean, Clive 2007, 'Election campaigns and television news coverage', *Australian Journal of Political Science*, vol. 42, no. 1, pp. 89–109.

Department of Communication, Information Technology and the Arts (DCITA) 2004, *Australia's Strategic Framework for the Information Economy 2004–2006*, DCITA, Canberra, <www.dbcde.gov.au/__data/assets/pdf_file/0018/20457/New_SFIE_July_2004_final.pdf> [14 January 2008].

Department of Defence 1976, *Australian Defence*, Australian Government Publishing Service, Canberra.

——1987, *The Defence of Australia*, Australian Government Publishing Service, Canberra.

Department of Foreign Affairs and Trade (DFAT) 1997, *In the National Interest: Australia's Foreign and Trade Policy White Paper*, Australian Government Printing Service, Canberra, <www.defence.gov.au/ARMY/LWD1/pdfs/docs/In_the_National_Interest.pdf> [22 February 2008].

——2003, *Advancing the National Interest: Australia's Foreign and Trade Policy White Paper*, <http://australianpolitics.com/foreign/elements/2003_whitepaper.pdf> [22 February 2008].

Department of Transport and Regional Services (DOTARS) 2006, *Local Government National Report 2005–2006*, DOTARS, Canberra, <www.dotars.gov.au/local/publications/index.aspx> [14 November 2007].

Detterbeck, Klaus 2005, 'Cartel parties in Western Europe?', *Party Politics*, vol. 11, no. 2, pp. 173–91.

DFAT, see Department of Foreign Affairs and Trade.

Di Francesco, Michael 2001, 'Process not outcomes in new public management? "Policy coherence" in Australian government', *Australian Review of Public Affairs*, vol. 1, no. 3, pp. 103–16, <www.australianreview.net/journal/v1/n3/difrancesco.pdf> [May 2008].

Diani, Mario 1992, 'The concept of social movement', *Sociological Review*, vol. 40, no. 1, pp. 1–25.

Dibb, Paul 1986, *Review of Australia's Defence Capabilities: Report to the Minister for Defence*, Australian Government Publishing Service, Canberra.

Dodd, Mark 2005, 'One has the key to one vote, one value', *Australian*, 29 April, p. 6.

Doig, Alan, Pfiffner, James, Phythian, Mark and Tiffen, Rodney 2007, 'Marching in time: Alliance politics, synchrony and the case for war in Iraq 2002–2003', *Australian Journal of International Affairs*, vol. 61, no. 1, pp. 23–40.

Donnelly, Kevin 2007a, 'Brave new words for education revolution', *Australian*, 24 December, p. 10.

——2007b, 'Students so much more than future cogs in the great GDP machine', *Weekend Australian*, 22 December, p. 17.

Downer, Alexander 2000a, Minister for Foreign Affairs, 'Government to review UN treaty committees', media release, 30 March, <http://pandora.nla.gov.au/pan/25168/20020910–0000/www.dfat.gov.au/media/releases/foreign/2000/fa024_2000.html> [4 March 2008].

——2000b, Minister for Foreign Affairs, 'Improving the effectiveness of United Nations committees', joint media release: 29 August, available at <http://pandora.nla.gov.au/pan/33012/20051107–0000/www.nationalsecurity.gov.au/agd/WWW/Attorneygeneralhome.nsf/Page/Media_Releases_2000_August_Improving_the_effectiveness_of_UN_Committees.html> [4 March 2008].

——2000c, Minister for Foreign Affairs, 'Government to review participation in UN Treaty committee system', transcript of interview with Kerry O'Brien on ABC *7.30 Report*, 30 March, <www.abc.net.au/7.30/stories/s114903.htm> [4 March 2008].

Doyle, Timothy 2001, *Green Power: The Environment Movement in Australia*, UNSW Press, Sydney.

Dryzek, John 2000, *Deliberative Democracy and Beyond*, Oxford University Press, New York.

Dye, Thomas 1972, *Understanding Public Policy*, 4th edn, Prentice-Hall, Englewood Cliffs, NJ.

Eardley, Tony, Abello, David and Macdonald, Helen 2001, *Is the Job Network Benefiting Disadvantaged Job Seekers? Preliminary Evidence from a Study of Non-Profit Employment Services*, SPRC Discussion Paper No. 111, January, Social Policy Research Centre, University of New South Wales, Sydney.

Economou, Nick 2006, 'A right-of-centre triumph: The 2004 Australian half-Senate election', *Australian Journal of Political Science*, vol. 41, no. 4, pp. 501–16.

Edwards, Kathy 2007, 'Introducing YES: Young people's democratic participation—towards developing a youth democratic voice' in *Are We There Yet? National Youth Conference Proceedings*, ed. Ani Wierenga, Peer reviewed papers, Youth Affairs Council of Victoria, Melbourne, pp. 37–44, <www.yacvic.org.au/includes/pdfs_wordfiles/YACVic_Conf_Papers.pdf> [31 March 2008].

Edwards, Kathy, Saha, Lawrence and Print, Murray 2006, *Youth Electoral Study Report 3: Youth, the Family and Learning about Politics and Voting*, <www.aec.gov.au/pdf/publications/youth_study_3/youth_electoral_study_03.pdf> [31 March 2008].

Edwards, Meredith 2001, 'Participatory governance into the future: Roles of the government and community sectors', *Australian Journal of Public Administration*, vol. 60, no. 3, pp. 78–88.

Edwards, Meredith and Henderson, Allan 1995, 'COAG—a vehicle for reform', in *Microeconomic Reform and Federalism*, eds Peter Carroll and Martin Painter, Federalism Research Centre, Australian National University, Canberra.

Eisenstein, Hester 1996, *Inside Agitators: Australian Femocrats and the State*, Allen & Unwin, Sydney.

Elder, Catriona 2007, *Being Australian: Narratives of National Identity*, Allen & Unwin, Sydney.

Emy, Hugh 1978, *The Politics of Australian Democracy*, 2nd edn, Macmillan Education, Melbourne.

Emy, Hugh and Hughes, Owen 1993, *Australian Politics: Realities in Conflict*, 2nd edn, Macmillan Education, South Melbourne.

Environment Protection Authority (EPA) 2006, *Who Cares about the Environment in 2006?*, <www.environment.nsw.gov.au/community/whocares2006.htm> [31 March 2008].

Errington, Wayne and Miragliotta, Narelle 2007, *Media and Politics: An Introduction*, Oxford University Press, Melbourne.

Evans, Chris 2006, 'The Senate corrupted, absolutely', *Labor E-Herald*, <http://eherald.alp.org.au/articles/0606/natp29-01.php> [31 March 2008].

Evans, Harry 2004, *Odgers' Australian Senate Practice*, 11th edn, Department of the Senate, Canberra, <www.aph.gov.au/senate/pubs/odgers/index.htm> [31 March 2008].

——2005, 'Executive and parliament' in *Howard's Second and Third Governments*, eds Chris Aulich and Roger Wettenhall, UNSW Press, Sydney.

——2007, 'The Senate' in *Silencing Dissent*, eds Clive Hamilton and Sarah Maddison, Allen & Unwin, Sydney.

Evans, Vanessa and Sternberg, Jason 1999, 'Young people, politics and television current affairs in Australia', *Journal of Australian Studies*, no. 63, December, pp. 103–9.

Evatt, Elizabeth 2001, 'How Australia "supports" the United Nations Human Rights treaty system: Comment', *Public Law Review*, vol. 12, March, pp. 3–8.

Everett, Sophia 2003, 'The policy cycle: Democratic process or rational paradigm revisited?', *Australian Journal of Public Administration*, vol. 62, no. 2, pp. 65–70.

Family First 2004, 'The truth about Family First—Setting the record straight', media release, 25 September.

Fenna, Alan 2004, *Australian Public Policy*, 2nd edn, Pearson Longman, Sydney.

Ferrari, Justine 2006, 'Themes emerging in school curriculum are straight from Chairman Mao—Education Minister Julie Bishop—Canberra to seize syllabus', *Australian*, 6 October, p. 3.

——2007, 'Audit to ensure that neediest log on first', *Australian*, 21 December, p. 5.

Fiebig, D., Savage, E. and Viney, R. 2006, *Does the Reason for Buying Health Insurance Influence Behaviour?*, CHERE Working Paper 2006/1, CHERE, Sydney.

Firth, Stewart 1999, *Australia in International Politics: An Introduction to Australian Foreign Policy,* Allen & Unwin, Sydney.

Fitzgerald, Julian 2007, 'The need for transparency in lobbying', Democratic Audit of Australia, Discussion Paper 16/07, Australian National University, <http://democratic.audit.anu.edu.au/papers/20070920fitz_lobbying.pdf> [31 March 2008].

Flew, Terry 2000, 'Down by Laws: Commercial talkback radio and the ABA "Cash for Comment" inquiry', *Australian Screen Education,* vol. 24, Spring, pp. 10–15.

Flitton, Daniel 2003, 'Perspectives on Australian foreign policy 2002', *Australian Journal of International Affairs,* vol. 57, no. 1, pp. 37–54.

——2008, 'Australia's cosy relationship with the US faces testing times', *Age,* 3 March, p. 15.

Flynn, Michael 2000, 'Lobbying into the new millennium: The gay and lesbian rights lobby 1988–2000' in *Queer City: Gay and Lesbian Politics in Sydney,* eds Craig Johnston and Paul van Reyk, Pluto Press, Sydney, pp. 64–83.

Fonteyne, Jean-Pierre 2002, 'Illegal refugees or illegal policy?', *Refugees and the Myth of the Borderless World,* Research School of Pacific and Asian Studies, Australian National University, Canberra.

Foucault, Michel 1995, *Discipline and Punish: The Birth of the Prison,* 2nd edn, A. Sheridan (trans.), Vintage Books, New York.

Franklin, Matthew 2008, 'Petitions to receive greater attention', *Australian,* 12 January, <www.theaustralian.news.com.au/story/0,25197,23040476-5013871,00.html> [31 March 2008].

Franklin, Matthew and Ryan, Siobhain 2007, 'Rudd's warm Kyoto reception', *Australian,* 4 December, <www.theaustralian.news.com.au/story/0,25197,22865700–601,00.html> [31 March 2008].

Fraser, Andrew 2007, 'Labor backs PM's history plan; Greens say mandatory curriculum is a "stunt"', *Canberra Times,* 12 October, p. 2.

Frost, Frank 2007, 'Perspectives on Australian foreign policy 2006', *Australian Journal of International Affairs,* vol. 61, no. 3, pp. 403–26.

Galligan, Brian 1987, *The Politics of the High Court,* University of Queensland Press, Brisbane.

——1989, *Australian Federalism,* Longman Cheshire, Melbourne.

——1995, *A Federal Republic: Australia's Constitutional System of Government,* Cambridge University Press, Melbourne.

Gallop, Geoff 2000, 'Identity 2000' in *Western Australia and Federation: Issues 2001,* State Library of Western Australia, <www.slwa.wa.gov.au/federation/iss/081_iden.htm> [21 January 2008].

Gamble, Seranie 2005, 'Criminal justice initiatives for indigenous offenders', *Indigenous Law Bulletin,* vol. 6, no. 14, pp. 8–9.

Gardiner-Garden, John and Chowns, Jonathan 2006, 'Media ownership regulation in Australia: e-brief', Australian Parliamentary Library, <www.aph.gov.au/library/intguide/SP/Media_Regulation.htm> [31 March 2008].

Garran, Robert 2000, 'No need for UN's help—PM', *Australian*, 31 August, p. 2.

Gauja, Anika 2005, 'The pitfalls of participatory democracy: A study of the Australian Democrats' GST', *Australian Journal of Political Science*, vol. 40, no. 1, pp. 71–85.

——2006, 'From Hogan to Hanson: The regulation and changing legal status of Australian political parties', *Public Law Review*, vol. 17, no. 4, pp. 282–99.

Gelber, Harry 1993, 'Australian interests: Politics and strategy towards the 1990s' in *Australia in a Changing World: New Foreign Policy Directions*, ed. Fedor A. Mediansky, Macmillan, Sydney, pp. 65–82.

Gelber, Katharine 1999, 'Treaties and intergovernmental relations in Australia: Implications of the Toonen Case', *Australian Journal of Politics and History*, vol. 45, no. 3, pp. 330–46.

——2001, 'Human rights treaties in Australia—empty words?', *Australian Review of Public Affairs*, Digest Section, posted 12 April, <www.australianreview.net/digest/2001/04/gelber.html> [May 2008].

——2003, 'A fair queue? Australian public discourse on refugees and immigration', *Journal of Australian Studies*, no. 77, pp. 23–30.

——2005, 'High Court Review 2004: Limits on the judicial protection of rights', *Australian Journal of Political Science*, vol. 40, no. 2, pp. 307–22.

——2006, 'High Court Review 2005: The manifestation of separation of powers', *Australian Journal of Political Science*, vol. 41, no. 3, pp. 437–53.

——2007, 'Hate speech and the Australian legal and political landscape', in *Hate Speech and Freedom of Speech in Australia*, eds Katharine Gelber and Adrienne Stone, Federation Press, Sydney.

George, Amanda 2003, 'Crime pays: Well, it does if you run the prison', *New Internationalist*, 1 April, p. 26.

George, Amanda and Lazarus, Sabra 1994, 'Private prison: The punished, the profiteers and the grand prix of state approval', *Australian Feminist Law Journal*, vol. 4, pp.153–73.

Gerth, H.H. and Mills, C. Wright (eds) 1948, *From Max Weber: Essays in Sociology*, Routledge & Kegan Paul, London.

Gilchrist, Michelle 2000, 'PM betrays women, says Lees', *Australian*, 30 September, p. 30.

Gillard, Julia 2007, 'Gillard details education revolution', *7.30 Report*, ABC TV transcript, 6 December.

Gillespie, James 1994, 'New federalisms' in *Developments in Australian Politics*, eds Judith Brett, James Gillespie and Murray Goot, Macmillan Education, Melbourne, pp. 60–87.

Goldsworthy, David 2001, 'An overview' in *The National Interest in a Global Era: Australian in World Affairs 1996–2000*, eds James Cotton and John Ravenhill, Oxford University Press in association with Australian Institute of International Affairs, Melbourne, pp. 10–30.

Goldsworthy, Jeffrey 1997, 'Originalism in constitutional interpretation', *Federal Law Review*, vol. 25, no. 1, pp. 1–50.

Goot, Murray 2002, 'Distrustful, disenchanted and disengaged? Public opinion on politics, politicians and the parties: An historical perspective' in *The Prince's New Clothes: Why Do Australians Dislike Their Politicians*, eds David Burchell and Andrew Leigh, UNSW Press, Sydney, pp. 9–46.

——2006, 'The Australian party system, Pauline Hanson's One Nation and the party cartelisation thesis', in *Political Parties in Transition*, ed. Ian Marsh, Federation Press, Sydney.

Goot, Murray and Rowse, Tim 2007, *Divided Nation? Indigenous Affairs and the Imagined Public*, Melbourne University Press, Melbourne.

Goot, Murray and Watson, Ian 2005, 'Immigration, multiculturalism and national identity' in *Australian Social Attitudes: The First Report*, eds Shaun Wilson, Gabrielle Meagher, Rachel Gibson, David Denemark and Mark Western, UNSW Press, Sydney, pp. 182–303.

Gordon, Michael 2007, 'Finally, after a lost decade, cause for optimism', *Age*, 12 October, p. 1.

Gordon-Smith, Michael 2002, 'Media ethics after "cash for comment"' in *The Media and Communications in Australia*, eds Stuart Cunningham and Graeme Turner, Allen & Unwin, Sydney, pp. 277–92.

Gough, Kristine 2001, 'Ambulance inquiry findings sent to DPP', *Australian*, 29 November, p. 5.

Grant, Bruce 2004, *Fatal Attraction: Reflections on the Alliance with the United States*, Black Inc., Melbourne.

Grant, Wyn 2000, *Pressure Groups and British Politics*, Palgrave Macmillan, Basingstoke.

——2004, 'Pressure politics: The changing world of pressure groups', *Parliamentary Affairs*, vol. 57, no. 2, pp. 408–19.

Grattan, Michelle and Tomazin, Farrah 2008, 'National plan to tackle education', *Age*, 31 January, p. 4.

Gray, Andrew and Jenkins, Bill 1995, 'From public administration to public managements: Reassessing a revolution?', *Public Administration*, vol. 73, no. 1, pp. 75–100.

Gray, Gwen 2004, *The Politics of Medicare: Who Gets What, When and How*, UNSW Press, Sydney.

——2006, 'Health policy' in *Government, Politics, Power and Policy in Australia*, 8th edn, eds Andrew Parkin, John Summers and Dennis Woodward, Pearson Education, Sydney.

Gray, John 1983, *Mill On Liberty: A Defence*, Routledge & Kegan Paul, London.

——1998, *False Dawn: The Delusions of Global Capitalism*, W.W. Norton, New York.

Green, Antony 2003, 'The new alternative party was great while it lasted', *Sydney Morning Herald*, 7 March, p. 6.

Greenpeace 2007, 'Howard's real APEC agenda spelled out in Newcastle coal protest', 1 September 2007, <www.greenpeace.org/australia/news-and-events/news/Climate-change/howard-s-real-apec> [31 March 2008].

Griffin, Gerard, Nyland, Chris and O'Rourke, Anne 2004, 'Trade unions, the Australian Labor Party and the trade-labour rights debate', *Australian Journal of Political Science*, vol. 39, no. 1, pp. 89–107.

Gunther, Richard and Diamond, Larry 2003, 'Species of political parties: A new typology', *Party Politics*, vol. 9, no. 2, pp. 167–99.

Gyngell, Allan and Wesley, Michael 2007, *Making Australian Foreign Policy*, 2nd edn, Cambridge University Press, Melbourne.

Hage, Ghassan 2006, 'Racism is not simply black and white', *Online Opinion*, 16 June, <www.onlineopinion.com.au/view.asp?article=4577> [May 2008].

Hague, Rod and Harrop, Martin 2001, *Comparative Government and Politics: An Introduction*, 5th edn, Palgrave, Basingstoke.

Hall, J.P. and Savage, E.J. 2005, 'The role of the private sector in the Australian health-care system' in *The Public-Private Mix for Health*, ed. A. Maynard, Radcliffe Publishing, Abingdon, pp. 247–78.

Hall, Richard 2000, 'The new politics of the High Court' in *The Politics of Australian Society: Political Issues for the New Century*, eds Paul Boreham, Geoffrey Stokes and Richard Hall, Longman, Sydney, pp. 141–58.

Halliday, Susan 2000, 'The fading vision of human rights pioneers', *Sydney Morning Herald*, 31 August, p. 12.

Halligan, John 1997, 'Labor, the Keating term and the senior public service' in *The Second Keating Government: Australian Commonwealth Administration 1993–1996*, ed. Gwynneth Singleton, Centre for Research in Public Sector Management, University of Canberra, and the Institute of Public Administration Australia, Canberra, pp. 50–62.

Hamilton, Clive 2001, *Running from the Storm: The Development of Climate Change Policy in Australia*, UNSW Press, Sydney.

Hammer, Chris 2008, 'Deal struck with PNG on carbon trading', *Age*, 7 March, p. 4.

Hancock, Linda 2006, 'Bringing in the community sector: Partnerships and advocacy' in *Beyond the Policy Cycle: The Policy Process in Australia*, ed. Hal Colebatch, Allen & Unwin, Sydney.

Hannan, Ewin and Baker, Richard 2005, 'Nationalists boast of their role on the beach', *Age*, 13 December, <www.theage.com.au/news/national/nationalists-boast-of-their-role-on-the-beach/2005/12/12/1134236003135.html> [31 March 2008].

Harris, Anita 2001, 'Not waving or drowning: Young women, feminism, and the limits of the next wave debate', *Outskirts*, vol. 8, no. 1, <www.chloe.uwa.edu.au/outskirts/archive/volume8/harris> [May 2008].

Harris, Anita, Wyn, Johanna and Younes, Salem 2007, 'Young people and citizenship: An everyday perspective', *Youth Studies Australia*, vol. 26, no. 3, pp. 19–27.

Harris, Ian 2005, *House of Representatives Practice*, 5th edn, Department of the House of Representatives, Canberra, <http://202.14.81.230/house/pubs/PRACTICE/index.htm> [31 March 2008].

Hartcher, Peter 2007, 'Waxing frugal, praise rings in Rudd's ears', *Sydney Morning Herald*, 20 November, <www.smh.com.au/news/federal-election-2007-news/waxing-frugal-praise-rings-in-rudds-ears/2007/11/19/1195321697328.html> [31 March 2008].

Hawke, Bob and Wran, Neville 2002, *ALP National Committee of Review Report*, <http://australianpolitics.com/parties/alp/02-08-09_hawke-wran-review.pdf> [May 2008].

Hawker, Bruce 2007, 'Lib's legacy of broken promises', *Australian*, 26 October, <www.theaustralian.news.com.au/story/0,25197,22648593-7583,00.html> [31 March 2008].

Hawker, Geoffrey 1975, 'The bureaucracy under the Whitlam government', *Politics*, vol. 10, 1 May, pp. 15–23.

Hay, Colin 2002, *Political Analysis*, Palgrave Macmillan, Basingstoke.

He, Baogang 2007, 'Democratization and federalization in Asia', in *Federalism in Asia*, eds Baogang He, Brian Galligan and Takashi Inoguchi, Edward Elgar, Cheltenham.

Head, Brian 2007, 'Community engagement: Participation on whose terms?', *Australian Journal of Political Science*, vol. 42, no. 3, pp. 441–54.

Hendriks, Carolyn 2002, 'Institutions of deliberative democratic processes and interest groups: Roles, tensions and incentives', *Australian Journal of Public Administration*, vol. 61, no. 1, pp. 64–75.

Henningham, John 1999, 'Media' in *Institutions in Australian Society*, ed. John Henningham, Oxford University Press, Melbourne, pp. 274–97.

Herald-Sun 2007, 'No regrets, says Downer', 31 December, p. 9.

Herman, Valentine and Lodge, Juliet 1978, 'The European Parliament and the "decline of legislatures" thesis', *Australian Journal of Political Science*, vol. 13, no. 1, pp. 10–25.

Hewett, Jennifer 2007, 'Aspirations in the air', *Australian*, 31 October, <www.theaustralian.news.com.au/story/0,,22675930-28737,00.html?from=public_rss> [31 March 2008].

Heywood, Andrew 2004, *Political Theory: An Introduction*, 3rd edn, Palgrave, Basingstoke.

Hillman, Mick 2002, 'Environmental justice: A crucial link between environmentalism and community development?', *Community Development Journal*, vol. 37, no. 4, pp. 349–60.

Hills, Rachel 2007, 'Net campaigns peeked behind the party scripts', *Age*, 25 November, <www.theage.com.au/news/federal-election-2007-news/net-campaigns-peeked-behind-the-party-scripts/2007/11/24/1195753377832.html> [31 March 2008].

Hirst, Christian 2007, 'Foresight or folly? RAMSI and Australia's post–9/11 South Pacific policies' in *Australian Foreign Policy in the Age of Terror*, ed. Carl Ungerer, UNSW Press, Sydney.

Hocking, Jenny 2004, *Terror Laws: ASIO, Counter-Terrorism and the Threat to Democracy*, UNSW Press, Sydney.

Hodge, Errol 1994, 'Radio Australia and the Dili massacre', *Australian Journal of International Affairs*, vol. 48, no. 2, pp. 197–209.

Hogan, David and Owen, David 2000, 'Social capital, active citizenship and political equality in Australia' in *Social Capital and Public Policy in Australia*, ed. Ian Winter, Australian Institute of Family Studies, Melbourne, pp. 74–104.

Hogan, Michael 1996, 'Advocacy and democratic governance' in *Keeping It Together: State and Civil Society in Australia*, eds Adam Farrar and Jane Inglis, Pluto Press, Sydney, pp. 155–81.

Hogwood, Brian and Gun, Lewis 1984, *Policy Analysis for the Real World*, Oxford University Press, Oxford.

Holland, Ian 2002, 'Members of Parliament (Staff) Act: Background', *Research Note 14 2002–03*, Australian Parliamentary Library, Canberra, <www.aph.gov.au/LIBRARY/Pubs/rn/2002–03/03rn14.htm> [31 March 2008].

——2006, 'Parliamentary committees as an arena for policy work' in *Beyond the Policy Cycle: The Policy Process in Australia*, ed. Hal Colebatch, Allen & Unwin, Sydney.

Hollander, R. 2006, 'National competition policy, regulatory reform and Australian Federalism: Research and evaluation', *Australian Journal of Public Administration*, vol. 65, pp. 33–47.

Holmes, Jean and Sharman, Campbell 1977, *The Australian Federal System*, Allen & Unwin, Sydney.

Horner, David 1993, 'The security dimension of Australian foreign policy' in *Australia in a Changing World: New Foreign Policy Directions*, ed. Fedor A. Mediansky, Macmillan, Sydney, pp. 83–101.

Hovell, Devika and Niemann, Grant 2005, 'In the matter of David Hicks: A case for Australian courts?', *Public Law Review*, vol. 16, no. 2, pp. 116–33.

Howard, Cosmo 2005, 'The policy cycle: A model of post-Machiavellian decision-making', *Australian Journal of Public Administration*, vol. 64, no. 3, pp. 3–13.

Howard, John 1997, speech to the Liberal Party NSW State Council, 24 May.

——2002, radio interview with Jeremy Cordeaux, 24 July, transcript <http://pandora.nla.gov.au/pan/10052/20080108–1314/livetest.pm.gov.au/media/Interview/2002/interview1762.html> [1 April 2008].

——2003, *Transcript of the Prime Minister the Hon John Howard MP—Closing Address to the Liberal Party National Convention,* Adelaide, South Australia, 8 June, <http://pandora.nla.gov.au/pan/10052/20030821/www.pm.gov.au/news/speeches/speech106.html> [23 July 2008].

——2005, 'Counter-terrorism laws strengthened', media release, 8 September, <http://pandora.nla.gov.au/pan/10052/20051121–0000/www.pm.gov.au/news/media_releases/media_Release1551.html> [23 July 2008].

——2006a, 'A sense of balance: The Australian achievement in 2006', transcript of the Prime Minister's address to the National Press Club, Parliament House, Canberra, 25 January, <http://pandora.nla.gov.au/pan/10052/20060321–0000/www.pm.gov.au/news/speeches/speech1754.html> [31 March 2008].

——2006b, 'National competition policy payment penalty for Western Australia: 2005–2006 water reforms', media release, 30 June, <http://pandora.nla.gov.au/pan/10052/20070823–1732/www.pm.gov.au/media/Release/2007/Media_Release24264.html> [22 January 2008].

——2007a, 'Joint statement by the PM and Premiers of NSW , Victoria and SA: Water contingency planning in the southern Murray Darling Basin', media release, 20 April, <http://pandora.nla.gov.au/pan/10052/20070823–1732/www.pm.gov.au/media/Release/2007/Media_Release24264.html> [23 January 2008].

——2007b, 'National plan for water security', media release, 8 February, <http://pandora.nla.gov.au/pan/10052/20070823–1732/www.pm.gov.au/media/Release/2007/Media_Release23896.html> [23 January 2008].

——2007c, 'Weekly message—water security', 2 March, <http://pandora.nla.gov.au/pan/10052/20070823–1732/www.pm.gov.au/media/Speech/2007/Speech24175.html> [23 January 2008].

——2007d, 'A national plan for water security', AAP Column, 30 January, <http://pandora.nla.gov.au/pan/10052/20070823–1732/www.pm.gov.au/media/columns/2007/aap_column_300107.html> [23 January 2008].

——2007e, 'Interview with John Laws, Radio 2UE, Sydney', 29 January, <http://pandora.nla.gov.au/pan/10052/20070823–1732/www.pm.gov.au/media/Interview/2007/Interview2347.html> [23 January 2008].

——2007f, 'Interview with Keith Conlon and Tony Pilkington, Radio 5AA, Adelaide', 30 January, <http://pandora.nla.gov.au/pan/10052/20070823–1732/www.pm.gov.au/media/Interview/2007/Interview2349.html> [23 January 2008].

——2007g, 'Moving forward on the national plan for water security', media release, 30 July, <http://pandora.nla.gov.au/pan/10052/20070823–1732/www.pm.gov.au/media/Release/2007/Media_Release24467.html> [23 January 2008].

Howlett, Michael and Ramesh, M. 2003, *Studying Public Policy: Policy Cycles and Policy Subsystems,* 2nd edn, Oxford University Press, Ontario.

Hughes, Owen 1998, *Australian Politics,* 3rd edn, Macmillan Education, Melbourne.

Human Rights and Equal Opportunity Commission (HREOC) 2005, *Face the Facts: Some Questions and Answers About Refugees, Migrants and Indigenous Peoples in Australia,* HREOC, Sydney.

Hume City Council (HCC) 2005, *Hume Social Justice Charter 2005,* <www.hume.vic.gov.au/Page/Download.asp?name=SocialJusticeCharter2005.pdf&size=467105&link=../Files/SocialJusticeCharter2005.pdf> [4 March 2008].

——2007, 'Council to engage community on social justice charter and bill of rights', media release, <www.hume.vic.gov.au/Page/Download.asp?name=Charter_and_Bill_Review.pdf&size=29292&link=../Files/Charter_and_Bill_Review.pdf> [30 October 2007].

Huntley, Rebecca 2006, 'Gen Y and politics', address to the Sydney Institute on 21 March, *Sydney Papers,* vol. 18, no. 2, pp. 128–35.

Industries Assistance Commission (IAC) 1989, *Annual Report 1988–1989,* Australian Government Printing Service, Canberra.

Inglehart, Ronald 1977, *The Silent Revolution: Changing Values and Political Styles Among Western Publics,* Princeton University Press, Princeton, NJ.

——1990, 'Values, ideology and cognitive mobilization in new social movements' in *Challenging the Political Order,* eds Russell Dalton and Manfred Kuechler, Oxford University Press, New York, pp. 43–66.

Intergovernmental Panel on Climate Change 2001, *Climate Change 2001: Synthesis Report,* IPCC, Geneva, <www.ipcc.ch/ipccreports/tar/vol4/english/index.htm> [31 March 2008].

Irving, Helen 1997, *To Constitute a Nation: A Cultural History of Australia's Constitution,* Cambridge University Press, Melbourne.

Iveson, Kurt and Scalmer, Sean 2000, 'Contesting the "inevitable"', *Overland,* vol. 161, pp. 4–13.

Ivison, Duncan 2002, *Postcolonial Liberalism,* Cambridge University Press, Melbourne.

Jackson, Keith 2006, 'Parliament' in *New Zealand Government and Politics,* 4th edn, ed. Raymond Miller, Oxford University Press, Melbourne.

Jaensch, Dean 1986, *Getting Our Houses in Order,* Penguin, Melbourne.

——1994, *Power Politics,* Allen & Unwin, Sydney.

——2006, 'Party structures and procedures' in *Political Parties in Transition,* ed. Ian Marsh, Federation Press, Sydney.

Jaensch, Dean and Mathieson, David 1998, *A Plague on Both Your Houses: Minor Parties in Australia,* Allen & Unwin, Sydney.

Jamrozik, Adam 2001, *Social Policy in the Post-Welfare State: Australians on the Threshold of the 21st Century,* Pearson Education, Sydney.

Johns, Gary 2000, 'Party democracy: An audit of Australian parties', *Australian Journal of Political Science,* vol. 35, pp. 401–26.

Johnson, Carol 2000, *Governing Change: Keating to Howard,* University of Queensland Press, Brisbane.

——2002, 'Australian political science and the study of discourse', paper presented at the conference of the Australasian Political Studies Association, Canberra, October, <http://arts.anu.edu.au/sss/apsa/papers/Johnson.pdf> [May 2008].

——2005, 'The ideological contest: Neo-liberalism versus New Labor', in *Mortgage Nation: The 2004 Australian Election,* eds Marian Simms and John Warhurst, API Network, Perth, WA.

——2007, *Governing Change: From Keating to Howard,* rev. edn, API Network, Curtin University of Technology, Perth, WA.

——2008, 'Civil unions in the closet: Rudd bows to the religious right', *Online Opinion,* 14 February, <www.onlineopinion.com.au/view.asp?article=6997> [May 2008].

Joint Standing Committee on Electoral Matters 2006, 'Dissenting Report 2—Senator Andrew Murray, Australian Democrats', *Funding and Disclosure Inquiry into Disclosure of Donations to Political Parties and Candidates,* Parliament of Australia, <www.aph.gov.au/house/committee/em/donations/dissentingreport2.htm> [31 March 2008].

Joint Standing Committee on Treaties (JSCT) 2004, *Report on the Optional Protocol to the Convention Against Torture and Other Cruel, Inhuman or Degrading Treatment or Punishment,* No. 58, <www.aph.gov.au/house/committee/jsct/OPCAT/report.htm> [4 March 2008].

Judge, David 1999, *Representation: Theory and Practice in Britain,* Routledge, London.

Karvelas, Patricia 2007, 'Full steam to 2010 win', *Australian,* 22 December, p. 14.

Karvelas, Patricia and McGarry, Andrew 2003, 'True-blue Liberals changing their colours', *Australian,* 18 February, p. 2.

Katz, Richard and Mair, Peter 1992, 'Introduction: The cross-national study of party organizations' in *Party Organizations,* eds Richard Katz and Peter Mair, Sage, London.

——1993, 'The Evolution of Party Organizations in Europe: The Three Faces of Party Organization' in *Political Parties in a Changing Age,* ed. William Crotty, Special Issue of the American Review of Politics.

——1995, 'Changing models of party organization and party democracy: The emergence of the cartel party', *Party Politics,* vol. 1, no. 1, pp. 5–28.

——2002, 'The ascendancy of the party in public office: Party organisational change in twentieth century democracies' in *Political Parties: Old Concepts and New Challenges,* eds Richard Gunther, José Ramón-Montero and Juan J. Linz, Oxford University Press, Oxford, pp. 113–35.

Kavanagh, Dennis 1983, *Political Science and Political Behaviour,* Allen & Unwin, London.

Kay, Adrian 2007, 'Tense layering and synthetic policy paradigms: The politics of health insurance in Australia', *Australian Journal of Political Science,* vol. 42, no. 4, pp. 579–91.

Keating, Michael and Weller, Patrick 2000, 'Cabinet government: An institution under pressure' in *Institutions on the Edge? Capacity for Governance*, eds Michael Keating, John Wanna and Patrick Weller, Allen & Unwin, Sydney.

Keating, Paul 2000, *Engagement: Australia Faces the Asia–Pacific*, Pan Macmillan, Sydney.

Keen, Sue 1993, 'The changing orientations of social science research in Australia', *Canberra Bulletin of Public Administration*, no. 75, December, pp. 35–9.

——1999, 'Servicing social capital? Service clubs in decline', *Third Sector Review*, vol. 5, no. 1, pp. 97–112.

Kell, Peter 2005, 'Cronulla beach riots: Making waves for the Asia-Pacific', *Online Opinion*, 19 December, <www.onlineopinion.com.au/view.asp?article=3976> [31 March 2008].

Kelly, Paul 1992, *The End of Certainty: The Story of the 1980s*, Allen & Unwin, Sydney.

——2003, 'Partners, friends and allies', *Australian*, 16 October, p. 1.

——2007, 'The Rudd agenda', *Australian*, 22 December, p. 1.

Kelton, Maryanne 2006, 'Perspectives on Australian foreign policy 2005', *Australian Journal of International Affairs*, vol. 60, no. 2, pp. 229–46.

Kenny, Mark and Henderson, Nick 2007, 'Sold down the river', *Advertiser*, 25 July, p. 1.

Kent, Ann 2001, 'Australia and the international human rights regime' in *The National Interest in a Global Era: Australian in World Affairs 1996–2000*, eds James Cotton and John Ravenhill, Oxford University Press in association with Australian Institute of International Affairs, Melbourne, pp. 256–78.

——2007, 'Australia and international human rights' in *Trading on Alliance Security: Australia in World Affairs 2001–2005*, eds James Cotton and John Ravenhill, Oxford University Press, Melbourne.

Kildea, Paul 2003, 'The bill of rights debate in Australian political culture', *Australian Journal of Human Rights*, vol. 9, no. 1, pp. 65–118.

Kildea, Paul and Gelber, Katharine 2007, 'High Court review 2006: Australian federalism—implications of the *Work Choices* decision', *Australian Journal of Political Science*, vol. 42, no. 4, pp. 649–64.

King, Rhianna 2007, 'National curriculum ready by 2010', *West Australian*, 13 December, p. 12.

King, Robert J. 2002, 'The Timor Gap, Wonosobo and the fate of Portuguese Timor', *Journal of the Royal Australian Historical Society*, vol. 88, no. 1, pp. 75–104.

Kingdom, John 1992, *No Such Thing as Society? Individualism and Community*, Open University Press, Philadelphia.

Kingsbury, Damien 2000, 'East Timor to 1999' in *Guns and Ballot Boxes: East Timor's Vote for Independence*, ed. Damien Kingsbury, Monash Asia Institute, Monash University, Melbourne.

Kingston, Margo 1999, 'Mate, Howard's hubris sank that sad preamble', *Sydney Morning Herald*, 8 November, p. 13.

Kinley, David and Martin, Penny 2002, 'International human rights law at home: Addressing the politics of denial', *Melbourne University Law Review*, vol. 26, pp. 466–77.

Kirby, Michael 1993, 'Reflections on constitutional monarchy' in *The Republicanism Debate*, eds Wayne Hudson and David Carter, UNSW Press, Sydney.

——1994, 'In defence of Mabo' in *Make a Better Offer: The Politics of Mabo*, eds Murray Goot and Tim Rowse, Pluto Press, Sydney, pp. 67–81.

Kirby, Simon 2007, 'NSW Police fear protest boil over during APEC climax', Australian Associated Press, 7 September.

Kline, Jodie 2002, 'The Andrews' Bill: Compromised citizenship or the protection of human rights?', *Journal of Northern Territory History*, no. 13, pp. 49–56.

Kollman, Ken 1998, *Outside Lobbying: Public Opinion and Interest Group Activity*, Princeton University Press, Princeton, NJ.

Krishnapillai, Sarojini 2002, 'Bad neighbour policy—Australia, Kyoto and the Pacific', *Arena*, no. 60, August–September, pp. 14–15.

Kukathas, Chandran, Lovell, David and Maley, William 1990, *The Theory of Politics: An Australian Perspective*, Longman Cheshire, Melbourne.

Lacey, Wendy 2001, 'In the wake of *Teoh*: Finding an appropriate government response', *Federal Law Review*, vol. 29, no. 2, pp. 219–40.

——2004, 'The end for *Teoh*? *Re Minister for Immigration and Multicultural Affairs; Ex parte Lam*', paper presented at the Constitutional Law Conference, Art Gallery of New South Wales, Sydney, 20 February, <www.gtcentre.unsw.edu.au/publications/papers/docs/2004/59_WendyLacey.doc> [28 May 2008].

Laffin, Martin 1997, 'Public policy-making' in *Politics in Australia*, ed. Rodney Smith, Allen & Unwin, Sydney, pp. 51–65.

Lasry, Lex 2007, *Final Report of the Independent Observer for the Law Council of Australia*, 24 July, Law Council of Australia, <www.lawcouncil.asn.au/hicksjustice.html> [14 January 2008].

Latham, Mark 2005, *The Latham Diaries*, Melbourne University Press, Melbourne.

Law Council of Australia (LCA) 2005a, 'Law Council's outrage at one week review for anti-terror laws', media release, 14 October, <www.lawcouncil.asn.au/read/2005/2417860179.html> [24 October 2007].

——2005b, 'Law Council launches final assault on counter-terror laws', media release, 4 December, <www.lawcouncil.asn.au/read/2005/2419087920.html> [24 October 2007].

Lawrence, Carmen 2007, 'Railroading democracy', Democratic Audit of Australia Discussion paper 6/07, <http://democratic.audit.anu.edu.au/papers/20070329_lawrence_railrddem.pdf> [31 March 2008].

Lawson, Kay 1988, 'When linkage fails' in *When Parties Fail: Emerging Alternative Organizations,* eds Kay Lawson and Peter Merkl, Princeton University Press, Princeton, NJ.

Leach, Michael, Stokes, Geoffrey and Ward, Ian (eds) 2000, *The Rise and Fall of One Nation,* University of Queensland Press, Brisbane.

Leaver, Richard 2007, 'The new trade agenda', in *Australian Foreign Policy in the Age of Terror,* ed. Carl Ungerer, UNSW Press, Sydney.

Lee, H.P. 2005, 'The "reasonably appropriate and adapted" test and the implied freedom of political communication' in *Law and Government in Australia,* ed. Matthew Groves, Federation Press, Sydney.

Legal and Constitutional Legislation Committee (LCLC) of the Senate 2005, *Report into the Provisions of the Anti-Terrorism Bill (No. 2) 2005,* November, Parliament House, Canberra.

Leigh, Andrew 2005, 'Economic voting and electoral behaviour: How do individual, local and national factors affect the partisan choice?', Discussion Paper No. 489, Centre for Economic Policy Research, Australian National University, Canberra, <http://econrsss.anu.edu.au/pdf/DP489.pdf> [31 March 2008].

Lenihan, Denis 2007, 'AWB: How the system let us down', *Public Administration Today,* April–June, pp. 66–71.

Lewis, Steve 2007, 'Pauline Hanson wins a bundle of cash for election bid', *Herald Sun,* 7 December, <www.news.com.au/heraldsun/story/0,21985,22881951–662,00.html> [31 March 2008].

Lijphart, Arend 2001, 'Australian democracy in comparative perspective' in *Elections: Full, Free and Fair,* ed. Marian Sawer, Federation Press, Sydney, pp. 189–201.

Linnell, Gary 2007, 'First time young voters have already tuned out', 3 November, *Daily Telegraph,* <www.news.com.au/dailytelegraph/story/0,22049,22693285–5001031,00.html> [31 March 2008].

Louw, Eric 2005, *The Media and Political Process,* Sage, London.

Lowe, Ian 2004, 'The environment' in *The Howard Years,* ed. Robert Manne, Black Inc Agenda, Melbourne.

Lucy, Richard 1985, *The Australian Form of Government,* Macmillan, Melbourne.

Lukes, Steven 2005, *Power: A Radical View,* 2nd edn, Palgrave Macmillan, Basingstoke (1st edn 1974).

Lyons, Mark 2001, *Third Sector,* Allen & Unwin, Sydney.

Macdonald, Emma 2007, 'NSW blocks expert from high school history panel', *Canberra Times,* 27 June, p. 5.

Macey, Jennifer 2007, 'E-voting to be rolled out for election', *ABC News,* 15 August, <www.abc.net.au/news/stories/2007/08/15/2005989.htm> [31 March 2008].

Maddison, Sarah 2004, 'New South Wales: January to June 2004 (Political Chronicles)', *Australian Journal of Politics and History,* vol. 50, no. 4, pp. 593–600.

Maddison, Sarah, Dennis, Richard and Hamilton, Clive 2004, *Silencing Dissent: Non-government Organisations and Australian Democracy*, Discussion Paper No. 65, Australia Institute, <www.tai.org.au/documents/dp_fulltext/DP65.pdf> [31 March 2008].

Maddison, Sarah and Partridge, Emma 2007, *How Well Does Australian Democracy Serve Australian Women?*, Democratic Audit of Australia Report No. 8, Australian National University, Canberra.

Maddison, Sarah and Scalmer, Sean 2006, *Activist Wisdom: Practical Knowledge and Creative Tension in Social Movements*, UNSW Press, Sydney.

Maddox, Graham 1992, 'Political stability, independents and the two party system', *Current Affairs Bulletin*, vol. 69, no. 1, pp. 20–7.

——1996, *Australian Democracy in Theory and Practice*, 3rd edn, Pearson Education, Sydney.

——2000, *Australian Democracy in Theory and Practice*, 4th edn, Longman, Sydney.

——2005, *Australian Democracy in Theory and Practice*, 5th edn, Pearson Education, Sydney.

Maiden, Samantha 2007, 'National curriculum would drive out sludge: Howard', *Australian*, 9 February, p. 4.

Mair, Peter 2005, 'Democracy beyond parties', Discussion Paper, Centre for the Study of Democracy, University of California, Irvine.

Mair, Peter and van Biezen, Ingrid 2001, 'Party membership in 20 European democracies: 1980–2000', *Party Politics*, vol. 7, no. 1, pp. 5–21.

Maley, William 2003, 'Asylum-seekers in Australia's international relations', *Australian Journal of International Affairs*, vol. 57, no. 1, pp. 187–202.

Manne, Robert 2002, 'Pale grey view of a genocide', *Age*, 16 December, p. 15.

Manning, Haydon 2002, 'Voting behaviour' in *Government, Politics, Power and Policy in Australia*, 7th edn, eds John Summers, David Woodward and Andrew Parkin, Longman, Sydney, pp. 247–76.

Marks, Gary 1993, 'Intra and extra familial political socialization: The Australian case and changes over time', *Electoral Studies*, vol. 1, no. 2, pp. 128–57.

Marr, David, 2005, 'Liberty is left in shaky hands when the High Court no longer defends it', *Sydney Morning Herald*, 31 March.

Marris, Sid 2008a, 'Gillard rejects state IR proposal', *Australian*, 26 January, p. 1.

——2008b, 'Put IR control to a vote: Kennett', *Australian*, 28 January, p. 1.

Marsh, Ian 1995, *Beyond the Two Party System: Political Representation, Economic Competitiveness and Australian Politics*, Cambridge University Press, Melbourne.

——2000, 'Gaps in policy-making capacities: Interest groups, social movements, think tanks and the media' in *Institutions on the Edge? Capacity for Governance*, eds Michael Keating, John Wanna and Patrick Weller, Allen & Unwin, Sydney, pp. 178–204.

——2002, 'The prospects for a new "federation settlement" (through a more consensual political system)', *Australian Journal of Public Administration*, vol. 61, no. 2, pp. 19–32.

——2006, 'Australia's political cartel? The major parties and the party system in an era of globalisation' in *Political Parties in Transition*, ed. Ian Marsh, Federation Press, Sydney.

Marsh, Ian (ed.) 2006, *Political Parties in Transition?*, Federation Press, Sydney.

Martin, Chelsey 2003, 'Howard: Protesters aid Hussein', *Australian Financial Review*, 21 February, p. 5.

Martin, Hannah 2007, 'Queensland losing its icon', *Courier-Mail*, 20 October.

Martin, Ian 2001, *Self-Determination in East Timor: The United Nations, the Ballot, and International Intervention*, International Peace Academy Occasional Paper Series, Lynne Rienner Publishers, Boulder, Colo.

Mascarenhas, R.C. 1996, *Government and the Economy in Australia and New Zealand: The Politics of Economic Policy Making*, Austin & Winfield, San Francisco.

Massicotte, Louis 2000, 'Second-chamber elections' in *International Encyclopaedia of Elections*, ed. Richard Rose, CQ Press, Washington DC.

Matthews, Trevor 1997, 'Interest groups' in *Politics in Australia*, 3rd edn, ed. Rodney Smith, Allen & Unwin, Sydney, pp. 269–90.

May, John 1996, 'The role of peak bodies in a civil society' in *Keeping it Together: State and Civil Society in Australia*, eds Adam Farrar and Jane Inglis, Pluto Press, Sydney, pp. 245–72.

Mayer, Kenneth 2006, 'Sunlight as the best disinfectant: Campaign finance in Australia', Democratic Audit Discussion Paper No. 31/06, <http://arts.anu.edu.au/democraticaudit/categories/polfin_gafrm.htm> [31 March 2008].

McAllister, Ian 1997, 'Political behaviour' in *Government, Politics, Power and Policy in Australia*, 6th edn, eds Dennis Woodward, Andrew Parkin and John Summers, Longman, Melbourne, pp. 240–68.

——2002, 'Political parties in Australia: Party stability in a utilitarian society' in *Political Parties in Advanced Industrial Democracies*, eds Paul Webb, David Farrell and Ian Holliday, Oxford University Press, Oxford.

McDonald, Geoff 2007, 'Control orders and preventative detention—Why alarm is misguided' in *Law and Liberty in the War on Terror*, eds Andrew Lynch, Edwina Macdonald and George Williams, Federation Press, Sydney.

McDonald, Matt 2003, 'Fair weather friend? Australia's approach to global climate change', paper presented at the Ethics and Australian Foreign Policy Symposium, School of Political Science and International Studies, University of Queensland, Brisbane, 3–4 July.

——2005, 'Perspectives on Australian foreign policy 2004', *Australian Journal of International Affairs*, vol. 59, no. 2, pp. 153–68.

McGinty, Jim, 2007, 'Human rights on the agenda for WA', media statement, 3 May, <www.humanrights.wa.gov.au/documents/media_release.pdf> [1 April 2008].

McGregor, Craig 2001, *Class in Australia*, Penguin Books, Melbourne.

McHugh, Michael 2005, 'The need for agitators: The risk of stagnation', Sydney University Law Society Public Forum, Sydney, 12 October.

McKee, Alan 2002, 'Textual analysis' in *The Media and Communications in Australia*, eds Stuart Cunningham and Graeme Turner, Allen & Unwin, Sydney, pp. 62–71.

McKinney, Bianca and Halpin, Darren 2007, 'Talking about Australian pressure groups: Adding value to the insider/outsider distinction in combating homelessness in Western Australia', *Australian Journal of Public Administration*, vol. 66, no. 3, pp. 342–52.

McKinnon, Gabrielle 2005, 'The ACT Human Rights Act 2004: Impact on case law, legislation and policy', *Democratic Audit of Australia Discussion Paper 7/2005*, <http://democratic.audit.anu.edu.au/categories/rightsfrm.htm> [31 October 2007].

McLelland, Robert 2007a, 'Strengthening the Australia-US alliance', media statement, 2 August, <www.alp.org.au/media/0807/msfa020.php> [14 March 2008].

——2007b, 'Labor's position on Iraq and regional security', Speech to Fairfax Community Forum, 3 October, <www.alp.org.au/media/1007/spefa030.php> [14 March 2008].

McMaster, Don 2001, *Asylum Seekers: Australia's Response to Refugees*, Melbourne University Press, Melbourne.

McMinn, W.G. 1979, *A Constitutional History of Australia*, Oxford University Press, Oxford.

Megalogenis, George 2007, 'Kevin follows the low road to GenY', *Australian*, <http://blogs.theaustralian.news.com.au/meganomics/index.php/theaustralian/comments/kevin_follows_the_low_road_to_gen_y/P50/> [31 March 2008].

Meikle, Graham 2002, *Future Active: Media Activism and the Internet*, Pluto Press, Sydney.

Melbourne Journal of International Law (MJIL) 2003, 'Advice on the use of force against Iraq', Special Feature, *Melbourne Journal of International Law*, vol. 4, no. 1, pp. 177–95.

Melucci, Alberto 1996, *Challenging Codes*, Cambridge University Press, Cambridge.

Meyer, David and Tarrow, Sidney 1998, 'A movement society: Contentious politics for a new century' in *The Social Movement Society*, eds David Meyer and Sidney Tarrow, Rowman & Littlefield, Lanham, MD, pp. 1–28.

Mill, J.S. 1991, *On Liberty and Other Essays* (first published in 1859), ed. J. Gray, Oxford University Press, New York.

Mills, Stephen 1986, *The New Machine Men: Polls and Persuasion in Australian Politics*, Penguin, Melbourne.

Milne, Christine 2007, Member of the Australian Senate, interview conducted by Anika Gauja, 14 August.

Milner, Anthony 2000, 'What is left of engagement with Asia?', *Australian Journal of International Affairs*, vol. 54, no. 2, pp. 177–84.

——2001, 'Balancing "Asia" against Australian values' in *The National Interest in a Global Era: Australian in World Affairs 1996–2000*, eds James Cotton and John Ravenhill, Oxford University Press in association with Australian Institute of International Affairs, Melbourne, pp. 31–52.

Miragliotta, Narelle 2006, 'One party, two traditions: Radicalism and pragmatism in the Australian Greens', *Australian Journal of Political Science*, vol. 41, no. 4, pp. 585–96.

Miskin, Sarah and Baker, Greg 2006, 'Political finance disclosure under current and proposed thresholds', Australian Parliamentary Library Research Note, No. 27, <www.aph.gov.au/library/pubs/rn/2005–06/06rn27.pdf> [31 March 2008].

Miskin, Sarah and Lumb, Martin 2006, 'The 41st Parliament: Middle-aged, well-educated and (mostly) male', Research Note No. 24 2005/2006, Australian Parliamentary Library, Canberra, <www.aph.gov.au/Library/pubs/rn/2005–06/06rn24.htm> [31 March 2008].

Moffatt, Ken, George, Usha, Lee, Bill and McGrath, Susan 1999, 'Advancing citizenship: A study of social planning', *Community Development Journal*, vol. 34, no. 4, pp. 308–17.

Moon, Jeremy and Sharman, Campbell 2003, 'Western Australia' in *Australian Politics and Government: The Commonwealth, the States and the Territories*, eds Jeremy Moon and Campbell Sharman, Cambridge University Press, Cambridge, pp. 183–208.

Moon, Jeremy and Sharman, Campbell (eds) 2003, *Australian Politics and Government: The Commonwealth, the States and Territories*, Cambridge University Press, Cambridge.

Morgan, Michael and McLeod, Abby 2006, 'Have we failed our neighbour?', *Australian Journal of International Affairs*, vol. 60, no. 3, pp. 412–28.

Morriss, Peter 2002, *Power: A Philosophical Analysis*, 2nd edn, Manchester University Press, Manchester.

Mulgan, Richard 2006, 'Government accountability for outsourced services', *Australian Journal of Public Administration*, vol. 65, no. 2, pp. 48–58.

Murphy, Mathew 2007, 'Rudd Kyoto promise pleases business', *Age Online*, 1 December, <http://business.theage.com.au/rudd-kyoto-promise-pleases-business/20071130–1e21.html> [31 March 2008].

Murray, Philomena 1997, 'Australia and the European Union' in *Seeking Asian Engagement: Australia in World Affairs, 1991–1995*, eds James Cotton and John Ravenhill, Oxford University Press in association with Australian Institute of International Affairs, Melbourne.

Murray–Darling Basin Commission (MDBC) 2006a, 'About the basin', <www.mdbc.gov.au/about/basin_overview> [23 January 2008].

——2006b, 'A brief history of the Murray–Darling Basin Agreement', <www.mdbc.gov.au/about/history_mdbc> [23 January 2008].

Nash, Kate 2000, *Contemporary Political Sociology: Globalisation, Politics and Power*, Blackwell Publishing, Oxford.

National Action Plan for Salinity and Water Quality (NAPSWQ) 2007, 'What is the NAPSWQ?', <www.napswq.gov.au/index.html> [22 January 2008].

National Farmers Federation (NFF) 2003, 'Biotechnology position statement', March, <http://archive.nff.org.au/pages/sub/biotechnology_position.pdf> [1 April 2008].

Nelson, Brendan 1997, 'Private health insurance: Sensible and vital protection against the unknown', *Healthcover*, October–November, pp. 52–7.

Nethercote, John R. 1996, 'The Australian public service as a career service: Past, present and future' in *New Ideas, Better Government*, eds Patrick Weller and Glyn Davis, Allen & Unwin, Sydney.

Nettle, Kerry 2003, Member of the Australian Senate, interview conducted by Ariadne Vromen and Nick Turnbull, 28 July.

Newman, Gerard 2002, *Federal Election Results 1949–2001*, Research Paper No. 9, 2001–02, Department of the Parliamentary Library, Canberra, <www.aph.gov.au/library/pubs/rp/2001–02/02RP09.htm> [May 2008].

——2005, 'Federal election results 1949–2004', Australian Parliamentary Library Research Brief No. 11, <www.aph.gov.au/library/Pubs/RB/2004–05/05rb11.pdf> [31 March 2008].

Newman, Jacquetta and Tanguay, Brian 2002, 'Crashing the party: The politics of interest groups and social movements' in *Citizen Politics: Research and Theory in Canadian Political Behaviour*, eds Joanna Everitt and Brenda O'Neill, Oxford University Press, Oxford, pp. 387–412.

Newspoll 2001, 'Asylum seekers poll', 4 September, <www.newspoll.com.au/cgi-bin/polling/display_poll_data.pl> [28 May 2008].

Nicholson, Brendan 2000, 'Women pressure PM on treaty', *Sunday Age*, 8 October, p. 6.

Nixon, Sherrill 2007, 'Push to reduce residential speed limit to 30kmh', *Sydney Morning Herald*, 22 October, p. 5.

Norberry, Jennifer 2003, 'The evolution of the Commonwealth franchise: Tales of inclusion and exclusion' in *Realising Democracy: Electoral Law in Australia*, eds Graeme Orr, Bryan Mercurio and George Williams, Federation Press, Sydney.

Norrington, Brad 2008, 'Rudd backs Iemma's power sell-off', *Australian*, 12 February, <www.theaustralian.news.com.au/story/0,25197,23198681–5013871,00.html> [15 February 2008].

Norris, Pippa 2001, 'The twilight of Westminster? Electoral reform and its consequences', *Political Studies*, vol 49, no. 5, pp. 877–900.

Norton, Andrew 2000, 'Liberalism and the Liberal Party of Australia' in *The Politics of Australian Society: Political Issues for the New Century*, eds Paul Boreham, Geoffrey Stokes and Richard Hall, Longman, Sydney, pp. 22–37.

O'Brien, John and O'Donnell, Michael 2002a, 'Towards a new public unitarism: Employment and industrial relations in the Australian public service', *Economic and Labour Relations Review*, vol. 13, no. 1, pp. 60–86.

——2002b, 'Introduction to symposium on the new public management and public sector employment relations: United Kingdom, the United States and Australia', *Economic and Labour Relations Review*, vol. 13, no. 1, pp. 1–6.

O'Connor, Tim, Chan, Sharni and Goodman, James 2006, 'Australian aid: Promoting insecurity?' in *Reality of Aid Reports 2006*, <www.realityofaid.org/roareport.php?table=roa2006&id=1> [7 March 2008].

O'Keefe, Michael 2007, 'Australia and fragile states in the Pacific' in *Trading on Alliance Security: Australia in World Affairs 2001–2005*, eds James Cotton and John Ravenhill, Oxford University Press, Melbourne.

O'Loughlin, Toni 2000, 'Howard move angers women', *Sydney Morning Herald*, 5 October, p. 2.

Oakes, Laurie 2006, 'You started it, Tony', *Nine MSN News*, 16 February, <http://news.ninemsn.com.au/article.aspx?id=86733> [1 April 2008].

Organisation for Economic Cooperation and Development (OECD) 2004, 'Private health insurance in OECD countries', policy brief, <www.oecd.org/dataoecd/42/6/33820355.pdf> [31 March 2008].

——2006, 'Are students ready for a technology rich world? What PISA studies tell us', OECD Programme for International Student Assessment, <www.oecd.org/document/31/0,2340,en_32252351_32236173_35995743_1_1_1_1,00.html> [14 January 2008].

Orr, Graeme 2007, 'Constitutionalising the franchise and the status quo: The High Court on prisoner voting rights', *Democratic Audit of Australia*, <democratic.audit.anu.edu.au/papers/20071019orr_prisonervotingrights.pdf> [May 2008].

Osborne, David and Gaebler, Ted 1993, *Reinventing Government: How the Entrepreneurial Spirit is Transforming the Public Sector*, Plume, New York.

Oztam 2007a, 'Top Twenty Programs Ranking Report, June 24–30', <www.oztam.com.au/documents/2007/E_20070624.pdf> [31 March 2008].

——2007b, 'Top Twenty Programs Ranking Report, October 14–20', <www.oztam.com.au/documents/2007/E_20071014.pdf> [31 March 2008].

Painter, Martin 1987, *Steering the Modern State: Changes in Central Coordination in Three Australian State Governments*, Sydney University Press, Sydney.

——1997a, 'Federalism' in *Politics in Australia*, 3rd edn, ed. Rodney Smith, Allen & Unwin, Sydney, pp. 194–215.

——1997b, 'Public management: Fad or fallacy?' in *Mangerialism: The Great Debate*, eds Mark Considine and Martin Painter, Melbourne University Press, Melbourne, pp. 39–43.

——1998, *Collaborative Federalism: Economic Reform in Australia in the 1990s*, Cambridge University Press, Melbourne.

Palmer, Bryan 2006, 'What is policy?', *Oz Politics*, <www.ozpolitics.info/guide/phil/policy/> [31 March 2008].

Panebianco, Angelo 1988, *Political Parties: Organization and Power*, Cambridge University Press, Cambridge.

Papadakis, Elim 2001, 'Social Movements: The Citizens in Action' in *Are You Being Served?*

State, Citizens and Governance, eds Glyn Davis and Patrick Weller, Allen & Unwin, Sydney, pp. 36–57.

Papadakis, Elim and Grant, Richard 2001, 'Media responsiveness to "old" and "new" politics issues in Australia', *Australian Journal of Political Science,* vol. 36, no. 2, pp. 293–308.

Papadopoulos, Yannis 2003, 'Cooperative forms of governance: Problems of democratic accountability in complex environments', *European Journal of Political Research,* vol. 42, pp. 473–501.

Parkin, Andrew 2003, 'South Australia' in *Australian Politics and Government: The Commonwealth, the States and the Territories,* eds Campbell Sharman and Jeremy Moon, Cambridge University Press, Melbourne.

Parkin, Andrew and Anderson, Geoff 2007, 'The Howard Government, regulatory federalism and the transformation of Commonwealth–State relations', *Australian Journal of Political Science,* vol. 42, no. 2, pp. 295–314.

Parkin, Andrew and Summers, John 2002, 'The constitutional framework' in *Government, Politics, Power and Policy in Australia,* 7th edn, eds John Summers, Dennis Woodward and Andrew Parkin, Longman, Sydney.

Parkin, Andrew, Summers, John and Woodward, Dennis (eds) 2006, *Government, Politics, Power and Policy in Australia,* 8th edn, Pearson Education, Sydney.

Parliamentary Joint Committee on ASIO, ASIS and DSD (PJCAAD) 2002, *Advisory Report on the Australian Security Intelligence Organisation Legislation Amendment (Terrorism) Bill 2002,* Parliament of Australia, Canberra, <www.aph.gov.au/house/committee/pjcaad/TerrorBill2002/Terrorindex.htm> [28 May 2008].

Parsons, Ian 1999, *Cripples, Coons, Fags and Fems: A Look at How Four Human Rights Movements have Fought Prejudice,* Villamanta Legal Service, Geelong.

Passey, Andrew and Lyons, Mark 2005, 'Voluntary associations and political participation' in *Australian Social Attitudes: The First Report,* eds Shaun Wilson, Gabrielle Meagher, Rachel Gibson, David Denemark and Mark Western, UNSW Press, Sydney, pp. 62–81.

Patapan, Haig 2000, *Judging Democracy: The New Politics of the High Court of Australia,* Cambridge University Press, Melbourne.

——2001, 'Church and state in Australia: Towards a new dialogue: Comment', *Public Law Review,* vol. 12, March, pp. 13–16.

Pateman, Carole 1979, *The Problem of Political Obligation: A Critical Analysis of Liberal Theory,* John Wiley & Sons, Chichester.

——1988, *The Sexual Contract,* Polity Press, Cambridge.

Patty, Anna 2006, 'Government has it wrong, expert says', *Sydney Morning Herald,* 7 October, p. 7.

Peake, Ross 2007, 'Rudd proposes national curriculum for schools', *Canberra Times,* 1 March, p. 5.

Perry, Michael J. 1994, *The Constitution in the Courts: Law or Politics?*, Oxford University Press, New York.

Pettafor, Emily 2003, 'Buying influence—are political donations gaining developers a sympathetic ear? You'd be green to believe it's largesse', *Australian*, 20 November, p. T01.

Pettit, Philip 1999, *Republicanism: A Theory of Freedom and Government*, 2nd edn, Oxford University Press, New York.

PJCAAD, see Parliamentary Joint Committee on ASIO, ASIS and DSD.

Plibersek, Tanya 2007, Member of the House of Representatives, interview conducted by Anika Gauja, 11 July.

Prasser, Scott 2007, 'Beattie retires', *Online Opinion*, <www.onlineopinion.com.au/view.asp?article=6392> [31 March 2008].

Print, Murray, Saha, Lawrence and Edwards, Kathy 2004, 'Youth Electoral Study Report 1: Enrolment and Voting', <www.aec.gov.au/pdf/publications/youth_study_1/youth_electoral_study_01.pdf> [31 March 2008].

Productivity Commission 2000, *Broadcasting*, Report No. 11, Ausinfo, Canberra.

Public Service Act Review Group 1994, *Report of the Public Service Act Review Group* (McLeod Report), Australian Government Publishing Service, Canberra.

Pusey, Michael 2000, 'Middle Australians in the grip of economic "reform" ... will they volunteer?' in *Volunteers and Volunteering*, eds John Warburton and Melanie Oppenheimer, Federation Press, Sydney, pp. 19–31.

Pusey, Michael and Nick Turnbull 2005, 'Have Australians embraced economic reform?' in *Australian Social Attitudes: The First Report*, eds Shaun Wilson, Gabrielle Meagher, Rachel Gibson, David Denemark and Mark Western, UNSW Press, Sydney, pp. 161–81.

Putnam, Robert 1995, 'Tuning in, tuning out: The strange disappearance of social capital in America', *PS: Political Science and Politics*, vol. 28, no. 4, pp. 664–83.

——2000, *Bowling Alone: The Collapse and Revival of American Community*, Simon & Schuster, New York.

Quiggin, John 2002, 'Contracting out: Promise and performance', *Economic and Labour Relations Review*, vol. 13, no. 1, pp. 89–104.

Ramsey, Alan 2001, 'Gloves are off over a shoddy advertisement for Australia', *Sydney Morning Herald*, 17 November, p. 38.

Ranck, Hutch 2007, 'Education overhaul will open door of opportunity', *Age*, 30 November, p. 10.

Rann, Mike 2005, 'Mike Rann calls for abolition of upper house', *The World Today*, ABC Local Radio, 24 November, <www.abc.net.au/worldtoday/content/2005/s1515919.htm> [31 March 2008].

Rasiah, Parameswary 2006, 'Does Question Time fulfil its role of ensuring accountability?', *Democratic Audit of Australia Discussion Paper 12/06*, Australian National

University, Canberra, <http://democratic.audit.anu.edu.au/papers/20060424_rasiah_qt.pdf> [31 March 2008].

Ravenhill, John 1997, 'Business and politics' in *Politics in Australia*, 3rd edn, ed. Rodney Smith, Allen & Unwin, Sydney, pp. 291–316.

——2007, 'Australia and the global economy', in *Trading on Alliance Security: Australia in World Affairs 2001–2005*, eds James Cotton and John Ravenhill, Oxford University Press, Melbourne.

Ray, Robert 2006, 'Are factions killing the Labor Party?', address to the Fabian Society Sydney, 20 September, <www.fabian.org.au/1077.asp> [1 April 2008].

Rees, John 1985, *John Stuart Mill's On Liberty*, Clarendon Press, Oxford.

Reilly, Ben 2001, 'Preferential voting and its political consequences' in *Elections: Full, Free and Fair*, ed. Marian Sawer, Federation Press, Sydney, pp. 78–95.

Reserve Bank of Australia (RBA) 2008, 'About monetary policy', <www.rba.gov.au/MonetaryPolicy/about_monetary_policy.html> [31 March 2008].

Reynolds, Andrew, Reilly, Ben and Ellis, Andrew 2005, *Electoral System Design: The New International IDEA Handbook*, Institute for Democracy and Electoral Assistance, <www.idea.int/publications/esd/upload/ESD_full_with%20final%20changes%20inserted.pdf> [May 2008].

Reynolds, Henry 2001, 'Whose story? From armband to blindfold', *Australian*, 14 March, p. 35.

Reynolds, Paul 1991, *Political Sociology: An Australian Perspective*, Longman Cheshire, Melbourne.

Rhiannon, Lee 2003, 'Green gains, Labor pains', *Arena*, no. 68, December, pp. 18–19.

Rhodes, Rod A.W. 1994, 'The hollowing out of the state: The changing nature of the public service in Britain', *Political Quarterly*, vol. 65, no. 2, pp. 138–51.

——1997, *Understanding Governance: Policy Networks, Governance, Reflexivity and Accountability*, Open University Press, Buckingham.

Richardson, Chris 2003, 'War not a budget breaker', *Business Review Weekly*, 8 May, p. 26.

Richardson, Jeremy 2000, 'Government, interest groups and policy change', *Political Studies*, vol. 48, pp. 1006–25.

Riley, Mark and Marriner, Cosima 2003, 'We didn't do Manildra any favours, says PM', *Sydney Morning Herald*, 18 August, p. 4.

Ritter, David 2006, 'The cricket tragic', *Online Opinion*, 23 November, <www.onlineopinion.com.au/view.asp?article=5183> [31 March 2008].

Robbins, Jane 2007, 'The Howard Government and indigenous rights: An imposed national unity?', *Australian Journal of Political Science*, vol. 42, no. 2, pp. 315–28.

Roberts, Jeremy and Walker, Jamie 2007, 'Father pleads: Let David get on with his life', *Australian*, 29 December, pp. 1, 6.

Roche, Maurice 2000, 'Rethinking citizenship and social movements: Themes in contemporary sociology and neoconservative ideology' in *Readings in Contemporary Political Sociology*, ed. Kate Nash, Blackwell Publishers, Oxford, pp. 209–37.

Rodrigues, Usha 2008, 'Blogging comes alive', *Hindu*, <www.thehindu.com/thehindu/mag/2008/01/13/stories/2008011350110400.htm> [31 March 2008].

Roy Morgan 2007a, 'Bans lifted as genetically modified food gains acceptance', Article No. 705, 6 December, <www.roymorgan.com/news/press-releases/2007/705/> [18 January 2008].

——2007b, 'Television remains main source of news and current affairs', <www.roymorgan.com/resources/pdf/papers/20070627.pdf> [31 March 2008].

Rudd, Kevin 2007a, 'Meeting of the Council of Australian Governments: Effective federalism for the future', media release, 10 December, <http://mobile.alp.org.au/media/1207/mspm100.php> [1 April 2008].

——2007b, 'Federal Labor campaign launch', 14 November, Brisbane, <www.alp.org.au/media/1107/speloo140.php> [11 January 2008].

——2007c, 'Ratifying the Kyoto Protocol', Australian Labor Party media statement, 3 December, <www.alp.org.au/media/1207/mspm030.php> [31 March 2008].

——2008a, 'Address to the Indigenous Welcome to Country, Opening of the 42nd Federal Parliament', 12 February, <www.pm.gov.au/media/Speech/2008/speech_0071.cfm> [15 February 2008].

——2008b, 'Apology to Australia's Indigenous Peoples', House of Representatives, Parliament House, Canberra, 13 February, <www.pm.gov.au/media/Speech/2008/speech_0073.cfm> [28 March 2008.]

Ruddock, Philip, 2007, 'Bills of rights do not protect freedoms', *Sydney Morning Herald*, 31 August, <www.smh.com.au/articles/2007/08/30/1188067275092.html> [31 October 2007].

Rudra, Natasha 2008a, 'National school curriculum steps closer', *Canberra Times*, 31 January.

——2008b, 'Gay, Lesbian couples toast end of long journey to recognition', *Canberra Times*, 21 May, <canberra.yourguide.com.au/news/local/news/general/gay-lesbian-couples-toast-end-of-long-journey-to-recognition/773847.aspx> [May 2008].

Sainsbury, Diane 2001, 'Rights without seats: The puzzle of women's legislative recruitment' in *Elections Full, Free and Fair*, ed. Marian Sawer, Federation Press, Sydney.

Sales, Leigh 2007, *Detainee 002: The Case of David Hicks*, Melbourne University Press, Melbourne.

Sanders, Will 2005, 'Never even adequate: Reconciliation and indigenous affairs' in *Howard's Second and Third Governments*, eds C. Aulich and R. Wettenhall, UNSW Press, Sydney.

Saunders, Cheryl 1990, 'The constitutional framework: Hybrid, derivative but eventually Australian' in *Public Administration in Australia: A Watershed*, ed. John Power, Hale & Iremonger, Sydney.

——1998, *It's Your Constitution: Governing Australia Today*, Federation Press, Sydney.

Savage, Shelly and Tiffen, Rod 2007, 'Politicians, journalists and "spin": Tangled relationships and shifting alliances' in *Government Communication in Australia,* ed. Sally Young, Cambridge University Press, Melbourne, pp. 79–92.

Sawer, Marian 1990, *Sisters in Suits: Women and Public Policy in Australia,* Allen & Unwin, Sydney.

——1998, *Mirrors, Mouthpieces, Mandates and Men of Judgement: Concepts of Representation in the Australian Federal Parliament,* Department of the Senate Papers on Parliament no. 31, June, Canberra.

Sawer, Marian 2002, 'Governing For the Mainstream: Implications for Community Representation', *Australian Journal of Public Administration,* vol. 61, no. 1, pp. 39–49.

——2003a, *The Ethical State? Social Liberalism in Australia,* Melbourne University Press, Melbourne.

——2003b, 'Down with elites and up with inequality: Market populism in Australia', *Australian Review of Public Affairs,* 27 October, <www.australianreview.net/digest/2003/10/sawer.html> [May 2008].

——2006, 'From women's interests to special interests: Reframing equality claims', *The Politics of Women's Interests,* eds Louise Chappell and Lisa Hill, Routledge, Oxford.

Sawer, Marian (ed.) 2001, *Elections: Full, Free and Fair,* Federation Press, Sydney.

Sawer, Marian and Zappala, Gianni (eds) 2001, *Speaking for the People: Representation in Australian Politics,* Melbourne University Press, Melbourne.

Sawyers, Traci and Meyer, David 1999, 'Missed opportunities: Social movement abeyance and public policy', *Social Problems,* vol. 46, no. 2, pp. 187–206.

Scalmer, Sean 2002, *Dissent Events,* UNSW Press, Sydney.

Scalmer, Sean and Maddison, Sarah 2006, *Activist Wisdom: Practical knowledge and creative tension in social movements,* UNSW Press, Sydney.

Scarrow, Susan 2000, 'Parties without members? Party organization in a changing electoral environment' in *Parties without Partisans,* eds Russell Dalton and Martin Wattenberg, Oxford University Press, Oxford.

Schmidt, Lucinda 2001, 'The Capital Hill mob', *Business Review Weekly,* 25 May, pp. 58–60.

Scholte, Jan Aart 2000, *Globalization: A Critical Introduction,* Macmillan, London.

Schwartz, Herman 2003, 'Economic rationalism in Canberra and Canada: Public sector reorganisation, politics and power', *Australian Economic History Review,* vol. 43, no. 1, March, pp. 45–56.

Scott, Claudia 2006, 'The policy process' in *New Zealand Government and Politics,* 4th edn, ed. Raymond Miller, Oxford University Press, Melbourne.

Segal, Jeffrey, Timpone, Richard and Howard, Robert 2000, 'Buyer beware? Presidential success through Supreme Court appointments', *Political Research Quarterly,* vol. 53, no. 3, pp. 557–73.

Selway, Bradley and Williams, John 2005, 'The High Court and Australian federalism', *Publius*, vol. 35, pp. 467–89.

Senate Environment, Communications and the Arts Committee 2004, *Report on the Kyoto Protocol Ratification Bill 2003 (No. 2)*, Department of the Senate, Canberra.

Senate Standing Committee on Community Affairs 2006, *Inquiry into Therapeutic Goods Amendment (Repeal of Ministerial responsibility for approval of RU486) Bill 2005*, Department of the Senate, Canberra, <www.aph.gov.au/SENATE/COMMITTEE/CLAC_CTTE/ru486/report/index.htm> [31 March 2008].

Sharman, Campbell 1989, 'Federal institutions and processes: A political science perspective' in *Australian Federalism*, ed. Brian Galligan, Longman Cheshire, Melbourne, pp. 98–115.

——1999, 'The representation of small parties and independents in the Senate', *Australian Journal of Political Science*, vol. 34, no. 3, pp. 353–61.

Sharman, Campbell and Moon, Jeremy 2003, 'One system or nine' in *Australian Politics and Government: The Commonwealth, the States and the Territories*, eds Jeremy Moon and Campbell Sharman, Cambridge University Press, Melbourne, pp. 239–62.

Sharman, Campbell and Moon, Jeremy (eds) 2003, *Australian Politics and Government: The Commonwealth, the States and the Territories*, Cambridge University Press, Melbourne.

Sheil, Christopher (ed.) 2001, *Globalisation: Australian Impacts*, UNSW Press, Sydney.

Shergold, Peter 2005, 'Coping with crisis: Personal reflections on what the public service learned from the tsunami disaster', *Public Administration Today*, October–December, pp. 43–8.

Sherman, Lawrence W., Strang, Heather and Woods, Daniel J. 2000, *Recidivism Patterns in the Canberra Reintegrative Shaming Experiments (RISE)*, Centre for Restorative Justice, Research School of Social Sciences, Australian National University.

Shields, John 2005, 'Setting the double standard: Chief executive pay the BCA way', *Journal of Australian Political Economy*, no. 256, pp. 299–324.

Simms, Marian and Warhurst, John (eds) 2005, *Mortgage Nation: The 2004 Australian Election*, API Network, Perth.

Simpson, Gerry 2005, 'The war in Iraq and international law', *Melbourne Journal of International Law*, vol. 6, no. 1, pp. 167–88.

Singleton, Gwynneth, Aitkin, Don, Jinks, Brian and Warhurst, John 2006, *Australian Political Institutions*, Pearson Longman, Sydney.

Skehan, Craig 2007, 'Pacific solution ends but tough stance to remain', *Sydney Morning Herald*, 8–9 December, p. 9.

Skinner, Quentin 1984, 'The idea of negative liberty: Philosophical and historical perspectives' in *Philosophy in History: Essays on the Historiography of Philosophy*, eds Richard Rorty, J.B. Schneewind and Quentin Skinner, Cambridge University Press, Cambridge.

Skotnicki, Tom 2003, 'Howard's high risk campaign', *Business Review Weekly*, 6 February, p. 10.

Smith, Hugh 1993, 'Internal politics and foreign policy' in *Australia in a Changing World: New Foreign Policy Directions*, ed. Fedor A. Mediansky, Macmillan, Sydney, pp. 17–42.

Smith, L. 1993, *Domestic Violence: An Overview of the Literature*, Home Office Research Study No. 107, London, HSMO.

Smith, Rodney 1994, 'Parliament' in *Developments in Australian Politics*, eds Judith Brett, James Gillespie and Murray Goot, Macmillan Education, Melbourne, pp. 106–31.

——1997a, 'Power' in *Politics in Australia*, 3rd edn, ed. Rodney Smith, Allen & Unwin, Sydney, pp. 17–34.

——1997b, 'The news media' in *Politics in Australia*, 3rd edn, ed. Rodney Smith, Allen & Unwin, Sydney, pp. 332–53.

——1998, 'Australia: An old order manages change' in *Political Parties and the Collapse of the Old Orders*, eds John K. White and Philip J. Davies, State University of New York Press, Albany, NY, pp. 113–35.

——2001a, *Voting and Elections: Hot Topics 34*, State Library of New South Wales, Sydney.

——2001b, *Australian Political Culture*, Pearson Education, Sydney.

——2003, 'New South Wales' in *Australian Politics and Government: The Commonwealth, the States and the Territories*, eds Jeremy Moon and Campbell Sharman, Cambridge University Press, Melbourne, pp. 41–73.

——2006, *Against the Machines: Minor Parties and Independents in NSW 1910–2006*, Federation Press, Sydney.

Smith, Rodney, Vromen, Ariadne and Ian Cook 2006, *Keywords in Australian Politics*, Cambridge University Press, Melbourne.

Smith, Tony 2007, *Gender Goes Missing from NSW Politics*, Democratic Audit of Australia Discussion Paper 8/07, Australian National University, Canberra, <http://democratic.audit.anu.edu.au/papers/20070525_smith_gendernsw.pdf> [31 March 2008].

Smyth, Russell 2003, 'Explaining historical dissent rates in the High Court of Australia', *Commonwealth and Comparative Politics*, vol. 41, no. 2, pp. 83–114.

Solomon, David 2007, *Pillars of Power*, Federation Press, Sydney.

Stanhope, John 2005, 'The Human Rights Act 2004 (ACT): Making a stand in the ACT', *Alternative Law Journal*, vol. 30, no. 2, pp. 54–7.

Stead, Victoria 2007, 'The unsatisfactory ending to the case of David Hicks', *Arena*, vol. 89, pp. 17–18.

Steketee, Mike 2008, 'How PM's red tape will bind recalcitrant states', *Australian*, 10 January, p. 1.

Stokes, Geoffrey 2004, 'The "Australian Settlement" and Australian political thought', *Australian Journal of Political Science*, vol. 39, no. 1, pp. 5–22.

Stone, Deborah 2002, *Policy Paradox: The Art of Political Decision Making*, rev. edn, W.W. Norton, New York.

Stone, Diane 1991, 'Old guard versus new partisans: Think tanks in transition', *Australian Journal of Political Science*, vol. 26, no. 2, pp. 197–215.

Street, John 2001, *Mass Media, Politics and Democracy*, Palgrave, Basingstoke.

Strutt, Jessica 2006, 'Liberals in revolt over Bishop policy', *West Australian*, 11 October, p. 9.

Sugita, Hiroya 1995, 'Challenging "twopartism": The contribution of the Australian Democrats to the Australian party system', PhD thesis, Flinders University, South Australia.

Sukma, Rizal 2006, 'Indonesia and the tsunami: Responses and foreign policy implications', *Australian Journal of International Affairs*, vol. 60, no. 2, pp. 213–28.

Summers, Anne 2003, *The End of Equality: Work, Babies and Women's Choices in 21st Century Australia*, Random House, Sydney.

——2004, 'Women's rights pushed back to the margin', *Sydney Morning Herald*, 15 November, p. 13.

Summers, John 2002, 'Parliament and responsible government' in *Government, Politics, Power and Policy in Australia*, 7th edn, eds John Summers, Dennis Woodward and Andrew Parkin, Longman, Sydney, pp. 23–48.

——2006, 'Parliament and responsible government' in *Government, Politics, Power and Policy in Australia*, eds Andrew Parkin, John Summers and Dennis Woodward, Pearson Education, Sydney.

Sunstein, Cass 1995, *Democracy and the Problem of Free Speech*, 2nd edn, Free Press, New York.

Swan, Wayne 2008, 'Productivity Commission to investigate paid maternity leave', ALP media release, 17 February, <www.alp.org.au/media/0208/msewrfcstres170.php> [31 March 2008].

Tadros, Edmund and Davis, Mark 2007, 'Rudd to select ministry', *Sydney Morning Herald Online*, 25 November, <www.smh.com.au/news/federal-election–2007-news/rudd-takes-dominant-role-over-ministry/2007/11/25/1195947545593.html> [31 March 2008].

Tarrow, Sidney 1994, *Power in Movement: Social Movements, Collective Action, and Politics*, Cambridge University Press, Cambridge.

Tasmanian Law Reform Institute (TLRI) 2007, *A Charter of Rights for Tasmania*, Report No. 10. TLRI, Hobart.

Tattersall, Amanda 2005, 'There is power in coalition: A framework for assessing how and when union–community colations are effective and enhance union power', *Labour and Industry*, vol. 16, no. 2, pp. 97–112.

Taylor, Robert 2006, 'Global warming is good for WA, says premier', *West Australian*, 4 November, p. 10.

Thatcher, Mark and Stone-Sweet, Alec 2002, 'Theory and practice of delegation to non-majoritarian institutions', *West European Politics*, vol. 25, no. 1, pp. 1–22.

The Hicks Legal Defence Team (THLDT) 2007, 'A fair go for Hicks?', *Bulletin: Law Society of South Australia*, vol. 29, no. 1, pp. 14–16.

Thompson, Elaine 1980, 'The "Washminster" mutation' in *Responsible Government in Australia*, eds Patrick Weller and Dean Jaensch, Drummond, Melbourne.

——1994, *Fair Enough: Egalitarianism in Australia*, UNSW Press, Sydney.

Thornton, Phil, Phelan, Liam and McKeown, Bill 1997, *I Protest! Fighting for Your Rights*, Pluto Press, Sydney.

Tiernan, Anne 2007, *Power without Responsibility*, UNSW Press, Sydney.

Tiffen, Rod 1989, *News and Power*, Allen & Unwin, Sydney.

——2000, 'The news media and Australia politics: Contemporary challenges for Australian democracy in the information age' in *The Politics of Australian Society: Political Issues for the New Century*, eds Paul Boreham, Geoffrey Stokes and Richard Hall, Longman, Sydney, pp. 175–91.

——2002, 'Political economy and news' in *The Media and Communications in Australia*, eds Stuart Cunningham and Graeme Turner, Allen & Unwin, Sydney, pp. 35–47.

——2006a, 'The press' in *The Media and Communications in Australia*, 2nd edn, eds Stuart Cunningham and Graeme Turner, Allen & Unwin, Sydney, pp. 97–112.

——2006b, 'The Geoffrey Boycott of Australian politics', *Australian Review of Public Affairs*, 23 February, <www.australianreview.net/digest/2006/02/tiffen.html> [31 March 2008].

Tiffen, Rod and Gittins, Ross 2004, *How Australia Compares*, Cambridge University Press, Melbourne.

Tilly, Charles 2004, *Social Movements: 1768–2004*, Paradigm Publishers, Boulder, Colo.

Toohey, Paul 2007, 'In the hot seat', *Bulletin*, 18 May, <http://bulletin.ninemsn.com.au/article.aspx?id=267198> [22 October 2007].

Topsfield, Jewel 2007, 'Teacher unions angry at Labor exclusion', *Age*, 2 March, p. 4.

Townsley, W.A. 1991, *Tasmania: From Colony to Statehood 1803–1945*, St David's Park Publishing, Hobart.

Tucker, Kerrie 2003, Member of the ACT Legislative Assembly, interview conducted by Ariadne Vromen and Nick Turnbull, 22 July.

Turnbull, Nick and Vromen, Ariadne 2006, 'The Australian Greens: Party organisation and political processes', *Australian Journal of Political History*, vol. 52, no. 3, pp. 455–70.

Turnbull, Sue 2006, 'Audiences' in *The Media and Communications in Australia*, 2nd edn, eds Stuart Cunningham and Graeme Turner, Allen & Unwin, Sydney, pp. 78–93.

Turner, Graeme, Tomlinson, Elizabeth and Pearce, Susan, 2006, 'Talkback radio: Some notes on format, politics and influence', *Media International Australia*, vol. 118, pp. 107–19.

Turner, Ken 1990, 'Parliament' in *Politics in Australia*, 2nd edn, eds Rodney Smith and Lex Watson, Allen & Unwin, Sydney.

Twomey, Anne 2004, *The Constitution of New South Wales,* Federation Press, Sydney.
Uhr, John 1998, *Deliberative Democracy in Australia: The Changing Place of Parliament,* Cambridge University Press, Melbourne.
Uhr, John and Wanna, John 2000, 'The future roles of parliament' in *Institutions on the Edge? Capacity for Governance,* eds Michael Keating, John Wanna and Patrick Weller, Allen & Unwin, Sydney
Ungerer, Carl 2007, 'Introduction' in *Australian Foreign Policy in the Age of Terror,* ed. Carl Ungerer, UNSW Press, Sydney.
Ungerer, Carl (ed.) 2007, *Australian Foreign Policy in the Age of Terror,* UNSW Press, Sydney.
United Nations Framework Convention on Climate Change (UNFCCC) 2008, *Kyoto Protocol,* UNFCCC, <http://unfccc.int/kyoto_protocol/items/2830.php> [31 March 2008].
Uren, David 2008, 'Time to cut the red tape: Treasurer', *Australian,* 11 January, p. 2.
van Acker, Elizabeth 1999, *Different Voices: Gender and Politics in Australia,* Macmillan Education, Melbourne.
van Biezen, Ingrid 2003, 'The place of parties in contemporary democracies', *West European Politics,* vol. 26, no. 3, pp. 171–84.
Van Onselen, Peter 2005, 'Western Australia's state election: Democracy in action?', Democratic Audit of Australia, ANU, <http://democratic.audit.anu.edu.au/papers/20050221_van_ons_wa.pdf> [31 March 2008].
Van Onselen, Peter and Errington, Wayne 2004, 'Electoral databases: Big brother or democracy unbound?', *Australian Journal of Political Science,* vol. 39, no. 2, pp. 349–66.
van Wanrooy, Brigid, Oxenbridge, Sarah, Buchanan, John and Jakubauskas, Michelle 2007, *Australia at Work,* Workplace Research Centre, University of Sydney, <www.wrc.org.au/documents/Australia@work_The_Benchmark_Report.pdf> [31 March 2008].
Viviani, Nancy 1993, 'The bureaucratic context' in *Australia in a Changing World: New Foreign Policy Directions,* ed. Feydor A. Mediansky, Macmillan, Sydney, pp. 43–62.
——1999, 'Australians and the East Timor issue: The policy of the Whitlam Government', in *East Timor and Australia: AIIA Contributions to the Policy Debate,* ed. James Cotton, Australian Institute of International Affairs, Canberra, pp 81–107.
Vromen, Ariadne 1995, 'Paul Keating is the prime minister, but who delivers the mail? A study of political knowledge amongst young people', *Australian Journal of Political Science,* vol. 30, no. 1, pp. 74–90.
——2003, '"People try to put us down …": Participatory citizenship of "generationX"', *Australian Journal of Political Science,* vol. 38, no. 1, pp. 78–99.
——2004, 'Three political myths about young people', *Australian Review of Public Affairs:*

Digest, 26 March, <www.australianreview.net/digest/2004/03/vromen.html> [May 2008].

——2005, 'Who are the Australian Greens? Surveying the membership', paper presented to the TASA Conference, University of Tasmania, 6–8 December.

——2008, 'Building virtual spaces: Young people, participation and the internet', *Australian Journal of Political Science*, vol. 43, no. 1, pp. 79–97.

Walliker, Annalise 2007, 'Aussies hooked on Facebook, MySpace and YouTube', *Herald Sun*, 31 December, <www.news.com.au/heraldsun/story/0,21985,22987962–662,00.html> [31 March 2008].

Wanna, John 2003, 'Queensland' in *Australian Politics and Government: The Commonwealth, the States and the Territories*, eds Jeremy Moon and Campbell Sharman, Cambridge University Press, Melbourne.

Ward, Ian 1992, 'Rich, wrinkly and rowdy politicians: Is this how teenagers "read" television news?', *Australian Journal of Political Science*, vol. 27, no. 3, pp. 213–29.

——1995, *The Politics of the Media*, Macmillan, Melbourne.

——1999, 'Federal government' in *Institutions in Australian Society*, ed. John Henningham, Oxford University Press, Melbourne, pp. 13–33.

——2000, 'One Nation: Organisation, party and democracy' in *The Rise and Fall of One Nation*, eds Michael Leach, Geoffrey Stokes and Ian Ward, University of Queensland Press, Brisbane, pp. 89–114.

——2002a, 'Media power' in *Government, Politics, Power and Policy in Australia*, eds John Summers, Dennis Woodward and Andrew Parkin, 7th edn, Longman, Sydney, pp. 401–14.

——2002b, 'Talkback radio, political communication, and Australian politics', *Australian Journal of Communication*, vol. 29, no. 1, pp. 21–38.

——2003a, '"Localising the national": The rediscovery and reshaping of local; Campaigning in Australia', *Party Politics*, vol. 9, no. 5, pp. 583–600.

——2003b, 'An Australian PR state?', *Australian Journal of Communication*, vol. 30, no. 1, pp. 25–42.

Ward, Ian and Randal Stewart 2006, *Politics One*, 3rd edn, Palgrave Macmillan, Melbourne.

Ware, Alan 1996, *Political Parties and Party Systems*, Oxford University Press, Oxford.

Warhurst, John 2003, 'Australian Capital Territory' in *Australian Politics and Government: The Commonwealth, the States and the Territories*, eds Jeremy Moon and Campbell Sharman, Cambridge University Press, Melbourne, pp. 209–23.

——2006, 'Euthanasia, stem-cell research and RU486: Conscience voting in the Federal Parliament', paper presented to the Australasian Political Studies Conference, University of Newcastle, NSW , 25–27 September.

——2007, *Behind Closed Doors: Politics, Scandals and the Lobbying Industry*, UNSW Press, Sydney.

Warhurst, John (ed.) 1997, *Keeping the Bastards Honest: The Australian Democrats' First Twenty Years*, Allen & Unwin, Sydney.
Warhurst, John and Parkin, Andrew (eds) 2000, *The Machine: Labor Confronts the Future*, Allen & Unwin, Sydney.
Weber, Max 1969, *The Theory of Social and Economic Organisation*, introduction by Talcott Parsons, 6th edn, Free Press, New York.
Webster, Elizabeth 1999, 'Job network: What can it offer?', *Just Policy*, no. 17, December, pp. 32–42.
Weiss, Linda, Thurbon, Elizabeth and Mathews, John 2004, *How to Kill a Country: Australia's Devastating Trade Deal with the United States*, Allen & Unwin, Sydney.
——2006, 'Free trade in mad cows: How to kill a beef industry', *Australian Journal of International Affairs*, vol. 60, no. 3, pp. 376–99.
——2007, *National Insecurity: The Howard Government's Betrayal of Australia*, Allen & Unwin, Sydney.
Weller, Patrick 2007, *Cabinet Government in Australia, 1901–2006*, UNSW Press, Sydney.
Weller, Patrick and Davis, Glyn (eds) 1996, *New Ideas, Better Government*, Allen & Unwin, Sydney.
Wesley, Michael 2002, 'Perspectives on Australian foreign policy, 2001', *Australian Journal of International Affairs*, vol. 56, no. 1, pp. 47–63.
Western, John and Tranter, Bruce 2005, 'Are postmaterialists engaged citizens?' in *Australian Social Attitudes: The First Report*, eds Shaun Wilson, Gabrielle Meagher, Rachel Gibson, David Denemark and Mark Western, UNSW Press, Sydney, pp. 82–100.
Western Australia Legislative Assembly 2005, 'One Vote One Value Bill 2005 debate', *Hansard*, 17 May, pp. 1611c–28a, <www.parliament.wa.gov.au/index.htm> [31 March 2008].
Whitlam, E.G. 1977, *On Australia's Constitution*, Widescope, Melbourne.
Willett, Graham 2000, *Living Out Loud*, Allen & Unwin, Sydney.
Williams, Caleb 1998, 'Protest, police and the green world view: The search for a brave new paradigm' in *Protest! Environmental Activism in NSW 1968–1998*, ed. Caleb Williams, Historic Houses Trust of NSW , Sydney, pp. 5–18.
Williams, Daryl 1999, Attorney-General, 'United Nations Committee misunderstands and misrepresents Australia', media release, 19 March, <http://pandora.nla.gov.au/pan/39423/20040414–0000/www.tisn.gov.au/WWW/attorneygeneralHome.nsf/Web+Pages/8C65BB3FF2EC8801CA256D590019BB6Df30d.html> [1 April 2008].
Williams, George 2002, *Human Rights Under the Australian Constitution*, Oxford University Press, Melbourne.
——2006, 'The Victorian Charter of Human Rights and Responsibilities: Origin and scope', *Melbourne University Law Review*, vol. 30, pp. 880–905.
——2007a, *A Charter of Rights for Australia*, 3rd edn, UNSW Press, Sydney.

——2007b, *Working Together: Inquiry into Options for a New National Industrial Relations System,* Office of Industrial Relations, NSW Government, <www.industrialrelations.nsw.gov.au/action/inquiry.html> [30 January 2008].
——2008, 'Thawing the frozen continent', in *Re-imagining Australia,* Griffith Review 19, ABC Books, Sydney, pp. 13–37.
Williams, John 1995, *In Search of the Federal Citizen: Andrew Inglis Clark and the '14th Amendment',* Federalism Research Centre Discussion Papers, November, Federalism Research Centre, Canberra.
Wilson, Shaun 2003, 'Obstructing government or stopping bullies: What do Australians think about government control of the Senate?', *Australian Review of Public Affairs Digest,* 13 June, <www.australianreview.net/digest/2003/06/wilson.html> [May 2008].
Wilson, Shaun and Breusch, Trevor 2004, 'Where the divides lie: Politicians, public opinion and anti-elite politics' in *Us and Them: Anti-elitism in Australia,* eds Marian Sawer and Barry Hindess, API Network, Perth, pp. 161–82.
Wilson, Shaun, Meagher, Gabrielle, Gibson, Rachel, Denemark, David and Western, Mark, 2005, *Australian Social Attitudes,* UNSW Press, Sydney.
Wilson, Shaun and Meagher, Gabrielle 2007, 'Howard's welfare state: How popular is the new social policy agenda?' in *Australian Social Attitudes 2: Citizenship, Work and Aspirations,* eds David Denemark, Gabrielle Meagher, Shaun Wilson, Mark Western and Timothy Phillips, UNSW Press, Sydney, pp. 262–85.
Wilson, Shaun, Meagher, Gabrielle and Breusch, Trevor 2005, 'Where to for the welfare state?' in *Australian Social Attitudes: The First Report,* eds Shaun Wilson, Gabrielle Meagher, Rachel Gibson, David Denemark and Mark Western, UNSW Press, Sydney, pp. 101–21.
Windschuttle, Keith 1984, *The Media,* Penguin, Melbourne.
——2002, *The Fabrication of Aboriginal History,* Macleay Press, Sydney.
Winterton, George 1992, 'Modern republicanism', *Legislative Studies,* vol. 6, no. 2, pp. 21–45.
Woodward, Dennis 2002, 'Economic policy' in *Government, Politics, Power and Policy in Australia,* 7th edn, eds John Summers, Dennis Woodward and Andrew Parkin, Longman, Sydney, pp. 417–38.
——2006, 'Political parties and the party system' in *Government, Politics, Power and Policy in Australia,* 8th edn, eds Andrew Parkin, John Summers and Dennis Woodward, Pearson Education, Sydney.
Yallop, Richard 2003, 'The Great Dissenter', *The Australian,* 3 October.
Yeatman, Anna 1997, 'The concept of public management and the Australian state in the 1980s' in *Mangerialism: The Great Debate,* eds Mark Considine and Martin Painter, Melbourne University Press, Melbourne, pp. 12–38.
Young, Liz 1999, 'Minor parties and the legislative process in the Australian Senate: A study of the 1993 budget', *Australian Journal of Political Science,* vol. 34, no. 1, pp. 7–27.

Young, Sally 2000, 'Why Australians hate politicians: Exploring the new public discontent' in *For the People: Reclaiming Our Government*, eds Dennis Glover and Glenn Patmore, Pluto Press, Sydney, pp. 171–82.

——2002, 'Spot on: The role of political advertising in Australia', *Australian Journal of Political Science*, vol. 37, no. 1, pp. 81–98.

——2007, 'Innovations in Australian government communication' in *Government Communication in Australia*, ed. Sally Young, Cambridge University Press, Melbourne, pp. 229–54.

Young, Sally (ed.) 2007, *Government Communication in Australia*, Cambridge University Press, Melbourne.

Young, Sally and Tham, Joo-Cheong 2006, *Political Finance in Australia: A Skewed and Secret System*, Report No. 7, Democratic Audit of Australia, Australian National University, Canberra.

Zanghellini, Aleardo 2007, 'Marriage and Civil Unions: Legal and Moral Questions', *Federal Law Review*, vol. 35, pp. 265–98.

INDEX

Page numbers in *italics* refer to tables